MW00459263

The Fervent Embrace

The Fervent Embrace

Liberal Protestants, Evangelicals, and Israel

Caitlin Carenen

NEW YORK UNIVERSITY PRESS
New York and London

NEW YORK UNIVERSITY PRESS
New York and London
www.nyupress.org

References to Internet websites (URLs) were accurate at the time of writing.
Neither the author nor New York University Press is responsible for URLs
that may have expired or changed since the manuscript was prepared.

Library of Congress Cataloging-in-Publication Data
Carenen, Caitlin.
The fervent embrace : liberal Protestants, evangelicals, and Israel /
Caitlin Carenen.
p. cm.   Includes bibliographical references (p.) and index.
 ISBN 978-0-8147-4104-7 (cl : alk. paper) — ISBN 978-0-8147-0809-5 (ebook)
 — ISBN 978-0-8147-0837-8 (ebook)
1. Christian Zionism — United States — History — 20th century.
2. Protestants — United States — Attitudes. 3. Evangelists — United
States — Attitudes. 4. Protestant churches — Political activity — United
States. 5. Protestant churches — Relations — Judaism. 6. Israel — Public
opinion — United States. 7. Public opinion — United States.   I. Title. II.
Title: Liberal Protestants, evangelicals, and Israel.
DS150.5.C36 2012
320.54095694088'270973 — dc23   2011041544

New York University Press books are printed on acid-free paper,
and their binding materials are chosen for strength and durability.
We strive to use environmentally responsible suppliers and materials
to the greatest extent possible in publishing our books.

Manufactured in the United States of America
10 9 8 7 6 5 4 3 2 1

For Patrick and Karl, with deepest gratitude

Contents

Acknowledgments

I have finished this book indebted to many people and organizations that have assisted me along the way. First, I thank the History Department, the Institute for Jewish Studies, and the Graduate School of Arts and Sciences at Emory University for their generous support of my graduate studies. The History Department was especially supportive, not just financially but professionally—the quality of the faculty, the academic rigor of my intellectual training, the professionalization assistance, and the congenial atmosphere of the department truly made my experience at Emory outstanding. Special recognition goes to Patrick Allitt, Eric Goldstein, and Frasier Harbutt, who offered extraordinary advice during the writing of this book. Patrick Allitt deserves additional recognition for his mentorship of my professional career as an academic. His tireless cheerfulness, teaching guidance, and tough criticism challenged me to constantly improve both my teaching and scholarship. His door was always open, his advice always thoughtful, and his support unwavering. He represents the very best this profession has to offer.

I also thank the Andrew W. Mellon Foundation, the Society for the Study of American Foreign Relations (SHAFR), and the Jacob Rader Marcus Center of the American Jewish Archives in Cincinnati for their support of my research. I am grateful as well to Jennifer Hammer, my editor at New York University Press, for her early interest in the project and her patience as she steered me through the process.

I am indebted to Michael McGarry, Rector of the Tantur Ecumenical Institute in Jerusalem, for his support during my two consecutive summers there as a Scholar in Residence. Living in East Jerusalem provided a unique opportunity to conduct my research. The Institute staff and the communities I encountered enriched my experiences as a scholar immeasurably. I also thank others in Israel who assisted me with my research, including Uri Bialer of Hebrew University for his valuable guidance on navigating the Israeli State Archives as well as his sound advice on the topic itself, Eyal Naveh of Tel Aviv University for his graciousness and helpful conversations about Reinhold Niebuhr and Messianism, and the staff of the Central Zionist Archives and the Israeli State Archives for their patient assistance.

I am also grateful for the warm welcome I have received as a junior faculty member at Eastern Connecticut State University. The university supported my research with grants and release time to work on the manuscript, and for that I am deeply grateful. The entire faculty and staff of the History Department offered the kind of support and friendship that has made my transition from graduate student to faculty member a pleasant one. I thank, in particular, Ann Higginbotham, Emil Pocock, Ania Kirchmann, and Jamel Ostwald for their support of the project and helpful advice.

Finally, I thank my friends who have made this process bearable. Thirteen years ago Karl Mechem offered wise advice in writing my first graduate school application, and he continued his support through the completion of this book. I am most deeply in his debt. Other friends deserve mention as well, including Candice Harrison (especially for meeting me at the Grand Canyon), Karen Houghton, Joe Renouard, Kate McGrath, and Marni Davis—thank you for being there from the beginning. I thank Dom DeBrincat for his friendship, support, and good humor—all of which has made life in Connecticut better. Adriana Buliga Stoian, the political science outlier, deserves my thanks for her dear friendship and support in the darkest days. Lastly, I thank Derek Morrissey for cheering me on and, most important, making me happy.

Introduction

Eleven minutes after Israel declared its independence on 14 May 1948, the United States granted it de facto recognition. President Harry Truman's memo was short and to the point: "This Government has been informed that a Jewish state has been proclaimed in Palestine, and recognition has been requested by the provisional government thereof. The United States recognizes the provisional government as the de facto authority of the new State of Israel." Truman's concise memo belied the drama behind its creation. Despite enormous pressure from Truman's State Department and members of his cabinet to withhold recognition, the president quickly offered it. Some scholars have argued that pressure from Jewish lobby groups explains Truman's speedy actions, but this alone does not fully explain the president's immediate support for the new Jewish state. What accounts for it, then? A significant part of the answer lies in the actions and lobbying efforts of an elite group of "mainline," or liberal, Protestant leaders who persuasively argued that the destruction of the European Jews during the Second World War necessitated support for Zionism. Historic Christian antisemitism helped to create the twentieth century's worst genocide, they insisted, and therefore its solution constituted a Christian responsibility. This powerful, well-connected mainline Protestant minority set about radically changing the nature of Protestant-Jewish relations and U.S. foreign policy over the course of the century.

In less than fifty years the Holocaust, the creation of Israel, and U.S.–Israeli foreign policy entirely changed American Protestant views toward Jews, Judaism, and Israel. Between 1933 and the turn of the twenty-first century, mainline Protestant leaders shifted attitudes away from antisemitism to a fervent embrace of Jews and Israel—an embrace later appropriated by evangelical and fundamentalist Protestants to advance their own prophetic theology. During these decades a powerful group of politically influential mainline Protestants supported the establishment of the State of Israel for humanitarian and geopolitically pragmatic reasons, and worked to create a strong U.S.–Israeli alliance. They also encouraged a greater religious ecumenism and improved Jewish-Christian relations in the United States, calling for a reevaluation of traditional Protestant theology to address the question of Judaism in the modern world. Their support for Israel's establishment and security in the first few decades of its existence proved to be an important step in the development of the special relationship between the United States and Israel.

Meanwhile, evangelical and fundamentalist Protestants in the United States, after a hiatus from politics following the Scopes Monkey trial in 1925, grew politically engaged in the prophetic implications of Israel's establishment. By the 1980s evangelicals had surpassed mainline Protestants in both numbers and political influence. This political shift proved important to the U.S.–Israeli alliance, as these Protestants supported Israel even more ardently than did their mainline counterparts but for entirely different reasons. Fundamentalist and evangelical Americans increasingly viewed Israeli security and prosperity as synonymous with U.S. security and prosperity and pushed for a tightening of U.S.–Israeli relations.

This book presents an analysis of American Protestants' changing attitudes toward Jews and Judaism between 1933 and the turn of the twenty-first century. It traces divisions in American Protestantism over reactions to the Holocaust, the establishment of Israel, and U.S. foreign policy toward Israel, and shows evidence of a significant shift away from widespread antisemitism among American Protestants toward a more friendly relationship. The book begins with Hitler's rise to power and concludes with a post–Cold War analysis of George W. Bush's administration. The Holocaust and Israel's establishment sparked a greater degree of ecumenism among mainline Protestants and American Jews, led to a reconsideration of traditional Protestant antisemitic theology, catalyzed general Protestant support for Israel, and inspired evangelicals to ardently advocate on Israel's behalf. This attitudinal change permanently altered the religious and political landscape of the United States.

In the mid-twentieth century few American opinion makers were more influential in shaping public opinion than theologically liberal Christians from the mainline Protestant denominations, particularly those from the Presbyterian, Methodist, Baptist, and Lutheran persuasion. These Protestants occasionally shaped national policy, too. They served not only on the faculty of both seminaries and secular universities but even in presidential cabinets. Policy makers often solicited their advice. Their concern for European Jews, although muted in the 1930s, during a time of sometimes outright antisemitism, did manifest itself in strong support for the establishment of the State of Israel and its survival after the Second World War.

Categorizing and evaluating the contribution of theologically conservative Protestants from the evangelical and fundamentalist traditions to Jewish-Christian relations and U.S.–Israeli foreign policy is more difficult than considering that of mainline Protestants.[1] This difficulty arises in part because defining the term "evangelical" poses serious challenges to which numerous studies have been dedicated. For the purposes of this book, the term "theologically conservative Protestants" refers to non-mainline Protestants of the evangelical tradition. The evangelical tradition may be subdivided further to include classical evangelicalism (derived from the Reformation), Pietism, and fundamentalist evangelicalism. The latter group is especially central to this book, as its adherents rejected modernity (specifically higher criticism of the Bible) and developed an apocalyptic theology, an end-of-times eschatology known as premillennial dispensationalism.[2]

Evangelicals tend to define themselves as adhering to three theological tenets. All believe in biblical inerrancy (infallibility of the Bible), the divinity of Jesus as Christ, and salvation through faith in Christ alone. All three tenets are reactions against the threat of modernity that arose in the late nineteenth century. Liberal (mainline) Protestants embraced these modernizing principles, provoking a reactionary reaffirmation of orthodox Protestantism among conservative Protestants.[3] American evangelicalism contains within it a remarkable number of variations and traditions; the four most common are the Baptist, the Holiness-Pentecostal, the Reformed-Confessional, and the Anabaptist.[4]

The definitions grew more complicated, however, as the century progressed, specifically because mainline Protestants decreased in numbers so significantly that they could no longer be considered mainstream. Although less well connected to national elites in the mid-twentieth century, by the century's end theologically conservative American Protestants far outnumbered their theologically liberal counterparts in American Protestantism. Theologically conservative Protestants became the new "mainstream" and, along with their ascendancy, definitions shifted as well. As one scholar notes, "Drafting a perfect definition of this mainstream is impossible; drafting a good working definition of it is not." By the late twentieth century evangelical mainstream Protestantism had generally come to be defined as "that network of born-again Christians associated with the Billy Graham Evangelistic Association, the National Association of Evangelicals, and Campus Crusade for Christ; with schools such as the Moody Bible Institute, Fuller Seminary, and Wheaton College; with publishing firms like Eerdman's and Zondervan; and with magazines such as *Christianity Today*, *Eternity*, and *Moody Monthly*."[5]

American Jews and the State of Israel have played a complex role in the theology of evangelical Protestantism. All branches of evangelical Protestantism believe that their efforts to convert the Jews reflect the command of the Great Commission—Jesus's command to his disciples to preach his gospel to the world, to convert the nonbelievers. In addition, many—particularly fundamentalists—believed that Israel's establishment was a harbinger of the "end times," when the scattered Jews would be reassembled in Israel and Christ would return to establish his millennium on Earth. Therefore evangelicals tended to vigorously endorse the establishment of Israel and, as they grew in numbers and political prowess, their ardent support for Israel gained political significance in the post-State era.

Jews did not passively observe these trends in American Protestantism. The transformation of American Protestantism's perspective on Jews, Judaism, and Israel was in part a reaction to the increasingly vocal and influential Jewish community around them. The Jews of Europe, Israel, and America helped shape their own destiny between 1933 and the turn of the twenty-first century, not least in vigorous exchanges with American Protestant intellectuals, leaders, and laymen. In these exchanges Jews attempted to counter antisemitic tendencies within traditional Protestant theology, asserted their legitimacy within the American mainstream, and rallied support for Israel. This book concentrates primarily on American Protestants, but it is mindful that America's own Jewish communities, descended from immigrants, were becoming an important element of the American population and a major segment of American intellectual life. Divisions in American Judaism between Reform, Conservative, and Orthodox Jews, however, resulted in a far from unified response to increased American Protestant interest in the Jewish-Christian dialogue and led to significant tensions in Jewish-Christian relations during the mid-twentieth century. Inside Israel, the debate over the role of religion in the state resulted in deep and sometimes acrimonious divisions that also affected Jewish-Christian understanding in the postwar world. Such transformations vitally affected American Protestants' understanding of Jewish affairs domestically and abroad.

No previous scholar has systematically examined the broad scope of American Protestant reaction to the Holocaust, Israel's establishment, and the U.S.–Israeli alliance during the course of the twentieth century. Prior work has tended either to focus on evangelicalism's complicated and somewhat sensational relationship with Jews and the State of Israel or to treat mainline Protestantism as monolithically antisemitic and anti-Israel. In fact, evangelical Protestants and mainline Protestants debated each other regarding antisemitism, the Holocaust, and Israel, and neither held uniform or uncontested positions.[6] Mainline Protestants were not monolithically antisemitic nor were evangelicals solely focused on prophecy. In light of the pressure of the Cold War to present a united front against atheistic communism, disagreements that emerged among American Protestants over the questions of theology and foreign policy highlight the importance of the issues to both groups and shatter our understanding of the postwar religious consensus. Moreover, the relationship between Protestants, Jews, Americans, and Israelis illustrates the increasing importance of religion in shaping U.S. foreign policy, particularly in the Middle East. The alliance between American and Israeli fates is so tightly formed now that the casual observer might not realize it was not always so. Understanding the role of religion in the formation of U.S. foreign policy toward Israel—what this book attempts to do—offers a partial explanation of how that happened. In an era when the role of religion in constructing Middle Eastern foreign policy has become a hotly contested issue, understanding the religious foundation of the U.S.–Israeli alliance is all the more important. The significance of individual activism in shaping policy, the impact of the Holocaust in reconstructing both Protestant theology and influencing Jewish-Christians relations, and the role prophecy plays in motivating a large number of American Protestants to become involved in foreign policy in the Middle East is worthy of close scrutiny. Such examination provides a deeper understanding of major shifts in American religious history and reveals the symbiotic relationship between personal piety and foreign policy.

List of Abbreviations

ACPC	American Christian Palestine Committee
ACJ	American Council for Judaism
ADL	Anti-Defamation League
AFL	American Federation of Labor
AIPAC	American Israel Public Affairs Committee
AIS	American-Israel Society
AJC	American Jewish Committee
AFME	American Friends of the Middle East
APC	American Palestine Committee
CCI	Christians Concerned for Israel
CCP	Christian Council on Palestine
CIO	Congress of Industrial Organizations
CMEP	Churches for Middle East Peace
FCC	Federal Communications Commission
IDF	Israeli Defense Forces
JTS	Jewish Theological Seminary
NCC	National Council of Churches
NCCJ	National Conference of Christians and Jews
NEA	Near East Affairs
PCUSA	Presbyterian Church of the United States of America
PLO	Palestinian Liberation Organization
TVA	Tennessee Valley Authority

American Protestants and
Jewish Persecution, 1933–1937

Jews should celebrate the birth of Christ—what is good for the
Christian, after all, is good for the Jew. At the end of the 1930s the Christmas
edition of the most important Protestant journal in the United States, the
Christian Century, issued this stern directive. Jews, the editors argued, should
celebrate the birth of Christ as a goodwill gesture to Christianity's universalism and American culture. "If the religion of Judaism is good for the Jews,"
it insisted, "it is also good for gentiles. If it is not good for gentiles, it is not
the best religion for Jews."[1] Religious differences, in other words, would not
be tolerated. Such a warning reflected the attitude of liberal Protestantism
in the United States during the 1930s—Protestantism *was* American culture.
Many scholars have argued that antisemitism in the United States marked
its high point during the decade of the 1930s. Isolationism and the trauma of
the Great Depression provoked both xenophobic attitudes and assimilation-
ist impulses.

At the same time, however, American Protestants were confronted by the
increasing persecution of Germany's Jewish population by the Nazi Party.
American Protestantism's hesitancy to directly confront and condemn the
persecution (a still unfolding development) reflected strong antisemitic tendencies in American society. Questions of acculturation and assimilation
collided with the great crises of the era—worldwide depression and reaction against modernity—to create a reactionary impulse in American Protestantism. Although some notable mainline Protestants called attention to
German persecutions of the Jews and others began mobilizing to support
the idea of a Jewish homeland in Palestine, few Protestants were concerned
about either issue. Isolationism and pacifism dominated political discussions
among Protestants.

Evangelical Protestants, a small minority in the 1930s, refrained from
political activism on behalf of the Jews. They invoked prophetic implica-

tions for the mounting persecution of the Jews in Germany and the growing numbers of Jewish immigrants to Palestine in the interwar period, but they did not politically engage these issues. Despite the lack of widespread reaction against Nazi persecutions, activism on behalf of the persecuted, or mobilization to support Zionism, American Protestantism lay on the cusp of dramatic changes that would transform the religious and political landscape of the United States in the decades to follow. The decade of the 1930s offers a stark contrast to the political mobilization that would follow in the next decade.

Protestants and Anti-Semitism

In 1933 mainline Protestant influence in American politics, education, and culture was unquestioned. The United States had always considered itself a Protestant nation. Although, in many ways, religious minorities found a safe haven in the United States, with its constitutional separation of church and state, they often—whether Jews or Catholics (the largest religious minorities in 1933)—found that their access to America's highest echelons of power was barred, including admission to the best schools, business opportunities, and representation in government, civic organizations, and clubs.[2]

American antisemitism was widespread. Recently historians of antisemitism have challenged the conventional argument that the history of American antisemitism is "exceptional," that "it was rarely more than a nuisance," rarely and weakly applied, and had no foundation in American laws, institutions, or ideology.[3] They argue that antisemitism in the United States stems directly from its Protestant heritage and "Christian sources" related to an anti-Jewish ideology inherent in Christian culture.[4] When Christian culture and tradition are at their strongest, their argument goes, so is antisemitism. This was particularly true in the interwar period of American history when antisemitism "was more widespread and profound than ever before . . . aggravated by several catastrophes, including the aftermath of the Great War, the Depression, and the international political crises of the 1930s."[5] Whether primarily religious or socio-cultural in nature, however, antisemitism reached its height in the 1930s.[6]

Particularly after the crash of the stock market in 1929, the United States found itself in the grip of a most serious assault on its American exceptionalism. The horrors of the Great War had already convinced most Americans to return to a policy of isolationism from European affairs. Such ardent isolationism, coupled with economic unrest, provoked an atmosphere of extreme nationalism in American society in the 1930s. The rise of fascist regimes in Europe in the following years, and the sense of purpose and unity in the face of economic and political woe they encouraged in their supporters, found sympathetic admirers among some worried Americans.

The particularistic aspect of Judaism found itself under assault from this new nationalism. Protestants warned Jews not to set themselves apart in any way from other Americans, even in their religious practices. The message they sent was clear: patriotism equaled Protestantism. Yet, paradoxically, religion was central to American identity. This centrality forced Jews to identify themselves religiously while simultaneously compartmentalizing aspects of their Jewishness. In the 1930s the Jewish community in the United States was still reeling from the second wave of immigration of Jews from Eastern Europe who had arrived in the later part of the nineteenth century. These orthodox Eastern European Jews struggled with their fellow Jewish Americans over questions of assimilation and acculturation in mainline America.[7]

While many Jews feared Jewish immigrants to America abandoned religious loyalties *too* quickly and integrated themselves *too* easily into American society, many American Protestants complained that the so-called melting pot was cooking too *slowly*. Even before the Great Depression, immigration restrictions in the post–Great War era had slowed Eastern European Jewish immigration from a flood to a small trickle. Between 1931 and 1936 only around four thousand Jews entered the country.[8] Antisemitism grew so quickly in the interwar period that, in 1936, *Fortune* magazine declared, "the apprehensiveness of American Jews has become one of the most important influences in the social life of our time."[9]

American Jewish organizations, worried about the rising tide of antisemitism, organized to combat it. In 1927 they sued Henry Ford for publishing the antisemitic and slanderous *Protocols of the Elders of Zion* and threatened to boycott his cars.[10] They also organized committees to address domestic antisemitism and the rise of fascist organizations. For example, in a letter to Roger Straus, the New York publisher and member of the American Council on Public Affairs and the National Conference of Christians and Jews (NCCJ), regarding the necessity of careful attention to fascist and antisemitic attitudes in the United States, Rabbi George Fox of Texas noted that "many of us have been greatly worried by what appears to be the rising tide of antisemitism in our land." Fox was concerned that, despite the proliferation of attacks on Jews, Jewish leaders and organizations remained ineffectual in addressing the attacks because the accusations of self-interest tended to negate Jewish efforts. For Fox, Christian activism offered the most effective means to combat antisemitism. He proposed that a non-exclusively Jewish organization, such as the National Association of Christians and Jews, address the problem and prepare a study on fascist and antisemitic organizations in the United States. "The matter is quite serious," he explained, "and of course we do not want to make the mistake of not trying to scotch this business before it gets too powerful."[11]

Straus acknowledged the grave situation but stopped short of offering more support, noting instead that NCCJ activism "is much more along the lines of positive, rather than negative action."[12] Eventually Fox proposed the formation of the National Foundation for the Preservation of Democracy whose sole purpose would be to combat, in an organized and systematic manner, the propaganda of antisemitic groups in the United States. Its first members included former president Herbert Hoover and other notables.[13] In its founding statement, the Foundation noted that, "whether from sincere desire to protect the United States from what . . . befuddled minds think are dangers, or from a desire to make money off gullible followers, some 248 so-called organizations have been created . . . to protect the land against Jews, Catholics, other minorities and Bolshevism, and to extol the so-called 100% Americanism of the white Protestant gentile."[14] In 1939 the National Foundation and the American Council jointly sponsored a report on antisemitic organizations in America. In his 1941 report for the American Council on Public Affairs, Douglas Strong, of the Department of Government at the University of Texas, surveyed eleven antisemitic organizations in a report titled *Organized Antisemitism in America: The Rise of Group Prejudice during the Decade 1930–1940*. Strong noted that the atmosphere of the 1930s proved to be fertile ground for antisemitic organizations.

Strong insisted that the growing power of these groups during the 1930s could not be ignored. Among the eleven groups he analyzed, fundamentalist Protestant Gerald Winrod's organization, The Defenders of the Christian Faith, served as the most potent example of the antisemitism among the extreme right-wing fundamentalist Protestants in America. Founded in 1925 by Winrod, the group targeted "modernity" as the great enemy of Christian America. Behind the push for modernity, Winrod argued, were "Jewish Bolsheviks." His organization's monthly magazine, the *Defender*, and its monthly newsletter, the *Revealer*, offered sensational "proofs" of the Jews' attempts to control the world. Winrod had endorsed the authenticity of the antisemitic *Protocols of the Elders of Zion* as the ultimate proof of international Jewry's attempts to gain global control through international business and finance. Strong estimated that between 1932 and 1936 Winrod distributed more than ninety-five thousand antisemitic tracts. The subscription rate of the *Defender* also increased dramatically during those years, from twenty-five thousand in 1930 to more than one hundred thousand by 1936. In 1938 Winrod, counting on widespread populist support, announced what would ultimately be an unsuccessful presidential run as a third-party candidate (after the Republicans refused to endorse his platform). Strong posited that the majority of Winrod's supporters came from those with "limited educational opportunities" who believed in a prophetic "interpretation of current world happenings in terms that the Bible has foretold."[15] This prophetic interest in the Jews grew increasingly as the decade progressed and would prove to be an important variable in Americans' changing views toward Jews. German persecution of the Jews was met with a divided response among American fundamentalists.

Some, like Winrod, endorsed antisemitic propaganda such as *Protocols*, including Arno Clemens Gaebelein, a leading fundamentalist theologian and editor of the fundamentalist journal *Our Hope*. In his book, *Conflict of the Ages*, Gaebelein offered a similar critique of world Jewry as communist agents who were intent on world control.[16] Gaebelein's assessment of the Jews as international conspirators found similar support among American fundamentalists like William Bell Riley of Minneapolis, Minnesota, editor of *The Pilot*, a fundamentalist journal. Riley also publicly endorsed the authenticity of *Protocols* and identified the Old Testament patriarch Joseph as the founder of "modern bolshevism." Not all fundamentalists agreed, however. J. Frank Norris, minister of the Temple Baptist Church in Detroit, Michigan, and First Baptist in Fort Worth, Texas, and editor of the *Fundamentalist,* challenged Riley and Gaebelein's assertion of the authenticity of *Protocols* and the idea of a worldwide Jewish conspiracy in the pulpit and in the pages of his journal. Transcripts of a public debate between Riley and Norris sold more than one hundred thousand copies and revealed a deep interest on the part of American fundamentalists over the place of the Jews in end-time eschatology. This growing interest in applying biblical interpretation to Jews was about to be ignited by events in Germany.

Fundamentalists' eschatological teachings about the end of the ages and Christ's return kept many from wholly endorsing such antisemitic platforms and served, in a modest way, as a moderating agent in the antisemitism of the 1930s. Even Gaebelein himself, as the decades progressed and the German persecution of the Jews became a campaign of annihilation, began to emphasize the necessity of kindness to the Jews as a prerequisite of any nation's blessings by God. As persecutions increased, these fundamentalists and their journals encouraged the modification of immigration laws to allow

Jews to come to the United States and supported Jewish immigration to Palestine—an idea endorsed by fundamentalists since the late nineteenth century.[17] Humanitarian and theological concerns collided in this reaction with Jewish persecution. Fundamentalist interpretations of Scripture insisted that a final "in-gathering" of Jews to Palestine would predate the return of Christ, and the then growing persecutions in Germany provided a humanitarian reason to support the increasing immigration to Palestine and resulted in a de-emphasis of the role of world Jewry in communist conspiracy theories. Moreover, the advocacy for increased U.S. immigration quotas reflected a reminder of the importance of Christian kindness toward God's chosen people as interpreted by fundamentalist Protestants.

This literal interpretation of biblical verses promising blessings to those who honored the Jews and destruction to those who did not distinguished fundamentalist Protestants from their mainline counterparts. Mainline Protestants, in their embrace of biblical higher criticism and modernity, had long since abandoned literal interpretation of scripture and, along with it, their belief in the relevance of the Jews to Christianity. Jews, with the crucifixion of Jesus, had negated their theological relevancy and their claims to particularism.

Prewar Interest in the Holy Land

Although political Zionism did not officially begin until Theodore Herzl's establishment of the World Zionist Organization in 1897, Jews, particularly from Eastern Europe, had already begun to migrate to Palestine in the 1880s. The second wave of Jewish migration to Palestine, again mainly from Eastern Europe, lasted from 1904 until the start of the Great War in 1914. During the Great War, the British seized pieces of the crumbling Turkish Empire, including Palestine. Zionist Jews viewed British control of Palestine as a possible boon to their hopes to reestablish a Jewish homeland there, and in the person of Lord Arthur Balfour, the then British foreign secretary, they found a sympathetic audience. The Balfour Declaration, issued in November 1917, stated that "His Majesty's Government views with favor the establishment in Palestine of a national home for the Jewish people, and will use their best endeavors to facilitate the achievement of this object, it being clearly understood that nothing shall be done which may prejudice the civil and religious rights of existing non-Jewish communities in Palestine, or the rights and political status enjoyed by Jews in any other country."[18] Viewed by Zionists as a huge victory in the struggle to establish a Jewish homeland, the Balfour Declaration galvanized the growing worldwide Zionist movement.

Although the earliest interest in Zionism can be traced to puritan minister Increase Mather, for most American Protestants active interest in Palestine as a home for the Jews had begun in the nineteenth century. Irish evangelical John Nelson Darby sparked the earliest Christian Zionist movement in the United States after several visits to the states after the Civil War during which he promoted his belief in premillennial dispensationalism—the idea that all human history is divided into distinct eras, or dispensations. The people and nation of Israel occupy a central role in this theology. According to dispensational premillennialism, the Jewish return to Palestine and the reestablishment of the nation of Israel would mark the beginning of the dispensation in which the final war of Armageddon will be fought and the kingdom of God on Earth inaugurated. Darby found two powerful converts to premillennialism with prominent fundamentalist ministers William E. Blackstone and Dwight L. Moody.

Blackstone and Moody worked together to influence American Protestants to support the return of the Jewish people to Palestine in fulfillment of biblical prophecy. Their initial efforts won the support of several significant Americans, including John D. Rockefeller, Charles B. Scribner, J. P. Morgan, and members of the U.S. Congress and the Supreme Court. Despite the organization's initial promise, however, the political efforts to effect U.S. policy in favor of a Jewish settlement in Palestine were short-lived and unsuccessful.[19] The historian Timothy Weber argues that, at this stage of premillennialism, human intervention in biblical prophecy was shunned by most fundamentalists who "watched from the sidelines," ever hopeful of the fulfillment of biblical prophecy but unwilling to work on its behalf.[20]

Although Christian Zionist activities in the Holy Land in the late nineteenth through the early twentieth century were minimal, Christian Protestant interest in missionary work among the Arabs was not. From the turn of the century through the 1930s Protestants had begun to establish missions for Arabs in an effort to win converts to Christ as well as to edge out the competition from other nations and Catholics, both of whom American Protestants feared would jeopardize American Protestant national interests. Missions, schools, and hospitals were established under these auspices. As historian Hertzel Fishman noted, "missionary sponsorship of [Arab schools like the University of Beirut] led, in time, to the identification of American Protestant missionary interests with Arab national interests."[21] This identification, combined with an upsurge in Protestant pilgrimage between the turn of the century and the 1920s, reflected an increased awareness of the Holy Land in the American Protestant consciousness. The trend was common enough for Mark Twain to joke about it. For example, in *The Innocents Abroad* he quipped: "There will be no Second Coming. Jesus has already been to Jerusalem and he's not coming back!"[22] Support for Arab nationalism in contrast to the growing British and French colonial presence found great resonance with many American Protestants who could combine a national belief in self-determination with missionary zeal.[23]

In 1917, when President Wilson and Congress overwhelmingly supported the Balfour Declaration, mainline Protestant leaders dismissed the idea of a Jewish homeland in Palestine. Many who were happy to hear that General Allenby had "taken Jerusalem from the Turks" and restored the holy sites once again to Christian control were less happy to hear of increasing Jewish intentions to immigrate.[24] Some wondered why Jews felt the need to have a homeland of their own. To them, the gates appeared wide open to American Jews, who had, in large numbers, already taken advantage of the economic and educational opportunities the United States offered its immigrants.

Yet American Jews still found the gates to the nation's best clubs, neighborhoods, schools, and even universities locked. While working for change in the United States, Jews began to cautiously support the Zionist movement to establish a homeland in Palestine—particularly in response to growing persecution in Europe. Great divisions existed among American Jews over the Zionist movement, divisions that often confused American Protestants who found themselves unsure of what to support in light of Jewish divisiveness. John Haynes Holmes, minister of the influential Community Church in New York City and co-founder of the National Association for the Advancement of Colored People, was one such Protestant who expressed his frustration.

In a 1937 letter to his good friend, Judah L. Magnes, President of Hebrew University in Jerusalem (and a supporter of a bi-national state in Palestine), Holmes expressed his "utter confusion" over the Zionist debates in the United States. While supporting the idea of a Jewish homeland in Palestine, Holmes did not support the militant attitude expressed by some members of the Zionist Organization of America. Magnes sympathized with Holmes's confusion. "To my mind," he replied, "there is one basic cause for their attitude and the confusion that it arouses not only with you but with me and with many others—and that is, the great majority of Zionists do not, up to this minute, realize the basic need of understanding with the Arabs." For Magnes, the most important issue was not Jewish sovereignty in Palestine but rather finding a place of refuge for the persecuted Jews in Europe.[25]

Mainline Protestants agreed with Magnes's condemnation of Zionist militancy and invoked biblical criticism in condemning the British policy of encouraging "aggressive Jewish claims to the country as a homeland for their people."[26] One article in mainline Protestantism's foremost journal, the *Christian Century,* insisted that, "it is the conviction of most modern biblical scholars that the Old Testament contains no anticipation of the restoration of Israel to its ancient homeland which can apply to the Jewish people in the present age."[27] At this point, the division between fundamentalist eschatological hopes for Palestine and resistance to Zionism among mainline Protestants marked a significant moment in the history of American religious attitudes toward Zionism. Mainline Protestants did not interpret the Bible through the same eschatological lens as the fundamentalists and so were far more willing to sever the biblical connection between modern Jews and historic Palestine than were their fundamentalist brethren. The divide between mainline Protestants and fundamentalists lay at its widest point.

Editor Charles C. Morrison also protested the movement on theological grounds. In an editorial written in May 1933 he admitted that "the Christian mind has never allowed itself to feel the same human concern for Jewish sufferings that it has felt for the cruelties visited upon Armenians, the Boers, the people of India, American slaves, or the Congo blacks under Leopold imperialism." He added, however, that "Christian indifference to Jewish suffering has for centuries been rationalized by the tenable belief that such sufferings were judgment of God upon the Jewish people for their rejection of Jesus."[28]

A Jewish claim to nationhood had been negated with the rejection of Christ, according to traditional mainline Protestant theology. Lest its readers conflate anti-Zionism with antisemitism, however, Morrison reminded his readers that the individual Jew should not be held responsible for the crucifixion. It was rather the Jewish *nationalistic impulse* that was responsible:

> He was crucified because he had a program for Israel which ran counter to the cherished nationalism of Israel's leaders—political and priestly. He opposed their nationalism with the universalism of God's love and God's kingdom. In the eyes of the Jewish rulers he was a seditious person, a menace to their fantastic nationalism and to their vested rights and prestige. It was nationalism that crucified Jesus. It was because he threatened by his teaching to upset their cherished ambition to make Israel and Israel's God the dominant power of the world that he came into collision with Israel's rulers.[29]

For some American Protestants, particularly those that distrusted nationalism of any kind, the solution to the increasing persecution of Jews in Germany was not to immigrate to Palestine but rather to pressure the German government to reform its behavior.[30]

In addition to the rejection of Jewish nationalism on theological principles, concern for Christian holy sites, not Arab or Jewish interests, influenced American Protestant reaction to increased Jewish immigration into Palestine under the British Mandate. The "Report of the Royal Commission on Palestine," published in 1936, noted that,

> The attention of the world has been concentrated on the issue as between Moslem Arab and Jews in Palestine to the practical exclusion of the Christian communities. And yet, the religious stake of the Christians in the Holy Places is just as great as that of Moslem or Jews. The Christian Communities constitute between 7 and 8 percent of the population. The 500 million Christians in the world cannot be indifferent to the position and well-being of their co-religionists in the Holy Land.[31]

Even the cautious endorsement of the creation of a Jewish state in Palestine by the ecumenical *International Review of Missions* expressed the hope that the Christian influence in the area would continue, and lead both Jews and Moslems by its example. It editorialized, in 1937, that "for twenty years [since the beginning of the British Mandate], we have had a Holy Land that was unholy because it was untrue, unreal. Now we are offered two non-Christian states [under the British Partition Plan] which will be real, and a new chance to make the Holy City what it ought to be: a focus of religious Christians, Muslims and Jews, under an administration that ought to be Christian enough to develop the best in all of them."[32] For the editors of the *International Review,* Palestinian or Jewish nationalism remained secondary to the promotion of Christian values.

Impressed by the Balfour Declaration, and the efforts of Jewish immigrants to Palestine to improve the land, a small group of mainline American Protestants had begun to show an interest in establishing a Jewish homeland in Palestine. The Pro-Palestine Federation, established in 1930, steadily worked to persuade other mainline American Protestants to support a Jewish homeland. Although it used biblical language to support Zionism, its three hundred members were mainly clergymen and educators less interested in eschatology and more concerned with humanitarian efforts to protect a vulnerable minority.[33] During the 1930s its support for Zionism found significant resistance among mainline Protestant leaders.

Nonetheless, Hitler's ascension to power increased the urgency of their mission. As persecution of the German Jews began in 1933, the Federation

worked on lifting British immigration barriers. In an effort to assist the fleeing Jews of Germany, in May 1936 its members wrote a letter to the British
prime minister Stanley Baldwin insisting that "the restoration of the Land of
Israel to the Children of Israel is the guiding star in this great struggle for a
better world and a better humanity."[34] The signatories included the Episcopal
bishop of Washington, the president of the Union of Congregational Colleges in America, and the president of the Federal Council of Churches of
Christ in America. Growing increasingly political in the face of continuing
persecution of German Jews, in 1936 it convened a Christian Conference on
the Jewish Problem. The conference, attended by state governors, university
presidents, senators, and clergymen, condemned the persecution of the Jews
in Germany and once more insisted that these "victims of barbarism" ought
to be allowed to "reach a land where their lives and inalienable rights may be
reasonably secure. Their natural place of refuge," wrote the conference sponsors, "is Palestine."[35]

German Events and "Non-Aryan" Christians

For mainline American Protestants and Americans in general, the primary concern of the early 1930s was not the idea of a homeland for Jews
in Palestine. Instead, most focused their attention on Hitler's rise to power
and the ensuing struggle between the Nazi state and the German Evangelical Church, a single government-sponsored church that existed in addition
to the Catholic Church in Germany. Following the conclusion of the First
World War, liberal Protestants had grown deeply pacifist. Most agreed in ret-
rospect that the Christian endorsement of the war had resulted in a loss of
credibility among the faithful in the wake of the war. Like most Americans,
they retreated into isolationism. The persecution of the Jews, though mildly
troubling, did not prompt calls for intervention. While some expressed early
concern for the implications for German Christians of Hitler's control over
the government, what would happen in Germany in the following years was
unclear and many American Protestants remained hesitant about condemning Hitler outright.

   "A thick fog still continues to lie all over this landscape," wrote German
theologian Karl Barth concerning the position of the German Evangelical
Church in 1934, a year after Hitler's ascension to power in Germany. Indeed,
the situation of the German Evangelical Church in the initial Nazi takeover
was far from clear. The murderous intentions of the Nazi Party remained
somewhat ambiguous even to those suspicious of national socialism. In the

early years of Hitler's reign, few people, including clergymen, recognized that the persecution of the Jews was only part, albeit a large one, of the larger plan to eliminate all those considered enemies of the Nazi state, including the churches. Deep divisions also plagued the German Protestant churches over the racial definitions newly imposed by the state with the 1935 Nuremberg Racial Laws. Outside the ominous significance these laws meant for the Jews, how should those Germans of Jewish ancestry who were Christian converts—now called "non-Aryan Christians"—be regarded? Immediately a split erupted within the Evangelical Church over this question. The German Christians, a denominational division that quickly came to power with the initial endorsement of Hitler in 1933, denied the religious equality of non-Aryan Christians and called for their expulsion from the Evangelical Church and for the purging of Jewish influence from all aspects of Christianity.

The Confessing Church, a splinter protest organization, formed in reaction and opposition to the German Christian call for a "racially pure" church. They upheld the traditional teachings of a Christianity that accepted the validity of baptism regardless of race. Yet, while the Confessing Church upheld the teachings of conversion, they, too, were infused with a nationalistic fervor and not immune to the influence of the national socialist state. In some cases they did distinguish between non-Aryans and Aryan Christians within their congregations, although never to the point of forceful exclusion or segregation as was the case in the German Christian movement. Although some effort was made to assist the oppressed, both Christian and Jew, as the persecution evolved from the political to the physical, little was done to protect the persecuted members even of their own congregations.

In the United States fellow Protestants watched the ensuing Church struggle with cautious reserve. Initially American Protestants were divided in response to the German Church struggle and the persecution of the Jews. Uncertain of the path the German Protestant Church would take, reaction among theologians and ministers varied as the Protestant press became increasingly hostile to the German Church's increasingly racist agenda. At this point, many ministers argued, it was too soon to speculate. Many German theologians also argued for moderation, some even condemning the mounting attack on Germany. As Wilhelm Adolf Visser't Hooft (later the president of the World Council of Churches), writing from Switzerland, argued in a 1933 article in the *Christian Century*, "At no other period since the Great War has there been such wholesale application of wartime methods to politics and journalism." While German Protestants faced terrific dilemmas in deciding the nature of the state's relationship with the church, the American Protestant press was guilty, Hooft insisted, of displaying an overzealous "enthusiasm for picking holes in another nation." Discrimination against the Jews might be "on a large scale," but the reasons for such a development were "to some extent justified," he explained. Furthermore, the Jewish question "is much more complex than outsiders seem to think." Ultimately, he insisted, there was no reason "to take it for granted that the worst antisemitic tendencies will finally prevail."[36]

Another German pastor, Ernst Modersohn, published an article in July 1934 in the fundamentalist journal *Moody Bible Institute Monthly* in an attempt to dispel the "lies about Germany [that] are being circulated abroad." Replying to the accusation that the plight of Jewish Christians had progressively worsened, he insisted that he did not know a "single case to sustain these reports." As to the concern over the elimination of the Old Testament from services (because of its Jewish origin), Modersohn quoted another pastor from Saxony who insisted that only "the compulsory reading is repealed."[37]

Fear of exacerbating the strained relations between the German Evangelical Church and the outside world, especially with America, was evident in the writings of some ministers and theologians in the United States. Author Henry Smith Leiper of the Federal Council of the Churches of Christ in America exemplified this cautious approach when he warned of issuing condemnations against the German church. "The process of splitting up the Church every time there is a disagreement has proved disastrous," Leiper wrote, and so, he explained, the worldwide ecumenical movement had "decided to remain in fellowship with the New Church [the Confessing Church] while at the same time expressing unalterable opposition to the racial discrimination and national domination."[38]

Other American ministers, writers, and theologians were less hesitant to confront the issue of nationalism and racism in the German church. Reinhold Niebuhr, one of the most important and influential theologians in the United States and a professor of Christian Ethics at Union Theological Seminary, blasted the German Christians as "a party of rather fanatical supporters of national socialism inside the church."[39] The leaders of the future Confessing Church were also chastised for their silence in the face of Nazi persecution of the Jews. In remarking on the ongoing church struggle for autonomy, Niebuhr wrote, "though the Church is making this heroic effort to preserve its independence, it does not seem to me that it has been equally brave in dissociating itself from the extravagances of nazi terror."[40] He blamed this failure on the preoccupation with the fight against state control, the increase in nationalistic fervor, and the traditional Lutheran teachings of separation of piety from politics. Such a separation of religion from politics had led to failure in the churches' stance on antisemitism. To those Christians who had protested against the German Christians' dismissal of non-Aryans from their congregations, Niebuhr argued that,

> In their very protest against antisemitism in the church they have by impli-
> cation allowed it in the state. They say in their protest, 'the state must judge
> but the church must save,' from which one can only draw the conclusion
> that they regard the antisemitic politics of the government as justified.[41]

Christians of Jewish descent took their protest over their exclusion in the German Evangelical Church to the American public. In an article in the *New York Times*, several non-Aryan clergy wrote: "We are Germans and we want to remain Germans."[42] Two days later another article in that newspaper discussed the creation of a non-Aryan advocacy group, the Reich Confederation of Christian-Jewish Citizens and Non-Aryans, whose purpose would be to "speak in the name of millions of non-Aryans and provide them with spiritual as well as material aid."[43]

American Protestants, both fundamentalist and mainline, noted with growing concern the measures taken against non-Aryan Christians, and as the measures against non-Aryans intensified in the next year, their protests grew louder.[44] The announcement by the German Christians that they would cease missions to the Jews entirely and establish non-Aryan churches provoked condemnation of so-called ghetto churches."[45] Protestants organized to assist Jewish converts to Christianity by establishing funds to provide social services and to assist some in their attempts to leave Germany.[46] The significance of Protestant activism on behalf of Jewish converts to Christianity only highlights the dearth of assistance or protest offered on behalf of persecuted non-converted Jews and reveals the depth of American antisemitism. Only Jews who had abandoned their religious particularism in favor of Christianity deserved assistance.

Not all Protestant journals expressed concern or sympathy for the plight of non-Aryan Christians, much less the Jews. The *Moody Bible Institute Monthly*, for example addressed the issue of the new ghetto church far less sympathetically. In an article in that journal, the editor argued that "Jews accepted baptism in the hopes that it would divorce them from the sorrows and problems of their race and make them and their children part of Germany."[47] The article concluded with a quote by an anonymous Jewish convert to Christianity: "A German Jew is, and always was, a conceited Jew hating his Polish and Russian brethren, for which reason God is using Hitlerism as a rod to unite them and make them one."[48]

Taking a prophetic turn that emphasized premillennial eschatology, the anonymous author concluded that Jews were being baptized only to "enter a college or for business reasons," and predicted that they would be punished by God "until they shall be forced to go back to Palestine and there accept our most loving Savior and Lord Jesus Christ." The article concluded with the editor's hope that such tribulations marked the end times when Christ would return. When considering the current persecution of the Jews, converted or not, the author wrote: "We rejoice with trembling."[49] Clearly, for these fundamentalists, the plight of the Jews remained an issue of utmost importance in their prophetic interpretation. From the fires of persecution, the desire for a return to Palestine would be forged. Mainline Protestants, however, did not actively encourage the idea of immigration to Palestine. For them, the future for the Jews remained in Europe, despite current persecutions.

Yet, if immigration should not be encouraged in Palestine, nor should it be in the United States. As American Jews and a small number of American Protestants lobbied for lifting immigration laws in light of Nazi persecutions, the *Christian Century* opposed this idea. Economic instability would combine with rising antisemitism and would do more harm than good to the Jewish community in America by making Jews likely scapegoats. "There is no ethical principle that requires either an individual person or nation to expose itself to a condition sure to involve a moral overstrain," the journal declared in 1938. "Our immigration laws should be maintained and even further strengthened. Christian and other high-minded citizens have no need to feel apologetic for the limitations upon immigration into the country."[50] The message was clear: the United States should not be unduly burdened by the influx of an inassimilable population, nor should it feel the need to justify its position.

As the decade progressed and persecution against Jews in Germany increased, the *Christian Century* continued its assault against Judaism. In editorials and articles, the journal warned Jews against maintaining a separate ethnic identity in the midst of Protestant America. In an editorial written in 1937, for example, the editors encouraged Jews to abandon Judaism's particularistic aspects in favor of its universalistic elements in the hope of "achieving a higher integration of social relationships in the United States."[51] Reflecting the inherent tensions between democracy and religion, another editorial insisted that maintaining religious particularity at the expense of a "higher synthesis" with Protestant America would only result in "the spirit of American tolerance shriveling up."[52] Such reaction against Jewish religious separatism within the United States could not help but inform American Protestantism's initial reaction toward Jewish Zionist impulses both before and during World War II.

Conclusion

A tradition of antisemitism—and its growth during the 1930s—would not disappear any time soon. When events in Germany crystallized the Jews' struggle there, this information was met in the United States by a handful of well-defined mind-sets, including antisemitic and prophetic ones. Only the plight of Jewish converts to Christianity catalyzed widespread activism from American Protestants, emphasizing all too clearly the lack of systematic concern for Jewish victims of Nazi persecution. Although American Protestants appeared more tolerant of Jews than did the German churches, they still focused on the question of Jewish assimilation and acculturation in American society. Entrenched in their own cultural hegemony, the idea that Jews might wish to remain distinctively Jewish and would perhaps even support the idea of Jewish nationalism would shock many Americans in the decades to come. Entrenched antisemitism, deep antipathy to any claim of Jewish nationalism, and cultural hubris characterized American Protestant attitudes toward Jews, Judaism, and Zionism in the 1930s. Such an assessment could not offer a starker before and after snapshot of American Protestant attitudes in the 1930s compared to those at the turn of the twenty-first century. It would take the attempted genocide of European Jews to alter the picture.

American Protestants Respond to Zionism and the Jewish Genocide in Europe, 1938–1948

In 1945, as violence mounted in the Middle East and Truman considered the fate of Palestine, members of the State Department's Near East Division sent him a secret memo warning him of the influence on Congress of a pro-Zionist Christian organization, the American Christian Palestine Committee. Made up of Christian politicians, clergy, and laity convinced by humanitarian impulses and Christian guilt to support the establishment of Israel, they had, a Near East Affairs (NEA) staffer warned Truman, "written all the members of Congress, asking them to write to you urging that now the war in Europe is over, steps be taken to implement a pro-Zionist policy regarding Palestine with the aim of opening the country to unrestricted Jewish immigration and creating a Jewish state." Moreover, the staffer added, "we have every reason to believe that a large number of the members of both houses will comply."[1] American Protestants had undergone a dramatic shift in attitudes—from ambivalence about Jewish suffering in the early 1930s to effective mobilization on behalf of the Zionist cause by 1945. The NEA memo to Truman signaled a significant moment not only in Protestant-Jewish relations but in the creation of what would become the special relationship between the United States and Israel.

Between 1938 and 1945, as the Jews of Europe were systematically massacred by the Nazis and their collaborators, the effects of what would later be termed the Holocaust reverberated across the world. Since the massacre of Jews was taking place in Christian Europe, American Protestants, in particular, reeled from the news. In a short time many began to reevaluate their theological assumptions about Judaism and to advocate for the establishment of a Jewish homeland in Palestine.

The transition from the dominant antisemitism of the 1930s to the growing American support of Jews and Judaism was not a smooth one, however.

It occurred in fits and starts, with some Protestant activists embarking upon intense public relations efforts to effect legislation and influence U.S. foreign policy on behalf of the Zionist cause and to rescue imperiled Jews in Europe. Others refrained from commenting on the situation of the Jews in Europe, resisted efforts to change immigration laws to allow Jews to escape Nazi Europe, and objected to the establishment of a Jewish state in Palestine. In the 1930s conservative fundamentalists, a growing minority, reported in their press with startling accuracy the imminent Holocaust, hesitantly supported Jewish immigration to Palestine, and yet viewed it all through the lens of biblical prophecy that emphasized the ultimate conversion of the Jews to Christianity.

American Protestants' thinking about the question of a Jewish homeland in Palestine continued to evolve in these years. Some Protestant circles remained resistant to the establishment of Israel as inter-Jewish disputes over Zionism influenced their thinking, even as the emergence of the politically powerful American Palestine Committee exerted enormous efforts on behalf of the Zionist cause. Despite significant initial hostility to Zionism within some American Protestant circles, by the end of the war the activities of pro-Zionist Protestant organizations had successfully persuaded Congress and many of their fellow Protestants to support the establishment of Israel. For different theological reasons, the fundamentalist premillennialists also joined in this effort, and their combined efforts fundamentally changed the nature of Jewish-Christian relations and U.S. foreign policy by 1948.

Kristalnacht and the British White Paper

The year 1938 marked a turning point in the Nazi persecution of the Jews, and mainline and fundamentalist Protestants alike acknowledged this reality. After *Kristalnacht,* or "The Night of Broken Glass," on 9 November 1938, many American Protestants understood that disenfranchisement could lead to destruction.[2] This realization led the editors of the *Christian Century* to acknowledge that the Jews needed a place of refuge—a haven from Nazi persecution—and even suggested allowing a small increase of Jewish immigration to Palestine, a position it had originally rejected. "Suppose that instead of merely subjecting Jews to economic and social disadvantages," the editor of that journal asked, "Nazi Germany should decide to massacre them? Is there an end to the world's tolerance?"[3]

Fundamentalists, who had in the previous decade embraced the antisemitic *Protocols* or shown deep ambivalence about Jewish persecution in Germany, abandoned such positions after November 1938. The confusion that had existed about Hitler's policies toward the Jews evaporated, and, as Timothy Weber notes, "by then it was clear to most dispensationalists what Hitler was up to, and equivocation stopped." The abandonment of the *Protocols* in fundamentalist circles had even begun before *Kristalnacht*. J. Frank Norris, a well-known fundamentalist Baptist preacher in Texas, argued that persecuting the Jews and alienating them from Christianity ran counter to God's purposes in the end of days. According to dispensationalist theology, Jews would convert to Christianity en masse in that time and become worldwide evangelicals. "Of all the peoples on Earth that ought not persecute Jews," he insisted, "it is that people called the Fundamentalist Baptists. Those who believe in the Premillennial coming of Jesus Christ should certainly do everything in their power to help the Jew because we believe when Christ comes the Jews will be converted, and become the world's greatest evangelicals—then why kill them off if they are to be the world's greatest evangelicals?"[4] The fundamentalist periodicals, though acknowledging the plight of the Jews of Germany, did not advocate mass immigration of Jewish refugees to the United States.[5] Many, however, pointed to Palestine as a place of possible refuge.

But in May 1939, six months after *Kristalnacht*, the British published the 1939 White Paper, an official foreign policy statement that restricted Jewish immigration into Palestine and effectively eliminated any hope for large-scale resettlement of European Jews there. The White Paper of 1939 was seen by many Americans as a default by the British on the promises made through the Balfour Declaration. Eventually, in the upcoming years, it would serve as a rallying point to unite both Jewish and Christian Zionist opinion in opposition against it. Only the *Christian Century* endorsed the White Paper. It assuaged the journal's fears of a Jewish minority dominating the Arab majority (and thereby jeopardizing both Christian control of holy sites and Christian missions to Arabs). "What today looks to many Zionists like black defeat will, in the light of history, turn out to be a glorious victory," *Century* editor Charles C. Morrison wrote. Let Palestine become a cultural and spiritual center for world Jewry—thereby avoiding inevitable clashes between competing groups. The White Paper, he wrote, "may turn out to be a blessing in disguise."[6] To some Protestants, the White Paper appeared to be an eminently reasonable solution.[7]

World events and shifting opinions were soon eclipsing the White Paper, however. As persecution in Germany grew more serious and immigration restrictions in Palestine more stringent, certain elements of the media reflected a growing interest in the Jewish settlements in Palestine. In 1939, for example, the *Christian Science Monitor* ran a series of articles describing them in glowing terms and praising the "highlight" of the new settlements—Zionism, "with its determination to colonize and redeem from decay the historic 'Land of Israel'" and the revitalization of "the Hebrew language."[8] The *Christian Science Monitor*, like many American Protestants, had begun to connect a biblical claim to Palestine with the efforts of Jewish settlers to establish a state.

The Holocaust Begins

After war broke out in September 1939, the main concern of mainline Protestantism centered not upon continuing developments in the Holy Land but on remaining neutral in the European war. In hindsight, the churches' enthusiastic endorsement of American involvement in World War I and the conflation of militarism with patriotism appeared to have been a horrific mistake—one they were not anxious to repeat. Calls for pacifism and isolationism dominated not only the churches but the popular consciousness of Americans in general. American Jews who increasingly, albeit cautiously, called for intervention were condemned as warmongers by many within the mainline Protestant community. A few months before the surprise attack on Pearl Harbor and American entry into World War II, an article in the *Christian Century* warned Jews that they would become scapegoats should they continue to agitate for American intervention in the European war: "Despite all attempts to gloss over the tension between Jew and Gentile in this land of freedom, the simple truth is that the spirit of tolerance is hardly more than skin deep. . . . The Jewish problem is not primarily a religious problem. It is a racial and social problem. Its explosive possibilities do not inhere in any conflict of religious forms or creeds, but in a tragic social unassimilability."[9]

In response to the increasing persecution of the Jews of Europe, New York Senator Robert F. Wagner established the bipartisan American Palestine Committee (APC) on 28 March 1941 in conjunction with the Emergency Committee for Zionist Affairs. Co-chaired by Senator Charles L. McNary, the APC, in its first press release, announced its "support of [the] Holy Land as an 'Outpost of Freedom and Social Justice'" and its intention to apply political pressure to bring about "large scale colonization of hundreds of thousands of Jewish refugees from war-torn European lands during the post-war period."[10] The APC would "endeavor to win public support for the program for the establishment of a Jewish National Home in Palestine." Both men were self-professing Christians who viewed antisemitism as a Christian problem, but Wagner also represented significant Jewish constituents. The establishment of the APC therefore satisfied a Christian obligation, a political problem, and Jewish voters.

The APC's first rosters included a veritable who's who of important American political and religious figures including "more than 300 outstanding government officials, legislators, Governors, educators, churchmen and civic leaders" dedicated to the fulfillment of the promise of the Balfour Declaration. Some of its most notable members included the then senator Harry S. Truman, the secretary of the interior Harold Ickes, Wendell Willkie, William Allen White, and Joseph W. Martin Jr., the minority leader of the House of Representatives and chairman of the Republican National Committee. "The American Palestine Committee," declared Senator McNary, "will aim to give expression to the interest, sympathy and moral support of the American people for this humane and statesmanlike cause."[11] McNary pointed to the growing Jewish refugee crisis in Europe as a motivating factor in the establishment of the APC.

At the outset of the APC, McNary also tied the Jewish plight in Europe directly to Christianity. He added that the problem of Jewish refugees was the anguish of Christians everywhere. "The solution of the age-old Jewish problem is as much the concern of enlightened Christendom as it is of the Jews themselves," he argued, adding, "American Jewry which is seeking to provide a haven for refugees made homeless by totalitarian brutality should be assured that in the promotion of this effort they can count on the good will and the moral support of their Christian fellow citizens."[12] In this case, American foreign policy in favor of a Jewish homeland in Palestine should find its base in the liberal Christian ethic of "the hope of the reunion of the Jewish people with the land of its ancient inheritance," argued Senator Wagner. Besides, Wagner pragmatically noted, "efforts to find territories" for displaced Jews elsewhere "have been fruitless. The ancient Homeland alone has been able to evoke the requisite spirit of sacrifice and pioneering qualities."[13] The pioneering efforts of the Zionist settlers would surely benefit the Arab population as well, Wagner argued, as they built up "agriculture, industry, and commerce" for the benefit of all inhabitants.[14] The argument that a Jewish state in Palestine would be an improvement for all living in the region, Jewish and Arab alike, would remain an essential part of APC propaganda efforts.

In a press release intended for the members of the Zionist Organization of America, the APC was quick to reassure pro-Zionist American Jews that it was "no mere complimentary body" to the Emergency Committee for Zionist Affairs. "The roster of its membership, the statements issued by its leaders, its historic background," the press release stated, "give[s] assurance that the Committee is not just a vehicle for making polite gestures to the Jewish people."[15] The "historic background" of the committee included the previous efforts of William E. Blackstone to petition the U.S. government to restore Palestine to the Jewish people. "Since that day," the press release noted, "the sympathy of America has been increasingly active and vocal." The release went on to note the joint resolution of the House and Senate in support of the Balfour Declaration in May 1922, and the establishment of the Pro-Palestine Federation "with the hearty blessings from Mr. Herbert Hoover, the President of the United States, and the late Charles Curtis, then Vice-President, and with former Senator William H. King of Utah, as Chairman."[16] "The American Palestine Committee," the press release concluded, "is calculated to awaken large hopes and expectations. It stirs the imagination." With the establishment of the APC, the United States was one step closer to fulfilling its "pre-destined role of arbiter of world affairs." Ultimately the question of a Jewish homeland in Palestine was one "in which no nation or individual in times of decision can escape. What word will America speak when the question of Zion stands before the nations, and what deeds will follow when that word has been spoken?"[17]

Protestant leaders called for change and also took action. In an effort to convince American Protestantism to throw off the ill-fitting garb of isolationism and pacifism, Reinhold Niebuhr, described by the *Christian Century* in 1939 as "without question the most vital personal force in American theology," established *Christianity and Crisis* in February 1941.[18] Frustrated by "liberal Protestants who believe that Christianity will shame the enemy into goodness," Niebuhr insisted that Christians had an obligation not only to fight fascism and Nazism, but to condemn the persecution of the Jews.[19] In the first issue Niebuhr wrote: "I think it is dangerous to allow Christian religious sensitivity about the imperfections of our own society to obscure the fact that Nazi tyranny intends to annihilate the Jewish race."[20] Between the first issue in February and the bombing of Pearl Harbor in December, Niebuhr consistently advocated U.S. intervention in Europe. Ten months after the first issue of *Christianity and Crisis* appeared, the Japanese bombed Pearl Harbor, Germany declared war on the United States, and the United States officially entered the Second World War.

Once the war began, both the secular and Protestant presses focused on winning the war and building a new and just world order after an Allied victory. Stories of Jewish persecution and efforts to establish a Jewish homeland in Palestine were eclipsed by concern for winning the war and establishing a just peace. Both presses appeared cautious about reporting on the increasing numbers of stories of Nazi death camps in the East. Plagued throughout the Second World War by disbelief in Nazi atrocities in the wake of the inaccuracies of World War I propaganda, the American secular press was hesitant to report about the existence of the Nazi extermination camps. Believing what they heard proved problematic since the stories appeared to be too similar to the false propaganda issued by the Allies during the Great War. It seemed too horrific to be real. Even when reporters did send such stories back to their editors, the editors often hesitated or outright refused to print it. They suffered from what Deborah Lipstadt terms "the show me syndrome."[21]

Suspicion of hyperbole restrained some Protestant press as well. In 1942, when Rabbi Stephen Wise, after consulting with Under Secretary of State Sumner Wells, informed the media of the mass exterminations of the Jews taking place throughout Eastern Europe, the *Christian Century* published an article questioning Wise's claim that "orders had been issued by the Germans to exterminate all Polish Jews by 1943. The exiled Polish government," it wrote, "has claimed only that orders have been issued to exterminate half of the Jews in Poland, not all, by the end of the year."[22] Such a response to Wise's statements angered many in the Jewish community.[23] Rabbi Theodore Lewis of Brooklyn, New York, for example, furious at the *Christian Century*'s attack on Wise, wrote to the journal: "Your editorial on the massacre of the Jews in Europe is anything but Christian. In fact, it is a heartless and unpardonable comment on one of the greatest tragedies of our day and one of the most gruesome experiences in the history of Israel." He went on to ask: "Just where is your Christian conscience? Is this the only answer you can give to the agonized cry of European Jewry facing death?"[24] Although the editors of the *Christian Century* remained unmoved, other Protestants did not.

In response to the reports of Nazi genocidal goals, many American Protestant leaders increased pressure on Congress to lobby the British to lift the ban on Jewish immigration to Palestine. Protestant leaders like Reinhold Niebuhr used their considerable public influence to advocate on behalf of the Zionist cause in mainline, secular periodicals. In late 1941 Niebuhr submitted a series of articles to *The Nation* about the plight of the Jews in Europe and the necessity of establishing a Jewish homeland in Palestine. Initially the editors expressed hesitancy to publish the controversial material, but they finally agreed in February 1942 to publish the first in the series.[25]

In these landmark articles Niebuhr advocated the establishment of a Jewish homeland in Palestine for morally pragmatic and politically pragmatic reasons. It was unfair, he argued, to ask the Jew to abandon his particularism in order to assimilate into whatever dominant culture he inhabited. "It is just as false," he wrote, "as if the command, 'Thou shalt love thy neighbor as thyself' were interpreted to mean that I must destroy myself so that no friction may arise between my neighbor and myself."[26] The disregard exhibited in Europe and the United States for ethnic differences among peoples constituted "unrealistic universalism or a conscious or unconscious ethnic imperialism." It was time, he wrote, to "support more generously than in the past legitimate aspiration of Jews for a homeland in which they will not be simply tolerated, but which they will possess." In a break with APC propaganda, however, Niebuhr did not support the Zionist claim that a Jewish homeland would bring benefits to both Jews and Arabs in Palestine. "It is absurd," he pointed out, "to expect any people to regard the restriction of their sovereignty over a traditional possession as 'just' no matter how many other benefits accrue from that abridgement."[27] High praise from Justice Felix Frankfurter followed the publication of *The Nation* article. "I would give a cookie," Frankfurter wrote to Niebuhr, "to see the letters that you have had on your Jewish articles. I hope very much that your articles will be put out in pamphlet form because, as I have told you, I know of nothing in print that faces the Jewish problem more trenchantly and more candidly."[28]

Henry Atkinson, member of the World Church Peace Union and an ardent Zionist, argued that a Jewish homeland was, in fact, a religious issue as well as a political one. He suggested, in 1943, that "a competent international Christian commission" be sent to Palestine to examine the best way to bring about the establishment of a Jewish homeland. "This is not 'Protestant Zionism.' It is an attempt to answer what is basically not a Jewish problem, but rather a Christian problem," he wrote.[29] By 1943 even the ardently anti-Zionist *Christian Century*, confronted with the reality of antisemitism in Europe, argued that "places of asylum and escape for those who can get away, with special consideration of the admission of more refugees to the U.S. and to Palestine" should be considered.[30] This sentiment grew rapidly among American Protestants, particularly as the mobilization effort of the American Palestine Committee began to take effect in Protestant America.

In 1943 the APC called on "Christian America to back up Jewish homeland." The APC, self-described as "Christian America's vehicle for the expression of sympathy for the Jewish aspirations in Palestine," now aimed "to enroll the broad mass of Christian Americans." In an indication that the APC agenda had made progress, Senator Wagner noted that "the initial response to our appeal for membership is highly encouraging."[31] Wagner justified this ambitious enrollment mission by claiming that the reality of Hitler's slaughter of the European Jews necessitated that America redeem its pledge to help rebuild the Jewish homeland in Palestine. Even as the APC worked to increase public awareness of the plight of the Jews in Europe and support for a Jewish homeland in Palestine, its members worried that these issues could be eclipsed by the nation's war mobilization. To prevent these issues from being ignored, the senators highlighted past U.S. nonpartisan support of the establishment of a Jewish homeland in Palestine and urged "practical action" in light of Allied plans for the postwar world. The promise of Palestine, made by the British with the Balfour Declaration, would be redeemed with American help, the senators pledged.[32]

Concern for the plight of European Jews, slowly spreading among American Protestants, helped to fill the ranks of the APC's newly founded subcommittee, the Christian Council on Palestine (CCP). Published a few months after its December 1942 establishment, the CCP's 1943 "Resolutions by the Executive Committee" set out eight recommendations to alleviate Jewish suffering in Europe. These included the insistence that "America takes the lead in helping to save millions of Jews from the horror created by the Nazi terror in Europe." The CCP also recommended lifting the immigration ban and urged an immediate repeal of the 1939 White Paper restricting Jewish immigration to Palestine. The Committee also recommended that an international commission be established to analyze the issues facing the Jewish-Arab problems in Palestine, as well as recommending that Palestine be placed under an "international mandate." Lastly, the Committee recommended that "provision be written into the peace treaty to make the outbreak of political antisemitism anywhere *prima facie* evidence of incitement to crime, and punishable as such under international law."[33]

In an effort to continue the massive public relations campaign on behalf of the Zionist cause and streamline the organizational structure, the leaders of the APC and CCP combined forces into the American Christian Palestine Committee (ACPC). The first agenda of the ACPC addressed the still very real problem of Christian antisemitism in the United States. Through the auspices of the Church Peace Union and the World Alliance for International Friendship through the Churches, Henry Atkinson and Carl Hermann Voss published pamphlets attacking antisemitism in no uncertain terms and suggested that an antisemite was simply an agent of Nazi Germany. Atkinson and Voss equated antisemitism with anti-patriotism and fascism. Collective security for the United States, they argued, could only be achieved after abandoning historic Christian antisemitism. Launching a "counter-attack" against such ideology constituted the responsibility of all patriotic Americans. Christians should form study groups and Sunday school programs that addressed the "nature and menace of antisemitism" as a necessary step in eradicating its evil. The authors also advocated isolating antisemites within their communities, called for legislation to make discrimination on "racial or religious groups" illegal, and called for a program of rehabilitation for the surviving European Jews in the United States and Palestine after the war.[34]

Moreover, their discussion of the Holocaust in the rest of the article proved surprisingly accurate and reveals mainline Protestant awareness of the details of the Nazis' ensuing genocidal campaign against the Jews. As early as 1943 Atkinson and Voss reported to the readers of the *World Alliance News Letter* that already three million Jews had been murdered under Hitler—"the greatest massacre of modern history, perhaps of all human history."[35] The authors warned against complacency and again offered a proactive program to assist the survivors. They suggested that the allied nations "intensify official threats of punishment for atrocities," aid the Jews left alive in the East by facilitating their escape through the neutral Balkans and Turkey, and provide refuge for survivors in the United States and Palestine.[36] Atkinson's and Voss's campaign marked a significant moment in Jewish-Christian relations in the United States. Rather than simply condemning antisemitism passively, they offered a proactive and energetic program with warlike rhetoric to eradicate its presence in American life and equated antisemitism with antidemocratic ideals.

In a convention held the following year at the Statler Hotel in Washington, D.C., the American Christian Palestine Committee joined forces with the American Federation of Labor (AFL), the Congress of Industrial Organizations (CIO), the Free World Association, the Union for Democratic Action, the Unitarian Fellowship for Social Justice, and the United Christian Council for Democracy to call for the "mobilization of American Christian sentiment in favor of free entry of Jews into Palestine and the reconstitution of that country as a free and democratic Jewish commonwealth."[37] Attendees included forty-eight delegates representing thirty countries, with the Reverend Henry Atkinson, Representative Helen Douglas, and Senator Robert Wagner representing the United States. Their purpose lay in "discussing the work being carried on by Christian pro-Palestine committees throughout the world" and in organizing the first International Christian pro-Palestine Committee.

Urging the passage of a bill then before Congress advocating a withdrawal of the British 1939 White Paper that called for severely limiting Jewish immigration to Palestine, Atkinson argued that the restriction of Jewish settlement conflicted "with American sentiment and American interests." Establishing a democratic Jewish homeland in the Near East would serve American foreign policy interests as well as humanitarian needs. The first resolution unanimously passed by the conference attendees included an affirmation of the right of the Jews in Palestine to form a state, recognized by international law through the United Nations. They further proposed a resolution that advocated the removal of all immigration restrictions against Jews trying to enter Palestine and a "repeal of the anti-Jewish land laws" implemented by the British. Both resolutions preceded a similar vote by the United Nations Special Committee on Palestine by two years.[38] Such efforts revealed the strategic mobilization orchestrated by politically powerful American Protestants to build support for a Jewish state.

The resolution adopted at the Statler Hotel Conference and immediately released to the media offered a clear relationship between proposed U.S. foreign policy in the post-war world and the importance of improved relations between Christians and Jews. The resolution declared that "the Christian world must rededicate itself to the heritage it has received from Judaism, the mother faith of Christianity," and called for repeal of the 1939 White Paper.[39]

It highlighted the efforts of the Jews of Palestine to assist the Allies. Palestine had become "an out-post of democracy" in the midst of a despotic and Axis-sympathetic Middle East. Appeasing the Arab population by restricting Jewish immigration was a failed policy and could not "provide the basis of an enduring and equitable solution of the Palestine problem." Appeasement, after all, "has failed to serve the cause of peace and democracy in other parts of the world." In conclusion, the resolution urged "the passage at the earliest opportunity by the Senate and the House of the Wagner-Taft and Wright-Compton resolutions now under discussion in Committees, so that these objectives may be the more speedily achieved."[40] Again tying the responsibility of American Christians to assist the Jews, Carl Hermann Voss, the executive secretary, reminded the audience that "it was the Christian's responsibility to help, because 'the Jewish problem' has been created by Christians: Persecutions of the Jews have almost without exception taken place only at the hands of Christians in so-called Christian countries."[41] Following the Statler Hotel Conference, the ACPC members set out a three-pronged approach to assist the Jewish victims in Europe and aid in the establishment of a Jewish homeland in Palestine. The ACPC encouraged "Christian churches all over America to continue to protest and work against anti-Jewish agitation, often leading to sheer brutality upon Jews by the enemies of democracy." Second, the ACPC argued that "a strongly established and recognized Jewish Homeland in Palestine offers the only real hope for most of the suffering men, women, and children of Israel in Nazi-occupied Europe."[42] Its emphatic insistence on the repeal of the 1939 White Paper restricting Jewish immigration constituted the third point. It was necessary to lift the immigration ban to accommodate those persecuted by Hitler in Nazi-occupied Europe. Notably it did not stop there. It advocated lifting immigration restrictions in the United States to assist the Jews, in contrast to the *Christian Century's* strong anti-immigration stance. It was, argued the ACPC, "the responsibility of America to accept more refugees so that the cry cannot be raised: 'Palestine for the Jews? Sure, send them all back to Palestine!'"[43]

The ACPC's efforts to educate American Protestants about the necessity of establishing the Jewish homeland in Palestine resulted in a flurry of radio addresses and a letter writing and mailing campaign in 1944. In multiple radio addresses, members of the ACPC and Jewish Zionists confronted the recurring issues that dominated American concerns about Jewish settlement in Palestine, including land sustainability, political tensions between Jews and Arabs, and American bipartisan support for a Jewish homeland.[44]

The campaign of the ACPC to convince mainline Protestant America to endorse the idea of a Jewish homeland in Palestine celebrated a victory when the Northeastern Jurisdictional Conference of the Methodist Church, representing more than one million Americans, unanimously passed a resolution endorsing the establishment of a Jewish nation in Palestine. The resolution called on the United States to "take appropriate action" to see that "international commitments made to the Jews may be fulfilled at the earliest possible time."[45] The fulfillment of the Balfour Declaration, the resolution continued, served "the interest of justice, humanitarianism and future world peace." The resolution further condemned "all racial and religious bigotry and intolerance as undemocratic and un-Christian."[46] Such justifications for support of a Jewish homeland clearly implied that to not support Zionism, to be undemocratic and un-Christian, meant allying with fascist or communist values.

During the years of Hitler's campaign against the European Jews, the fundamentalist periodicals, such as *Our Hope*, the *Weekly Evangel*, the *Sunday School Times*, the *Moody Monthly*, and others, approached the persecution quite differently from their mainline counterparts. The periodicals consistently and accurately reported the statistics and details of the persecution. But unlike pro-Zionist mainline Protestants, fundamentalists saw the persecution of the Jews in a prophetic light and, for the most part, eschewed human efforts to intervene. They condemned Hitler's campaign against the Jews, even while acknowledging that the persecutions helped to fulfill biblical prophecy—namely, pushing more Jews toward Palestine. One fundamentalist noted ironically in a *Moody Monthly* article that "by driving the preserved people back into the Promised Land, Hitler, who does not believe the Bible and who sneers at the Word of God, is helping to fulfill its most outstanding prophecy."[47] Furthermore, most dispensationalists, though quick to point out that those who persecuted the Jews would be punished by God, nonetheless insisted that such persecutions were a necessary part of God's plan for the Jews.

In *Our Hope,* Gaebelein noted that of the estimated ten million Jews living in Europe, more than half were the subject of increasing antisemitism, and noted particularly the plight of Jews in Germany and Poland. It was proof, he insisted, that "their own God-inspired Scriptures are being fulfilled." This persecution could not be solved with human endeavors, and, perhaps in a reference to the efforts of the ACPC, he argued, "nor can a united front with Gentile nominal Christians bring about change. The change will come when 'they shall look upon Him whom they pierced' and acknowledge Christ as their Saviour-King."[48]

Many fundamentalists viewed the persecution of the Jews in Europe as an opportunity to witness.[49] As the *Moody Monthly* pointed out in April 1943, "The terrific persecutions in Europe, the troubles in Palestine, and the ever-increasing antisemitism throughout the world have softened their hearts and make them long for security and rest of soul."[50] Even though the conservative press offered far more details of Jewish destruction than their liberal counterparts, they nonetheless interpreted these statistics through a uniquely prophetic perspective which emphasized that the divine purpose of Nazi persecution lay in Jewish conversion to Christianity.[51] For example, the *Moody Monthly* argued that the persecution of the Jews in the Warsaw Ghetto had resulted in mass conversions of Jewish children. "Perhaps that is the reason the Devil saw to it that Warsaw was wrecked and the Jews scattered," one contributor suggested.[52] Nonetheless, nations who wreaked such destruction on God's chosen people would surely face divine judgment, "the wrath of God Almighty."[53]

In contrast to the editors of the *Christian Century*, Gaebelein and the editors of other fundamentalist periodicals did not question the reports of persecution coming from Europe and felt it their responsibility to report them to their readers. As the war progressed, these periodicals continued to apprise readers of the fate of the Jews of Europe. Gaebelein addressed the false propaganda reports of the First World War that now prevented many Americans from believing the atrocity stories they now heard but insisted that "this is far from being true in this war of barbarism. If anything, the number of Jews killed is underestimated. Reliable sources," he continued, "mention not less than two million Jews murdered since Hitler went on his devil-controlled mission."[54]

As the war progressed and the plight of the Jews trying to escape persecution in Europe worsened, Gaebelein increasingly focused the attention of the readers of *Our Hope* to the question of a Jewish homeland in Palestine. Since the "barbed fist of persecution is crushing the Jews, or trying to do so," he concluded, "where will Israel go? To THE LAND PALESTINE."[55] Gaebelein reported the protests of Dr. Chaim Weizmann regarding the plight of Jewish refugees trying to enter Palestine to the British government. After a refugee ship carrying 760 Jewish escapees sank in a failed effort to land in Palestine, Weizmann protested the British government's refusal to permit their landing in Palestine. "The only alternative," Gaebelein wrote, "was to return to the Gestapo in Romania." These "unfortunate," including sixty children, he explained, were "living like rats in their 200 ton ship." Such policies, Gaebelein argued, stemmed from the British government's attempt to "curry favor with the Arabs."[56] In 1943 *Our Hope* clearly articulated a concern for the establishment of Israel for both humanitarian and religious reasons, and decried the 1939 White Paper and British immigration policies.

Yet for American fundamentalists the question of a Jewish homeland in Palestine was of religious significance at least as much as it was a pragmatic humanitarian issue. Fundamentalists rejected the idea of a Jewish homeland divorced from its religious roots. In describing a recent fund-raising dinner sponsored by the American Jewish Congress in New York, Gaebelein highlighted this conviction. "Notable was the omission," he concluded, "of any mention of the God who brought Israel out of the land of Egypt, and Who will one day, as He has promised, lead 'the seed of the house of Israel'" to "'dwell in their own land.'"[57] Whether Palestine would prove to be an immediate haven of refuge was "a question" unanswered. Surely "they will return one day in belief," he reminded his readers. But whether the goals of Zionism would coincide with the time line of the end times which called for a restoration of Israel, remained to be seen.[58] The hesitancy to fully associate the socialist Zionist agenda in Palestine with the promised restoration of Israel explains the cautious support for Zionism during the war period and its immediate aftermath. In some ways the Zionist movement appeared too exciting to dismiss as less than prophetic, but the movement's decidedly socialist, secular moorings gave pause to some fundamentalist leaders.

Protestants and Anti-Zionism

Not every Protestant—mainline or fundamentalist—was onboard with Zionism or new Christian-Jewish relations, of course. The increasing effectiveness of the American Christian Palestine Committee and the organization's close relationship with Zionist organizations in America prompted the anti-Zionist American Council for Judaism (ACJ) to launch its own public relations counter-activities. For many mainline Protestants, hesitation to endorse the Zionist cause stemmed from the divisiveness of the issue among American Jews. Although some American Jews such as Stephen Wise and Abba Hillel Silver welcomed and encouraged Protestant support for the Zionist cause, many American Jews resented Protestant interference in a cause that so divided them.

Nowhere was this more evident than in a pamphlet produced by the American Council for Judaism in 1944. Founded in 1942 in an effort to counter the increasing influence of Zionism among American Jewry, the Council insisted that Judaism was simply a religion, not an ethnicity. According to an internal State Department report, the Council "takes the position that Judaism is a religion rather than a national force, in other words that American Jews are Americans first and Jews second, just as is the case with American Catholics or American Baptists."[59] Although the ACJ never represented a majority of American Jews, its influence on Protestants who were unsure of whether to support the Zionist cause remained a significant issue in redefining Jewish-Protestant relations and support for Zionism both before and after the war. The ACJ sought to divorce Zionism from American Judaism in an effort to stave off charges of dual loyalty and stem the tide of American antisemitism by emphasizing Jewish assimilation into the dominant American culture.

Moreover, the ACJ resented Protestant support for the Zionist cause. On 30 April 1944 the ACJ printed an editorial in several major newspapers in an effort to elucidate to Protestants the different views of Zionism among American Jews. In the editorial the ACJ condemned the British White Paper of 1939 and supported increased Jewish immigration to Palestine but also insisted that Zionism was contrary to the spirit of American Judaism. The editorial argued that "because of the hitherto unchallenged Zionist claims, many Gentiles were led to believe that friendship for the Jews necessitated the acceptance of the Zionist formulas; and so they made that acceptance, although with misgivings."[60] The Council decided to mail the editorial to several hundred Christian clergy and educators and solicit their response to it. They received more than 150 letters, "the vast majority of them," the Council pointed out, "welcomed our statement as clarifying a confused situation." The Council then turned the responses into a pamphlet titled, "Christian Opinion on Jewish Nationalism and a Jewish State." It was important, noted Morris S. Lazaron in his foreword to the pamphlet, "for Gentiles to know that among Jews themselves there is a considerable and growing judgment that Jewish nationalism and the Jewish State are not the way to go."[61]

Most Protestants who responded agreed with the Council that Judaism was a religion, not an ethnic group deserving of its own nation. Many condemned nationalism of any sort. Carolus P. Harry, president of the Board of Education for the United Lutheran Church in America, wrote: "In these days when the nationalism of the last century has so clearly revealed its inability to direct the affairs of humanity peacefully and progressively, to seek to establish another national sovereignty on a racial basis is very foolish." H. Richard Niebuhr, professor of Christian Ethics at the Yale Divinity School and Reinhold Niebuhr's brother, also objected to Zionism for its nationalistic impulses. "To this unity [of all races] under God," he wrote, "Jews and Christians have given testimony through the ages, partly by words but also by being communities of a definitely international or supranational character. At this moment in world history nothing would be more tragic than the nationalization of these religious communities." Niebuhr conceded that "as a method of relief the creation of a national Jewish state may have its points," but he added that "as a method of realizing the one thing that is all important now, the actual human community, it seems a retrogressive step."[62]

Henry Sloan Coffin of the Union Theological Seminary in New York objected to Jewish claims to nationhood at the expense of the Arabs—a common concern among many liberal Protestants, who, for reasons discussed in the previous chapter, believed that a Jewish state would jeopardize missionary work and the human rights of Arabs. A letter written by James Mullenberg of the Pacific School of Religion in Berkeley, California, noted that a Jewish state would exacerbate antisemitism in America: "I do not think it is too much to say that the aggressiveness of certain Jewish and Christian groups is proving a boomerang and actually inspiring greater antisemitism." Horace J. Bridges of the Chicago Ethical Society also worried that "for Jews to argue that there is a 'Jewish people consisting of all Jews' is to play straight into the hands of their enemies. For the first argument of antisemitism is that a man can't be a patriotic citizen of two nations at once."[63]

American Protestants who were unsure about Zionism, or opposed to it outright, found reassurance from members of the American Council for Judaism that anti-Zionism did not equate with antisemitism. Ardent anti-Zionist Protestants like Virginia Gildersleeve, Dean of Barnard College, argued that Zionism trampled over the rights of Arabs in Palestine to determine their own government and endangered American foreign policy interests in the Middle East. Convinced of the danger that a pro-Zionist position presented to American interests, she would later form the Committee for Justice and Peace in the Holy Land in 1948 to try to counteract the influence of the ACPC on American foreign policy. She would be joined in this effort by several notable mainline Protestants, including Coffin, Daniel Bliss, Bayard S. Dodge of the American University in Beirut, Harry Emerson Fosdick, and Paul Hutchinson and Garland Evans Hopkins, both of the *Christian Century* editorial board.[64]

As mentioned earlier, even among American Protestants who did support the cause of Zionism, the bitter divides among both Protestants and Jews often caused tension. In a series of letters to Judah Magnes of Hebrew University in Jerusalem, John Haynes Holmes, an ardent Zionist and civil rights activist, confessed his frustration at the increasingly hostile situation. Magnes's endorsement of a bi-national state with equal rights for both Palestinians and Jews created a firestorm of controversy within the Jewish community in America. Holmes, both a pacifist and a Zionist, was often caught in the crossfire. "You say that you are 'utterly confused' concerning the attitude of the majority of the Zionist Organization. I well understand your confusion," Magnes wrote to Holmes. "To my mind there is one basic cause for their attitude and the confusion it arouses—and that is, the great majority of Zionists do not, up to this minute, realize the basic need of understanding with the Arabs."[65]

Holmes, who remained a dedicated pacifist throughout the war, endured criticism from the Jewish community for his stance against the war. In one letter to Magnes, Holmes confessed: "As an incorrigible pacifist, I am beginning to get the full brunt of misunderstanding and denunciation. Would you believe it, I am even being denounced as an antisemite, and only last week received the threat of picketing my church in protest against my antisemitism. What do you think of that?" Still, despite Holmes's lament against the "controversy over the Zionist problem [which] rages here with increasing bitterness," he remained "as ardent a Zionist as ever, and am, wholeheartedly, with those who seek prosperity and happiness of Zion."[66]

A Jewish Homeland

By the war's conclusion, many religious organizations were reaching the consensus that a Jewish homeland should be created, but in Washington the issue was far from settled. The effective lobbying efforts of the American Christian Palestine Committee worried members of President Truman's administration—many of whom were veterans of the Roosevelt era. Evidence from State Department documents suggests that many in Roosevelt's administration had expressed concern over the direction of U.S. foreign policy in the Middle East. Roosevelt had often issued contradictory statements about the Zionist movement, and, as a result, Truman inherited an ambiguous legacy of U.S. policy in the Middle East. For example, in a memo from Vice Consul Parker T. Hart, of the American Consulate in Dhahran, Saudi Arabia, a meeting between Roosevelt and King Abdul Aziz, the vice consul revealed that Roosevelt had been won over to the anti-Zionist viewpoint by the King of Saudi Arabia: "The President had planned to attempt to modify the King's attitude regarding Palestine, but was instead convinced by the King of the Arab point of view." Furthermore, the Vice Consul noted, "the President assured the King that he would not support the Zionist movement for a Jewish National Home in Palestine."[67] At the same time Roosevelt had given both Stephen Wise and Senator Robert Wagner of the ACPC his assurance that their efforts to support a Jewish homeland in Palestine enjoyed his full support.

Immediately after Truman became president, the decidedly anti-Israel State Department pressured him to take a definite stand on the issue of Palestine and to abandon the Janus-faced policy Roosevelt had thitherto held.[68] On 14 April 1945, on the occasion of the impending visit from the Regent of Iraq, Paul H. Alling, of the Department of State, Division of Near Eastern Affairs, wrote a memo to Truman in which he noted that the visit provided a "suitable occasion for you to make public the assurances you have given the Arabs on several occasions that in the view of this Government there should be no decision affecting the basic situation in Palestine without full consultation with both Arabs and Jews." Alling added that a statement by Stephen Wise on 16 March, in which Wise publicly announced that Truman supported the establishment of a Jewish homeland in Palestine, complicated the situation. "We believe it essential," he told the president, "that this Government should adopt now a definite public stand on Palestine." Ambiguity on the issue hurt American interests in the Middle East, Alling insisted: "Every indication from our missions in the fields is that our standing in the entire Near East is being undermined by recurring indications of pro-Zionist sentiments in the U.S. Unless this tendency is speedily and effectively counteracted, our ability to protect our interests in the area will be seriously prejudiced."[69] One member of the State Department reflected the hope of the Department that Truman would avoid commenting on the situation entirely when he wrote to the U.S. ambassador in Iran: "My personal impression is that . . . now that he knows the difficulties and dangers, we will hear much less on the subject of Palestine in the near future unless there is something important and well-considered to say."[70]

As much pressure as members of the cabinet exerted on Truman to abandon a pro-Zionist stance on Palestine, equal pressure emanated from pro-Zionist American Jews and Christians who were intent not to let the issue diminish in the postwar planning. Indeed, the effective lobbying efforts of the ACPC alarmed Truman's cabinet members and prompted one to warn the president against its influence in a secret memo dated 28 May 1945. In the letter attached to the memo, Loy W. Henderson, of the Division of Near East Affairs, explained that the memo was necessary to call President Truman's "attention to the pressure campaign being launched on Capital Hill by the American Christian Palestine Committee, with a view to getting all members of Congress to petition the President regarding Palestine." According to Henderson, "any such move would have very serious adverse effects, particularly at the present time."[71] In a memo to Truman, Joseph C. Grew of the State Department's Near East Affairs Division explained that the ACPC's political pressure had grown particularly intense, and would surely result in a request by Congress to endorse unrestricted immigration and a Jewish state. Grew urged the president to remember that any position along pro-Zionist lines "desired by the American Christian Palestine Committee" would make the situation in Palestine worse.[72] President Truman, however, while still senator, had served as a member of the American Palestine Committee, and in the coming months would prove more receptive to the pro-Zionist position than his predecessor.

As the Second World War drew to a close, the ACPC continued its foreign policy efforts to aid the cause of a Jewish state in Palestine. In June 1945, only a few months after the conclusion of the war in Europe, the ACPC sponsored a national seminar that included a variety of speakers, educators, political analysts, journalists, clergy, and civic leaders, including David Ben-Gurion. Its purpose, the organizers declared, was to kick off a nationwide series of regional seminars that would address Christian support of the Jewish settlement in Palestine. As part of the conference, Democratic Congresswoman Helen Gahagan Douglas of California addressed a crowd of young Christians at Christ Church in New York City, where she quoted Harry Truman who, in a speech he had delivered in Missouri regarding the postwar world, had declared: "We may make mistakes. We may have difficulties, but I am asking you to exercise that admonition which we will find in the gospels and which Christ told us was the way to get along in the world: 'Do by your neighbor as you would be done by!'"[73] According to Douglas, "if we are to attempt to remake our world in the image of true Christian faith, we cannot fail to see as one of the test problems confronting us, the question of the future of the Jewish people." She continued, exhorting her audience to remember that:

> It was out of Judaism that Christianity grew; it was on the Old Testament as well as the New that this country and democracy throughout the world were based. It was because of their undeviating adherence to their Old Testament heritage that Jews remained a group apart through the ages, and it was because their life was so bound up with the words and the vision of the Book of Books that during twenty centuries of dispersion they continued to see the goal of Jewish history as the restoration of Jewish national life and the renaissance of Jewish ethical and cultural values in the promised land of their ancestors, the Land of Israel—Palestine.[74]

She continued, "Jews in Palestine today are making the Bible's prophecies come true," and added that remaining European antisemitism made it impossible for Jews to stay there. But the question was more than religious or humanitarian. It was in America's best interest from a foreign policy standpoint to encourage the spread of democracy by supporting a Jewish state in the Middle East.

In a speech delivered at the Press and Radio Luncheon, a part of the National Seminar, Reverend Wendell Phillips addressed the political situation in the Middle East with a searing indictment of the state of political affairs there. It was perhaps "national policy" to allow poor Arabs to remain poor in order to allow despotic rulers to go unchallenged. Zionism and the West provided an easy target for Arab leaders unwilling and unmotivated to better the lot of their subordinates.[75]

Ecumenical Reassessments

Even before the war had ended, mainline Protestants had begun a nascent reevaluation of traditional Christian teachings about Jews and the relationship between Judaism and Christianity. These ecumenical responses to current events were voiced in publications and conferences around the country.

In a *Christian Century* article, writer and feminist activist Katherine Hayden Salter insisted that there was no "Jewish problem"—only a Gentile Problem. That Jews had not embraced Christianity should come as no surprise. The hostility, violence, and persecution Christians exhibited toward Jews who refused conversion could only but confirm the Jews' decision to remain Jewish. She reminded readers that the measure of the quality of Christians was the treatment of minorities among them. Salter concluded by reminding her readers of the significance of Judaism to Christianity and the world.[76]

Such arguments were echoed in a sermon preached by John Haynes Holmes at his Community Church in New York City. The sermon was reprinted by Christian and Jewish groups alike and distributed in mass mailings around the United States. In the sermon, Holmes argued that Christians must acknowledge Christianity's inheritance from Judaism. Christianity owed a heavy debt to Judaism, Holmes insisted, and it could begin to repay it by fighting against and ending antisemitism. Holmes argued that Christians must do everything they could to assist Jewish refugees as part of the repayment of its debt. "To succor the Jews in this their hour of greater distress than they have endured since Jerusalem fell to Titus, this is our plain duty," he charged. "And it should be our welcome opportunity to discharge the debt which all too long has gone unpaid."[77] In the aftermath of the war, these initial efforts to reassess Christianity's relationship with Judaism only intensified and found expression mainly in national and international ecumenical conferences that addressed questions of Christian antisemitism.

By the end of 1946 the general public acknowledged, with varying degrees of incomprehensibility, six million as a realistic estimate of the number of Jews murdered by the Nazis. Between 1945 and 1949 the mainline newspapers dedicated considerable space not only to the liberation of concentration camps across Europe and the resulting problem of two million displaced persons but also to religious issues and even increased coverage of religious organizations, conferences, and institutions dedicated to eradicating bigotry and antisemitism.

An analysis of both the secular and religious responses to the reality of Christian antisemitism offers a glimpse into the dynamics of secular and religious post-Holocaust discourse and suggests ways in which secular discussions informed religious issues. Between 1945 and 1949, for example, the *New York Times* promoted both national and international interfaith understanding and dialogue that addressed approaches to eradicating antisemitism at home and abroad. Mainline American Protestants attended such conferences in droves, and memberships in organizations like the National Conference of

Christians and Jews dramatically increased after the war. The secular press, like the religious press, was covering new approaches to Jewish-Christian relations in response to the Holocaust.

Even before the end of the war, the *New York Times* began to print articles that promoted the need for an increased understanding between Christians and Jews. The first discussion of the necessity for improved dialogue between Christians and Jews appeared in an article published on 9 February 1945. The article reviewed a lecture held at the Institute of Human Relations in New York, during which the speakers called for "action against intolerance by pulpits, press and men and women in every walk of life."[78] Under the general theme of "Re-Education of America," a lecture series, sponsored by the National Conference of Christians and Jews, called on America to "examine its own record in matters of racial and religious tolerance."[79] One of the featured speakers, Sigmund Livingston, acknowledged the difficulty of eradicating antisemitism from American consciousness by pointing out the persistence of the belief in the validity of the notorious *Protocols of the Elders of Zion* despite proof of its forgery. "The remedy for prejudice is to conquer prejudice," he insisted, "[and] such a victory would do more for man than a complete victory over Hitler."[80]

The secular press revealed concern for the continuing persecution of Jews in postwar Europe. One *New York Times* article quoted "leaders in the National Conference of Christians and Jews" who warned that, unless proactive measures were taken, "attacks against Jews . . . and other minority groups would increase further in the post-War years." In order to stem the threatening tide of antisemitism and bigotry, the National Conference authorized a $2 million budget for "racial and religious cooperation."[81] By the end of the year, however, the projected budget had increased tremendously. In November Everett R. Clinchy, president of the National Conference of Christians and Jews, announced a budget of $10 million allocated for an annual education program designed to eradicate antisemitism.[82] Certainly an increase of $8 million from the projected budget within a matter of months signified an increased interest and motivation of Americans in the elimination of antisemitism through the cooperation of interfaith organizations.

The National Conference of Christians and Jews, established in 1928, took on an increasingly active role in 1946.[83] The *New York Times* dedicated significant print space to covering the conferences, workshops, and educational programs initiated by the NCCJ to promote religious understanding between Christians and Jews, including national American Brotherhood Week, the establishment of an International Conference of Christians and Jews in order to "devise a world plan for combating religious intolerance."[84] In a show of inclusiveness, the international committee moved to "include provisions for full representation of Jews" within its organizational structure.[85]

In fact, the elimination of what the Archbishop of Canterbury, another conference participant, called "the rise of antisemitism" in postwar Europe defined the aims of the conference.[86] Reports from behind the Iron Curtain indicated that Jews who had survived the Holocaust often returned to their homes and villages to face undiminished antisemitism from their neighbors and fellow countrymen. In Poland, in particular, reports of Jews massacred there worried the West. This concern translated into improving interfaith communication and efforts to eliminate antisemitism at home. Clinchy cited "unprecedented civic cooperation between Protestants, Catholics and Jews," and noted that "Jews today, who watched 6 million Europeans of their faith systematically liquidated, no longer want to go it alone."[87] Israel Goldstein, former president of the Zionist Organization of America, expressed his gratitude that through this international conference "statesmen were seeking and finding one another in endeavoring to achieve spiritual brotherhood."[88]

The mainline Protestant press, too, noted the importance of interfaith cooperation in the postwar years. In continuing to promote international interfaith cooperation, the Protestant periodicals focused attention on the World Council of Churches international convention held in February 1946 in Geneva. *Christianity and Crisis*, the *Federal Council Bulletin*, and the *Christian Century* published in full the resolutions fashioned by the World Council of Churches including Resolution Three: "On Antisemitism and the Jewish Situation" which acknowledged "with penitence the failure of the churches to overcome in the Spirit of Christ those factors . . . which have created and now contribute to this evil [antisemitism] which threatens both Jewish and Christian communities." The resolution urged "cooperating with Jews in a reciprocal attempt to remove the causes of friction in personal and community relationships."[89]

Much of the mainline Protestant press perceived the establishment of the International Conference of Christians and Jews as a necessary step in healing Jewish-Christian relationships in the wake of the war.[90] As the postwar years progressed, the major focus of the religious news continued to be the increase of interfaith organizations, both national and international, and the need to continue to fight antisemitism within the churches and nation. Participation in and publicity for National Brotherhood Week increased dramatically as a consequence of this emphasis. President Truman retained the title of "honorary chairman" of the NCCJ and again urged national observance.[91]

Truman's call for national observance in 1947 reflected worldwide tensions emerging at the start of the Cold War. First in reaction against fascism in World War II, now in reaction against communism, the emphasis on shared religious values proved to be a useful weapon in the Cold War arsenal. In a pattern that would continue in the coming years, Truman insisted that "democracy rests on Brotherhood justice, amity, understanding and cooperation among Catholics, Protestants, and Jews throughout the nation. [These] are cornerstones of democracy, even as they are requirements of brotherhood."[92] Mainline Protestants appeared willing to embrace ecumenism on behalf of the nation's unity in the Cold War—adapting their theology and minimizing denominational and doctrinal differences among themselves. This unity belied a deeper fracture in American Protestantism, however. Even as mainline Protestants united, their very attempts to minimize distinctiveness repelled conservative orthodox Protestants who increasingly wondered what made them distinct. In the decades to come, particularly over the issue of the supremacy of Jesus in the role of salvation—an issue American Jews highlighted as a barrier to interfaith dialogue—evangelical and mainline Protestants would find themselves increasingly at odds. In the immediate outbreak of the Cold War, however, Truman's call for unity met with cooperation.

Beyond the calls for interfaith cooperation, the secular press revealed an increased interest in theological implications of the Holocaust and reported several incidents of doctrinal modifications to traditional Protestant theology and reformulations of traditional mission practices to the Jews. For example, one New York Times article noted the radical decision by Reverend J. Earle Edwards, pastor of the Queens Baptist Church, to modify his own interpretation of New Testament scripture. The article reported that Edwards, after deciding that the New Testament contained multiple antisemitic references, had informed his congregation that he would "henceforth substitute the word 'people' for the word 'Jews' whenever the latter word is used in the Old Testament in a disparaging way."[93]

A reevaluation of the language of Christian theology continued on an international scale in 1947 when the International Emergency Conference to Combat Antisemitism convened in Seelisberg, Switzerland, and advocated "a radical revision in religious instruction and preaching by both Christians and Jews." The conference approved a report issued by a religious subcommittee that "emphasized the tragic fact that certain theologically misleading presentations of the Gospel of Love, while essentially opposed to the Spirit of Christ, contribute to the rise of antisemitism."[94] It is necessary for Christians, the subcommittee urged, to "emphasize the close bond that exists between Christianity and Judaism, to present the Passion Play in such a way as to not arouse animosity against the Jews and to eliminate from . . . preaching and teaching the idea that the Jews are a people under a curse."[95]

The reevaluation of traditional Protestant teachings about Jews and Judaism in the immediate wake of the war were not numerically significant yet, but reflected the first stirrings of the postwar Protestant conscience. The threat of atheistic communism and the dawning realization of what the consequences of antisemitism had wrought in Christian Europe motivated mainline Protestants to embrace interfaith activities and interfaith relations with a passion unknown before the war. Much was at stake in the new Cold War era for both American Protestants and Jews. Agreement on how to respond, particularly over the question of Zionism, would prove elusive.

Jewish Refugees

The growing emergency of the plight of 250,000 displaced Jews across Europe garnered support for Zionism among many Protestants. "Hitler set out to annihilate the Jewish people," wrote an anonymous Protestant chaplain in an article that appeared in *Christianity and Crisis* in 1945, "and he very nearly accomplished his purpose. For years now in righteous Christian indignation, we have preached 'deliverance of the captives,' and at last we have 'set at liberty them that are bruised.' Now with indifferent heartlessness, we condemn these same people to the impossible exile of homelessness." To encourage Jews to return to their prewar homes, as some suggested, would be folly, the chaplain argued. "Central Europe," he insisted, "is not redeemed from antisemitism, and the Jews should not be condemned to remain therein."[96] Palestine, many Protestants argued, must be a haven, a refuge for the survivors.

In the postwar period the fate of "stateless" ships filled with homeless Jewish refugees attracted international attention to the problem of displaced persons. In one such case of the *Fede*, a ship filled with more than one thousand Jewish refugees, the Christian Council on Palestine began an active letter-writing campaign to persuade the president and the British to allow their entry into Palestine. In a telegram to President Truman, the Council urged that "the only way we can move toward a solution to the problem of the 1,014 refugees [of the *Fede*] lingering in misery and ignominy and of the great problem of the displaced Jewish people throughout Europe is to insist that the gates of Palestine be opened immediately for free Jewish immigration." The authors of the telegram reminded Truman that "the toll of six million dead Jews during these recent years should shock the Christian world into an awareness of Christian responsibility for Jewish national homelessness."[97] Earlier the fate of the *Exodus,* a ship filled with refugees that arrived in Palestine only to be turned back by the British, led to overwhelming international condemnation of the British immigration policies in Palestine. Even in the postwar era, however, the British remained desperate to prevent continued warfare between the Jewish settlers of Palestine and the Arab Palestinians and so continued to deny further Jewish immigration into Palestine.

Arno Gaebelein, of *Our Hope,* also remarked upon the emergency situation of the displaced Jews in Europe who were desperate to enter Palestine. "The poor Jews!" he exclaimed in 1945, "6,000,000 of them died under Nazi persecution. Had Palestine been open many of them might have escaped." But for Gaebelein and his premillennialist fundamentalist readers, however, the cause of a Jewish homeland posed theological difficulties. "That they will come back to their land those who believe the Bible know. The present movement to that end is a return in unbelief, however."[98] Still cautious in its support of Palestine as a place of refuge for the surviving Jews, Gaebelein and other fundamentalists refused to join with other Christians who supported the establishment of Israel, such as the ACPC in lobbying the U.S. government. God's will for the Jews in Palestine would come to pass with God's timing—not through human intervention. The crimes of the Nazis, however, should be punished through human efforts. To do so would be obedience to God's commands to "vindicate Israel as God's peculiar people" and by so doing garner "eternal life and blessedness for the righteous" among the Gentiles.[99] Here again the fundamentalist leaders tied the idea of God's blessings for the United States as "righteous among the nations" to support for the Jewish people—in this case, U.S. responsibility for the prosecution of crimes against the Jewish people by another nation. The promise of blessings for the nation through its support of Jews, and later Israel, would become an increasingly significant motive for fundamentalist support for the future U.S.–Israeli alliance.

For the first time in fundamentalist history, antisemitism found unambiguous rejection in the pages of the most popular evangelical journals. Even more than the mainline Protestants, the fundamentalists recognized the failure of Christianity to fulfill the commandment to love one's neighbor when it came to the plight of the Jewish refugees of Europe. While the refugee crisis offered the tantalizing promise of the Jewish people returning to Palestine— a fulfillment of biblical prophecy— the fundamentalists met the crisis from a humanitarian perspective as well. Refugees should be provided for—either in Palestine or the United States. It constituted a Christian duty.

The Anglo-American Committee of Inquiry

The problem of Jewish refugees in Europe was not the only problem facing leaders in Washington and London. There were Jews on boats en route to Palestine, increasing number of Jews in settlements there, and, of course, many Palestinian Arabs who were unhappy about the prospect of a Jewish state. The establishment of the Anglo-American Committee of Inquiry in 1945 signaled increasing British and American concern for addressing these problems and the need for a reevaluation of the 1939 White Paper. At the end of the war the situation of displaced Jewish refugees grew to one of primary concern, particularly for the British in light of the refugees' almost unanimous desire to immigrate to Palestine. A telegram to Secretary of State James Byrnes from the British Foreign Secretary's office warned that "the situation in Palestine appears to be moving swiftly toward a crisis period with Jews determined to send there as many refugees as possible, and Arabs preparing to resist the new influx, there is risk of serious bloodshed at any moment. Behind this situation," the telegram noted, "lays one of the most tragic stories of history, and that while Nazis failed in their purpose of reducing mankind to subjection, they did succeed to great extent in their war against the Jews. Only a small fraction survives."[100]

Those who had survived, particularly in Eastern Europe, were still in danger from "the poison of antisemitism injected by Hitler [which] is still widespread." It was only natural "that they turn with desperate longing to [the] only spot on earth where they would not be regarded as intrusive refugees." Such a situation called for assistance from all the allied nations, particularly the United States. Shared responsibility and an internationally agreed upon solution to Palestine should be a necessary part of the post-war agenda.[101]

At the behest of British Foreign Secretary Bevin, Lord Halifax, the British ambassador to the United States, met with U.S. Secretary of State James Byrnes on 19 October 1945 to discuss the formation and purpose of the Anglo-American Committee. Lord Halifax explained that the Committee would "be set up immediately with rotating chairmanship to study and report on the general question of the position of the Jews, first of all in British and American occupied Europe, and the possibility of relieving the position in Europe by immigration into other countries outside Europe, including Palestine."[102]

Comprised of six Britons and six Americans, the Committee visited Washington, D.C., London, Vienna, Cairo, and Palestine before convening in Switzerland to make its final report in 1946. Various individuals testified before the Committee in regard to both the refugee problem and the problem of Jewish immigration to Palestine. While in Washington, two American

Protestant leaders were asked to testify before the committee as representatives of mainline American Protestantism. They were Daniel Poling, editor of the *Christian Herald* and member of the American Christian Palestine Committee, and Reinhold Niebuhr. Unlike Niebuhr, who viewed the establishment of a Jewish homeland in Palestine as a politically pragmatic necessity, Poling argued for the Zionist cause from a religious perspective. Although not a dispensationalist fundamentalist himself, Poling nonetheless echoed a similar theological view in his testimony before the committee. He insisted that "Christians believe overwhelmingly that Palestine was divinely selected as the site of the Jewish nation. I am trying as the representative of the Christian groups to present what is, we believe, the Christian viewpoint. I may say," he continued, "this viewpoint has been and is now being, with increasing fervor, expressed by representatives of the Evangelical Christian peoples of this country." When questioned by committee members about whether such a statement was representative of American churches, he replied: "I would say again, overwhelmingly, in my opinion and the opinion of my associates, Christians in the U.S., preferably Palestine should be a Jewish State."[103]

Though supportive of the idea of a Jewish homeland in Palestine, Niebuhr's testimony, given two days after Poling's, was less religiously oriented and more pragmatic. For Niebuhr, Jewish resettlement in Palestine was the "logical" choice that should result in a Palestinian state with a Jewish majority. Jews had already invested "lives and treasure" in Palestine, improving the land upon which they settled. "There is," however, Niebuhr warned, "no way of finding a perfectly just solution for the conflict of rights and priorities between the Arabs and the Jews in Palestine. There is, in fact, no perfectly just solution of any political problem." But, for Niebuhr, "the fact that the Arabs have a vast hinterland in the Middle East, and the fact that the Jews have no where else to go, establish the relative justice of their claims and of their cause."[104]

Upon questioning by the committee, Niebuhr conceded that the question should ultimately be settled by a trusteeship supervised by the United Nations and again reiterated that any solution would be viewed by the Arabs as "unjust:" "I don't know of a way of solving this problem without the loss of some sovereignty in some part of Palestine." He also argued that the Western powers ought to be more aggressive in finding homes for the displaced Jews of Europe and noted that the Arab world could say with some rectitude: "You are trying to push off a problem that you are not willing to consider in your world, on us."[105] Referring to Niebuhr's *Moral Man, Immoral Society*, a committee member asked Niebuhr if the Zionist movement would ultimately become another selfish and oppressive society. He replied:

I disagree with my Christian and Jewish friends who take an individualistic, liberalistic attitude and say Jewish nationalism is egotistic. This seems to me to be very unrealistic an approach. That is, a group has as much right to live as an individual has. Through its survival impulse, perhaps it is morally neutral, but it gets to be selfish. The will to power develops out of the survival impulse, but I don't think that a group that is established can very well say to a culture which lives in a very precarious position, that is, a nation without a base, it is very difficult to say to them, "It is a selfish thing for you to want to be established."

But why a Jewish state? Why not just allow immigration into Palestine to continue? the committee member asked. "Could you put it like this?" Niebuhr answered, "The Jews have survived as a people, so presumably they will survive even if they don't have a Jewish state, but the price is terribly high. The spiritual and physical price is terribly high. The physical price is very high because they were almost liquidated. The price will continue to be high because the group has to maintain itself in a minority position wherever it is."[106]

High praise from Rabbi Stephen Wise followed Niebuhr's testimony. In a letter to Niebuhr written the day after his testimony, Wise conveyed the comments of a leading attorney for the Zionist case: "He made the finest presentation of the Zionist case that I have ever heard. . . . He showed why the Jewish State in Palestine was a necessity not only for the Displaced Jews of Europe, but for all Jews, including Jews in America and Britain. He lifted the question completely out of the realm of refugee-ism and revealed the philosophy of Zionism and its need."[107]

In May 1946 the Anglo-American Committee made its final unanimous recommendation. It urged that the 1939 White Paper restricting Jewish immigration to Palestine be lifted and that one hundred thousand displaced Jews be granted immediate access. It further urged Britain to continue governing Palestine until a U.N. trusteeship could be established in its place. Truman, unsurprisingly in light of the intense lobbying efforts of the powerful ACPC, endorsed the findings immediately. Britain, however, angered by Truman's quick judgment and the burdens the committee's findings would place on an already strained government, did not.

The American Protestant reaction was mixed. Some Protestants argued that the committee had gone too far in encouraging the immediate immigration of one hundred thousand Jewish refugees to an area already rife with Arab-Jewish tensions. Other groups, like the ACPC, appeared unhappy that the committee did not favor the immediate establishment of a Jewish state and blasted the committee's concern for ensuring Christian rights in Palestine. One report of the ACPC condemned the committee's emphasis on what it considered to be a non-issue: "As Christians we protest this effort to create an issue out of a situation which has never been a problem, and thus obscure the real issue at stake, which is not only to create a haven for homeless Jews, but to build a national home for a homeless people."[108] The ACPC did, however, praise Truman's "courageous forthright request" that Britain allow for immediate immigration for Jewish refugees to Palestine.[109]

In preparation for the committee's findings and the imminent United Nations debate over the question of Palestine, the State Department in October 1945 had studied the feasibility of four possible outcomes: Palestine as a Jewish Commonwealth, Palestine as an Arab state, a partitioned Palestine, and an international trusteeship. The State Department, noting the strategic advantages of keeping the Arabs happy in the Middle East with the establishment of an Arab state, nonetheless rejected the possibility of Palestine as an Arab state outright: "It would seem probable that large segments of the non-Jewish Christian peoples of the world would be sympathetic to the cause of the Palestinian Jews." Furthermore, the report noted, President Wilson's endorsement of the Balfour Declaration and "President Roosevelt's published letter to Senator Robert Wagner dated October 15, 1944, in support of the Zionist cause . . . would make this proposal . . . a political issue in the United States of very serious import. If this settlement were to be either proposed or agreed to by the Executive Branch of the United States Government, there would be the very grave likelihood of strong opposition in Congress."[110]

One year after Britain rejected the findings of the Anglo-American Committee, the United Nations used the study to propose a solution to the question of a Jewish homeland in Palestine. On 29 November 1947 the General Assembly approved the partition of Palestine. It suggested that two independent states be created, with Jerusalem under international control, and imposed an arms embargo to prevent the outbreak of war. According to public-opinion surveys conducted by the State Department, Americans generally approved of the U.N. partition plan with some commentators hailing it as a "historic achievement."[111] The State Department noted limited opposition "to U.S. action supporting partition," but those who objected decried the "'bitter behind-the-scenes battle being waged in Washington over Palestinian policy."[112] Within a few months, such notable public figures (and ACPC members) as Eleanor Roosevelt, Sumner Welles, Herbert Lehman, and Philip Murray argued that the United States should take a leadership position in support of the U.N.'s partition plan, establishment of an international police force to keep order, and the lifting of an arms embargo to help arm the Jewish militias.[113]

While the Jews reluctantly accepted the U.N.'s recommendation, the Arabs refused it. Meanwhile, the situation for the British in Palestine had become unbearable. Under siege from both increasingly militant sides, the Mandate ended and the British left. On 14 May 1948 Jews in Palestine declared Israel's independence.

Conclusion

The establishment of Israel was hailed as a victory by both pro-Zionist mainline Protestants and their fundamentalist brethren. The American Christian Palestine Committee rejoiced to see the efforts of its labor come to fruition on 14 May 1948. While Israel's establishment would pose a moral dilemma to some mainline Protestants still reeling from the theological implications of the Holocaust, the coming Palestine refugee problem would prevent some from offering their wholesale support of Israel. The ACPC, assuming its task was complete with Israel's establishment, would suddenly find itself on the defensive, working in conjunction with the new state to counter charges of Israeli aggression as Israel struggled for both survival against its decidedly anti-Zionist neighbors and for the favor of world opinion. Liberal American Protestantism reflected these tensions, which would soon lead to internal divisions, hardening views, and louder voices on the issues of Israel and U.S.–Israeli relations in the ensuing Cold War.

Meanwhile, on the American religious front, mainline Protestantism was in flux. During the late 1930s and the war, it underwent a major shift in its views toward Jews and Judaism. This change was brought on by consideration of the Holocaust and a Jewish homeland. Protestantism was also facing an ascendant evangelical movement. This shift brought to the forefront of American politics increasingly well-organized evangelicals, many of whom were fundamentalists and saw the fulfillment of biblical prophecy in Israel's establishment. This new wave of Christian Zionism was a different creature altogether than the burgeoning and fragile mainline Protestant support of Israel. As the decades advanced, the numerical and political decline of Niebuhr's Protestant establishment resulted in the pro-Israel torch being passed to another group of Christians whose theological justifications of the new Israeli state were, in many ways, anathema to the values of the liberal Protestants who had preceded them.

The Myth of Christian Intervention, Christian Guilt, and the Martin Niemöller Controversy

As American Protestants wrestled with the guilt of Christian responsibility for the Jewish genocide in Europe, the controversy surrounding the invitation from the Federal Council of Churches, in 1947, to German pastor Martin Niemöller to speak in the United States as a "hero" of Christian resistance to the Nazis illustrated the church's difficulty in coming to terms with historic Christian antisemitism. The Niemöller controversy highlighted both the individual's action (and inaction) and revealed the guilty conscience of Christendom in the face of the reality of the Holocaust. Niemöller was a singular example of Christian resistance to the Nazis, and hope for religious redemption lay in elevating his story beyond its worth. Moreover, the decision of the Federal Council of Churches to invite Niemöller to conduct a speaking tour in the United States helped perpetuate the myth of Christian intervention and, for a time, set back interfaith dialogue between Protestants and Jews in the United States.

As early as June 1945 one can observe in the secular and Protestant press the initial overemphasis of Christian intervention against Hitler's genocidal policies.[1] Under the optimistic headline, "Jews Future Seen Better in Europe," *New York Times* contributor Virginia Lee Warren concluded, "aside from the Italian immunity to the more virulent forms of antisemitism, two factors contributed greatly to the fact that the majority of this country's Jewish population escaped irreparable harm." The most important factor, she argued, was "the magnificent work of the Catholic and Protestant clergy in hiding the haunted."[2]

The Protestant press emphasized the role of Christians across the world in the fight against antisemitism by highlighting the efforts of the small, dissenting German Confessing Church in the Christian fight against Nazism. The Confessing Church, established on 22 April 1934 by German Protestants to counteract the growing influence of the Nazi state in matters of the church, openly challenged the legitimacy of the Nazi influence in religious matters. In the years following the war, the Confessing Church garnered praise from American Protestants who viewed its members as heroes who had challenged the majority and influence of pro-Nazi German Protestants (self-described "German Christians"). In one example, the Confessing Church[3] received glowing praise from Reinhold Niebuhr, editor of *Christianity and Crisis.* Niebuhr commended the chaplaincy service for carrying the fight against antisemitism into the German army. He highlighted the discovery of a pamphlet circulated throughout the army barracks in which a German chaplain called on all Christians to resist Nazism. The pamphlet boldly declared:

> The Church must not keep silent. It must not say the settlement of the Jewish problem is a civil matter, and one in which the state is entitled to authority. . . . Nor must the Church say the Jews are now receiving the punishment they desire for their sins. There is no such thing as moderate Christian antisemitism . . . Christianity must repent and acknowledge its own guilt.[4]

Praise for the role of the churches across Europe dominated discussion of the Holocaust through 1945. The Protestant press promoted the idea of the church as a hero in the fight against Nazism with such headlines as "Dutch Churches Praised for Uncompromising Stand against Persecution of the Jews" and "France Praises Interfaith Cooperation."[5] The latter article described Marc Boegner, president of the French Protestant Church Federation traveling to Indianapolis for a meeting of the World Council of Churches, as a guardian of French Jews. "He spoke with great emotion," the article noted, "of the persecution of the Jews and of the efforts of the French church on their behalf."[6] One article suggested a feeling of gratitude on the part of Dutch Jews toward the Christians of Holland. In another article, "Jewish Congregation in Holland to Help Rebuild Catholic Churches," the Jewish congregation in Maastricht, "whose only synagogue was virtually destroyed during the war," the author noted, "has contributed eight-hundred dollars toward rebuilding damaged Catholic churches in the Roermond diocese."[7] Like the secular press, Protestant periodicals in 1945 filled their pages with articles that presented a picture of ardent Christian resistance to the destruction of the Jews and mutual interfaith appreciation of that effort.

In an interview published in October 1945 in many Protestant periodicals, one of Germany's most famous dissenting Lutheran pastors—and Protestant hero—Martin Niemöller responded to questions regarding his protest of the Jewish genocide. Niemöller, founding member of the Confessing Church, initially endorsed the Nazis by joining their organization in 1933 but subsequently rejected their ideology and spent several years imprisoned in Dachau for his resistance to Nazi influence in the churches. In the interview U.S. Army Chaplain Ben Rose pointedly asked: "Then the Confessional Church did speak out against concentration camps, persecution of the Jews, etc.?" Niemöller responded unequivocally: "Yes, it spoke out against them to Hitler in no uncertain terms."[8] In a message of the Evangelical Church to the German people, again Niemöller proclaimed the Church's boldness in resisting Nazism. In the message, he lamented the failure of Christians in Germany to prevent the genocide of the Jews. Yet, he wrote, despite the

> shortcomings of the Church . . . the Church took its responsibilities seriously [by speaking] up against the crime of the concentration camps; it spoke up against the mistreatment and murder of the Jews and of the sick; it tried to prevent the seduction of the youth . . . [but] the public was not allowed to listen to its word."[9]

At the conclusion of the war both the *New York Times* and the Protestant periodicals overwhelmingly hailed Niemöller as a champion of the oppressed. The extent and effectiveness of Church resistance would later become a hotly contested issue in both the church and academia, and, in the immediate postwar years, a firestorm of controversy gathered around the figure of Niemöller himself.[10] The debates that ensued reveal a Protestant conscience under siege.

Apparently inundated by letters from American Protestants critical of his initial support for the Nazis and, later, his lack of ardent resistance to Nazi racial policies (he was imprisoned for his resistance to Nazi encroachments upon the freedom of the church—not for his protest against the Nazi policies against the Jews) before and during his eight-year imprisonment in Dachau—Niemöller published a letter of response in *Christianity and Crisis* in July 1946. In the letter he questioned the right of American Protestants to criticize the failure of German Protestants to protest Nazi policies in as large numbers as had the Catholics.[11] Yet he offered no explanation for the discrepancy and claimed that, unless one had endured the camps as he had, judgment should be withheld.[12] American Christians and Jews rejected such an explanation, and Niemöller found himself continually plagued by questions of guilt, responsibility, and Christian failure. Many could point to the fate of

Dietrich Bonhoeffer, another member of the Confessing Church, who had been executed a few days before the end of the war for his role in the assassination attempt against Hitler, as a figure more deserving of hero status. Bonhoeffer had not only courageously challenged Nazi influence in the churches, but he had, from the beginning of the Nazi era, unequivocally protested the persecution of the Jews.

Nonetheless, the Federal Council of Churches extended an invitation to Martin Niemöller to conduct a speaking tour of the United States in January 1947 as the Council's guest. General Secretary of the Council Samuel Cavert tirelessly worked to secure permission first from the U.S. Army officials occupying Germany and then from the U.S. government to allow Niemöller into the United States. Cavert argued that the purpose behind Niemöller's visit lay in "strengthening the normal and natural contacts between the German Church and the other churches of the world" and, by showcasing Niemöller's heroism in the face of Nazi fascism, "influence the German Church along the democratic lines we desire it to follow."[13] Niemöller and his wife accepted the invitation and began their tour of the United States in January 1947 with his first appearance in New York City where he preached to an audience of six thousand at the invitation of the Protestant Council of New York, the Federal Council of Churches, and the American Committee for the World Council of Churches.

In his first address Niemöller proclaimed: "Hitler never succeeded in silencing the church in Germany. The loss of our peace was worth more to us than peace with Hitler would have been."[14] Although the church resisted the temptation to declare its innocence and instead declared "its solidarity of guilt with the starving German people," Niemöller noted that "among thinking people Christianity has gained in esteem, because under Hitler's totalitarian rule, the Christian churches stood firm when confronted by a hard and severe test. They came out of this test strengthened."[15] No doubt the two thousand people assembled for the speech cheered Niemöller's confidence in the health and vitality of the churches in the post-Nazi era which allowed listeners to believe in the myth of Christian intervention.

Protest erupted immediately. C. Montieth Gilpin, director of the Society for the Prevention of World War III, issued a statement condemning it as "another effort on the part of apologists to make the world forget Germany's crimes against humanity."[16] Reporters and critics pointed to more unsavory aspects of Niemöller's background as evidence of misjudgment on the part of the Federal Communications Commission (FCC) to use Niemöller as a role model for German Christians. Niemöller, a submarine captain in the First

World War, had voted for the Nazi Party in 1924 and again in 1933. Even after being sent to Dachau in 1937, when World War Two began in 1939 Niemöller again offered his services as a submarine captain to the Germany military. Critics also insisted that Niemöller's imprisonment, however courageous and heroic, stemmed from his protest against state infringement on the churches rather than Nazi racial ideologies. Eleanor Roosevelt protested Niemöller's visit in her *New York Times* column, warning of the dangers of glorifying Niemöller and, in the process, forgetting where guilt lay—with the German people. "We do not have to ignore the fact that there were Germans who struggled against cruelty," Roosevelt acknowledged. "But," she reminded her readers, "we have to remember the results of the coming to power of the type of men who brought on a war that devastated many lands; and we must guard against forgetting where the responsibility lies when, in any nation, such men are allowed to become dominant."[17] Cavert replied immediately to Roosevelt's column. In a letter to her, Cavert insisted that "if you were well informed about what he has been saying you would welcome him as an ally." He included excerpts from Niemöller's addresses that claimed Germans must face their collective guilt as a nation, to iterate the point. Roosevelt was not convinced. In her reply to Cavert, she pointedly noted, "I am afraid I cannot agree with you. I think it is bad for us to grow sympathetic to the Germans."[18]

As the press published additional information about Niemöller's background, individuals flooded Secretary Cavert's mailbox with letters protesting the FCC's sponsorship of Niemöller's tour and supportive of Roosevelt's stance.[19] Several people wrote to Cavert to request that their names be withdrawn from the FCC's membership and to inform him that they would no longer provide financial support for the Council. One woman noted, "No man who holds no quarrel with fascism, and with its manifestations in Germany or elsewhere, except insofar as it attacks the church and religion, alone, in their purely clerical sense, is a man to be entrusted with the guidance of human beings."[20] Another, more pointed letter condemned the FCC's "very grand reception [of] Nazi Neimueller [*sic*]."[21] As more Americans grew uncomfortable with Niemöller's visit to the United States, Niemöller himself increased the controversy when he declared in a sermon preached on January 20 that antisemitism was dead in Germany.

The next day, in a *New York Times* article, Niemöller explained that "his opposition to the Hitler regime was not based solely on the anti-clerical measures of the Government, but as an affirmation of the rights of man as expressed in the Ten Commandments."[22] He continued his defense with the explanation that "antisemitism has come to an end and will not recur."

Indeed, he argued, the belief that "compassion, pity for the Jews, and a feeling that what has been done to the Jews has been revenged, not by the Allies, but by God, is the outstanding psychic reaction in [Germany]."[23]

Swift reaction followed Niemöller's claim of the end of German anti-semitism. *New York Times* journalist Delbert Clark described the increasing opposition within both the religious and secular ranks to Niemöller's comments as representative of German mentality. In an interview with influential New York Rabbi Balfour Brickner, Clark noted Brickner's response to Niemöller's claim: "Antisemitism in Germany is as strong as ever and if the Reverend Martin Niemöller denies it exists, he has lost touch with the people." While on tour in Europe as chairman of the Committee on Army and Navy Religious Activities, Brickner had testified to "the many evidences of antisemitism he said he had seen and heard of while here." Rabbi Brickner further objected to Niemöller because, he argued, he "had never recanted his nazism" and suggested that "the minister was in no position to speak for Germany on antisemitism."[24] Individuals again wrote letters of protest to the FCC. One man noted that "the press reports him as saying that antisemitism has ceased to exist in Germany and that the Germans today have nothing but pity for the Jews. This, I venture to say, is a complete lie, and in view of it," the author suggested, "one can only have the gravest misgivings as to the real purposes of Pastor Niemöller's visit and public addresses here."[25] Another wrote to the FCC to say that on the same day he read Niemöller's remarks declaring the end of antisemitism, he "got a letter from a friend . . . still living in the French Zone of Germany and she reported that the Germans have been destroying Jewish Cemeteries as they did during the Nazis regime."[26] Most people writing to the FCC questioned the wisdom of jeopardizing the organization's prestige to sponsor such a controversial figure as Niemöller.

Under siege, Cavert composed a pamphlet titled "The Truth about Niemöller," in which he addressed the charges leveled against the German pastor.[27] He noted that Niemöller had, indeed, voted for the Nazi Party from 1924 through 1933, and had declared: "I am confident that Hitler will support collaboration between Church and State." But Cavert justified this voting history and comment by noting that Niemöller's support for the Nazis in the early stage came before he realized the evil intentions of the party, and his votes took place in "minor elections" only. Cavert also acknowledged that Niemöller had volunteered his services to the German military in 1939 at the start of the Second World War but suggested that Niemöller's intention was to make contact with the German underground through military service and that he did not have "accurate knowledge of Hitler's foreign policy or of the international situation." Many observers did not seem convinced by Cavert's defense. *PM* remarked, in an editorial, that Niemöller might not have "had a Party card in his pocket, but until Hitler stepped on his personal toes, he had the Swastika engraved on his heart."[28] One veteran of the Second World War wrote to the Federal Council to suggest that Niemöller's visit could damage postwar efforts to bring justice to Europe. "This Mephistopheles of German intellect is more dangerous than an outright Nazi whose attitude you know at least," he explained. "By using religion as his cloak he is going to make a fool of us unless he is stopped right now." [29] This letter writer was not alone in his concern. The large crowds of Americans who gathered to see Niemöller also worried those outside the United States. Jan Masaryk, the Czechoslovakian foreign minister mentioned the visit, at a press conference in Paris on February 11, as evidence of continuing German propaganda. "He was greeted as if he were Mahatma Gandhi. In Los Angeles 50,000 persons turned out to hear him," Masaryk complained. "Mrs. Roosevelt telephoned me that I should write some sort of article to counteract him," he added. "It was sad."[30]

Perhaps one of the most significant aspects of the Niemöller controversy is the degree to which the Federal Council's endorsement and sponsorship of Niemöller damaged Jewish-Protestant relations in the United States. Ecumenical efforts to improve interfaith dialogue had begun in the wake of the war but suffered a setback when disagreements between leading Protestants and Jews over Niemöller turned heated. Stephen Wise, one of the most well-known Jewish leaders in the United States and president of the American Jewish Congress, wrote to Cavert to protest Niemöller's visit. Hoping that his protest would not "be regarded as unduly intrusive," Wise nonetheless argued that Niemöller "has not so borne himself throughout the unspeakable Hitler years as to merit the respect or confidence of Christian peoples in America." Surely, Wise remarked, other Christian leaders in Germany or Europe were more deserving of praise. Wise also suggested that Niemöller's insistence that antisemitism had been eradicated in Germany would lead to "softer" treatment of a country undeserving of such consideration.[31] Wise published his letter to Cavert in the *New York Times*.[32]

Protestants who had worked to support Niemöller responded angrily, including Wise's friend Reinhold Niebuhr. Although Niebuhr noted that "there is a regrettable tendency to overestimate the Christian resistance to Nazism for propaganda purposes on the part of both Catholic and Protestant special pleaders," he nonetheless candidly suggested that American Jews not interfere with the business of American Protestants.[33] Other leaders such as the *Christian Herald* editor Daniel Poling wrote columns in support of Niemöller in an effort to counteract the negative publicity.[34] The *Christian Century* published its own plea: "Play Fair with Niemöller!" Reiterating the idea of significant Christian resistance to Nazi party ideology, it asked, "why not repay to Hitler's most famous prisoner a little of the debt we owe to many hundred thousand resolute Germans and citizens of other nations who bore the brunt of the first costly resistance to the nazis?" Jews should appreciate Niemöller, the editorial continued since "the Jews had a share in making him what he became and have good reason to appreciate what he tried to do." The *Christian Century* claimed that "a motive for the attack on Niemöller is hatred of Christianity" by "secular-minded radicals who are ideologically committed to systems of materialism which proclaim themselves rivals of Christianity."[35] Some Protestants reacted even more violently to Wise's perceived "intrusiveness." Pastor Emeritus Gottlieb Hafner of the First Evangelical Reformed Church of Portland, Oregon, wrote to the Federal Council of Churches to complain. "Has it come to this, that a Jewish Rabbi assumes the authority of the Federal Council upon himself, and dares to say whom the Council may or may not invite to speak in Christian churches?" Hafner asked. "What arrogance and impudence! I wish that Dr. Cavert would write to the Rabbi and put him in his place," he concluded. Cavert did indeed write to Wise to argue that he was "misinformed" about Niemöller and that, once he was better acquainted with the whole story, he would, no doubt, "subsequently modify your present opinion."[36] Other Protestants wrote to Wise as well, less diplomatically. "As one of the 'Christian people of America' whom you presume to advise, permit me to take strong exception to your letter," H. C. Furstenwalde of New York wrote to Wise. "I am tempted to retaliate with some advising of my own," he continued, "and would recommend to you, as distinctly worthy of your attention, the words of the admirable Rabbi Beck anent the 'small Jews' with which I assume you are familiar."[37] The *B'nai B'rith Messenger* retaliated by deeming Niemöller's visit "an arrogant subversion of the ideal of brotherhood" and accused Niemöller of "smoothly and suavely spreading by negation the same ideas that Goebbels and Rosenberg instilled by blood and iron." Niemöller's claim that antisemitism had ended in Germany could only produce one conclusion, the *B'nai B'rith Messenger* insisted: "that Martin Niemöller is lying. And lying for a cause—the cause of another German Reich and another Hitler!"[38] By mid-February the press surrounding Niemöller's visit had grown so contentious that Cavert felt compelled to write Niemöller to suggest that he not extend his visit to the United States. "It is becoming clear to me that the longer you stay the more criticism you will encounter from those persons who assume that you are trying to carry on 'propaganda' for Germany."

Yet even as American Protestants celebrated acts of Nazi resistance by German Protestants, the Protestant press, as the details of the Holocaust horror mounted, found itself humbled by the failure of humanity in the face of evil and civilization's rejection of moral law. Unlike the *New York Times* coverage of the extermination camps, which focused on the details of the camps, the Protestant press largely, although not exclusively, caged in its reaction in moral tones that underscored the weaknesses of human nature. In May 1945 an editorial that appeared in *The Christian Century* declared that "the horror of the nazi concentration camps is the horror of humanity itself when it has surrendered to its capacity for evil." The problem was one of all humanity, for, as the author continued, "in the nazis and beyond them we are looking into the very pit of hell which men disclose yawning within themselves when they reject the authority of the moral law."[39] Ultimately, the author concluded, "Buchenwald and the other memorials of nazi infamy . . . reveal that the salvation of man, the attainment of peace, the healing of the nations is at last a religious problem."[40]

American Protestants' reaction to Martin Niemöller's visit and his statements about Christian resistance to the Nazis revealed the ambiguities surrounding the initial knowledge of the Holocaust. Many Protestants wanted to ignore the reality of weak Christian resistance to Nazi genocidal plans in Europe and did so by looking for examples of heroism and resistance, and elevating these examples beyond their context. American Jews often rejected this attempt, as exemplified in their response to Martin Niemöller's visit to the United States. It would take some time before American Protestants could fully realize the enormity of the Holocaust and face the reality of widespread Christian accommodation to Nazism in Europe.

The Challenges of Statehood, 1948–1953

Israel's establishment excited Americans. Israelis' creation of their independent state in May 1948 was met with a generally positive reaction in the United States. In public opinion assessments conducted by the State Department leading up to, and after, the Israeli Declaration of Independence, more than 90 percent of "public comment mail" sent to the State Department concerned Palestine. The Department noted that most of the mail came from "organized pressure" groups in "areas of crucial importance in American politics."[1] Although noting that most of the organizations were Jewish, the Department repeatedly pointed out the influence of one non-Jewish group—the American Christian Palestine Committee—and its members on public opinion. Two years later its influence clearly remained strong. In a March 1950 public opinion assessment, the State Department noted that interest in the Near East had prompted the creation of an unusually large number of "specialized organizations" whose purpose lay in "appealing to public opinion and to press for certain policies in the region." It continued: "Their interests and scope of activity are broad, and their ultimate influence is evidently pervasive and strong. They include the Zionist organizations, the American Christian Palestine Committee, the *Nation* Associates and others." Although the report noted that opposition groups had "sprung up to press the interest of the 'other side,' in Palestine," it concluded that "these have not had the influence that the Zionist-supporting organizations have had."[2] Opposition came mainly from business interests and from a small number of Christian groups who had close missionary ties in the Middle East and the Arab world.[3] As is clear from the Department of State's assessment, opinion among mainline Protestants appeared fractured over political support of Israel. But this chapter will show that for the first five years of Israeli statehood, pro-Israel mainline Protestants continued to outmaneuver the anti-Zionist Protestants, providing crucial support for the nascent U.S.–Israeli alliance.

Mainline Protestants who had worked closely with Jewish Zionist organizations undoubtedly experienced a sense of relief and accomplishment. The celebrations, however, only served as a temporary respite. In the immediate aftermath of the Israeli Declaration of Independence and the war that followed, Protestant organizations dedicated to tempering American enthusiasm for Israel arose to remind Americans of the Palestinian plight, the dangers of ardent nationalism, and the importance of not alienating the Arab Middle East. Organizations arose in the 1950s, such as the American Friends of the Middle East, to counterbalance the politically powerful American Christian Palestine Committee, which continued its lobbying efforts on behalf of the new state. Other equally fierce pro-Israel mainline Protestant organizations emerged, such as Christians Concerned for Israel (CCI), which became the self-appointed watchdogs of American Protestant attitudes toward Israel.

Israel's establishment posed a theological stumbling block for mainline Protestants as they struggled to come to terms with new political and religious realities. Meanwhile, despite a far from unified response to the establishment of Israel, an emphasis emerged in the following two decades within the mainline churches on reevaluating traditional Christian theology toward Judaism. Scholarly investigations of antisemitism began an earnest effort to understand the connection between the Holocaust and Christian history. The urge to root out theological antisemitism from mainline Protestant theology, particularly the belief in supercessionism, informed these theological undertakings.

Meanwhile fundamentalists, excited about the establishment of Israel, began to take an active interest in determining how and in what ways its establishment fulfilled prophecy. Fundamentalist prophecy watchdogs gradually abandoned their initial hesitancy to support the secular Zionist state, which, according to them, and in contrast to their interpretation of biblical prophecy, had been founded in "unbelief." Gradually excitement built among these Protestants who began to view the new Jewish state with growing anticipation.

The Truman Administration

On the political front, Harry Truman became the first world leader to offer de facto recognition of the new country, despite bitter debate in his State Department. American Jews who had supported the Zionist efforts during the war celebrated the victory of Israel's establishment and the immediate recognition of the state by the United States. Historians have argued that Truman's decision came solely as a result of pressure from U.S. Zionist organizations and stemmed from the fear of losing the Jewish vote, particularly in New York, and that Truman and those who worked in the State Department's Near East Division were themselves overwhelmingly antisemitic.[4] Others have argued that Truman recognized Israel out of humanitarian and religiously inspired impulses, and point to Truman's acknowledgment of the horror of the Holocaust, his concern for the treatment and fate of displaced Jews after the war, and his own Protestant upbringing as evidence to support their claims.[5]

What is certain, however, is that Truman found the situation frustrating. Although he had served as a member of the American Christian Palestine Committee while still a senator, the incessant lobbying of both the ACPC and the Zionist organizations in the United States created a situation Truman found most difficult to negotiate around. A few months before Israel declared its independence, Truman wrote a letter to his friend Edward Jacobson, who was living in Key West, Florida. Jacobson had hoped to arrange a visit with Chaim Weizmann while Truman visited Florida, but Truman, though expressing his regrets that the meeting could not take place, added that "there wasn't anything he could say to me that I didn't already know, anyway. . . . The situation has been a headache to me for two and a half years." Besides, he noted, "the Jews are so emotional, and the Arabs are so difficult to talk with, that it is almost impossible to get anything done. The British, of course, have been exceedingly non-cooperative in arriving at a conclusion. The Zionists, of course, have expected a big stick approach on our part, and naturally have been disappointed when we can't do that."[6] In a personal and confidential letter to Dean Alfange on the evening before Israel's declaration, Truman again reiterated his frustration with the incessant lobbying of pro-Zionists for Israel: "The main difficulty with our friends, the Jews in this country," he wrote, "is that they are very emotional—they, the Irish and the Latin-Americans have something in common along that line. The President of the United States has to be very careful not to be emotional or to forget that he is working for one hundred and forty-five million people primarily and for peace in the world as his next objective."[7]

Truman's comments reflected the challenges he faced in balancing domestic and political concerns—both of which were tinged with religious significance. Divisions in the State Department reflected both pragmatic geopolitical concerns and divisions in American society over the issue of Israeli statehood. In the coming years pro-Israel Protestants would work to overcome fellow Protestants' objections to, and concerns about, Israel's existence while simultaneously increasing grass-roots support for the new state.

The years between 1947 and 1954 brought many events that forced political changes in the United States, in both domestic and foreign policy. The emerging Cold War made the Middle East an important focus in the democratic versus communist struggle for global influence. The new Israeli state had the unusual opportunity to create a foreign policy from scratch, but it was shaped, of course, by Israel's practical needs.[8] Historian Uri Bialer argues that Israel, desperate for allies, immigrants, and money, found itself in an ideological no-man's land.[9] Aware of his country's dual needs—material aid and immigrants—David Ben-Gurion, Mapai's charismatic leader and Israel's first prime minister, once said of Israel's non-alignment policy: "I refuse to give up my soul, but I will give up my pants."[10] Increasing American financial and political support for the new Israeli state during its first few decades must be viewed in this context. Although much of the earliest and loudest support of Israel came from liberal Protestants, and later evangelicals, American concern over Israel would be dictated by current events. The fight against communism and the superpowers' contest for global influence were quickly leading to a pro-Israeli foreign policy.

In the post-Independence years, Israel also dedicated much of its time and attention to religious diplomacy—mainly focused on securing recognition by the Vatican and simultaneously thwarting its attempts to push for the internationalization of Jerusalem.[11] Yet the Ministry of Religious Affairs and other Ministry departments did not neglect American Protestants, many of whom had worked tirelessly to support Israel's independence and to persuade fellow Protestants to support the new state religiously, militarily, and politically. Israel worked closely with Zionist organizations in the United States and their allies, namely, the American Christian Palestine Committee, to improve relations and promote Israeli interests in the United States. The government kept careful records of major Protestant denominations and the numbers of affiliates of each, including subdivisions in the denominations (for example, Northern Baptists, Southern Baptists, the National Baptist Convention USA, and the National Baptist Convention of America all delineated with membership numbers listed for each).[12] The state also fielded interest and inquiries from evangelical Americans who, after Independence, grew increasingly interested in the theological significance of the rebirth of Israel.

The Mainline Protestant Press

As evangelicals increasingly united behind Israel, mainline Protestants further fractured. As mentioned above, some mainline Protestants had rejected the idea that the displaced Jews of Europe should make Palestine a Jewish homeland. Within this group, discussion of the issue usually centered on concern for the protection of Christian landmarks, the plight of Arab refugees fleeing the influx of Jewish settlers, and concern over the government courting Jewish votes to the detriment of U.S. foreign relations.[13] In an effort to advocate for the Arab Palestinian cause, Virginia Gildersleeve, dean of Barnard College in New York, established the Committee for Justice and Peace in the Holy Land in February 1948. Its initial membership included Henry Sloan Coffin; Bayard S. Dodge, president of the American University of Beirut; Harry Emerson Fosdick, pastor of Riverside Church in New York City; and Paul Hutchinson and Garland Hopkins, both of the *Christian Century*. Gildersleeve, alarmed by what she considered "a great many American Christians" advocating for the establishment of Israel, argued that "some . . . advocated [for] the project because it would relieve us of doing anything ourselves to help the exiles. These unworthy Christians did not want to admit any more refugees into America."[14] In this context, Gildersleeve's anti-Zionism could be interpreted as concern *for* the Jews and condemnation of U.S. immigration policy.

While debate among mainline Protestants over the question of Arab rights and secular Zionism continued, fear regarding the Vatican's interest in the area also arose. The editors of the *Christian Century* noted a recent article in the Vatican's newspaper, *Osservatore Romano*, which claimed that the Holy Land was only so for Christians, not Arabs or Jews. The article posed this question: "If Palestine's holy places are only such for Christians only, and if the Roman Church—as it asserts—is the only true Christian body, can this mean that the Vatican is starting to lay the groundwork for a claim to administer the U.N.'s reserved portions in Jerusalem and Bethlehem which are to be in neither Arab nor Jewish territory?"[15] Such concern echoed the old fear among American Protestants that the Catholic Church would win the race over missions and influence on Arab populations in the Middle East—a fear that had prompted American interest in the Holy Land at the turn of the century.

Once Israel declared its independence in 1948, some mainline Protestants condemned its aggressively nationalist, secular attitude. One *Christian Century* article acknowledged that "the harrowing experiences undergone by

European Jews during Hitler's systematic campaign to annihilate them have left deep spiritual scars on world Judaism," and such scars had undoubtedly contributed to the militaristic stance of the new nation. But the author deplored this "Jewish toughness," which he compared to "nazi toughness," and concluded by asking the reader: "How long will Judaism, with its message of peace, continue to find satisfaction in believing that Israel is feared?"[16] In another article in the *Christian Century,* the editors decried the lack of "ascription to God for the formation of the Zionist nation" in Israel's Declaration of Independence. "Not only does the declaration open with no ascription of gratitude, it closes with no appeal to Him for justification and support." Clearly, the authors concluded, "Zion without God has become Israel without God. It is an ominous portent."[17]

Correspondents criticized the editorial. In fact, Israel's Declaration of Independence *did* contain a reference to God and was completed hours before the Jewish Sabbath in order to keep its observance. As Rabbi Benjamin Kreitman of Congregation Beth El in New London, Connecticut, wrote in a letter to the editor: "As a religionist, I was deeply disturbed by your accusation, both out of concern for my religion and the people who bear its name, and the fearful effect that such an accusation may have on organized Protestantism." [18]

Members of Virginia Gildersleeve's Committee for Peace and Justice in the Holy Land consistently argued that the only just solution for Palestine would be the creation of a federation governed by both Arabs and Jews, and explained their stance in multiple articles published in the sympathetic *Christian Century.* In one article Committee member Daniel Bliss, grandson of the founder of the American University in Beirut and a consistent critic of the Zionist movement, insisted that both Jews and Arabs had equal claim to the land—one should not supplant the other—and, as such, "the principles of self-determination and federalism among sub-states or cantons" could be "applied successfully to Palestine with the only hope of bringing lasting peace there."[19] Others argued that Jewish nationalism only compounded the problem of antisemitism and drew a correlation between them. Millar Burrows, an ordained Presbyterian minister and director of the American School of Oriental Research in Jerusalem, argued that antisemitism would be partly eradicated only when "Jews learn that they are themselves in part responsible for antisemitism." Burrows echoed the earlier mainline Protestant warning against Jewish particularism when he added: "There are better ways of fighting [antisemitism] than extravagant and excessive publicity with incessant stress on the fact that they are Jews and on their sense of being different from other people." In fact, Burrows asserted, "the present resurgence of Jewish nationalism is a repetition of the same fateful error that caused Israel's rejection of Jesus. It is the focal point at which Christian opinion, in all brotherly love, should make clear and emphatic its disagreement with the dominant trend in contemporary Judaism. The Christians' final attitude," he concluded, "must be that of Paul: 'Brethren, my heart's desire for Israel is that they might be saved.'"[20]

The approximately seven hundred thousand Palestinians displaced before, during, and after the 1948 War, and Israel's refusal to allow their return, posed an enormous humanitarian crisis and remained a stumbling block for mainline Protestant support of Israel. In June 1949 Garland Evans Hopkins, associate secretary of the Board of Missions and Church Extension of the Methodist Church, secretary of the Committee for Justice and Peace in the Holy Land, and editor of the *Christian Century*, issued a public condemnation of the new Israeli state. After visiting Jerusalem and Tel Aviv, Hopkins met with Pius XII in Rome and declared that the conditions for refugees in "Palestine" were "serious." Israel, which at the time was engaged in a diplomatic battle with the Vatican, took interest in the American Protestant's charge that "the State of Israel will not make the concessions necessary for peace in the Middle East."[21] While some Israelis recognized that they must change their hard-line approach to the Arabs in order to peacefully coexist with the surrounding nations, Hopkins noted, "fanatical elements, both in Palestine and America, are preventing the establishment of a policy based on friendly intercourse. They demand instead a policy of further political and economic aggression."

Fearing that such policies would result in turning potential American allies "towards other alignments," Hopkins charged that "the time has come for the United States to take a firm stand against further aggression and for the immediate return of refugees to their homes." Calling the current condition of Arab refugees "pitiful," Hopkins insisted that the Israelis had violated the United Nation's Charter of Human Rights. The solution, Hopkins argued, must be the internationalization of Jerusalem and an investigation into the destruction of the Holy Places by the Israelis, which, he noted was "far greater" than officials in Israel admitted. Such a declaration reflected the Vatican's own agenda: that Jerusalem was an "Open City" and that its Holy Places were to be in the control of the United Nations. Israel desperately wanted to prevent such an outcome.

Articles critical of Israel's treatment of the Palestinian refugees and the Christian holy places appeared in the *Christian Century* and *Christianity and*

Crisis on the heels of Hopkins's public announcement. Henry Sloan Coffin, elected to the editorial board of *Christianity and Crisis* in February 1949, began his editorial stint with a first-page feature editorial in the 21 February 1949 issue. Titled, "Perils to America in the New Jewish State," Coffin denounced Israel as a creation of "fanatical Jewish nationalism." The creation of Israel embroiled the United States in "new perils" since Israel was an economic parasite that alienated other Middle Eastern nations and created a burden of dual loyalty among American Jews. "No greater blunder," Coffin concluded, "could have been made by American Jewry than to espouse Zionism if it wished to do away with antisemitism in this country."

From a foreign policy standpoint, Coffin argued that Israel's location in the center of the unstable Middle East put it in a prime place to allow the Soviets who "thrived on chaos" to wreak diplomatic havoc. Israeli fanatics would continue to expand their borders and "will not stop their ruthless thrusts against unhappy peaceful Moslem and Christian Arabs whose misfortune it is to live within areas on which they have set covetous eyes." Conceding that for the "present we can do nothing but accept the fact of this new nation," Coffin concluded the editorial by warning Christians to stay vigilant about Jewish attempts to influence American foreign policy in favor of Israel and at the expense of the United States' best interests. "Our foreign policy must be designed in the interests of this country and of the commonweal of mankind, not of any other state—Eire or Israel or what not—for which some group of partially Americanized Americans profess a sentimental attachment."[22]

Response to Coffin's editorial from *Christianity and Crisis* readers was furious. The editors dedicated the entire correspondence section of 21 March 1949 to angry letters from readers, including Rabbi H. A. Fischel, director of B'nai B'rith Hillel Foundation in Tuscaloosa, Alabama, Karl Baehr of the American Christian Palestine Committee, former Secretary of the Interior Harold Ickes, S. Ralph Harlow of Smith College, John Haynes Holmes, A. Roy Eckardt, and Reverend Clark Walter Cummings of the Metropolitan Church Federation of St. Louis, Missouri. The conclusion of the correspondence section included a note from the periodical expressing its apologies that "the limit of space makes it impossible to publish all the letters received on this question." Only two short letters affirmed Coffin's arguments—the rest were critical.

Many expressed shock that the normally friendly stance the periodical had taken toward Israel appeared reversed. Rabbi Fischel began his letter of protest by indicating his "astonishment, since it deviates considerably from the theological perspective which makes *Christianity and Crisis* indispensable even to the Jewish reader."[23] Karl Baehr echoed Fischel's criticisms of the journal in his response: "This editorial is hardly in keeping with the high standards of your paper, for one would have to go to the antisemitic press to find an article more extravagantly unfair to Israel and all Zionists. . . . Not only does he call Jewish Nationalists 'fanatical' nationalists, but, it would seem, the many thousands of Christian Zionists are also considered insane."[24]

Not content that his letter to the editor sufficiently addressed the Coffin article, Baehr sent a mass letter to members of the American Christian Palestine Committee and the Israeli government decrying Coffin's editorial. Baehr's decision to alert members of the ACPC about the negative editorial and his response to it, complete with instructions to write periodicals critical of Israel (making sure to keep carbon copies of letters to editors), defines the general approach of the pro-Israel Protestants in the periodical wars over Israel in the Protestant press. Editorials and articles critical of Israel were used, in turn, to incite pro-Israel Protestants to write letters of protest and pro-Israel articles, if possible, to counterbalance the negative publicity.

Problems concerning the reasons for Arab flight, the numbers wishing to return, and the economic and security obstacles to implement full reintegration, plagued policy makers in Israel and the United States. Still, Baehr noted that during his trip to Israel, impressed by efforts of both Jewish and Arab Israelis to cooperate, he found much to commend in Israel.[25] Arab Israelis voted in the past election and three representatives now had seats in the Knesset. Despite the problems that remained, Baehr argued that "every effort is being made to integrate the various peoples in Israel into the life and structure of the new state."[26] Ultimately, Baehr concluded, "Israel deserves the complete support of the United States and the United Nations."[27]

Although other Protestant presses did not engage in intense editorial debates, they nonetheless offered a perspective on the refugee crisis. The *Lutheran*, for example, while dedicating much print space to solving the crisis of Jewish displaced persons still living in Europe in the years following the war, also highlighted the plight of Arab refugees, the problem of the internationalization of Jerusalem, and concern for the protection of the Arab Christian minority living under Israeli control. Noting that "somebody at least as wise as King Solomon would have to be found to be the governor of Jerusalem," an editorial highlighted the "loud unwillingness" of both Arabs and Jews to relinquish control of the Old City to the United Nations. The editorial offered no opinion or solution to the problem but concluded the article by quoting the report of the six ACPC members who charged that internationalization was "dangerous and unnecessary."[28] The *Lutheran* did criticize the new Israeli state in preventing its missions work from proceeding in Israeli-occupied Bethlehem, however.

Several articles appearing in 1949 and 1950 discussed the challenges one Lutheran minister, Edwin Moll, encountered in running the Syrian Orphanage, a church institution and the largest training school for boys in the Middle East in Bethlehem. In several interviews with the *Lutheran*, Moll told its readers that the influx of Palestinian refugees into these areas following the 1948 War added to the financial burden of Lutheran missionaries offering services and humanitarian aid and overwhelmed the physical infrastructure of Lutheran orphanages and schools for refugees.[29] "The effect of the Palestinian Arab disaster, especially on children," reported Elias Haddad, a Lutheran missionary in Bethlehem, "has been very grave indeed." He noted that "hundreds of children who two years ago were properly cared for are now in a pitiable state of neglect, not only physically, but mentally, morally and spiritually."[30] The *Lutheran* refrained, however, from offering a political solution to the problem—their concern rested solely on provided humanitarian aid to its missions.

Throughout the first five years of Israeli independence, concern over the plight of Palestinian refugees dominated the discussion of Israel and Zionism in the major mainline Protestant presses. While some journals, such as the *Lutheran*, offered no political statements about the crisis, other journals' editorials, feature articles, and letters to the editor served as the staging ground for written altercations. The *Christian Century* consistently highlighted the plight of Arab refugees and voiced its humanitarian concern for them while couching these concerns in decidedly hostile language toward Israel and pro-Zionists, both Jewish and Christian, whom they felt were jeopardizing America's interests in the Middle East. The editorial board of *Christianity and Crisis*, divided about the question of Israel, thus printed more varied articles, some positive and others, as in Henry Sloan Coffin's case, decidedly critical of the new state. These divisions reflected the intense disagreements among mainline American Protestants over the establishment of Israel and the resulting refugee crisis. Some Protestants considered the Palestinian refugee crisis reason enough to withhold support for the new state; others offered concern for the humanitarian plight of the refugees but withheld political commentary; still others believed that the challenges Israel and its Arab neighbors faced in regard to the refugees could be resolved in time and did not constitute a reason to withhold political support for Israeli statehood.

Beyond the Protestant Press: The Christian Pro-Israel Lobby

The Protestant discussion of Israel was not confined to the written word, of course. Outside the editorial disagreements in the Protestant periodicals, the American Christian Palestine Committee continued to hold annual seminars and workshops around the country to educate clergy and other Christian leaders about the importance of American Protestant support for the Jewish state. Travel itineraries included a five-week visit to the West Coast by members of the executive committee to speak for the United Jewish Appeal and the ACPC. Karl Baehr traveled to Seattle, Portland, San Francisco, San Diego, Los Angeles, Denver, and Kansas, speaking before groups of local ACPC members, Jewish organizations, and Christian communities. In each city Baehr held press conferences, was interviewed by local radio stations, made important political contacts, and met with local university and college faculty. "The great majority were impressed with our thesis that one *must* be *pro-Israel* and *pro-Arabs* for," he explained, "in that democratic context, the problems faced by both peoples can be resolved." Even when encountering hostile questions from the audience regarding the ACPC's stance on refugees and Arab rights, Baehr reiterated his argument: "The formula I've worked out for these seminars works beautifully! How can they attack us when we plead for both the Jews and the Arabs? For democracy, freedom, and opportunity for the masses of both people? For the West, and against communist infiltration?" The results of such a stance appeared effective to Baehr. "The audience was with us at least 90 percent. I received some of the most enthusiastic comments I've yet received," he wrote of his meeting in Denver.[31]

Generally pleased with the reception he received and the enthusiasm of his audiences for support for Israel, Baehr nonetheless encountered challenges to the ACPC agenda, primarily from the anti-Zionist American Council for Judaism, just as it had in the pre-Independence years. Even after Israel's establishment, the ACJ remained skeptical of Zionism and concerned about the consequences of a Jewish state in the Middle East for the status of Jews in other countries. "The strong force of the Council for Judaism helps to keep the Christians neutralized," he wrote in an internal memo about his meeting in Portland. In San Francisco he encountered similar pressures from the ACJ. "The Council for Judaism continues to be aggressive in besieging Christians with their literature the moment that they express an interest in Israel by speaking on its behalf, selling bonds, etc.," he wrote. Jewish supporters of the ACPC had encountered pressure from the ACJ members who dominated local boards of the National Conference of Christians and Jews.

Also, the close ties between the Zionist organizations and the ACPC alarmed some supporters who cautioned Baehr that close connections could do more harm than good by making the effort of Christians on behalf of Israel appear as a front for Jewish organizations.[32] "The Jewish people . . . are timid about pushing the Zionist program and especially timid about pushing it among Christians . . . lest it appear that the Jewish community was putting undue pressure on the Christian community," he noted in an internal memo.[33]

For their part many Christians, too, expressed concerns to Baehr about the pressure they felt from the pro-Israel Jewish community and the constant charge of being "antisemitic" for not endorsing Zionism. Regarding these concerns, Baehr noted, "if a conclusion is in order here, I do think that something ought to be done to get the Jewish community to be very much more cautious in using the term 'antisemitic.' Instead they ought to assume that the offending person just does not have all the facts and that he would undoubtedly appreciate receiving them. Thus a friendly contact can be made, on the basis of giving him some supplementary information and, almost naively, expecting him to take these facts into account. This approach," he concluded, "is more apt to succeed than driving a person completely into the opposite camp by branding him or labeling him."[34]

While Zionist organizations supplied funding for the American Christian Palestine Committee, local Christian organizations also supplied funds for study tours to Israel for members of their congregations, and local ACPC communities contributed to their expenses. Although historian Fishman has argued that the ACPC served simply as a front for Jewish organizations and fulfilled its purpose with the establishment of Israel,[35] in reality the establishment of Israel did not lessen the ACPC's importance; if anything, the organization found itself in greater demand as the need for continued American support for the new state mounted. Moreover, the dedication to the work of the ACPC by its Protestant members and leadership—despite Zionist funding—reveals the sincerity of their efforts and their desire to make, as Voss would later describe it, "spiritual atonement" for the centuries of Christian antisemitism that culminated in the Holocaust. Especially significant about the work of the ACPC in the post-Establishment decades is the degree to which the Israeli government assisted and relied on the organization to wage effective propaganda on its behalf, the close cooperation of Jewish and Protestant organizations in working together to increase grassroots support for Israel, and the fierceness with which the ACPC addressed organizations and publications it viewed as hostile to the cause of a close U.S.–Israeli alliance.[36]

The Land Reborn, published by the American Christian Palestine Committee in 1950, was the group's pro-Israel publication which it used for propaganda purposes and to counterbalance what it perceived to be the negative publicity of the *Christian Century*. Its pages contained a hodge-podge of information. Sections highlighted quotes from senators and members of Congress supportive of Israel and particularly critical of Britain's desire to sell arms to Egypt and other Arab nations hostile to Israel with the use of U.S. loans. It published clippings from other newspapers and journals that described Israel in a positive light. It included testimonies from recent visitors to Israel and new immigrants' stories of their adventures. It advocated technological and agricultural developments in Israel by noting civil engineering and infrastructure projects undertaken by the Israeli government.

In April 1949 the ACPC held its annual meeting in Israel and worked closely with Israel's Ministry of Religious Affairs and the Emergency Zionist Council in America to plan and coordinate the visit. The Israeli government, experiencing hard economic times in the wake of the 1948 War and unable to help fund the annual meeting, recognized the importance of the visit to Israel by the members of the ACPC and other prominent American Protestant leaders. In a reference to the frustration Karl Baehr expressed about the activities of the Committee for Peace in the Holy Land and the need for counter-propaganda in the United States, Eliahu Elath, Special Representative of the Israeli Embassy, noted: "I fully agree with you as to the seriousness of the anti-Israeli propaganda being carried on under the guise of Christian humanitarian activities." Unfortunately, he added, "the present condition of our Treasury is such that not a single penny could be spent in financially supporting such activities." While noting that all assistance would be given to the visitors upon their arrival, he added that "it is for the Zionist organizations [in the United States] to find the funds for their journey."[37]

In a confidential letter sent to local Zionist Emergency Council leaders regarding the plans and arrangements for the visit, Abba Hillel Silver, chairman of the executive committee of the Emergency Zionist Council, noted that participants in the ACPC seminar would be chosen directly from local Zionist communities. Silver asked local chapters to donate funds to "defray travel, hotel and personal expenses of their delegates for this important and unprecedented public relations project." Money should not be sent to the Emergency Council or the ACPC "under any circumstances." Instead, funds would be sent to the travel agency chosen by the ACPC to arrange the trip. Support for non-Jewish delegates to visit Israel would provide an essential service to improving American-Israeli relations, Silver informed his readers.

"The Executive Council of the ACPC believes," he went on, "that the American people need firsthand reports of Israel today . . . we are still beset by hostile propaganda groups working to undermine the State of Israel by false accusations. The ACPC delegates to Israel will be in a position to counteract these hostile influences, after an intensive study of conditions in Israel, under sponsorship of Israeli experts."[38] Clearly the Israeli government believed that its assistance to the ACPC was important for courting American Protestant support in opposing the internationalization vote in the U.N., even if funds could not be spared for the cause.

Instead, it dedicated considerable time to organizing the delegation's schedule and preparing for the delegation to meet with significant political figures in Israel. The executive council of the ACPC and the local Zionist organizations chose six Christian leaders to visit Israel in 1949. During their two-week trip these Protestants met with Israeli officials and toured holy sites and also spoke with Palestinians. They returned home and, as the Zionist organizations and the Israeli government had hoped, set about lecturing and writing about their experiences in Israel in a positive light. They also published a follow-up report to their earlier letter to Truman opposing the Vatican's internationalization scheme in Jerusalem.[39] Based on their experiences in Jerusalem, the fact-finding group unanimously concluded that "the United Nations plan to internationalize the Jerusalem area is dangerous and unnecessary" and urged that a "United Nation's Commission with no territorial sovereignty be established in order to ensure the free accessibility of the Christian world to the Holy Places of Jerusalem." The nine-page report detailed meetings with Christians in Jerusalem, most of whom, according to the delegates, opposed internationalization.[40]

Although most of Israel's attention to the Christian world in the years following Independence focused on its tumultuous relationship with the Catholic Church and the Internationalization movement, Israeli ministers recognized the importance of fostering positive interactions with American Protestants. The Ministry of Religious Affairs in Israel therefore expended a great deal of time and effort cultivating these relations by working closely with members of the ACPC to encourage religious exchange programs and good press in the United States. In addition, Israel consistently sent high-level representatives to the United States to work as ambassadors for the ACPC's various public relations campaigns.[41]

In September 1949 American Jewish Zionist organizations and the Israeli government worked together to promote the ACPC's platform. Jerome Unger, executive director of the American Zionist Council, urged the Israeli delegate to the United Nations, Aubrey S. Eban, to attend a meeting in New York of the ACPC's "top Christian leadership." Noting that the members of the ACPC had been "so valuable in our work," Unger asked for a thirty-minute presentation on the issues facing Israel in the United Nations over the question of the internationalization of Jerusalem. "I need not point out to you how valuable this will be for us," Unger wrote in urging Eban to attend.[42]

The ACPC continued to work closely with the Israeli government in launching its public relations campaign with a weekly Sunday radio broadcast in the United States. Its first broadcast, titled "American Christians Present Israel," was aired on 13 November 1949. The ACPC announced, in a press release, that the fifteen-minute weekly program would be chaired by Voss and would feature guest speakers "conversant with the subject of Israel." Esther Herlitz of the Israeli Ministry for Foreign Affairs, in the United States as a member of the Israeli delegation, was the first guest speaker.[43] Also, in 1949, the ACPC launched a program titled "TVA [Tennessee Valley Authority] on the Jordan," beginning with a dinner to discuss the idea of a joint Israel-Arab venture to tap the energy resources of the Jordan River. This plan, according to the ACPC, would benefit both Jordanians and Israelis. Notable speakers for the event included the chief engineer for the Tennessee Valley Authority C. E. Blee, Congressman Hugh Mitchell, Senator James E. Murray, and Walter Clay Lowdermilk. Israeli president Chaim Weizmann sent a telegram praising the effort to be read at the dinner, as did Reinhold Niebuhr, Eleanor Roosevelt, former president Herbert Hoover, Senator Arthur Vandenberg, Sumner Welles, and Bishop G. Bromley Oxnam. More than one hundred notable American leaders attended the event, and radio, press, and magazines covered the story.[44]

The following year, bolstered by "the successful report" of the six Protestants who had visited Israel earlier, the Israeli government decided to broach the idea of another visit by Protestant leaders in 1950. This visit reflected Protestants' concern over the Vatican's attempts to internationalize Jerusalem through the United Nations. It also reflected their unease over the December 1949 resolution issued by the executive committee of the Federal Council of Churches calling on Israel to fulfill the following principles: assurance of human rights, freedom of religious observation to all groups, and the restitution of, and compensation for, property. This time the Israeli government wanted the representatives not only to be members of the ACPC but to represent a larger swath of prominent American Protestants.

Enlisting the help of the executive editor of *The Nation* magazine—a periodical that had shown sympathy to the Israeli cause and a willingness to coordinate American visits to Israel and Protestant-Jewish relations in the United States—the embassy in Washington and the government decided which representatives to invite. "The proposal is that our Minister of Religions should invite the heads of the main denominational branches of the Federal Council of Churches to proceed to Israel in order to study the position in all three of these issues," the Israeli official wrote. Chosen among the six delegates were O. Bronley Oxnam, the Methodist bishop of New York; Reinhold Niebuhr; Samuel Cavert, general secretary of the Federal Council of Churches in America and a prominent Presbyterian; Henry Hobson, the Episcopal bishop of Southern Ohio; Arthur Cushman McGiffert, president of the Chicago Theological Seminary and a Congregationalist; and Fredrick Eliot, president of the American Unitarian Association. "In all, except the case of Dr. Niebuhr, who has no organization to sponsor him, we should leave the Churches concerned to defray the expenses of the visit, since I believe this would give them a greater sense of impartiality and avoid any suspicion of contamination."[45]

However much Israeli officials wished to display impartiality to the outside world, Ministry officials recognized that the tension among American Protestants and Catholics could be exploited to Israel's advantage in religious diplomacy circles and therefore offered to invite the six delegates as Israel's guests. Lilly Schultz of *The Nation* contacted Ambassador Elath to outline the plan for the delegation's visit to Israel and emphasized the need to avoid any hint of pressure upon the delegates to view Israel favorably. Clearly, however, the goal of the trip from both Schultz's perspective and that of the Israeli Foreign Ministry and Ministry for Religious Affairs would be to persuade the Protestant visitors to reconsider the Federal Council Resolution of December 1949 in light of their experience in Israel and to return to the United States ready and willing to speak positively on Israel's behalf in important religious and political circles. Moreover, the Israeli government, desperate to avoid a U.N. resolution internationalizing Jerusalem, wanted to persuade these influential visitors to support Israeli control over Jerusalem.

The visitors, therefore, were chosen carefully. Schultz considered Oxnam to be the most significant member and pointed to Cavert, the general secretary of the Federal Council of Churches, as particularly important. Schultz added in a handwritten note to the ambassador that "Oxnam thinks that the Baptists are not too important, though Truman is a Baptist. Still we feel a Baptist should be included so that there is no exclusion."[46] Above all, Schultz insisted, the project must appear to be completely free of pressure and any hint of propaganda. The delegates would be guests of Israel, and therefore incur no expenses of their own, but should believe that their opinions would be freely shaped by their experiences. Schultz added, however, that "of course all of this is related to the Jerusalem question, yet in the invitation none of that must appear. Also, once they get to Israel, the persons who clear the way for them and guide them must be most carefully chosen and care taken too that they are not being pressured. In other words," she concluded, "they should see what they are prepared to see, reach the proper conclusions, but without seeming to be led to them by any outside influence."[47]

Shortly after Schultz's letter reached the ambassador, invitations were sent to the six previously chosen delegates to visit Israel, as guests of the state, by Foreign Minister Moshe Sharett. Within a week three negative responses almost derailed the project. Oxnam seemed favorably disposed to the trip, but Cavert expressed grave reservations about being sponsored by Israel and suggested that non-Federal Council members go instead.[48] The sentiment seemed to spread among the group. Schultz quickly rushed a letter to Elath, asking that the negative responses be ignored—that all, in fact, were onboard thanks to the intervention of Niebuhr and Oxnam.[49] The initial negative responses frustrated the Israeli officials, however. "It would not only be a pity if these particular people will not be able to visit Israel, but would have a bad effect on future operations of this kind," Elath warned Schultz. "I need not tell you how vital it is for us to proceed with the mobilization of our friends in [the United States] in order to continue our battle for Jerusalem and I am confident that this projected visit will be an important step forward," he added.[50]

The trip planned for 1950, however, would never take place. In June of that year Schultz contacted Moshe Karen, counselor to the Israeli Embassy, with the news that the two most important participants—Oxnam and Niebuhr— would have to postpone the trip because of health reasons. "When this delegation was first proposed," she wrote, "we had in mind a specific group, one which, had it gone and seen for itself the developments in Israel, could have influenced Protestant thinking in a most substantial way, and with it American policy." She recommended delaying the trip until the following year, with Oxnam agreeing to lead a delegation from the World Council of Churches, as a "substitute proposal for the original plan." Although conceding that it "is possible to send a very distinguished Christian delegation this summer to Israel," she suggested that the Ministry wait until Oxnam could travel the next year for two reasons. "To extend invitations to countless delegations seems to us to place the Israel government on the defensive," she pointed out, " as if it is apologizing for what it has done, and is looking for supporters for its position, in a vulnerable way."[51] Second, Schultz argued that the press and public opinion in the United States opposed the internationalization of Jerusalem, making the immediate purpose for the delegation's visit moot. Explaining why other delegations should not be sent in place of Oxnam's, Schultz emphasized the importance that the support of significant Protestant leaders would have on the government, and added:

> It is conceivable that various groups, going to Israel, coming back and expressing their views will have reflection in the press and among organizations. But . . . the focal point is not public opinion. The focal point is the government of the United States, and a particular section of the American public, the Protestant church. What is needed is to create a counterbalance to the Vatican, and to Catholic pressures, which in turn would have an effect upon the government. Since this particular delegation cannot go to Israel, we shall have to carry on our efforts to influence the Protestants and the government without the trip to Israel.[52]

Progress had been made in that regard, Schultz reassured Karen, and pointed out a letter to the president signed by 285 "distinguished Americans, and particularly leaders of the Protestant organized community," in opposition to the internationalization of Jerusalem. More efforts would follow, she concluded, and reassured Karen that Oxnam's delegation would plan for a trip the following year.

Schultz's claim that only the most important Protestant leaders should be invited to Israel did not resonate with other Protestants, namely, those of the American Christian Palestine Committee. The ACPC wished to continue its study tours in Israel with the support of the Foreign and Religious Affairs Ministries. After sending off a six-member study tour, the Jerusalem Fact-Finding Commission, under the auspices of the ACPC, Carl Hermann Voss wrote to Karen of the Israeli Consulate to remind him of the importance of welcoming lesser-known American Protestants to Israel. Voss sympathized with Israel's "understandable desire to present in the minds of your associates and ours that we secure as many 'top names' as possible." But, he pointed out, the schedules and responsibilities of such people as Oxnam and Niebuhr made it hard to secure their participation and, once they returned, would prevent them from writing or speaking much on the issue. Referring to Oxnam, Niebuhr, and Daniel Poling, he added, "they are really of little value to us in publicizing the truth about Israel or the virtues of Zionism . . . they say little that is novel or provocative." Ultimately Voss pointed out, "securing

'Big Names' may . . . be self-defeating."[53] Although the members of the current Jerusalem Fact-Finding Tour did not enjoy the same name recognition as other proposed participants, they were immensely more valuable—speaking, writing, lecturing, and touring for free—and could reach a larger audience. "They reach deep into American life, especially into areas where the 'Big Names' are little known," Voss explained, adding that "they are in great demand in their local communities through the country."

Moreover, their ecumenical reach was far greater: the six delegates currently visiting Israel represented a much wider swath of American Protestantism, Voss pointed out, including "the Presbyterian Church . . . the southern liberals and churchwomen . . . vast numbers of Bible Belt Baptists and Negroes . . . missionary–minded (and thus anti-Zionist) circles of my own Congregationalist church . . . [and] the usually untouched Evangelical and Fundamentalist groups." The Israeli government agreed and, although it did not financially support the study tours organized by the ACPC, did cooperate in organizing events, interviews, and itineraries for the next two decades. Furthermore, at the request of Daniel Poling, the Israeli government allowed Karl Baehr to remain in the country during the summer of 1951 in order to influence American Christian visitors to Israel on behalf of the Zionist cause. "A new situation presents itself," Poling explained, "many American Christians visiting the Middle East (including Israel) have returned home with unfriendly reactions to the new Jewish state and its people because they have been convinced that Israel is responsible for the tragic Arab refugee problem."[54] After consulting with "a number of Israelis and American Zionists," Poling urged that American Christian visitors be accorded "special attention" while in Israel to counteract the "intensive programs arranged for them when they are in the Arab lands."

While visiting other countries in the Middle East, these Christians encountered missionaries and "trained Arab propagandists" who highlighted the refugee problem and "many other troubles which plague their countries 'as a result,' they contend, 'of the establishment of Israel as a state.'"[55] Poling argued that Baehr's role would be to serve as a guide to visiting American Christians, study the life of modern Israelis to use for propaganda purposes, send regular reports and photographs back to the United States that "would be of special interest to the Christian press," and "cultivate Christian leaders resident in Israel." Recently unfriendly articles in the *Christian Century* (which Poling included in his letter), only added to the urgency. He concluded by requesting funds for Baehr's extended stay. The Zionist Emergency Council agreed to the request and coordinated the details with the Israeli government—further indication that the support of American Protestants for Israel concerned both American Zionists and Israelis.

In the meantime, the Israeli government and Zionist groups in the United States relied heavily on the public relations skills of the ACPC. On multiple occasions the Israeli Consulate relied on materials prepared by the ACPC to assist Zionist groups speaking to Christian audiences, answer questions, and prepare appropriate talking points.[56] In the years after the War of Independence, the government relied heavily on the ACPC and *The Nation* associates to counteract negative publicity regarding the plight of the Arab refugees, particularly Christian Arabs in Bethlehem. Reports of restrictions of religious freedom of Palestinian Christians in Bethlehem and other occupied towns (by making travel by Arabs difficult to undertake) worried American Protestants.

The Israeli Embassy in Washington and the government in Tel Aviv found themselves under assault in the Protestant and secular presses over concern for the freedom of religion of Hebrew Christians and Arab Christians and ran stories of the persecution of these groups. James M. Watkins, general manager of the Conferences of the Churches of God and the National Bible Institution, wrote Ambassador Elath regarding reports from missionaries in Bethlehem that their missions were "finding disfavor with some of the government officials in Israel" and expressed his concern that freedom of religion, promised by the Israeli constitution, was not being observed in Bethlehem. He concluded his letter by asking the ambassador to provide information about the "attitudes of local authorities to [missionary activity] in Bethlehem."[57]

In fact, as historian Uri Bialer has recently revealed, the Israeli government privately expressed a negative attitude toward missions of any kind targeting the Jewish population. Israeli Jews, harboring a deep skepticism and even hostility toward Christians in light of thousands of years of persecution at their hands, hesitated to allow Christian organizations a free hand in missionary activities, despite the existence of freedom of religion in the Israeli constitution. Emotional resentment and years of Christian antisemitism influenced unofficial policy. Yet, as Bialer argued, while unofficial policy condemned missionary activities, the Israeli government shrewdly recognized that such a public policy would no doubt—fairly or unfairly—impede its attempts at religious diplomacy at the Vatican and in Protestant circles around the world. Hostile attitudes toward freedom of religion certainly found disfavor in the United States.[58] Americans—Jews and Protestants—retained concern over the secular nature of the Israeli state. Religious freedom, an important element in a democratic society, could not be curtailed without serious repercussions for a close U.S.–Israeli alliance.

Fundamentalist Protestants Show Cautious Interest

Fundamentalists, excited by the rebirth of Israel in the Holy Land, nonetheless approached the prophetic implications of the new nation with caution. The Jews were returning to Palestine, now Israel, in "unbelief"—in contrast to the fundamentalist understanding of biblical prophecy. But to these close watchers of biblical prophecy, the reestablishment of the Jewish state could hardly be viewed without excitement. Predictions were readjusted to fit the secular nature of the Jewish state as most prophecy students continued to watch, with intense interest, the birth pangs of the Zionist state. Sermons, pamphlets, and journals that celebrated the efforts of the Israeli pioneers to make the "desert bloom like a rose" and consolidate land in the 1948 War abounded. Now that Israel was indeed a state, the next step, according to prophecy watchdogs, must be the consolidation of Jerusalem under Israeli control. The division of the Old City between Jordan and Israel following the 1948 War troubled premillennial fundamentalists who argued that the city must be united and under Israeli control in order for the mosque on the Dome of the Rock to be razed and the temple rebuilt to usher in the end times.

In April 1949 the *Pentecostal Evangel,* a charismatic periodical, published an editorial lamenting the divided nature of the city. Emphasizing that the consolidation of Jerusalem under Jewish rule would mark the "end of the time of the Gentile," one of the important dispensation markers of the end times, the editorial noted that "Jews are entering Israel at the rate of 25,000 a month" in accordance with "Bible prophecy." "A million Jews are on the move," it continued. "They are coming from Moslem lands, and from Holland, France, and Belgium, as well as from Eastern Europe. The world is witnessing the fulfillment of the ancient promise in Jeremiah 31:10: 'He that scattereth Israel will regather him.'"[59] The following month, while reminding readers that "because of perpetual rejection of God's commandments, Israel . . . became a vassal to Gentile powers," author U. S. Grant declared that such subservience had surely ended. Celebrating the recent land acquisitions of the 1948 War, Grant predicted that Israel would "continually wage successful gains until God's original promise is fulfilled completely." To date, he added, "thirty Gentile nations" had officially recognized Israel, once again concluding that "the times of the Gentiles is about fulfilled!"[60]

Excitement over the fulfillment of prophecy led one self-professed "evangelist" from Missouri to write Chaim Weizmann to ask if animal sacrifices by Orthodox Jews had resumed in Jerusalem, as rumors had indicated. "We understand this has taken place recently," layman James Reeves wrote, "perhaps about October 19th, 1949. We are very much interested and would be very grateful to you for full details as to the date that the daily sacrifice was renewed."[61] His letter was forwarded to the Ministry for Religious Affairs which responded by disclaiming the renewal of animal sacrifices in Jerusalem. "I have the honor to inform you that, according to the Jewish law, no sacrifices may take place before the rebuilding of the Temple," wrote E. Etayen, an Information Officer of the Ministry for Religious Affairs. He added: "In view of this, I regret to state that your information regarding the renewal of the Daily Sacrifice is, apparently, based on some error."[62] Nonetheless, Reeves's letter demonstrates the enthusiasm and excitement that a growing number of fundamentalist premillennialists demonstrated toward the "reestablished" Israel.

The *King's Business*, another fundamentalist periodical dedicated to issues of prophecy, joined with other fundamentalist periodicals and preachers who now unequivocally considered the "regathering and establishment of Israel in Palestine" to be the prophetic fulfillment. Louis Bauman, a premillennialist minister in the conservative Brethren domination and a regular contributor to the *King's Business*, continued his study of prophecy and Palestine in the years following Israeli Independence. He renamed his series, "Israel Lives Again!" to reflect what he considered the literal fulfillment of biblical prophecy, as he had predicted in his pre-Independence series, "Ezekiel 36: Palestine and Russia." "For more than fifty years, I have studied the great prophecies of the Scripture," he wrote. "And if those years of study have taught me anything, it is that to [the] world of men, no trustworthy sign has been given and will not be given, unless the Jew is in the picture."[63] All other worldly events were of little significance outside their relationship with Jewry.

Denying the traditional mainline Protestant claim that Israel could now only be viewed as a "spiritual" nation, not a physical one, Bauman countered that "since the sun does not rise in the west and set in the east, 'physical Israel' remains a *nation* before the Lord, no matter what the attitude of the nations towards that ancient people may be." Furthermore, he insisted, how individuals and nations treated the Jews and Israel would be the measure by which God would, in the end of days, judge the world. In a warning that would be echoed in later decades and used as justification for pro-Israel foreign policy in the Middle East, Bauman insisted that those who wished to be faithful to God's plan for history would be faithful to the nation of Israel.[64] All things worked according to a divine plan—even Hitler's persecution of the Jews served the purpose of "aiding the children of Jacob to realize their dream—a return of their ancient home in Palestine."

The progress and success of the Jewish settlers in Israel only testified to the fulfillment of prophecy and could be contrasted with the lack of development in the Arab areas. "The turbaned (Esau) Arab still sits on the ground amidst squalid surroundings, working only with his ancient stick for a plow, jealous and despising Jacob," Bauman wrote.[65] Bauman's assessment of the plight of the Arabs reflected a consistent attitude among fundamentalists toward the Palestinians. At best, to these Protestants, the Palestinians represented a despotic people, unwilling to improve their land, and therefore existing solely as a contrast to the efficiency and hard work of the Jewish settlers. At worst, they were a hindrance to the expansion of Israeli territory according to the fulfillment of prophecy and deserved no consideration of territorial claims or rights.

In March 1952 an editorial in the *King's Business* laid out the necessary steps that should happen in accordance with biblical predictions after Israel's establishment. "Next in order for Israel," it explained, "will be the complete jurisdiction over Jerusalem, the destruction of the Mosque of Omar, the building of a great temple and the reestablishment of their ancient worship. This generation now living," the editorial confidently concluded, "will probably witness those thrilling events."[66] Opposition to this plan by the United Nations only confirmed fundamentalists' suspicions of the organization. Many believed that the United Nations heralded the coming of a satanic one-world government with a supreme ruler (the Antichrist) as foretold in the book of Revelation. In Bauman's last article before his death, which included a photo of a flag-raising ceremony at the U.N. General Assembly, he echoed earlier warnings against resisting God's plans for the State of Israel: "Thus, the nations that have held the flesh and blood of the Jews so cheaply, will be drawn into the valley of Jehoshaphat for their final judgment . . . and these nations will be judged on the ground of their treatment of the Jew."[67] Nations would be judged, but so, too, would individuals, Bauman reminded his readers and, in a departure from the legacy of fundamentalist antisemitism in the previous decades, asked, "How can any child of God permit himself to be impregnated with the virus of antisemitism?"[68] Bauman's final message to the readers of *King's Business* encouraged them to support Israel, despite worldly pressure to do otherwise.

In their sermons, other well-known fundamentalist preachers, such as J. Frank Norris, president of the Directors for the Bible Baptist Seminary in Fort Worth, Texas, and Reverend W. O. H. Garman, echoed Bauman's excitement and the call to support Israel. In a radio address broadcast by the American Broadcasting Company in the wake of Israeli independence, Garman noted the significant events taking place in the world—the rise of Russia and the establishment of the United Nations and the World Council of Churches—and explained that these events set "the stage thereby for the reign of the Anti Christ and the worship of the Beast." Israel's establishment, too, echoed prophecy, and Garman, like many fellow fundamentalists, reminded his listeners that the Jews remained God's chosen people and the establishment of their nation of Israel put into place an important part of the prophecy puzzle.[69] Before the reestablishment of Israel, Jewish distinctiveness in the Diaspora, he argued, carried a special significance, because "God has declared in His word that the Jewish race will never lose its identity nor be swallowed up by the Gentile nations."

Adhering to traditional fundamentalist theology, Garman explained that because of Jewish disobedience to God's laws, they had been cursed and dispersed and were now restored to their ancient homeland. Zionism should be supported by all Christians, since the "Jew is going back home in preparation for the closing events of this dispensation, and the return of our Lord Jesus Christ." Despite the punishment the Jews had endured for their disobedience and failure to recognize Jesus as the Messiah, all was not lost, Garman told his listeners. "During the [coming] Kingdom reign of their Messiah the Jew will not only be fully restored to his earthly inheritance but to God's favor." Again emphasizing the fundamentalist theological position on the Jews, he concluded that "their only sure hope is the return of the Lord. They will never come into their own until He has come as their accepted Messiah."[70]

Another sermon, delivered by Norris to a crowd of twelve hundred people, attracted the attention of Samuel Newman of the American Zionist Council. In a letter to Norris, Newman thanked him for his sermon about "Palestine and Israel in the light of prophecy" and added that "your deep insight into Jewish problems and warm sympathy with the Zionist movement exceeded my expectations."[71] Leaping across ecumenical divides, Newman concluded his letter to the fundamentalist preacher by asking if he could give his name to the ACPC. "The American Christian Palestine Committee, numbering more than 20,000 members," Newman concluded, "feels keenly the responsibility of Christians and Christendom for the evils and shame of anti-Jewish persecutions throughout our tragic history."[72] Such a request indicated Newman's belief that Norris, as a person whose interest in Israel created a commonality with an organization made up of Protestants Norris might otherwise eschew, might be willing to work across denominational divides to help Israel.

Despite the growing religious interest in the establishment of Israel and the event's place in the prophetic puzzle of the end times, fundamentalist Protestants still did not advocate political lobbying for American support of Israel after 1948. Instead, their focus remained on the religious aspect. Preachers, pamphleteers, and periodicals praised Israel's birth, predicted further developments, and patiently awaited the fulfillment of prophecy.

Ecumenical Efforts, Theological Considerations

The plight of the Jews during the Holocaust initiated some ecumenical efforts, but postwar realities spurred them even further. Just as the Cold War was heating up and pitting two cultures against each other, the creation of Israel ensured that religion would play a role in world politics. The National Conference of Christians and Jews, which had benefited from official government endorsement and dramatic increases to its budget, continued to operate conferences, workshops, and seminars around the country in the postwar decades. Motivated in part by the continuation of antisemitic propaganda and persecution in formerly Nazi areas of Europe, the NCCJ also pointed to America's own antisemitic legacy during the 1930s and 1940s as a motivation for its mission. "In view of the menace that threatened world society and human relations in our own country the National Conference stepped up its educational program," Robert Ashworth of the NCCJ declared in a 1950 pamphlet.[73] Its roundtable discussions and workshops attracted crowds as large as nine thousand people, and members of the NCCJ who participated in its events included such notable figures as Oswald Garrison Villard, content editor of *The Nation*, J. Roscoe Drummond, executive editor of the *Christian Science Monitor*, and Henry Luce, the publisher of *Time, Fortune,* and *Life* magazines. With aid from the Warner Brothers Studios in California, the NCCJ continued its tradition of sponsoring a national "Brotherhood Week," as it had since 1934. Now, however, Cold War considerations informed the agenda.

Unity in the face of atheistic communism dominated brotherhood activities. The immediate conclusion of the Second World War found the allies engaged in another struggle—this time against communism. The theme of the 1946 Brotherhood Week that year reflected these new concerns.[74] David O. Selznick, who had produced and directed previous films for the Brotherhood Week, produced another, three-minute film titled "The American

Creed" in 1946. Famous American film actors and actresses—"the brightest constellation of stars in moving picture history"—declared their support for the cause of brotherhood. Edward G. Robinson (an American Jew) read a pledge that affirmed "the basic ideal of my country—fair play for all" and promised to "keep America free from the disease of hate that destroyed Europe." The film concluded with Jimmy Stewart calling all viewers to sign the pledge. The film appeared in ten thousand movie theaters, and conference members distributed eleven million pledges nationwide.[75]

Its official poster for the 1947 Brotherhood Week declared: "Brotherhood: Democracy's Strongest Link."[76] The NCCJ also worked to internationalize the movement with cold war allies and, in August 1947, sponsored a workshop in Seelisberg, Switzerland, to "study antisemitism" in the churches, in Jewish-Christian relations, schools and universities, and civic and social services. The conference attracted sixty-three leaders from seventeen countries.[77]

While attempts at ecumenical understanding flourished in the postwar years, theological reevaluations moved more cautiously. For some American Jews, the era of modernism in American Protestantism provided an opportunity for interfaith discussion. Rabbi Jacob Chinitz, of Congregation B'nai Israel in Pontiac, Michigan, noted in an address before the Pontiac Ministerial Association—an interfaith organization—that "in the era of rationalized faith and the sophisticated notion of 'multiple revelations,' some conversation between the faithful on both sides exists."[78] Yet Chinitz's address echoed reservations about the validity and practicality of ecumenism. Quoting H. L. Mencken's remark that "religions tolerate each other only when they don't take themselves seriously," Chinitz reminded his listeners that for the orthodox practitioners of Christianity and Judaism, real obstacles remained in the way of interfaith relations. Historic memory on both sides, the reality of little Christian resistance to Hitler, and the problem that "to one type of Jew, any new approach to Christianity involves a desecration of saintly memories and the wasting of sacrifice" offered daunting challenges to ecumenism.[79] But for the contemporary era, Chinitz argued, no greater obstacle existed for "liberal Protestantism" than the reality of the State of Israel's existence and the fact that Judaism remains a living religion. To acknowledge this, he argued, would mean a break with the traditional Protestant teachings of supercessionism, and real "communion" between the faiths would require "the assumption that Sinai still stands for the Jews as the only revelation, never abrogated, never replaced." Furthermore, Chinitz explained, "part of the recognition by Christians of Judaism as a living religion would have to be its acknowledgment of Israel as a living people. The establishment of the

State of Israel," he correctly concluded, "must have come as a concentrated shock to orthodox Christian theologians." After all, he noted, "here is a living refutation of the Wandering Jew, a fulfillment of prophecy in a rather unexpected literal form, a turning back of the clock to a situation which had always seemed so ancient."[80]

Ultimately, until Christianity addressed these new religious and political realities, ecumenical efforts would necessarily be limited. Each faith needed to approach the other cautiously, not anticipating the abandonment of distinctiveness.[81] Chinitz's call for theological fidelity and Protestant acknowledgment of Israel's political and religious reality ironically echoed the fundamentalists' platform—a group that typically eschewed the ecumenical gathering that Chinitz addressed. Yet Chinitz's call for Protestants to abandon supercessionism and acknowledge Judaism as a living faith and Israel as a real capital would indeed present a stumbling block to his intended audience who were, as he correctly surmised, stunned by the theological implications of Israel's rebirth.

For many American Jews, concerns over Jewish-Protestant relations centered on the familiar issue of Protestant missions to the Jews in the United States. In January 1949 the Anti-Defamation League of B'nai B'rith prepared a special issue of its monthly publication, *The Facts,* to address the problem (a copy of which was sent to the Israeli Ministry for Religious Affairs). The report outlined the major missionary organizations in American Protestantism, and though it noted that "the majority of Christian missionaries affiliated with established churches . . . are sincere religionists . . . [and] so far as it is known, most of the legitimate church-sponsored committees are guilty of no deliberate antisemitism," it also added that two organizations posed concerns for the Jewish community.[82] The report highlighted, as particularly problematic, A. D. Michelson's Hebrew Evangelicalization Society and Joseph Hoffman Cohan's American Board of Missions to the Jews. While noting that statistics concerning the "success" of proselytizing efforts were difficult to obtain, the report suggested that the missionary activities had been largely unproductive. "Many Jews," the report concluded, "consider any attempt to proselytize a kind of 'higher antisemitism' which, wittingly or otherwise, tends to disrupt harmonious relations between Jews and Christians."[83] The report noted that "in recent years there has been a decrease in proselytizing activities," and pointed to a growing divide among mainline Protestants over the issue of converting the Jews. Although the World Council of Churches had cautiously upheld the principle of converting Jews, other significant Protestant figures had "gone on the record as strongly opposing the continuation of organized attempts to convert Jews."

A. Roy Eckardt, theology professor at Lehigh University, also publicized his opposition to Christian missions to the Jews in a book titled *Christianity and the Children of Israel*. In it Eckardt called for a reevaluation of the relationship between Christians and Jews in light of the Holocaust and offered a historical analysis of the long relationship between the two religions, calling for Christians to reexamine their historically hostile approach to Judaism. According to Eckardt, the Jews retained their special covenantal status with God—a covenant separate from Christianity—and therefore ought to be respected by Christians. Furthermore, Eckardt argued, Jews existed not only as religious adherents but also as an ethnic and cultural people who deserved the right to preserve their distinctiveness. Echoing Niebuhr's testimony before the Anglo-American Inquiry in 1946, Eckardt argued that Eretz Yisrael offered ethnic and cultural security to preserve the special distinctiveness of the Jewish people.[84] Despite Eckardt's condemnation of the *Christian Century's* consistent call for Jews to integrate themselves at the cost of their cultural distinctiveness, the periodical gave the book a positive review. W. E. Garrison, writing for the *Christian Century*, noted the book's criticism of the periodical but considered the book a "competently written treatise." "Personally, I do not accept the idea that the Jews of today rest under some 'special judgment of God' that applies uniquely to them," he wrote. "But if they do—and here the author agrees—certainly it is not the business of Christians to execute that judgment," he concluded.[85] Ultimately, however, calls for the reevaluation of Christian theology toward the Jews and Judaism were rare in the years immediately following independence. Albeit cautiously, the World Council of Churches endorsed continued missions to convert Jews, and theological and ecumenical journals expressed the same intent.

The political realities of Israel's establishment, however, sparked intense debate in religious periodicals. In one anonymously written article that appeared in the *Ecumenical Review*, the author, while praising many aspects of the new Israeli state, lamented the lack of concern for the Arab population and the lack of religious adherence among Israelis. The Protestants working as missionaries in Israel were failing at their job of serving the spiritual needs of the Israelis. The author argued that they suffered from their tendency to "see Israel as the literal fulfillment of Old Testament prophecy, and therefore blind themselves to its imperfections." The author continued, "Israel is for them so very much the fulfillment of the expressed will of God that it cannot fail. One of them put it bluntly to me, 'It is silly to talk as if Israel might go bankrupt. When one remembers that all this is foretold in Scripture, it is clear that God will not allow it to happen."' [86] Apparently, for this author, Protestant excitement over Israel's establishment had muted missionary fervor.

Regarding the Arabs, the author noted that "there is almost no attempt to understand the Arab point of view, or even to admit that they have one, and the children in school learn quite surprisingly little about them." Such a tactic would no doubt lead the Arabs to communism, the author surmised: "the Arabs . . . are almost driven into the arms of the Communists, feeling that there is no one else left in the world to help them."[87]

Such remarks reflect a general American tendency to underestimate the conflict between atheistic communism and Islam but reveal profound geopolitical fears. Most important, these remarks expose several shared concerns of mainline Protestants: that the evangelical view of Israel's establishment as the fulfillment of biblical prophecy posed a barrier to an honest assessment of geopolitical realities, and that the evangelicals' growing tendency to uncritically support Israel for prophetic reasons alienated the Arabs of the Middle East at a time when such alienation could only pose risks for Cold War strategies and American interests in the region.

American Friends of the Middle East: The Anti-Israel Christian Lobby

It did not take long after 1948 for critics of Israel to organize and begin lobbying the U.S. government for a different foreign policy. Their arguments came to describe much of the opposition to Israel that a vocal minority of Americans—including mainline Protestant leadership—would hold over the next few decades. Established in 1951 by Dorothy Thompson, a one-time supporter of a Jewish homeland who became a critic of nationalistic Zionism, the American Friends of the Middle East (AFME) began as an attempt to counterbalance the successful propaganda efforts of the American Christian Palestine Committee to influence U.S. foreign policy. While members of the ACPC (and historian Hertzel Fishman) argued that the AFME consistently took an anti-Zionist, anti-Israel stance, motivated mainly from Protestant missionary activities in the Middle East and the humanitarian concern for the plight of the Arab refugees, the reality of Cold War politics dictated many of the group's concerns. The AFME worried that U.S. policies toward Israel, influenced by the active propaganda of Zionist organizations in the United States—both Jewish and Christian—would prove detrimental to U.S. policies in the Middle East and, by extension, its national interests. The AFME feared that the close ties between the United States and Israel would alienate potential Arab allies at a time when the Soviet Union actively courted possible Arab satellites. Just as Israel's foreign policy alignment proclaimed its neutrality in the early years of its establishment, so, too, did the Arab nations appear ripe for influence.

The AMFE advertised itself as an organization dedicated to improving relations between the United States and the rest of the Middle East. To that end, it sponsored its own study tours to nations (other than Israel), sent out newsletters, sponsored academic exchanges with Middle Eastern scholars, sponsored seminars, and heavily advertised its agenda in major newspapers around the country. Its executive branch, headed by Thompson, also claimed several prominent Protestants, including Garland Evans Hopkins, a Methodist and former editor of the *Christian Century*. Of the sixty-three members of its national council, however, only eighteen were Protestant clergymen.[88] The AMFE claimed no members of Congress but nonetheless worked to influence U.S. foreign policy—and to counter the successful efforts of the ACPC. Its members, Hopkins argued, "have helped to create the climate in American public opinion which once again allows newspapers and radios to present the Middle East in its proper perspective. They have given the lie to half truths and unfactual propaganda spread by special interest groups. They have had a real part in restoring the American way in America."[89]

Clearly, to members of the AFME, the propaganda of the ACPC jeopardized U.S. interests abroad and failed to accurately explain the situation to the average American. When Russia sold arms to Egypt in 1955, Hopkins declared this to be a direct result of a misdirected U.S. policy in the Middle East—one that ignored the Arab nationalist movements to the detriment of the United States and further antagonized the Arabs by supporting Israel. In the AFME's Fifth Annual Report, Hopkins wrote:

> It is high time the American public began to demand why this had happened; to discover how so few people have been able to block the best interests of the United States in that strategic area. . . . This requires a reappraisal of American policy in the area—a reappraisal based on America's best interests rather than one formulated as a result of pressure from any special interest groups or any foreign power.[90]

In its public relations campaign, the AFME relied heavily on the assistance of the anti-Zionist American Council for Judaism and particularly the help of Rabbi Lazaron who campaigned on behalf of the organization. Yet, however much the AFME wished to spark a reversal of U.S. policy toward Israel, it suffered from low membership and a lack of financing. Although Fishman argued that the AFME represented "the most potent of American anti-Israel organizations," he also conceded that the ACPC "was far larger in recorded supporters and was tied to, and supported by, an indigenous American Jewish citizenry deeply concerned with Israel's security and future."[91] However small its grass-roots and financial support may have been, the establishment of the AFME certainly captured the attention of the ACPC and its Jewish supporters, who correctly viewed its agenda as a direct threat to their own.

After learning of the establishment of the AFME and its full-page advertisement in the *New York Times*, Voss wrote to Abe Harman of the Israeli Office of Information (and copied the Israeli Consulate) with the suggestions that the ACPC infiltrate the membership councils of the AFME to keep tabs on the organization and to help plan a counterattack.[92] While alarmed that such notable figures as Thompson, Hopkins, and Harry Emerson Fosdick sat on the executive council, Voss advised proceeding with caution in countering the group. He noted that their full page advertisements in the *New York Times* and *New York Herald Tribune*, while highlighting the plight of refugees as the group's primary concern, did not explicitly mention Israel. To immediately counterattack, he argued, would be counterproductive without a specific attack against Israel: "Too often in the past, we have been too hasty and too denunciatory. Let us be very careful in this instance." He insisted that the ACPC not allow "Zionist groups, either Jewish or Christian, throughout the country to engage in trigger-action denunciations or attacks, for such an approach would be disastrous." He concluded by reminding Harman that if the ACPC would "give our enemy enough rope he will surely hang himself."[93]

Yet, for a brief time, it appeared as though the AFME and the ACPC might have similar agendas, or at least Karl Baehr thought so. While concerned from the beginning about the AFME's agenda, members of the ACPC met with members of the AFME to discuss their goals. One ACPC member met with Eric Bethman, AFME's director of publications, in order to assess the program's aims. The ACPC member explained that their organization was "eager to promote any program which will be of positive humanitarian benefit to all the peoples of the Middle East" and asked if the AFME would be interested in joining forces with the ACPC if they shared similar goals. Bethman replied that the AFME "has only a positive program which is not anti-Israel . . . only pro-peace for the Middle East" and were interested in "practical solutions for the anti-West problems of the area." Furthermore, Bethman added, "the handling of this Israel business was entirely wrong, and will result in trouble." Despite their efforts to organize programs that included all the major nations of the Middle East, as soon as the Arab nations learned that Israel had agreed to participate, those nations withdrew, forcing the AFME to "set up regional conferences with Arabs alone. . . . We are broader in concepts than ACPC, and therefore have to take more care with the Arabs, which are in the majority." When asked about the connection of the American Council for Judaism, Bethman replied that the ideas of Elmer Berger, the director of the ACJ, and Morris S. Lazaron "completely coincide with ours."[94]

Still, Baehr held out hope that Garland Hopkins would not become an enemy of the ACPC and met with him on several occasions. He reported that they did not agree on all issues. He noted that Hopkins, impressed by the freedom of speech in Israel, nonetheless worried that "this freedom had engendered fear in the Arabs, because they constantly read letters in the Israel press demanding all of Palestine, all of Jordan, and even some demanding parts of Syria." Hopkins also articulated a concern of the AFME that the United States "stop playing favorites" in the Middle East and charter a more neutral policy there.[95] On another occasion, Hopkins complained to Baehr that the Arab Nations of the Middle East rarely received adequate media attention in the United States, unlike Israel. The problem, Hopkins insisted, lay in the unwillingness of the Arab nations to sponsor public relations campaigns. One Egyptian told him that "if the Americans want our point of view, let them pay for it." Still, Baehr reported that he "was impressed with the friendliness of Hopkins and the fact that he has moved considerably in our direction [by agreeing that Israel should receive financial aid from the U.S.]."[96] His initial impressions, however, proved premature in the following years.

Over the next few years the ACPC kept careful tabs on the actions of the AFME, sending an infiltrator who sent regular reports back to ACPC headquarters about the meetings and plans of the organization. In addition, Voss and Baehr engaged Hopkins in debates about Middle East policy on more than one occasion—keeping the conversations discreet and sending confidential memos to the ACPC regarding the nature of their conversations. Such a policy kept with Voss's warning to maintain a low profile about the organization and only counterattacking it when specific references were made about Israel in the press. In February 1953 Garland Hopkins invited Samuel Margoshes of the Jewish National Fund (whose stated purpose was "to redeem the soil of Palestine as the inalienable property of the Jewish people") and James H. Sheldon, executive director of the anti-Nazi League, whom Margoshes described as a "Christian friend of Jews," to lunch to discuss their recent public criticisms of the anti-Israel platform of the AFME with the hope of "enlightening" Margoshes and Sheldon about the AFME's purposes.[97] Describing him as possessing a "cruel mouth," Margoshes reported that Hopkins began his comments by describing himself as a "Methodist minister, who was released by his congregation to do Christian work in the Middle East." The purpose of the AFME lay in "making friends in the Middle East for America and the West which had lost considerable ground in that are due chiefly to the pro-Zionist stand of President Truman."[98]

Eisenhower's administration presented an opportunity for those concerned with the ramifications of a policy too closely aligned with Israel in the area to enact changes. "An open policy of conciliation with Israel would only antagonize the Arabs," Hopkins explained, and added that the AFME has "embarked on a course of cultivating Arab friendships, hoping in this way they would be able, at some future time, to influence the Arabs to make a settlement with Israel."[99] Developing friendships with the Arabs marked an important step in securing the West against the Soviet Union, he explained, and noted that "the Arab states are essential to any defensive plan in the Middle East and that their goodwill is of primary importance in the cold as well as a hot war with Russia." Hopkins then began to complain about the influence of American Jews and Christian Zionists on U.S. policy, according to Margoshes. He wrote: "The Jews of America should know, he added with a laugh, that Truman is no longer in the White House and that there is an American administration in Washington." He condemned the failure of the press and media to adequately cover the programs of the AFME and said this was due to Jewish control of the major newspapers in the United States. "Finally came his clear threat," he wrote:

> If, he warned, America is ever embroiled in a war in the Middle East because of the intransigence of Israel and the support of Israel's position by the Jews of the United States, the American people can be counted on to react most violently to such a situation, and he wouldn't be surprised at all, if there was a wave of antisemitism of an unprecedented character in this country, resulting possibly in excesses.[100]

Shocked by this statement, Margoshes replied that he would "be prepared to go on with my Zionism and take my chances with the American people," to which Hopkins replied that Margoshes might be staking "too much on the American character, for he has seen Americans when aroused." Sheldon, Margoshes reported, "was truly magnificent, both in his righteous indignation as a Christian at hearing the kind of talk that came from a Methodist minister, as well as in his rejoinder to Hopkins's argument. At times it seemed as if the two men would come to blows."[101] Whether Margoshes accurately represented Hopkins's position or not, he left the meeting convinced that "Hopkins and his friends are afraid of the Zionist influence, which they terribly overrate and that in Hopkins and in the American Friends . . . we have a strong and dangerous enemy that will not stop at anything to hurt Israel and American Jewry as well."[102]

In January 1953 Dwight Eisenhower ushered in a new Republican administration. Eisenhower and John Foster Dulles, his secretary of state (both Presbyterians), introduced a new approach to Middle East foreign policy that alarmed pro-Israeli Protestants and excited Protestants critical of U.S. pro-Israeli policies.[103] Any earlier hope that the AFME and the ACPC could find common ground disappeared during the Eisenhower administration. The two organizations found themselves at cross purposes: the AFME believed that current pro-Israeli foreign policy supported by the Zionists had only hurt U.S. relations in the Middle East at a time when the United States could ill afford to make enemies. The Zionists—Christians and Jews—continued to push for U.S. support of Israel for humanitarian and religious reasons, just as they had in Truman's administration.

Conclusion

The celebrations over Israel's establishment and Truman's recognition were short-lived by pro-Israel Protestants. Far from believing that their support for Israel was no longer necessary, in the first five years of Israel's existence pro-Israel Protestants continued their public relations efforts to reach grass-roots organizations and lobbied on behalf of Israel. Politically pro-Israel mainline Protestants outmaneuvered the anti-Zionist liberal Protestants. Mainline Protestants were less divided, however, over the importance of increased ecumenism in the Cold War atmosphere and reevaluations of traditional theology toward Judaism. Meanwhile fundamentalists, excited about the establishment of Israel, began to take an active interest in determining how and in what ways its establishment fulfilled prophecy. Those who had eschewed political mobilization on Israel's behalf continued to remain politically dormant but grew increasingly excited by events unfolding in the Middle East. When Israel captured the Sinai Peninsula following the Suez Crisis in 1956, these Protestants viewed the event as nothing less than a continued fulfillment of biblical prophecy. Protestants critical of Israel, such as the American Friends of the Middle East, condemned the actions of Israeli and her British and French allies and approved of Eisenhower's response. Members of the ACPC found themselves facing new challenges in their efforts to increase mainline support for Israel and pro-Israel policies in the Congress in the following years.

Political and Theological Dissent, 1953–1967

Karl Baehr, chairman of the American Christian Palestine Committee, was worried. Upon receiving notification that the pastor of the National Presbyterian Church of Washington, D.C., Edward L. R. Elson, planned to tour the Middle East, including Israel, Baehr contacted Alisa Klausner Ber of the Israeli Foreign Office to request that the government take note of the visit. Pro-Israel Protestants viewed Elson as hostile to Israel's interests and worried about the implications of his visit to his very famous parishioners. "It is extremely important," he wrote, "that he [Elson] be given the 'VIP' treatment, realizing full well that he is not at all a friend of Israel. He will probably be most eager to have his beliefs that Israel is basically an expansionist nation and that she treats her Arabs as second-class citizens and so forth substantiated." Elson's influence was not to be taken lightly, Baehr advised, since "Elson will have the opportunity to report to both [President] Eisenhower and to [Secretary of State] Dulles, for both are members of his church."[1]

Despite overwhelming American support for the establishment of Israel and Truman's decision to offer de facto recognition following Israel's Declaration of Independence, the Eisenhower administration approached foreign policy in the Middle East with a decidedly neutral stance. Pro-Israel American Protestants often found themselves at odds with the administration's policies, a situation that peaked during the Suez Crisis of 1956 and pitted members of the ACPC against the administration. Protestants critical of Israel made concerted efforts to affect American public opinion about Israel and the nature of the relationship between the United States and the Arab nations of the Middle East. These Protestants found more fuel for their attack in the perceived aggression of the Israeli state and filled the pages of their periodicals with praise for the policies of Eisenhower and John Foster Dulles and condemnation of Israel's actions. Despite the fractiousness of mainline Protestant reaction to the U.S.–Israeli alliance, however, by the eve of the 1967 War, those mainline Protestants who had worked to sway public opinion to the Israeli cause felt confident that they had succeeded in their mission. Meanwhile, mainline Protestants showed an increase in interest in the Holocaust and its implications for traditional Protestant theology. In the 1950s American Protestants began to reevaluate supercessionist theology and embraced increased interfaith communication with Jews.

At the same time evangelicals grew increasingly interested in the Middle East. They watched the Israeli takeover of the Sinai Peninsula with excitement—another piece of the biblical map of the Holy Land now belonged to Israel—but still refrained from active political engagement. While evangelicals also refrained from the theological reevaluations embraced by their mainline Protestant counterparts during these years, their discussions of the significance of Jews and Judaism to history took on a new tone—gone was any trace of the antisemitism that had tainted their discussions of Jews in the 1930s. Now the focus shifted to the important role Jews would play in the end of history and the importance of recognizing the religious significance of Judaism to Christianity.

The Eisenhower Administration

In 1952 Dwight D. Eisenhower won the presidency. Formerly the Supreme Allied Commander of the Allied Forces in the Second World War, Eisenhower came to office with extensive foreign policy experience and widespread support. Furthermore, his experiences in the Second World War liberating Jews from Nazi concentration camps had made him sympathetic to their humanitarian plight in the aftermath of the war. Yet Eisenhower's presidency took place during the first few decades of the Cold War, and his pragmatic foreign policy platforms testified to his insistence that the United States exercise "neutral and impartial friendships" toward the nations of the Middle East. Like Truman before him, Eisenhower initially refused to offer more than economic aid to Israel, and, observing the shipments of military aid to the Israelis by the French and West Germans (as a form of reparations payments), authorized sales of military weapons to Arab nations in an attempt to avoid alienating Western alliances in the unstable Middle East.

Concerned for the growing Soviet influence in an area experiencing emerging nationalist movements, Eisenhower and his secretary of state, John Foster Dulles, crafted a Near East foreign policy that sought to avoid charges of favoritism. The fear of Soviet influence engulfing Arab nations such as Egypt, which, under the leadership of Colonel Gamal Abdul Nasser, struggled to throw off the mantle of British colonialism, encouraged a careful, middle-of-the-road approach to Israel and the Arab world. For example, Eisenhower's government offered aid to Egypt in building the Aswan Dam, a huge infrastructure project on the Nile River. Twice in 1953 Eisenhower did not hesitate to speak out against Israel at the United Nations: first, by condemning an Israeli military action against Syria in the Jordan Valley and Golan Heights; and, second, by supporting a U.N. Security Council resolution that threatened economic sanctions against Israel for the massacre of the Qibya Palestinian refugee camp in Jordan.[2] For the United States, national and international interests were best served with a U.S.–Middle East policy that ensured U.S. access to oil and shipping routes, avoided war between Israel and her enemies, and prevented undue Soviet influence in the area. Those policy objectives would be repeatedly tested throughout Eisenhower's two terms in office.

Mainline Protestant Organizations

Concern for the fate of the U.S.–Israeli alliance in the new Eisenhower administration prompted ACPC Chairman Karl Baehr to testify before the Senate Foreign Relations Subcommittee on the Near East on 25 May 1953. Foremost on the agenda was the charge to address the U.S. response to the plight of the Arab refugees and the question of continued American financial support for Israel. Baehr provided testimony on behalf of continued support for Israel and suggested that his experience traveling in the region—speaking to Israeli and Jordanian officials, refugees in camps and U.N. officials—allowed him a unique and well-traveled perspective on the issues. The testimony served as a privileged soapbox for Baehr and the ACPC to express their pro-Israeli Protestantism and their political views.

Baehr immediately made clear that the Arabs should take the majority of responsibility for the refugee crisis. "The Arab war against the United Nations decision [to partition Palestine] created not only the Arab refugee problem . . . but made inevitable the expansion of the Jewish refugee problem, for it made untenable the position of substantial Jewish communities in the Arab world."[3] He pointed out that the hostilities between Israel and her Arab neighbors had forced Jews from those nations to flee and that the plight of such refugees fell solely to Israel to address—the U.N., in other words, had ignored the financial crisis that the resettlement of Jewish refugees in Israel presented to the new state and had focused all its attention and financial assistance to the Arab refugee crisis alone. Such a burden on Israel necessitated continued U.S. financial support, Baehr argued.

Israel, Baehr claimed, had done well with the financial assistance provided by the United States, and its success in handling a myriad of problems offered a "profound spiritual experience [to observers] as they help to implement the many projects which increase production, create new jobs and . . . help in the difficult but exciting job of rebuilding a wasted land and redeeming rejected peoples. Literally," he testified to the Senate Foreign Relations Committee, "the Bible is, with American aid, being fulfilled in Israel today."[4] Eventually the money Americans spent would result in financial, economic, and social stabilization in Israel. The Arab refugee problem, however, appeared less hopeful.

Baehr argued that the huge amounts of international financial relief, the land resources, the financial compensation offered by Israel, and the vast oil incomes should have produced positive results for the Palestinian refugees. "The basic reason" why the Palestinian refugees remained unsettled, Baehr concluded, "is that the Arab states have not accepted the existence of Israel" and continue to use the refugees as political pawns—ignoring true improvement possibilities in order to exact political capital from the U.N. against Israel.

He urged the Committee to recognize that a failure to support Israel financially would signal to her enemies that the United States approved of their hostilities. He recognized that the fear of communist influence in the Middle East prompted concern among policy makers but insisted that such claims constituted scare tactics and that, when pressed, Arab officials recognized the disadvantage of inviting Soviet influence into their countries. America must continue to pledge "her support to both Israel and the Arab states. To follow a sell-out policy for either Jews or Arabs would be to deny the basic American principles of fair play and of a democratic concern for people in need, no matter what their background, race or religion."[5]

Baehr insisted that the only reasonable tactic for the United States and the United Nations to take with regard to the refugee problem was to recognize the impracticality of Palestinians returning to Israel and to press the Arab nations to resettle these refugees—with outside economic aid—immediately into the countries where they now lived. The refugees themselves, Baehr pointed out, hardly languished in the camps and often fared better than did the Arabs in the surrounding areas outside the camps. He pointed out that the birth rate was as high as, if not higher than, surrounding countries, including a lower infant mortality rate, that most refugee children had access to free education (unlike their Arab neighbors), and that the caloric and protein intake, thanks to U.N. rations, remained superior to most Arab citizens.

Of course, they could not remain indefinitely in the camps, Baehr conceded. As he concluded his testimony, he reminded the Committee that, "above all, America must insist upon resettlement as the only logical and humanitarian solution."[6]

Less than a year later, the ACPC held its tenth annual meeting in Washington, D.C. Dominating the conference proceedings was the continued concern that Eisenhower's stated intention to offer "sympathetic and impartial" friendship for all sides in the U.S. Near East policy signaled a shift away from Truman's support for a strong U.S.–Israeli alliance. Attended by more than three hundred delegates, the conference attracted senators, university administrators, congressmen, judges, professors, and ministers from ACPC branches across the country. Foremost on the agenda, the U.S. decision to sell arms to Arab nations hostile to Israel as an act of neutrality and impartiality elicited passionate condemnation from speakers and attendees in conference sessions. Senator Guy M. Gillette (D., Iowa), urged the administration to withhold military assistance from "Arab States hostile to Israel."[7] A close alliance with Israel had, in the previous administration, served as a "defense system against Soviet aggression" in a strategically important area—the land bridge between Asia and Africa. Now new policies proposed by John Foster Dulles and Eisenhower threatened that security and marked the first time in U.S. history that "plans are going forward to ship arms to friendly countries which are in a state of war with another country friendly to the United States."[8] Gillette and other speakers emphasized Israel's geographic and military use as a strategic ally in the Cold War and a potential contributor to Middle Eastern security from communist aggression.

The alliance was not only important for geopolitical strategy but also for the spiritual well-being of Americans, according to some speakers. Maurice N. Eisendrath, president of the Union of American Hebrew Congregations, reminded his listeners in the closing session that "the sympathies within the spirit's core of America cannot but bind us inseparably, inextricably, to the people of Israel who are striving, like unto ourselves, to build a democracy based upon the spiritual impulses and inspiration of our common Scripture." Eisendrath's emphasis on "common Scripture" reflected the growing trend in American society to emphasize the common bond of the "Judeo-Christian tradition" in the face of atheistic communism.[9]

At the conference's end, twelve delegates of the ACPC presented the conference's final resolutions to Henry A. Byroade, Assistant Secretary of State for Near Eastern Affairs. The final resolutions reaffirmed its commitment to support anticommunist influences in the Middle East and noted the "importance of the area in defending and strengthening the free world." But the concern expressed in the resolutions over Eisenhower's promise to offer "sympathetic and impartial" friendship for all sides in its Near East policy prompted a resolution urging "this nation to stand steadfast upon those fundamental principles that have thrust our country into world leadership . . . [o]ur national interests can be served only through firm support of those principles of self-determination and national sovereignty which both Jew and Arab have been seeking in this region for more than a generation."[10]

Such a statement signaled concern that the Eisenhower administration's stance might prove detrimental to the special support Israel had received under the Truman administration and the ACPC's determination to prevent an erosion of the new alliance. By advocating support of "self-determination" and "national sovereignty," the ACPC placed its platform within the recognized language of Cold War rhetoric. For the ACPC, positioning Israel as a valuable Cold War ally in an unstable region of the world served to strengthen the need for American political and financial support for Israel. Other resolutions from the annual conference emphasized the need to develop infrastructure projects (such as the TVA on the Jordan, which would benefit both Israelis and the surrounding Arab nations) and address the plight of Arab refugees. Repeatedly throughout the resolutions, the ACPC emphasized the hostile tone of the Arab nations toward Israel and highlighted the danger to the Middle East posed by such rhetoric. Fear of the growing tensions in the Suez Canal over Israeli shipping rights and the continued warlike rhetoric of Arab leaders prompted the committee to call for a condemnation of such action by the U.N. Security Council.

Support for Israel had grown more complicated for the ACPC since its original mission in 1944 to support a Jewish homeland, as it had articulated a decade previously. Once the goal of Israel's establishment became a reality, the complications of such a reality presented the committee with countless new challenges. A new administration publicly committed to neutrality further spurred the ACPC into more politically savvy action.

Even as the Eisenhower administration augured a more neutral tone in Middle East foreign policy, putting the ACPC on the defensive, members of the ACPC executive board hoped to continue cordial relations with its newest rival—the American Friends of the Middle East. In January 1952 Karl Baehr discussed a recent lunch appointment with Garland Evans Hopkins. Baehr, who was also joined by Carl Herman Voss at the luncheon, described Hopkins as "most congenial and eager to develop friendly relations with us."[11] Recognizing their common interests in U.S. foreign policy in the Middle

East, Hopkins invited Voss and Baehr to join his organization. He insisted that acceptance of Israel's existence constituted a basic platform of the AFME and noted that "the conditions under which Israel would cease to exist would be unthinkable." Yet Hopkins conceded to Voss and Baehr that the organization, while anxious to present "an objective platform," would nonetheless consider itself "pro-Arab" in its interpretation of the events in the Middle East. Hopkins, well connected to the *Christian Century*, also "admitted that [the journal] carries on biased journalism." Hopkins agreed (according to Baehr) that "perhaps they had gone 'overboard' in attempting to 'write the balance' vis-à-vis Zionism in America."[12]

Hopkins's comments revealed two major concerns of the AFME: that the activities of the ACPC and other pro-Israel Protestants dwarfed the Arab point of view in American society and promoted a Zionist agenda to the detriment of U.S. policies in the area. The consistently hostile attitude toward Israel displayed in the pages of the *Christian Century* represented a defensive viewpoint rather than a representative position of liberal American Protestants. From the ACPC's standpoint, the lunch meeting resulted in reinforcing the expectation that the two organizations, though fundamentally opposed to each other's goals, might avoid the bitter vitriol that characterized debates about Israel and U.S. foreign policy. Yet Baehr also left the meeting with the sense that the AFME's financial backing came from mysterious sources that Hopkins appeared unwilling to disclose. "It appears obvious," he wrote, "that this organization has secured considerable financial support. No doubt, the oil companies have a very close relationship to it."[13] Hopkins, while recognizing that cooperation between the two organizations would be limited, nonetheless expressed hope for a cooperative attitude that would benefit the Middle East.

Congeniality aside, after consulting with the executive board of the ACPC and the Emergency Zionist Council, Baehr decided to plant "observers" at all advertised AFME events, who then reported back the details of the events in the form of memos to the ACPC. Signing the memo "Observer A" and "Observer B" for the next few years, ACPC members engaged in observing AFME activities and provided a firsthand account of the organization's guest speakers, lectures, "coffee hours," and college seminars.

On 14 October 1953 one anonymous observer reported on the "coffee hour" meeting of invited guest speaker Professor Samuel A. Bergman of Hebrew University in Jerusalem. Invited to address the AFME because of his sympathy to the anti-Zionist American Council of Judaism, Bergman discussed the problems of the Israeli-Arab conflict in Jerusalem. The question-and-answer session proved eventful. Questions involving the feasibility of the "return of Palestinian Arabs to Jerusalem" and the redemption of "Zion" through Israel's establishment prompted less than ideal responses for the AFME's platform. Bergman insisted that a return of refugees could never happen. The return of the Arabs "would create a vast minority, which would be, in the opinion of the Israelis, a fifth column." In responding to the question of redemption, Bergman referred to Ben-Gurion's famous insistence that Israel's establishment "is the beginning of the beginning of redemption."[14] In concluding his remarks, Bergman explained that "in order to understand Israel today you had to realize that 6 million Jews had been horribly killed. This did something to a people," he added, "hardening them spiritually—so that in trying to understand them you needed to remember this." Another "observer" noted in his report that "those present at the meeting . . . who are pro-Arab showed by facial expressions their dislike of the speaker's replies to questions." One audience member confided in the observer that "she was puzzled at Miss [Dorothy] Thompson's bringing over anyone so pro-Jewish."[15]

Over the following two years concern about the AFME's possible anti-semitism gave way to increasing hostility from ACPC members. On 28 May 1954 Hopkins published a letter titled "Memo to Americans" under the auspices of the AFME. In the letter Hopkins decried the "multi-million dollar lobby" of Zionists who now "dictate U.S. Government policy" and prevented Americans from understanding the importance of cultivating goodwill with Arab nations. "I am convinced, beyond all reasonable doubt, that Hopkins is bent on doing a hateful piece of work and that he must not be permitted to do it unopposed," Baehr confided to a fellow Zionist.[16]

However much the ACPC and its supporters may have speculated about Hopkins's true intentions toward Jews and Israel, publicly the AFME aimed to present a neutral platform for their perspective on U.S. foreign relations in the Middle East. They did not hesitate to recruit members of the ACPC in their endeavors to create a more pro-Arab foreign policy perspective. S. Ralph Harlow, Smith College professor and ACPC member, received an introductory membership into the AFME, at the suggestion of two former students. The letter of membership explained the urgency of the AFME's mission: "Only a few years ago the United States was trusted and respected throughout the Middle East, but our relations with the area have deteriorated dangerously." The letter continued: "We believe that every effort should be made to regain the friendship and confidence of the people of that vast and vital region."[17]

Rectifying the perceived imbalance of American pro-Israel sympathies, the AFME sponsored several college conferences and invited students from the Middle East studying in the United States to attend. Katherine Sellers, director of the Midwest Region of the AFME and former professor at the Beirut College for Women, insisted in a letter to members of the AFME that cultivating goodwill with foreign students would have serious implications in later years. "In the United States," she wrote, "there are some 3,000 students from the countries of the Middle East—many in our Midwest Region. In a few short years they will be leaders of their own countries. The effect of the friendships that they enjoy while students will, many a time, be deciding factors when they form national and world policies." Preserving U.S. interests abroad (and combating the appeal of communism), in other words, began with cultivating goodwill among Middle Eastern students. The AFME also hoped, through its own study tours, to extend cooperation between Arabs and Americans traveling to the Middle East. Like the ACPC, it recruited prominent clergy to participate in such tours and publicized the event in the press, including Edward Elson's visit to the Middle East in 1956. His tour included a stop at the American Colony in Jerusalem (then occupied by Jordan) where he would donate $500 to assist in refugee relief programs. The AFME capitalized on Elson's visit by describing his plans in a press release to major newspapers.[18]

How to handle the Arab refugee crisis and the consequences that the failure to do so equitably would have on U.S. interests in the Middle East remained the most significant divisive factor among liberal American Protestants. The Arab refugee crisis surfaced early in the first few years of Israeli statehood and remained a stumbling block for attaining full liberal Protestant support for Israel. Both the AFME and the ACPC recognized the importance of the issue but differed considerably in their recommendations for its solution.

Consideration of the problem of the Arab refugees, who, according to U.N. estimates, numbered 750,000 by 1953, occupied much of the United Nations' attention in the decade following Israeli independence. On 14 December 1950 the U.N. adopted a resolution that established a "reintegration fund" to help Arab refugees integrate themselves into the surrounding Arab nations that had absorbed them after the 1947 War. Two years later the U.N. reiterated its position that Arab refugees should adjust to life in the countries in which they now found themselves and dedicated $250 million to that purpose. While in principle the resolutions acknowledged the Arab right to return to Israel, in practice they offered immediate help for Palestinian refugees to permanently acclimate to their new societies—financial assistance accepted by the Arab nations affected.

However directed, financial assistance to the Arab refugees did not solve the problem of long-term agreements between the Arab nations and Israel regarding the right of return—the right of all Palestinians who fled in the 1947 War, and their progeny, to return to their homes in Israel. The Arab nations' insistence on right of return and their rejection of Israel's right to exist, coupled with Israel's refusal to agree to any measure that would overwhelm its Jewish population and create a potential security threat, doomed the United Nations Palestine Conciliation Commission. Its purpose lay in forcing a permanent resolution of the refugee crisis, but by November 1951 (three years after its establishment) it disbanded, explaining that "the present unwillingness of the parties fully to implement the General Assembly resolutions . . . have made it impossible for the Commission to carry out its mandate."[19] The problem of Palestinian refugees would remain a thorn in the side of the international community to the present.

Both the AFME and the ACPC offered solutions to the problem. The ACPC supported the report of nineteen independent American citizens (many of whom were sympathetic to the aims of the ACPC to increase U.S. support for Israel) submitted to the U.N. General Assembly, a pamphlet titled "The Arab Refugee Problem: How It Can Be Solved." In the paper the group advocated that the U.N. allocate $25 million to expedite the refugees' resettlement in surrounding Arab nations and emphasized the impracticality of retaining an absolutist platform regarding the right of return. Dealing with the realities of daily life for Palestinian refugees by offering a new start in neighboring Arab countries provided the most compassionate response to their plight, the group charged. In response, Fayez A. Sayegh, the acting director of the Arab states' delegation, published a pamphlet financed by the AFME titled "The Palestinian Refugees" that included a foreword by Virginia Gildersleeve, dean of Barnard College and former founder of the Committee for Peace and Justice in the Holy Land. Sayegh attacked the veracity of the first paper and charged that the plight of the Palestinian refugees and the justice they deserved were subverted to promote the "official Israeli position." He insisted that "the only just and lasting solution of the refugees' problem lies in the direction of repatriation. Repatriation is the absolute right of all the refugees and must be made a practical responsibility for every refugee willing to return home." The AFME sent copies to all registered members of the ACPC in an attempt to present a different perspective on an issue that troubled American Protestants concerned with events in the Middle East.

By the beginning of 1956 growing worries about general U.S. policy in the Middle East overshadowed the plight of the Arab refugees. Early in Eisenhower's presidency, he had stated that the United States must exercise "neutral and impartial friendship" toward the nations of the Middle East—a statement that worried Zionist groups in the United States, including the ACPC. Essential in crafting Eisenhower's neutral Middle East strategy, John Foster Dulles urged Americans to take the Arab-Israeli dispute out of domestic politics and place it in the realm of international politics, where it belonged. While the *Christian Century* supported such a suggestion, other Protestant and secular presses roundly criticized the secretary of state for his perceived anti-Zionist bias.[20] Yet those who supported Dulles's appeal received a boost to their claims of undue Zionist influence in American policy when, in his memoirs, Truman disclosed that during deliberations about the establishment of Israel, he had "never known as much pressure and propaganda aimed at the White House." As discussed above, Truman's decision to recognize the new state met with almost unanimous disapproval from the members of the State Department's Near East division.

Dorothy Thompson and the AFME seized upon Truman's disclosure as evidence that he had been "threatened" by Zionists until his "own position was thoroughly prejudiced by Zionist propaganda." One article in the *Christian Science Monitor* noted that the AFME, led by Thompson, had placed an ad in the *New York Times* in support of Dulles's statement. "One of the signers . . . is the Rev. Edward L. R. Elson, pastor of the National Presbyterian Church, of which President Eisenhower is a member," journalist Mary Hornaday noted.[21] In a speech to AFME supporters, Thompson, according to Hornaday, "declared that successful foreign policy-making in the United States must be concentrated in the executive." Thompson explained that "there is an extremely pertinent reason why, under our constitutional distribution of powers, the conduct of foreign policy is put into the executive department: An erroneous foreign policy, setting events in train outside our jurisdiction and therefore out of our control, can seldom be reversed."[22] Clearly, for Ms. Thompson and the members of the AFME, foreign policy decision making should only be the work of the executive branch; the representative branch, not having as much access to intelligence and more susceptible to lobbying influences, could not be trusted to formulate wise, long-term decisions regarding policy.

ACPC members flatly denied such a stance and, as a lobby group, worked to effect policy from a grass-roots level. The ACPC continued its tactic of running full-page advertisements to increase public awareness of its policy concerns. The ACPC's growing concern over Eisenhower's perceived coolness to the young Israeli–U.S. alliance prompted such an advertisement in the *New York Times* of 27 January 1956. The full page announcement noted that where Israel had failed in living in peace with its neighbors, "that failure has been due in large measure to the inordinate provocation which, we feel, no nation in similar circumstances would have tolerated with so much patience." The more than three hundred signatories urged Eisenhower to "stand firm in support with vigor our sister democracy of Israel." They asked that because of communist military support for Egypt, the United States should "make available to Israel without delay the legitimate means for its self-defense." They urged the United States to make "security treaties" with Israel and other peaceful Arab nations to guarantee their "present frontiers against alteration by force."[23]

The American Friends of the Middle East responded to the ACPC ad a month later by sending letters to the most prominent signatories, urging them to reconsider their stance. Hopkins sent Baehr copies of the letter that the AFME mailed to the signatories, at Baehr's request.[24] The letter, which was accompanied by general information about the AFME, noted the recipient's "interest in the area where we are at work" and pointed out that the organization agreed that "the United States must stand firm in its support of Israel." Hopkins wondered, however, "if you have considered the total picture of the area in the request you have addressed to our government." He reminded the reader that the ACPC received considerable funding from the Zionist Council of America, and that the *New York Times* advertisement would only increase Zionist influence and pressure on the U.S. government. "There is nothing inherently wrong in Christian and Jewish American citizens announcing their support of these views," he conceded, but added that "there is an element of misrepresentation involved in labeling such a Committee as Christian." Hopkins then reiterated the AFME's stance that questions of foreign policy should be removed from domestic policies and concluded the letter by urging the reader, after "more mature reflection" on the issue, to write to the president to disavow the advertisement, sign a petition urging the separation of domestic politics and foreign policy, and join the AFME.[25]

The growing tension between the ACPC and the AFME reflected mainline Protestants' inability to unite in support of Israel. Far more influential and better funded, the ACPC nonetheless struggled to counteract the AFME's propaganda efforts among Protestants and rejected the AFME's assertion that religious interests should be eliminated from domestic policies and domestic policies divorced from foreign policy concerns. The struggle between the ACPC and the AFME exacerbated fissures in mainline Protestantism in the years preceding the Suez Crisis. The members of the ACPC, while continuing their efforts to elicit grass-roots support for Israel among mainline Protestants, grew increasingly concerned about Eisenhower's neutral approach to Middle East affairs.

The Suez Crisis

The growing concern over tensions in the Middle East took on a new fervor in October 1956. The past few years had witnessed struggles between Israel and her neighbors over questions of water resources in the Jordan Valley and shipping rights through the Strait of Tiran. Now, in 1956, questions over shipping rights and access to the Canal devolved into an Egyptian ban on all Israeli shipping. The Suez Canal had proven to be a stumbling block not only to the stranded Israelis but a source of frustration for Western nations as well.

After pledging Nasser over $270 million to assist with the development of Aswan Dam, Britain and the United States froze the account when Nasser turned to the Soviet Union for $300 million worth of arms. The United States and Britain had hoped that assisting the Egyptians with their internal infrastructure project would prevent Soviet influence from developing in Egypt. The relationship between Britain and Egypt had been rocky—the Egyptians under the leadership of Nasser pushed hard for British withdrawal from both the Sudan and the military bases they occupied in the Canal Zone. But Nasser still appeared willing to accept Western dollars for the project, with the understanding that Egypt would develop its growing nationalist impulses with a British withdrawal from the area. The Soviet arms deal (done in exchange for Egyptian cotton) alienated the United States and Britain.

Frustrated by frozen aid, Nasser decided to nationalize the Suez Canal and support its development through toll and tax collection. In control of the Sinai Peninsula, Nasser closed the Strait of Tiran in 1955, blocking all Israeli shipping from their southern port in the Gulf of Aquaba. The French, angered by Nasser's support of anti-colonialist forces in the French colony of Algeria, joined the British and the Israelis in launching an offensive in the Sinai to regain control of the Canal (and, for the Israelis, to capture land in the Sinai).

On 29 October 1956 Israeli forces launched a major ground offensive into the Sinai and Gaza and within a week captured Gaza and the entire Sinai Peninsula. The French and British attacked from the air, wiping out the majority of the Egyptian air force. After two weeks, and mounting disapproval from the United Nations and the United States, a cease-fire ended the campaign. Meanwhile, both Nasser and the British and French had sunk several ships in the Canal, rendering it useless. The United States condemned the military campaign, particularly since the British, French, and Israelis did not inform their ally of the plan to attack. The Soviet Union threatened military intervention in the region, and the U.N., led by the future Canadian prime minister Lester B. Pearson, threatened sanctions unless the fighting stopped. Nasser managed to remain in power and emerge as a hero to the Arab world, Anthony Eden, Britain's prime minister resigned in disgrace, and the cease-fire forced the Israelis to relinquish all land captured during the offensive.

Despite Eisenhower's public condemnation of Israeli aggression, the United States viewed the Israeli position with some sympathy. The Eisenhower administration recognized that the Soviet arms deal with the Egyptians brought Soviet influence to the borders of the small state. Furthermore, Soviet Premier Nikolai Bulganin's threat of military intervention against the British, French, and Israelis worried Eisenhower. Acknowledging Israeli concerns about being surrounded by Soviet arms prompted the United States to publicly guarantee Israeli access to an open Strait of Tiran. Also, in response to the events in the Middle East, Eisenhower issued his own Doctrine. In an address before Congress on 5 January 1957 Eisenhower noted that, "all this instability has been heightened and, at times, manipulated by International Communism."[26] The "free nations of the Mid East need, and for the most part want, added strength to assure their continued independence" and to fight off communist influence and aggression, Eisenhower explained. In order to assist these countries, he proposed four principles that the United States would enact to achieve stability in the Middle East, even as he recognized that to do so would require "a greater responsibility" from the United States. Eisenhower proposed to provide "development of economic strength" to bolster independence and thwart communist infiltration, and offered "military assistance and cooperation with any nation or group of nations which desires such aid." Such military aid could include "employment of the armed forces of the United States to secure and protect the territorial integrity and political independence of such nations . . . against overt armed aggression from any nation controlled by International Communism." Such potential military action would necessarily work in accordance with both the U.N. Charter and the recommendations of the Security Council. Finally, Eisenhower added that these proposals would "authorize the President to employ . . . sums available under the Mutual Security Act of 1954 . . . without regard to existing limitations."[27]

These policy proposals, Eisenhower explained, would be used as another weapon in the Cold War struggle against communism. "If power hungry Communists should either falsely or correctly estimate that the Middle East is inadequately defended, they might be tempted to use open measures of armed attack," he declared to Congress.[28] Preventing the circumstances that might encourage such a deduction would undoubtedly promote peace. While Israel was not explicitly mentioned—in fact, the Eisenhower Doctrine intentionally avoided partiality in addressing individual countries—the implications remained clear: the United States would designate economic and military aid to independent nations resisting either influence or aggression from nations under Soviet influence. For Israel, the bitter pill of public U.S. rebuke following the Suez crisis considerably sweetened with Eisenhower's promise of aid. Hope that such aid would include armament deals prompted Israel and her American allies to increase pressure on the U.S. government to negotiate deals favorable to Israel.

The Protestant Press Reacts to the Suez Crisis

Protestant journals revealed an uncertainty among American Protestants over the continuous tension in the Middle East. Both readers and editors evinced mixed reactions to the Suez crisis and Eisenhower's new Doctrine. In the months leading to the crisis, R. Park Johnson, in a feature article in *Presbyterian Life,* argued that the United States should avoid partiality in the conflict, siding with neither the Arabs nor Israelis and should prevent shipments of arms to either side.[29]

Several weeks before Israel's incursion into the Sinai, the *Christian Century* condemned recent Israeli attacks on refugee camps in Jordan in response to "Arab provocations." The editorial condemned the "massive blows" Israel returned to its attackers: "The old law of an eye for an eye has apparently been supplanted in Israel's ideology by a more savage rule: a head for an eye." The editorial worried that such activity on the Jordanian border could spread to other Arab nations in an already volatile atmosphere.[30] In keeping with its criticism of Israeli behavior, the *Century* wholly condemned Israel, France, and Britain after the outbreak of war—the former for its territorial aggression and the later two for their archaic colonialism. It praised Eisenhower's firm response to "the aggressors" and his willingness to preserve Egypt's borders from offensive military action—even against the United States' own traditional allies.

Not all Protestant journals expressed such wholly positive views of the United States in the aftermath of the war. The *Christian Herald* agreed with the *Century's* position that the Israeli, French, and British reaction should be condemned, but, unlike the *Century*, the *Herald* reminded its readers that Israel had been provoked by Egypt's Nasser. Although the *Herald's* editorial board agreed that Nasser had "'the right'" to nationalize the canal, waterway rights were "something very close to an international right of eminent domain" and, as such, all nations had a vested interest in working out the conflict.[31] Another editorial pointed out that although France and Britain had overacted since they had not yet, in fact, been denied passage through the canal, Israeli passage had been denied for some time.[32]

Christianity Today echoed other journals' condemnation of Israel, France, and Egypt and praise for Eisenhower's response. In contrast to the *Christian Century*, however, it offered criticism of the United States' deference to the United Nations. Such behavior revealed "an excessive trust in the power of colossal human organization as the potential resolver of all major world disputes."[33] The following month *Christianity Today* offered point-counter-point articles on the validity of Israel's existence, perhaps in response to the past months' events. In an essay critical of Israel, the Rev. Oswald T. Allis of Princeton Theological Seminary offered a summation of traditional liberal Protestantism's theological rejection of the biblical principle of restoration.

The birth of Israel, Allis wrote, "is an amazing situation" brought about by "Zionist agitation in England and America [and] widespread sympathy for the Jews because of the inhuman treatment they received in Europe during World War II." Yet, Allis claimed, Israel's existence was not a political question, "but a religious one." "Do the promises of the Old Testament to which the Zionists appeal support their claim to the possession of land?" Allis asked. He argued that, to the contrary, the disobedience of the Jewish people negated any claims to Palestine: "This basic principle, that possession of the land and prosperity in it was conditioned on obedience, is stressed again and again," Allis insisted. The dispersion of the Jews, a punishment "for their sin of rejecting and slaying their long-promised Messiah," would end only with repentance. Such repentance remained a "prerequisite" to return to Palestine.

Moreover, the birth of Christianity eliminated Jewish claims of nationalism, rendering the "land no longer important," according to Allis: "It is quite true, and to the Church's shame be it said, that for many centuries and even in our day she has failed to welcome the Jew into her communion. Instead she has hated him and 'ghettoed' him. But despite her unfriendly attitude, many thousands of Jews have found their Messiah through the Church; and for all such the Jewish problem has been largely or wholly solved."[34] Jews who refused to convert and insisted on a return to the land of Palestine based their desire on "racial pride and nationalistic aspirations" and ignored the "many open spaces in the world, many friendly nations, in which oppressed Israelites can find a refuge and a home without imperiling the peace of the world." Ultimately, Allis argued, "the attempt to restore the Jews to Palestine has proved to be unjust in itself and highly dangerous to the peace of the world." "Does the Israeli cause deserve to succeed?" Allis asked in conclusion. He answered: "We believe the verdict of history will be, No!"[35]

As much as Allis's argument exemplified traditional liberal Protestant supercessionist theology that denied Jewish nationalistic aspirations, the opposing article by Wilbur Smith, a professor at Fuller Theological Seminary, represented the growing premillennialist interest in Israel as a fulfillment of prophecy. He wrote: "One's attitude toward Palestine as a future Land of Promise will be determined, primarily, by his attitude toward two eschatological themes: will there be a millennial reign of Christ on this earth, and is there a special place for Israel as a nation at the end of the age?" Smith highlighted scripture verses that emphasized the permanence of God's promises of the land of Palestine to the Jewish people—a promise that superseded human mandates.[36]

Aside from the permanence of God's promise, the improvements to the land by the Israelis justified their possession. "Palestine needed the Jews for posterity and plenty. Anyone who saw the pitiful barrenness and poverty of that land even thirty years ago . . . recognizes that the Arab was a curse to the land, showing no advancement in agricultural methods for two thousand years," Smith argued.[37]

Some Protestant journals such as *Presbyterian Life* and the *Lutheran* avoided assessing the legitimacy of either side, but still offered comprehensive coverage of the major events of the Crisis and the policy proposals of the Eisenhower Doctrine that followed.[38] While all journal articles expressed dismay at the outbreak of war in the Sinai, they offered different approaches in their coverage of the event; some editorialized, others simply commented. The editorials and point-counterpoint style of the *Christian Century* and *Christianity and Crisis* reaffirmed the lack of consensus among mainline Protestants about U.S. interests in the Middle East.

Protestant Organizations after Suez

In December 1956 the ACPC sent a letter to Eisenhower urging him to press both the Israelis and Arabs for a negotiated peace settlement that would allow all countries in the region to ship their goods through the Suez, prevent Egyptian remilitarization of the Sinai, and keep U.N. peacekeeping forces on the ground in the Peninsula to ensure that all objectives for the region had been achieved.[39] After Eisenhower announced the new Doctrine for Middle East policy, the ACPC again wrote to the president to express its concerns about the new policy implications. "We welcome your decision to undertake a new diplomatic initiative in the Middle East," Baehr wrote on behalf of the ACPC. But solving the internal problems of the Middle East, Baehr noted, should be considered as much a priority as repulsing external Soviet influences. Baehr highlighted the continued Palestinian militia attacks on Israel in defiance of U.N. resolutions and the perceived imbalance of U.N. responses to Israel, France, and Britain versus Nasser and his allies.[40]

The AFME applauded Eisenhower's rebuke of Israel, France, and Britain and considered it a harbinger of a more balanced approach to Middle Eastern affairs. In 1957, as it had after Eisenhower's first inauguration, the AFME considered the president and his administration more sympathetic to their concern for enhanced Arab-American cooperation. On 17 January 1957 Garland Evans Hopkins resigned his position as director of the American Friends of the Middle East. According to Hopkins, a "physical breakdown" the previous spring had prompted his resignation from the helm of the AFME, "whether or not the time was propitious."[41] His farewell speech, delivered before the National Council of the AFME, offered a candid assessment of the AFME's achievements and revealed both a cautious optimism about the Eisenhower Doctrine and concern that it would fail to achieve a balanced policy toward the Middle East.[42] He hoped that the "waning influence of Zionism in Washington" would allow the oil companies greater influence on policy. "I have never thought the oil industry evil or its money contaminated," Hopkins noted, and added: "I hope the oil companies will provide in the future more than in the past the substance on which the Zionist can base their charges."[43] Hopkins condemned lobbyist pressure on the government to enact policies favorable to Israel. "Not only the AFME but all Americans," Hopkins insisted, should "declare open warfare against all individuals and agencies who would sell our birthright for a mess of political pottage."[44]

Yet Eisenhower's presidency had inaugurated a more favorable climate for AFME's platform, Hopkins explained, and through the president's recent refusal to back England, France, and Israel, America "gained back a considerable amount of our lost prestige in the area." In a letter to Eisenhower congratulating him on his response to the Suez Crisis, Hopkins wrote: "America has not lost the Middle East only because you refused to be cowed by Zionism and its few but vocal supporters. But," Hopkins added, "we have not yet won the partnership of the Middle East." In a clear indictment of the Eisenhower

Doctrine, Hopkins insisted that "military force or economic enticements" would not win friends in the Middle East, only "moral persuasion based on a policy of complete impartiality in intra–Middle Eastern disputes" would effect change in the relationship between the Middle East and the United States.[45]

Under the new leadership of Harold Minor, former U.S. ambassador to Lebanon, former chief of the Division of Middle Eastern Affairs in the State Department during World War II, and former government relations officer for the Arabian American Oil company in Saudi Arabia, the AFME continued to sponsor conferences and college seminars around the country. Its fifth annual conference, held on 25 and 26 March 1957 in New York City, attracted an array of speakers. Rabbi Elmer Berger, the executive vice president, and Rabbi Morris S. Lazaron, the honorary vice president of the American Council for Judaism addressed the participants. Other speakers included notable Middle Eastern dignitaries, including H. E. Moussa al-Shabandar, the Iraqi ambassador to the United States, H. E. el-Mehdi Ben Aboud, the Moroccan ambassador, and H. E. Mohammed Ali, the Pakistani ambassador. Significant U.S. political figures including the Honorable Cornelius Van H. Engert, secretary-treasurer of the AFME and former U.S. minister to Afghanistan and Ethiopia, chaired panel discussions. Edward Elson, the pastor of Eisenhower's National Presbyterian Church, and Dorothy Thompson hosted the final banquet dinner of the conference.

The ACPC continued to keep a watchful eye on the activities of the AFME as well. Its anonymous observers continued to attend AFME functions. One such function, a regularly scheduled "Afternoon Tea," featured the guest speaker Freda Utley, author of "Will the Middle East Go West?" The ACPC mole described the event, adding that "there was fruit punch for the Moslims and sherry for the infidels." The observer cattily added, "Freda snuggled up to the sherry." The "gist" of Utley's talk, according to the observer, centered around the argument that "the biggest obstacle to working out Middle East problems is the continued inordinate focus of the West on Israel, and this in spite of the terrible things the Jews have done to the Arabs." During the question-and-answer period of Utley's appearance, one audience member asked: "How can Americans see the Arab side of the problem when our newspapers play up shipment of a few arms from Russia to Egypt while hardly mentioning the fact that Israel bought arms from Czecho-Slovakai?" Her answer echoed the long-standing concern of the AFME that press support and coverage of Israel disadvantaged Arab nations when she replied, "This is serious because the chief media—the press is controlled." The observer added, "Miss Utley implied that the audience knew by whom."[46]

No action, conference, letter to the editor, or published document of the AFME escaped notice and comment by the ACPC. Each time the AFME made a public plea for its platform, the well-organized and attentive ACPC responded with a rebuttal, usually public. In September 1958, for example, the AFME published a report by Professor William Ernest Hocking of Harvard and Dean Virginia Gildersleeve, Emeritus of Barnard College, which argued that "the Arab-Israeli dispute is a principal cause of the crisis in the Middle East and is threatening to set off World War III." Reverend Edward Elson of the National Presbyterian Church sent a copy to all members of the AFME along with a cover letter explaining the importance of the Hocking-Gildersleeve analysis of U.S.–Middle East relations.

The "Hocking Report," as the ACPC dubbed it, elicited a firm rebuttal from both Karl Baehr and Samuel Guy Inman who sent a five-page response to members of the AFME and ACPC who had received the report. In their response, Baehr addressed the charge that American support for Israel stemmed solely from Zionist pressure groups in the United States. "Such a charge," he wrote, "represents an insult to those thousands, if not millions, of Christians who supported the creation of the State of Israel out of genuine Christian and humanitarian motives." Politicians who had supported Israel through their activities with the ACPC and in Congress did so from personal conviction, Baehr insisted. "Senator Owen Brewster ardently supported the idea of an Israel reborn though he had no 'Jewish vote' to speak of, let alone to bow down to."[47] The Hocking Report's hostility to Israel advocated a dangerous position to Middle Eastern nations flirting with communist sympathies. Hocking and Gildersleeve's report "played right into the Communist camp because it keeps the conflict boiling and it in essence tells the Arab world to keep up hope for Israel's destruction because there are Christians in America who support the same hostile outlook on Israel as the Russians."[48]

Despite the AFME's attempts to improve Arab-American relations and sway American public opinion away from U.S. support of Israel, American public support for Israel appeared firmly entrenched by the end of 1958. Membership numbers of the AFME remained low, and even its most notable members encountered resistance to their ideas in the national arena. The journalist Dorothy Thompson, the AFME's founder and most recognizable figurehead, found her syndicated column "On the Record" discontinued after twenty years. In her final column, she claimed that her political positions and perceived "anti-Israeli" positions had prompted the cancellation of her column.[49] As for Israel, Thompson wrote, it "must go back to the ideas of a great, enlightened Western Jew, Judah Magnes, and not promote with American Jewish support the Ghetto-Chauvinism of David Ben-Gurion."[50] Other members of the AFME recognized that their support for Nasser's pan-Arabism had alienated the American public. Erich Bethmann, the AFME's head researcher, acknowledged this failing in a private conversation with an ACPC mole.[51] Bethmann conceded that the AFME faced "accusations of being unpatriotic . . . because of their continued support of Moslems like Nasser who are attacking the USA and the West generally."[52] By the end of 1958 groups that had supported the efforts of the AFME began to withdraw their support. In December Miriam Jackson of the ACPC informed the American Zionist Council that the American Committee to Help Arab Refugees had "severed" its connections with the AFME. Jackson added that she would soon meet with the chairwoman of the organization directly, in the hope of directing their efforts through the ACPC.[53] By the beginning of the 1960s, though the ACPC still monitored the AFME, it no longer considered it a major threat to its platform and mission. In fact, American public support for Israel appeared so secure to ACPC members that the ACPC also decreased its activities. Other organizations arose to continue its efforts in the following two decades but on a smaller scale.

On the eve of the Six-Day War the ACPC had greatly reduced its lobbying activities and now primarily focused on organizing study tours to Israel and assisting the Israeli government in public relations efforts among American Christians.[54] Meanwhile, in the wake of public criticism of its perceived anti-patriotism in response to its continued, vocal support of Nasser, the influence of the AFME had declined along with its membership numbers. Karl Baehr, no longer working exclusively on ACPC programs, became director, in 1961, of the America-Israel Society (AIS), a division of the larger America-Israel Cultural Foundation. Founded in 1954 by Maryland's then governor Theodore R. McKeldin, the America-Israel Society mimicked its sister organization in Jerusalem, the Israel-America Society. The AIS advertised in form letters to ministerial associations that its primary purpose lay in "fostering understanding and friendship between the people of the United States and the people of Israel—two peoples who share a common spiritual and democratic heritage." The programs of the AIS included the earlier proposed program, now called the Institutes for the Clergy, study tours to Israel, bulletins, and featured speakers at local religious organizations. "Our efforts in friendship-building for Israel are designed to reach a cross section of the American public with a special emphasis on reaching the Christian and grass-roots sectors of our land," Baehr explained in an internal AIS memo.[55]

The Speakers Bureau Division of the AIS would provide speakers for Protestant congregations and organizations interested in fostering ecumenical dialogue. The purpose of such speakers appearing at local congregations would be to "present a positive image of Israel and to counteract Arab propaganda that is being disseminated throughout the country by . . . the American Council for Judaism." The grass-roots effort extended beyond the churches, however, to include universities, World Affairs Councils, meetings with the editors of major newspapers across the country, civic clubs, and high schools. In addition to local Zionist leaders, the organization invited a variety of notable Israelis to address audiences. A prolific organization, the Speakers Bureau organized 2,440 engagements across the country in a single year.[56]

Theological Exchanges

The shift in propaganda efforts by the Zionist organizations in the United States reflected a larger national trend. In the face of communist aggression, Americans felt the need to bond together in their religious counterattack. Cold War warrior Eisenhower had said as much himself in 1952 in a speech before the Freedoms Foundation in New York. "Our form of government has no sense unless it is founded in a deeply felt religious faith," he declared, "and I don't care what it is. With us of course, it is the Judeo-Christian concept but it must be a religion that all men are created equal."[57] Historian Mark Silk argues that emphasis on a common religious heritage between Judaism and Christianity emerged first in response to the threat of fascism in World War II and then grew stronger in response to opposition from the Soviet Union during the Cold War. Defeating their enemies abroad required Americans to embrace religious unity at home.[58]

Mainline Protestants, often under the auspices of the still-active National Conference of Christians and Jews, continued to emphasize national ecumenism through celebration of the Judeo-Christian tradition (in contrast to atheistic communism) with its annual National Brotherhood Week. More dramatic theological reevaluations began to emerge, however, in the late 1950s and early 1960s that reflected concern over the legacy of traditional Protestant antisemitism and theological hostility to Judaism. Moreover, the publicly televised trial of former Nazi SS Lieutenant Colonel Adolph Eichmann in Jerusalem for crimes against the Jewish people in 1961 offered a public forum for discussion of the Holocaust, created an interest in Holocaust studies, and reiterated to American Protestants the need to improve Jewish-Christian relations in the United States.

On 19 November through 5 December 1961 the World Council of Churches met in New Delhi, India, to convene its Third Assembly. One of the issues under consideration concerned a resolution, "The Christian Approach to the Jews," first written in 1948 but not passed. Now, however, the Council adopted the resolution which recommended abandoning the collective charge of deicide against the Jewish people. The resolution "called upon all the churches we represent to denounce antisemitism, no matter what its origin, as absolutely irreconcilable with the profession and practice of the Christian faith. Antisemitism," the resolution concluded, "is sin against God and man."[59]

Between 26 April and 2 May 1964 the Department of World Mission of the Lutheran World Federation convened a conference, "The Church and the Jewish People," which echoed the earlier resolution of the World Council of Churches.[60] It, too, condemned antisemitism and urged Lutheran churches everywhere to "examine their literature for possible antisemitic references" and "work to prevent national and international manifestations of antisemitism," and also called upon congregations to "love their Jewish neighbors as themselves; to fight against discrimination and persecution of Jews."[61]

On 5 June 1964 the General Board of the National Council of Churches of Christ in America followed suit with its own call for a reevaluation of antisemitic tendencies in the Church. In a "Resolution on Jewish-Christian Relations," the board affirmed the resolutions of the Third Assembly of the World Council of Churches and urged its members to support and engage in "true dialogue" with the Jewish community. Moreover, in October 1964, the House of Bishops of the Protestant Episcopal Church convention adopted a resolution, "Deicide and the Jew," that condemned antisemitism from a theological perspective. Jews could not collectively be held responsible for the Crucifixion, the resolution continued, because "the Christian understands that all men are guilty of the death of Christ."[62] One year later, under the auspices of the Second Vatican Council, the Catholic Church amended its own teachings on the relationship between the Church and Jews, eliminating references to "the perfidious Jew" and the centuries-old teaching of deicide.

The Jewish community in the United States took note of the resolutions passed by significant Protestant organizations and the Catholic Church, and published a pamphlet, distributed to the mailing list of the Anti-Defamation League's *Christian Friends Bulletin,* recounting the major events of the Protestant organizations and Vatican II and expressing the hope that such changes would result in deepening, authentic dialogue between the two faiths. Clearly, to the Anti-Defamation League, Christian acknowledgment of culpability in the perpetuation of the Holocaust prompted the new changes in Christian teaching. "All developments in Jewish-Christian relations since the Nazi holocaust have been motivated and spurred, at least in part, by the awful specter of that tragedy," the bulletin explained.[63]

Alarmed by a 1966 report by the University of California, Berkeley, that revealed the persistence of antisemitism in the United States as a result of Christian theology, the *Christian Century* addressed the issue of Christianity's relationship with Judaism and echoed the Anti-Defamation League's call for deeper dialogue and an honest assessment of the role of Christianity in perpetuating antisemitism. In one article Jeffrey Hadden noted the report's findings that "a great deal of antisemitic sentiment, in this nation at least, stems directly from teaching of the Christian churches."[64] The study noted that among the most orthodox churches, antisemitism appeared to be most prevalent. Such a finding posed a dilemma to the churches: Should they abandon "orthodoxy" to eliminate antisemitism? Hadden answered negatively but agreed that "antisemitism is not dead and the churches, however unwittingly, are helping to keep it alive."[65] Another contributor to the article, Bruce Vawter, conceded that "the ghetto and the yellow star were decreed by church councils and popes before the Nazis ever thought of them. The Christian today who wants to be a bigot has a tradition ready made for him." Still, Vawter expressed hope that "the Christian churches have, by and large, both repudiated the tradition and are making sincere efforts to reverse it."[66]

Other theological journals of the 1950s and 1960s also revealed an increasing interest in examining the relevance of Judaism to Christianity and reassessing traditional doctrines. In a *Theology Today* article theologian Markus Barth argued against the idea that the "new covenant" made by God with the Church replaced the "old covenant"—challenging the teaching of supercessionism that Protestants had used to discount the relevance and legitimacy of Judaism after Jesus.[67]

Other theologians, though not abandoning supercessionism entirely, treated it more gently by focusing on the enormous debt Christianity owed Judaism.[68] In the 1960s the theological journal *Interpretation* ran a series of articles addressing the question of Israel's role in Christianity. In one such article T. F. Torrance argued that, indeed, the covenant between God and Israel had been broken at the Crucifixion: "In the ultimate act of union between God and Israel, and in the ultimate conflict which that entailed, in Israel's refusal of the Messiah, the rejection of Israel had to take place."[69] "Israel rejected [the Incarnation] in the crucifixion of the Messiah, and in so doing shattered itself on the Cross—theologically, the complete destruction of Jerusalem and the Temple in A.D. 70 had to follow upon the crucifixion of the Son of Man," Torrance noted in an affirmation of supercessionism. Yet Israel, even in her rejection of the Messiah, had played a divine role, worthy of Christian appreciation.[70] Such realization should impact Jewish-Christian relations, Torrance continued, for "we are his [the Jew's] debtors in Christ."[71]

Moreover, according to Torrance, the rebirth of the State of Israel must be viewed as "surely the most significant sign given in God's dealings with his covenant people since the destruction of Jerusalem." The "ancient struggle between Israel and its Lord is renewed" in the tension between Israel's secular, atheistic foundation and its religious heritage. The Church should serve the modern State of Israel by trying to remind it of its covenant with God. The Church would be unable to assist Israel, however, until it acknowledged the great debt it owed the Jews, "that it can only exist as church grafted on to the stock of Israel and at the expense of Israel."[72]

Mainline Protestants, however slowly, began to reconsider traditional Protestant supercessionism in light of Israel's existence. No uniform conclusion would be drawn at this point, but the attempt stood in stark contrast to the resistance of evangelicalism to significantly alter its interpretation of the significance of Judaism. For evangelicals, however, a shift of emphasis—from passive observers of world affairs to active engagement with the eschatological significance of Israel—signaled their own theological innovations.

Evangelical Protestants

Unlike their mainline brethren, and in opposition to the hopes of the Jewish community in the United States, the evangelical and fundamentalist Protestants eschewed theological reevaluations of Judaism within their own journals and rejected the idea of Judeo-Christian unity in America. They remained certain of the centrality of Christ to human salvation and the necessity of conversion for all non-Christians. Yet, unlike the liberal Protestants, they encountered no trouble in engaging in theological assessments of the significance of Israel's reestablishment. Whether one believed that the modern State of Israel fulfilled biblical prophecy, evangelicals and fundamentalists believed that there *was* prophecy to be fulfilled and that the Jews would play *some* role in that fulfillment—whether in belief or unbelief.

For example, *Bibliotheca sacra,* the oldest conservative fundamentalist theological journal in the United States, published multiple articles in the 1950s and 1960s reaffirming the premillennialist interpretation of the end times and the belief in an unbroken covenant between Israel and God that would be revealed in the last days through Jewish conversion to Christianity. It celebrated Israel and Judaism as central to Christian eschatology and worthy of study, prayer, and support.[73]

In 1957 William Hull, an American Protestant minister living in Jerusalem published the book *Israel—Key to Prophecy: The Story of Israel from the Regathering to the Millennium as Told by the Prophets*. It was heralded with warm reviews from notable figures including David Ben-Gurion and editors of the *Jewish Spectator, American Judaism*, the *Moody Monthly*, the *Sunday School Times* and the *Christian Herald*. The book also reflected the continued and growing interests of fundamentalist Protestants in Israel. Marc Tanenbaum's expressed hope to Samuel Newman that fundamentalist eschatology might begin to appreciate a wider, ecumenical interpretation would receive an unsympathetic response from most American fundamentalists. Since Israel's establishment in 1948 and the Suez crisis in 1956, evangelicals and fundamentalists had only grown increasingly convinced that they were living in "the end of days" and that Jews and Israel would occupy center stage in the coming apocalypse. The possibility that Israel might again occupy the Sinai Peninsula catalyzed a hope among fundamentalists that Israel might once again occupy the entire Holy Land, as promised to them by God, according to fundamentalist interpretation.

Given Hull's fundamentalist persuasion, *Israel—Key to Prophecy* employed a strictly literal interpretation of Scripture to predict the future role Israel would play in the end of times. He began his work by explaining how prophecy had already been fulfilled in the "regathering" of Jews to Israel.[74] Even the Suez crisis had been predicted by the prophets, Hull claimed. "The nineteenth chapter of Isaiah, verses 17 and 18, speak of a war between Israel and Egypt.[75] The Cold War, too, could be viewed through prophetic lenses, Hull explained. Conflict with Russia—"the forces of the North"—had already been foretold in the Book of Revelation. The remainder of his book takes a futuristic tone in describing the possible events that could take place on the world stage in fulfillment of prophecy, including a Catholic takeover of the presidency, the House of Representatives, and the Senate in service to a one-world government administered by the pope/Antichrist.[76] Not only would the Catholics serve the Antichrist's purposes but so, too, would the Arabs, particularly the Palestinian refugees, Hull argued. In the telling of his futuristic interpretation of the end of days, Hull wrote that "[the persecution of the Jews in the end of days] began, at first, among a few of those who had formerly lived there [Israel]." Eventually "the fury and the wrath of Satan was revealed as he urged on the Arab leaders in their hatred of the Jews and determination to annihilate them."[77]

After the return of Christ, the defeat of the Antichrist, and the restoration of God's Kingdom on earth, the nations of the world would be judged based on "the actions of these nations toward the Lord's brethren, the Jews, and their treatment of the Jews in their midst during the centuries of Israel's exile." Hull continued his description of this judgment:

> Now was revealed before all, the intensity of Jewish suffering and the hatred that Satan had inspired against them. Men hung their heads in shame as they realized how terrible had been their feelings and actions against the Jews. They were amazed and ashamed that they had permitted God's enemy to deceive them and mislead them.[78]

Such a scenario certainly would have given Hull's American fundamentalist readers pause in considering U.S.–Israeli foreign policy (and might explain the book's warm reception in Israel despite its prediction that the surviving Jews of Israel would convert to Christianity). Hull's warning that the nations of the earth would be judged according to their treatment of Israel would be a theme evangelical leaders in the following decades would use to great effect in generating evangelical support for Israel.

Countless articles in fundamentalist and evangelical newspapers also addressed the theme of Genesis 12:3—"I will bless them that bless thee and curse him that curseth thee." An article in the *Sunday School Times* argued that this promise of blessings and curses to nations that helped or abused Jews could be seen in the fate of nations such as Egypt, the Persian Empire, Spain, Germany, and even England. When England prospered as it did under Queen Victoria and her prime minister Disraeli, it did so because it had assisted the Jews, namely, by creating the Palestine Mandate that provided a home for the Jews in their ancestral land. When, however, "the rulers of Britain who either did not know their Bible or disregarded God's sure promise of blessing . . . threw in their lot with the Arabs and strengthened them rather than helping the Jews," financial ruin and the loss of the empire resulted.[79] In the wake of the Suez crisis, the author concluded by asking: "Is the United States to be the next nation to fall from her present exalted position through her failure to help Israel in this crucial hour when she is surrounded by foes bent on her destruction?"[80] The author continued: "Will the lessons of history fall on deaf ears here in America? Is the oil of the Middle East more important than the blessing of God?"

Such an article signified an important shift for evangelical Protestants. Prior to the Suez crisis, discussions of Israel centered on the fulfillment of prophecy in its rebirth. Now, however, the emphasis shifted from simply an observation of prophetic fulfillment to action. The author ended his article with the request that the readers "pray earnestly that our leaders may have the right attitude toward the State of Israel in this her hour of crisis, and so bring forth blessing to our own, beloved land."[81] Although the command to pray for political leaders was not followed by a call to write, or vote, it nonetheless signified a subtle shift—a more active engagement that had not occurred in the preceding decades. If evangelical political engagement in the late 1970s and early 1980s signaled, as historian Timothy Weber argues, "their willingness to go beyond their spectator status" and enter the game of geopolitics, perhaps the post–Suez crisis reaction prompted evangelicals to rise to their feet and contemplate entering the game for the first time.[82]

Not all fundamentalists, however, viewed Israel with increasing prophetic excitement. The fundamentalist *Bible Baptist Tribune*, a weekly newspaper published in Springfield, Missouri, published a series of articles, in the late 1950s and early 1960s, highly critical of Israel.[83] The prophetic concern that secular Israel had been reestablished in "unbelief"—a concern that many evangelicals and fundamentalists increasingly ignored—prompted a highly critical assessment of Zionism and Israel in the *Tribune*.[84] Although some critics conceded that modern Israel appeared to fulfill some aspects of prophecy, and suggested that more fulfillments would come in the end times, the *Tribune* generally reiterated the conservative theological tradition of supercessionism and offered a constant reminder to its readers that the Jews had rejected the Messiah, that all Jewish suffering could be explained by this rejection, and that instead of founding Israel as a theocracy, as Israelis should have according to biblical prophecy, Israel remained a secular, atheistic Zionist state—unworthy of American support.[85] Jews themselves were divided over the question of Zionism. Smith noted Alfred M. Lilienthal's recently published book, *What Price Israel?* (also praised by the American Friends of the Middle East) as evidence that American Jewry did not fully support Israel. The Zionist strategy regarding Israel "was to treat the Israeli crisis as if it were the crisis of the Jewish people all over the world," Lilienthal wrote, "But if the political problems of Israel continue to be the political responsibility of Jews of the United States, disaster must follow."[86]

Still, Smith, as a student of biblical prophecy, could not resist highlighting the role that the secular, atheistic State of Israel would play in the end times. "The State of Israel gives the nations of the earth, for the first time in 2,000 years, a center. Israel is at the geographic center of the earth. It is going to increasingly become the political and religious center as well," he wrote in a 1961 article. Most important, Smith insisted, "it will be at the center of the Great Tribulation . . . and beyond that terrible time, the State of Israel will be the center of the righteousness of the earth."[87] Students of prophecy would be wise to pay attention to world events there, Smith urged, since "the great majority of Christians . . . are blind to what is taking place before their eyes—blind because they have turned from the Scriptures to their own traditions."[88]

Many evangelicals, like Smith, refused to engage in the ecumenical dialogues of their mainline brethren and insisted on reaffirming traditional Protestant teaching of the necessity of salvation through Christ for all people—Jew or otherwise. Although unyielding in this basic tenet of theology, many evangelicals nonetheless attempted to address the historical problem of antisemitism within their traditions, even while continuing to evangelize the Jews. In an article appearing in the *Bible Research Monthly,* F. Kenton Beshore argued that antisemitism should find no place in the Christian worldview. While God intended to judge the Jew "until he turns to God in belief," Christians who practiced antisemitism were taking "a position against God and His will."[89] He concluded by reminding his readers that "it is important that we as Christians help Israel to realize her God-given destiny, by giving her the Gospel now."[90]

In another article, Beshore insisted that Christians should continue to evangelize, out of obedience to the Great Command and because eventually, 144,000 Jews who survived the Apocalypse in Israel would eventually serve as the great missionizing force to convert the rest of the world in the end times. Beshore reaffirmed the significant role Israel would play in the end times, and, because of this, God had not revoked his promise of blessings to the Jewish people. "He gave His glory to Israel, and makes it clear He will not take that glory away from her, and confer it upon another. How erroneous for Bible teachers to say God is through with the Jewish nation," he argued in effusively philo-semitic language.[91]

Missionary tracts designed to convert Jews reflected condemnation of antisemitism and celebration of the important role Israel and the Jews would play in the last days. One such tract, published by the Friends of Israel Society in Philadelphia, began with an acknowledgment by the Christian missionary author Roy Grace who declared that "all that is most precious in our Christian faith and life has come to us from the Jewish race."[92] Like Beshore, Grace also argued that God was not through with the Jewish people and identified "two developments" that proved the argument: "one is political and territorial—the Jewish return to the Land of Israel. In fact, the State of Israel is an amazing reality." The other development, Grace argued, was the development of a universal religion Jewish in origin and Christian in its faith in Jesus as Messiah. Grace ended his missionizing appeal to the Jewish reader with the "prophecy" that "some day the Jewish people will be believers in Jesus as Messiah."[93]

The evangelical journals clearly reiterated the theological and eschatological importance of Israel. For them, while missions remained a crucial part of the Great Commission, reaffirming the importance of the modern State of Israel remained a high priority. The tone of the journals' assessment of the Jewish people had dramatically shifted by the late 1950s. Abandoning all vestiges of traditional antisemitism, these journals promoted a strong alliance with Israel for theological reasons and did so by emphasizing the historic link between Judaism and Christianity and dismissing the tendency of mainline Protestantism to embrace supercessionism. The Jews were still chosen, as far as evangelicals were concerned, and would continue to play a relevant role in history.

A Political Shift

A friendlier attitude toward Israel—initiated first by Eisenhower's Doctrine and the beginning of a negotiated arms deal for Israel—continued with the election of John F. Kennedy. to the White House in 1960. In the last years of his administration, Eisenhower and members of the State Department had grown increasingly frustrated by Nasser's aggressive behavior in the region and his continued flirtation with the Soviet Union. In 1957 and 1958 the Middle East had once again been rocked by instability—stemming mainly from pro-Nasser rebels attempting to overthrow King Hussein of Jordon and gain control of Jordan's West Bank and a brief pro-communist radical overthrow of the Syrian government. In 1958 Syria joined Egypt in creating the United Arab Republic—a union dedicated to expelling Western influence in the region and destroying Israel. In May of that same year pro-Nasser militants attempted a coup in Lebanon to oust the cautious Lebanese government and replace it with a pro-Nasser, anti-Israel regime, and again attempted an overthrow of King Hussein. Eisenhower responded by sending U.S. Marines into Lebanon to restore order, and the British sent troops to Jordan to bolster the King. Israel's willingness to allow the British to move through their airspace and to withhold direct military intervention in Lebanon earned the thanks of both Dulles and Eisenhower. Now the White House increasingly viewed Israel as a strategic ally rather than a liability.[94]

Shimon Peres of the Israeli Ministry of Defense responded to American thanks with a request for a defensive Hawk missile arms deal. The Eisenhower administration remained hesitant about offering a major military package to

Israel for fear of upsetting the delicate balance of U.S.–Middle East foreign policy, but by the summer of 1959 the administration agreed to provide "$100 million in technical and financial assistance over the next two years, a sum," argued historian Douglas Little, "larger than all previous American aid to Israel since 1948."[95] Yet the increased cooperation and hint of military deals to come at first appeared to wither in the hot desert sands of the Negev, where the Israelis, with French assistance, had begun building a nuclear reactor at Dimona. State Department officials feared that the idea of a nuclear Israel would no doubt send Nasser straight into the arms of the Soviets, who would certainly offer to assist Egypt in developing its own nuclear program.

Nonetheless, the arms deal proposed by Israel during Eisenhower's second term found ardent support in the young President Kennedy. Kennedy had publicly expressed his support for Israel during the presidential campaign, and during his short tenure in office had worked to bring the arms deal to fruition by tying it to assurances that the Dimona reactor would only be used for peaceful purposes and that the Israelis would work to bring the question of Palestinian refugees to a satisfactory conclusion. Yet the growing concern that the Israelis intended to "go nuclear" by building a reactor at Dimona, coupled with encroaching Soviet influence upon the unpredictable and often militant Nasser as well as the instability of King Hussein's reign in Jordan, prompted Kennedy to confirm the arms deal without Israeli concessions. Such a decision moved the United States closer to a U.S.–Israeli alliance and away from the publicly neutral stance of the Eisenhower administration.

Despite Kennedy's increased rapprochement between Israel and the United States during his tenure, Little argued that the administrations of *both* Eisenhower and Kennedy "laid the groundwork for closer relations with the Jewish state."[96] The close relationship developing between Israel and the United States found a stronger advocate still in Kennedy's successor, Lyndon B. Johnson, who told an Israeli official after Kennedy's assassination: "you have lost a great friend, but you have found a better one."[97] Johnson had publicly expressed his admiration for Israel over the course of his career. Historian H. W. Brands argued that Johnson, "while majority leader in the Senate during the 1950s had distinguished himself as a loyal and powerful friend of Israel; that he did so coming from a state without a conspicuous Jewish constituency distinguished him further."[98] Johnson solidified the special relationship by becoming the first president to secure an offensive weapons deal for Israel, in the form of American tanks and A-4 fighter bombers. Furthermore, in the midst of the Vietnam War, Johnson found much to admire in Israel's military prowess. The coming war in 1967 would only increase Johnson's admiration.

Conclusion

By the eve of the Six-Day War, mainline Protestant supporters of Israel had grown confident of U.S. support—both militarily and politically. They no longer believed in the necessity of ardent political lobbying on Israel's behalf. By the time Carl Hermann Voss spoke before an audience at Hebrew University in Jerusalem in 1966 regarding American Protestant support for Israel, the ACPC had disbanded. Reflecting back on the history of the ACPC before his Israeli audience, Voss explained the motivations, challenges, and successes of the organization during the past few decades.

The organization's basic purpose, he informed his audience, lay in arousing "Christian concern, trying to point out the plight of European Jewry, this during the war, and after the war, that there was almost this unanimous desire on the part of the remnant of Jewry to go to Palestine. And we were also trying to note the historic ties of the Jewish people to Palestine—something which many American Christians had forgotten, overlooked, or not even known."[99] The motivation for "all of us who took part in the committee," he claimed, came from a belief that their participation constituted "something of an act of atonement."[100]

When asked by an audience member to assess the "pro-Jewish state feeling among grassroots Americans," Voss pointed to the success of Zionist efforts, both Christian and Jewish, in fostering widespread American support for Israel. "The informed intelligent grassroots person, the farmers, at least, they understood the issues, and reacted positively and well, and there was an innate idealism in these Americans, a sense of wanting to have justice done, of having a wrong righted that prevailed among them." Beyond the grass-roots efforts, political pressure in Washington, D.C., also worked. "I could go on at great lengths about the kind of influence we had on Congressmen," Voss explained, "by starting letter writing campaigns and telegraph campaigns . . . [and] during those times, if they had external pressure brought upon them by Jews and Christians, they reacted positively."[101] Even President Truman had been persuaded by the efforts of Daniel Poling, Voss claimed. "I would say that Dan Poling had more influence on President Harry Truman, and whatever pro-Zionist moves Truman made, than anybody else." Roosevelt, Voss added, "didn't have the kind of knowledge of the Bible that Truman had; he didn't have the kind of dogged, persistent, almost primitive faith that Truman had.[102]

Voss recounted the enormous challenges that the ACPC faced, including opposition from the American Council on Judaism and the American Friends of the Middle East, the former having posed the greatest difficulty in the early years. The American Council on Judaism was "well financed, quite well-run, and provided the major source of confusion in the Jewish community, to such an extent that in the Christian churches people would turn to them and say that the Jews can't make up their own mind on the question . . . Sometimes I'm amazed at how much we got done, considering what had to be done," Voss added. Nonetheless, he concluded, eighteen years later, "it was important for us to have this kind of thing going on, and it did play its part."[103]

The satisfaction Voss experienced before his Israeli audience signified an important transformation. The American Christian Palestine Committee—the most powerful pro-Israel Christian organization in the United States—had, on the whole, succeeded in its mission to develop a solid grass-roots basis for Protestant support for Israel in the United States. Division might remain among some liberal Protestants, but, on the eve of the 1967 War, Voss remained convinced that the majority of American Protestants fully supported Israel, as he noted, in an effort to correct a "historic wrong." Theological transformations had begun, dialogue between Jews and Christians had surely improved, and the burgeoning evangelical interest in Israel would only solidify the pro-Israel base among American Protestants. The events of June 1967 would test these assumptions.

"Of course, down in Virginia, you do have to worry about Southern Baptists"

Samuel Newman, American Protestants, and the Post–World War II Jewish-Christian Dialogue

The demand for theological reevaluations stemmed not only from Protestantism itself, but in one remarkable example came from a single Holocaust survivor, now an American, who was offended by the Southern Baptist Conventions' pamphlet "Winning the Jew" which asserted that Jews who did not convert to Christianity "are lost without hope." Samuel Newman, a physician from Danville, Virginia, launched an extraordinary twelve-year letter-writing campaign to hundreds of Protestant leaders around the country calling for "theological integrity and sophistication." He wrote to more than one hundred "outstanding spokesmen of Christian denominations," including a wide variety of theologians, seminarians, and editors of religious journals, in a one-man effort to redefine the terms of dialogue between Christians and Jews. The responses he solicited reveal an American Protestantism in the throes of theological transformation regarding the relationship between Judaism and Christianity and between Jews and Christians.

Newman protested the idea that Jews were lost without conversion and asked for responses from various Protestant denominational ministers and theologians regarding their position on the salvation of Jews. The answers he elicited reveal a split between liberal and conservative denominations over the relationship of Jews to God and salvation, and the role of the Holocaust in their responses. As he discovered, the Baptists themselves could not agree on the statement that claimed "5 and a half million Jews are lost without Christ" (a phrase he used as a catalyst for dialogue). Such disparate responses testified to the fractured nature of American Protestantism and the inability to exact a comprehensive representative statement supporting the legitimacy of Judaism as a valid way to God.

In his cover letter, Newman asked if such teachings represented the "normative Christian teaching or the teaching only of the Southern Baptist Convention?" He added, "Antisemitism antedates the rise of Christianity; however, serious and devoted Christian thinkers and writers are of the opinion that Christianity has been a major factor in fostering antisemitism for the last 1900 years."[1] Newman concluded by adding that such teachings of the "lost" Jew "may unintentionally foster antisemitism. Surely," he noted, "when a Jew is thought to be 'lost,' it must be assumed that in some respect—morally or spiritually—he is inferior to the person that believes himself 'saved.'" His letter, he explained to the recipients, "is written with feelings of pain and humiliation and in a spirit of earnest search for religious truth."[2]

The responses of hundreds of ministers, theologians, and journal editors to Newman's campaign for clarification on Protestant teachings toward Jews and Judaism reveal a religion in transition. Fewer mainline Protestant leaders' responses echoed the supercessionism of previous traditional Protestant theology. Responding to Newman's letter, Harry Emerson Fosdick of New York wrote that such a statement was "shocking. To say that all faithful Jews are damned unless they become Christians is an insult to the character of God. I never heard such a thing said by any Christian."[3] William Hamilton, professor of sociology and ethics at the Colgate-Rochester Divinity School insisted that he knew "nothing of, and care [sic] less for Southern Baptists, who are nearly as sick as Northern ones. Your passage quoted is neurotic, sick and deeply un-Christian." Hamilton urged Newman to publish his responses from Protestants regarding this issue and compile them into an article to be published. "Good luck," he added.[4]

The dean of Harvard's Divinity School apologized to Newman about the statement. "I am sorry to say that there is a certain parochialism that still exists in the world and expresses itself in rather rigid prejudices of such a nature that not only you, but I and many others, are deeply and profoundly embarrassed."[5] R. Paul Ramsey, head of the Department of Christian Ethics at Princeton University also apologized and noted that such statements regarding the salvation of the Jews reflected an archaic element in Christianity and pointed out that "the most orthodox Christian theologian today—Karl Barth—who is accused of 'Christocentrism' in all his thinking, nevertheless believes in universal salvation. And about a year ago," Ramsey continued, "the outstanding American theologian Reinhold Niebuhr came out in opposition to any specific endeavors to 'convert' the Jews." Ramsey concluded his letter by adding, "Of course, down in Virginia, you do have to worry about Southern Baptists."[6]

The president of the Southern Baptist Convention, H. H. Hobbs, initially responded to Newman's letter by noting that "the quotations which you have listed do not exemplify the Christian spirit" but added that "the persecution which your people underwent in Europe in the last few decades was not of a Christian, but a pagan, origin." Moreover, Hobbs added, "I do know that our Southern Baptist people have only the highest regards for you and your people. As we understand the New Testament, all people, whether Jew or Gentile, who have not believed in Jesus Christ as their Savior are lost. So the word 'lost,'" Hobbs concluded, "does not in any sense reflect upon you as inferior."[7] Newman responded to Hobbs's letter with a request for an elimination of such a statement in Baptist literature as unrepresentative of Christian theology. "In this conviction I am strengthened by the fact that authentic spokesmen: Baptist, Roman Catholic, Protestant Episcopal, Presbyterian, Methodist, Congregationalist and Disciples, do not approve of that statement, and some were shocked by it."[8] Hobbs responded by reminding him that "no 'authoritative body' to which a plea could be presented" existed for Southern Baptists. "We have no Baptist creed," he explained to Newman. As to Newman's charges that such statements incited and reflected antisemitism and the charge of deicide, he again reiterated his earlier argument that "we do not believe that the Jew is any more guilty because of the crucifixion of Jesus than is the Gentile." Hobbs argued that "the sins of all of us" crucified Jesus. Hobbs concluded his letter by informing Newman that he would pray "that you will come to know Him as I do, as your personal Savior."[9]

Other responses from conservative denominations affirmed Hobbs's position—in varying degrees of gentleness. David M. Stowe, of the Department of Interpretation and Enlistment of the American Board of Commissioners for Foreign Missions, though noting that "our attitude is quite profoundly different from that of the Southern Baptist Convention," nonetheless upheld the belief in the need of Jews to convert. "We believe," he explained, "that some of our Jewish friends might find fuller life, deeper peace, and a clearer sense of purpose, through such conversion to the Christian faith." He concluded, however, that "we make no judgments about those who do not take this step. That is a matter between God and themselves, so far as we are concerned."[10] Harold Lindsell, editor of *Christianity Today* (subtitled "Protestantism's Fortnightly Magazine of Evangelical Conviction"), also affirmed the evangelical theological position of the necessity of conversion. He explained to Newman that "Paul in the Book of Romans asserts that the Jews who do not keep the Law of God are lost and without hope. . . . If a Jew can honestly assert that he has kept the Ten Commandments perfectly then he is not lost. However," he added, "I have never found a Jew who could so assert." Since Jews who did not keep the Mosaic Law were, indeed "lost," the only answer lay in conversion to Christianity. "I do not think that what you read in the pamphlet of the Southern Baptist Convention is different from what any evangelical Christian would say," he concluded.[11]

John H. Gerstner, professor of church history at Pittsburg Theological Seminary, echoed Lindsell's assertion that evangelical Christians believed in the necessity of conversion to Christianity for salvation, and his comments reveal the growing tension between mainline Protestantism and the increasingly disgruntled evangelicals. "The historic teaching of the general Christian Church is that no one can be saved apart from faith in Christ. There is much defection from orthodoxy today, and many in the 'mainline Christian denominations' no longer believe what their creeds profess," he noted.[12] Others were even blunter in their response to Newman. One minister of the Zion Baptist Church in Philadelphia curtly noted: "the statement to which you refer is unilaterally or universally accepted by all Christians."[13] Another minister explained to Newman that he "would like to caution you against taking the statement of the track as an example of antisemitism." Like other evangelical ministers, he believed that salvation must be a universal goal—regardless of ethnicity or culture. "Christian people, unless it should be some in the liberal tradition, believe that faith is necessary, but this is not a demand made of some men and not of others. It is made of all," he concluded.[14]

Six years into the campaign, Newman wrote Rabbi Marc Tanenbaum, director of the Interreligious Affairs Department of the American Jewish Committee (AJC), and explained his quest to alter the statement of the Southern Baptist Convention. Tanenbaum's response clearly illustrates the tension between evangelical Protestants intent on missionizing the Jews and Jews who wished to be left alone. "Because of the nature of their theology," Tanenbaum explained to Newman, "I do not believe that it is realistic to expect them to give up their hope of conversion. . . . All of us have visions of the end of days and if they will accept this eschatological view more centrally, then I am prepared to live with that. All I want of them," he explained, "is to leave the Jews alone and stop insulting us with their constant pressures and attitudes which see Jews as unfulfilled Christians."[15]

Newman's letter-writing campaign offers a glimpse into the changing theological persuasion of mainline Protestantism's attitude toward Jews and

Judaism. Responses to Newman's letters reveal significant divisions between the mainline and conservative branches of Protestantism over the issues of missions, universal salvation, and the centrality of a personal relationship with Jesus. Increasingly letters from Protestant clergy revealed that the mainline Protestant denominations were abandoning the idea of the centrality of Christ for salvation, while more orthodox denominations retained its importance in their theology. Perhaps a reflection of the Eichmann trial, the reality of the Holocaust, or simply in response to the pressures of modernity, American Protestantism found itself increasingly fractured in its evaluation of traditional theology.

The Tide Turns, 1967–1973

The outbreak of war in the Middle East in the early morning hours of 5 June 1967 surprised no one. The sweeping Israeli victory in six days, however, did. By 8 June Israel had taken control of the entire Old City of Jerusalem, including the Western Wall. As a rabbi blew the shofar to a crowd of emotional Israeli soldiers and civilians, American evangelical and fundamentalist prophecy watchdogs rejoiced as well. The end times had begun. Writing for the *Moody Monthly* John F. Walvoord, president of the Dallas Theological Seminary, could barely contain his excitement: "This return constitutes a preparation for the end of the age, the setting for the coming of the Lord for His Church and the fulfillment of Israel's prophetic destiny."[1] Israel may have returned "in unbelief," but this newest "piece of the prophetic puzzle" could hardly be ignored. Interpreters of prophecy scriptures outdid one another in their attempts to link the 1967 War with biblical verses. Whether it was the fulfillment of prophecy or not, however, the war certainly heralded a new age in U.S.–Protestant–Israeli relations, as the growing political power of evangelicals coincided with their increasing excitement over Israel. Although Israeli land acquisitions and the refugee crisis following the war would provide another political stumbling block for mainline liberal support of Israel, evangelicals professed no such reservations. Israel was back in the Holy Land, and its boundaries began to look increasingly like those maps in the back of their Bibles.

Yet even as the geopolitical landscape changed in the Middle East, the religious landscape in the United States was also undergoing dramatic transformations that would have a serious impact upon the U.S.–Israeli alliance. While the 1950s witnessed a surge of religiosity in American society, with record-high church attendance, profound internal controversies in Protestant denominations resulted in denominational splintering that created newer, more orthodox churches. The mainline Protestant denominations that had adapted to the sweeping societal changes of the 1960s and adjusted their doctrines accordingly (women's rights, gay rights, civil rights, and abortion), faced declining memberships.

Disillusioned by the increasing loss of theological distinctions between most mainline denominations and their abandonment of orthodoxy in favor of modernity, American Protestants in the late 1960s began to establish their own churches. A move into the suburbs to newer homes and newer church buildings, coupled with a reactionary return to orthodoxy, created a profound shift in American Protestantism. Mainline Protestants were now the "liberals," and evangelicals and fundamentalists gradually became the dominant group of American Protestants. This religious realignment had profound implications for American politics, and especially for U.S. foreign policy. The mainline American Protestants who had supported Israel for pragmatic and humanitarian reasons were increasingly replaced in numbers and influence by evangelical and fundamentalist Protestants who viewed Israel through an eschatological lens. Certainly the importance of having an ally in the unstable Middle East appealed to these Protestants, but more important than that was the prophetic role Israel would play in the end times. Whereas the reaction to the Suez crisis in 1956 had marked the beginning of a change in political activity, the evangelical response to Israeli military prowess and land acquisitions between 1967 and 1979 permanently altered evangelical Protestant political behavior and set the foundation for the dynamic political engagement that would characterize evangelical Protestants in the 1980s.

The War of 1967

In the months leading up to the outbreak of war the United Nations had been inundated with complaints filed by both Israel and Syria about constant border skirmishes and aerial dogfights between the two nations. In May Nasser, leading the United Arab Republic and twelve other Middle Eastern countries, had called for the total mobilization of military forces along the border with Israel and, on 18 May, demanded the removal of U.N. peacekeeping forces stationed in Gaza and the Gulf of Aquaba. To worldwide surprise, U.N. Secretary General U Thant complied with Egypt's request and removed the U.N. forces. On 22 May Nasser implemented a total blockade of the Gulf of Aqaba, preventing the free passage of Israeli ships. The U.N. security measures implemented after the Suez crisis had enforced the right of Israeli ships to pass through the gulf. In response, the Israelis declared the new blockade a violation of international law and considered it "an act of aggression against Israel." Israel began mobilizing its forces in preparation for war—a war that both the Arabs and Israelis did little to prevent and, in fact, appeared eager to commence.

The superpowers were less eager for a Middle Eastern war. Both the Soviet Union and the United States issued cautious statements and called for Security Council emergency meetings to alleviate the crisis. Nasser publicly announced, on 29 May, that "negotiated peace is out of the question" and warned Israel that an attack would result in a united Arab effort, whose "main objective will be the destruction of Israel." Furthermore, boasting of Soviet support for the Arab war effort, Nasser publicly announced that he had assurances that the Soviets would block U.S. intervention on Israel's behalf. With the Security Council paralyzed by the Arabs' and Israelis' unwillingness to negotiate, and the refusal of the United States and the Soviet Union to negotiate over their Middle Eastern allies, the War of 1967 began with an Israeli preemptive strike against the Egyptian Air Force.[2]

Within several hours in the early morning of 5 June the Israeli Defense Forces (IDF) had completely destroyed the Egyptian Air Force. The Israelis quickly capitalized on the surprise attack and pressed their advantage with sweeping ground attacks on all fronts. The Egyptians and Jordanians, on 6 June, publicly charged the United States and Great Britain with aiding the Israelis—a charge both nations denied vigorously, but Egypt cut all diplomatic ties with the United States and England and declared a total blockade of the Suez Canal and a cessation of all oil shipments to the United States and Britain. By the next day, however, the Israelis had broken through the Sinai and captured the Suez Canal, effectively ending the blockade. The same day Jordan, suffering heavy losses in the West Bank, agreed to a cease-fire, ending the war on the Jordanian-Israeli front. On 8 June, one day later, Syria and Egypt agreed to a cease-fire, although sporadic fighting continued between Israel and Syria. On 10 June the Israelis and Syrians ended hostilities in a separate cease-fire agreement and brought the war to an end. Israel found itself in possession of the Sinai Peninsula, the Gaza Strip, the West Bank, and in total control of the Old City of Jerusalem. It declared immediately that it would not return to its 1948 boundaries.[3]

The world had watched the events of the Six-Day War closely. For the first time the hotline between Moscow and Washington, D.C., had been used for purposes other than sending baseball scores and lines of poetry, as each tried to gage the other's intentions. Although both superpowers had resisted involvement—instead issuing benign ambiguous statements—the Israelis' sweeping and swift success had provided Washington with diplomatic ammunition in the United Nations. The superpowers had avoided direct conflict in the war, but at the war's conclusion the United States worked to press its advantage on behalf of Israel. The U.N. Security Council, despite Soviet pressure, refused to condemn Israel as the aggressor.

In England and the United States individuals rallied to Israel's side during the war. In England fights broke out among hundreds of Britons over available seats on El Al flights in order to fly to Israel to fight for the Israelis. Winston Churchill's grandson, covering events in Jerusalem for *News of the World*, donated blood to the Israelis during the national blood drive on the eve of the war.[4] In the United States fear for Israel's safety prompted widespread support for the Jewish state. Franklin Graham, the evangelist Billy Graham's son, rushed to Israel to join the war effort, and famed American author James Michener sent a telegram to the Israeli government pledging his support in any way the nation might request it. More important, Jewish organizations across the United States sent so much money to Israel that the government had trouble recording it. Congressmen who had increasingly voted against appropriations for the Vietnam War, voted for U.S. support for Israel during the crisis. It turned out to be unnecessary. U.S. intelligence studies of Israeli military preparedness had twice confirmed, in the months leading up to the war, that Israel, despite fewer numbers and less equipment, was nonetheless better prepared than her Arab neighbors and would surely defeat them in a confrontation.[5] Yet the swiftness of the victory surprised many military experts.

The Israeli victory, surprising or not, inspired the American people. Despite the fact that on 8 June Israeli torpedo boats and fighter jets attacked an American warship, the USS *Liberty*, cruising in international waters in the Mediterranean Sea, killing 34 sailors and wounding 172, American support for the Israelis in the Six-Day War remained unfazed.[6] Bogged down in the quagmire of the Vietnam War, the idea of a David versus Goliath struggle in the Middle East (however inaccurate that comparison might have been) sparked a great deal of fist-pumping and wistful calls for Moshe Dayan, the celebrated military general of the IDF, to lead the U.S. offensive in Vietnam. One letter to the editor of the *Boston Herald* encapsulated American popular response to the Six-Day War: "If I were the Israelis (and how I dearly wish we had a Moshe Dayan in Viet Nam) I would not yield one yard of conquered territory till there were ironclad guarantees for the safety and peace of Israel." Furthermore, the writer added, "I am not of Jewish faith or extraction, but an old line Yank, whose lineage is rooted in the Northern Kingdom. The daring courage and valor of the Israeli people as they smashed the aggressors thrilled me beyond words and taxed my emotions to the breaking point."[7]

The 1967 War permanently altered the U.S.–Israeli alliance, as Americans, swept up in the euphoria of Israel's rapid and sweeping victory, cheered for the perceived underdog and cemented the alliance.

Liberal Protestants React

Despite continued hostilities between Israel and her Arab neighbors, when Carl Hermann Voss of the American Christian Palestine Committee discussed the development of American support for Israel before an audience of Israelis at Hebrew University in Jerusalem in 1966, he did so confident that Americans stood fully behind their Middle Eastern ally. The American public reaction to the Six-Day War illustrated the verity of such a belief. Yet it also proved problematic for the liberal Protestants who had only just begun addressing the theological significance of Israel and reevaluating historic antisemitic tendencies in Protestant theology. Many perceived Israeli aggressiveness in refusing to return land acquired during the conflict as verification of extreme nationalism and disregard for the worsened plight of the Palestinian refugees. The year 1967 was a high water mark for mainline Protestant confusion over Israel.

While these Protestants struggled to make sense of events in Israel, they were soon criticized for not being pro-Israel enough. American Jews, while celebrating Israeli victory, pointed to the silence of the mainline churches on the eve of the war when Israel appeared to be on the brink of destruction as proof of continued antisemitism and anti-Zionism, and likened such silence to the failure of the Churches to protest the Holocaust.[8] The initial gains in interfaith dialogue made during the previous decade appeared jeopardized, even as the rest of the world struggled to come to terms with the new geopolitical realities of the Middle East. The mainline Protestant support for Israel that Voss and other ACPC members had worked so hard to build prior to 1967 fractured in the aftermath of the war, splitting apart the fragile alliance. Ultimately, however, the support that mainline Protestants had offered Israel in the building of the initial U.S.–Israeli alliance would be superseded in numbers and strength by the newly electrified evangelical base.

Concern for war refugees dominated many mainline Protestants' initial reaction to the war. The Lutheran World Federation, for example, immediately launched an appeal for half a million dollars to assist Syrian and Jordanian war victims.[9] Several weeks later the *Lutheran* reported that "church groups" had called for Arab recognition of Israel, international control of Jerusalem, and water-rights guarantees for all neighbors in the region as part of a proposal for long-term solutions in the area.[10] The *Lutheran* reiterated the objections of the mainline churches to Israeli acquisition of land acquired during the fighting and noted that "Israel would make a mistake if it annexed conquered territory without negotiation."[11] But in an acknowledgment of the damage done to interfaith relations by Protestant "silence" on the eve of the war, it also noted the criticisms of American Jews who "chided Christians for failing to support the Israeli cause" during the war.[12] Early in the aftermath of the 1967 War, then, mainline Protestants recognized this profound rupture to their relationship with American Jewry. Such recognition catalyzed a greater push for theological reassessment of Jewish nationalism and the profound role Israel now played in Jewish identity.

As it had in 1948, the fate of Jerusalem once again divided mainline American Protestants. The National Council of Churches (NCC) issued a statement calling for international control of a city sacred to all three of the world's major religions. The NCC could not "condone by silence" Israeli claims to territories seized during the war, but the organization did call for Arab recognition of Israel and secure territorial borders for all Middle Eastern nations to be enforced by the "entire international community."[13] The *Christian Century* echoed the call for the internationalization of Jerusalem. J. A. Sanders of Union Theological Seminary, writing for the journal, argued that "the likelihood of Jerusalem's reverting to Jordanian administration under massive U.N. presence should be anticipated and, if need be, supported by the American Christian community."[14]

Other Protestants appeared less cautious about an Israeli victory. For example, the National Conference of Christians and Jews, in joint cooperation with major Jewish American organizations, sponsored a massive pro-Israel rally in Washington, D.C., to raise money to help Israel.[15] In addition, sixteen prominent Americans including Reinhold Niebuhr, Martin Luther King Jr., Krister Stendahl of Harvard Divinity School, and Jerald Brauer, dean of the Divinity School at the University of Chicago, issued a statement in support of Israeli control over Jerusalem. "During the past 20 years," they wrote, "the City of David has experienced an artificial division. We see no justification in proposals which seek once again to destroy the unity which has been restored."[16]

Indeed Niebuhr's journal, *Christianity and Crisis,* symbolized the split among mainline Protestants over reaction to the war. In an editorial Niebuhr echoed mainline America's celebration of the Israeli victory. Writing before the final cease-fire had been imposed, he criticized both the decision of U Thant to withdraw peacekeeping forces from the Suez and the inability of the Security Council to prevent the hostilities. Niebuhr addressed Israeli preemptive action sympathetically, noting that "obviously a nation that knows . . . it is in danger of strangulation will use its fists."[17] Perhaps peace between Israel and her Arab neighbors would, as Abba Eban noted earlier, rest upon the nations finding "their own way to conciliation and peace," Niebuhr concluded. Citing the "new cold war atmosphere" between the United States and the U.S.S.R., Niebuhr predicted that the National Security Council Committee on Middle Eastern problems "will have its hands full." Ultimately, Niebuhr added, "all of us will cheer its efforts."[18] Niebuhr's analysis reiterated the reason why many mainline Protestants had supported Israel since 1948—the Cold War necessitated U.S. support for a democratic ally in the unstable but oil-rich region. Israel's strategic importance remained essential to Cold War interests and would require cooperation between the United States and the U.S.S.R.[19]

In the weeks following the war *Christianity and Crisis* ran a series of articles that further addressed the interfaith fallout from the crisis and the Christian responsibility in addressing the problems between American Protestants and Jews. Alan Geyer noted in one article that the Israeli victory and the American Jewish response to the war had sparked "a profound stirring . . . that is at once a religious event and a political phenomenon of astonishing poignancy and power." Rejecting the charge from the American Jewish community that Christians had remained largely silent about the war and its consequences and causes, Geyer pointed to the widespread pulpit support for "the policies of the Israeli government" and noted that the war "has mustered an instinctively sympathetic response from some of our most visible churchmen. Religion and politics," Geyer concluded, "have always provided a highly combustible if inevitable and necessary mixture."[20] To Geyer, interpretation of biblical prophecy in favor of Israeli land acquisitions should be roundly rejected by modern theologians.

American Jews rejected Geyer's assessment of mainline pro-Israeli behavior. Rabbi Balfour Brickner, the director of the Commission on Interfaith Activities of the Union of American Hebrew Congregations, a Reform organization, argued that "Christians saw what happened in and to Israel as a political problem with little or no real theological implications or overtones."[21] Brickner was critical of the Christian response to the war and pointed out that the silence of the churches on the eve of the conflict and Protestant claims that the issue was geopolitical, and not religious, astonished Jews in America who viewed Arab threats to "exterminate Zionists, Jews, and Israelis (with no distinction made between these groups)" as a threat to all Jews' ethnic and religious being. Problems with Zionism in general, never fully resolved, Brickner charged, had once again become the focus of the debate in the aftermath of the war. Most Christians were "stateless," Brickner explained, but noted the interest of the "theologically conservative groups" who "do share the general Jewish conviction about Jerusalem but for different reasons."[22] After the 1967 War many American Jewish and Israeli organizations slowly began to embrace the "theologically conservative groups" that offered their ardent support as some mainline Protestant leaders withdrew theirs.[23]

Apart from the damage done to Jewish–mainline Protestant relations in the United States, the 1967 War alarmed many mainline Protestants for theo-political reasons. Geyer's concern that a literal interpretation of Scripture might be gaining ground among mainline Protestants worried some who feared its foreign policy implications. Willard G. Oxtoby, a professor of religion at Yale University and active member of the National Council of Churches, criticized American Protestants for their "hypocritical" response to the Israeli victory. Any other war that resulted in such dramatic territorial acquisitions would have outraged Americans, Oxtoby pointed out. Yet, with Israel, "Americans seemed hardly to mind." Such incongruent responses had generated an increasing double standard among American Christians toward the Arabs, "by which," Oxtoby argued, "Arabs can be judged bloodthirsty from their rhetoric no matter how little they could actually do, while Israel could do no wrong no matter how far its conquests exceeded its provocation."[24]

Oxtoby identified three reasons for such Christian reaction: humanitarian concern stemming from the Holocaust, evangelical support for Israel as the fulfillment of biblical prophecy, and the lessening of antisemitism and improved interfaith relations between Christians and Jews in America.[25] Moreover, the evangelical belief that Israel existed as a sign of prophecy fulfillment (ignoring, Oxtoby argued, the traditional Protestant teaching that "the promise [to Israel] had been fulfilled in antiquity and [now] applied by the New Testament to the church as the New Israel") had influenced "liberal Christians" who "are subtly swayed by claims that modern Israel enjoys a historic right, a divine destiny that is above criticism."[26] Acknowledging that while "pockets of petty prejudice remain," Oxtoby insisted that "among an educated younger generation it is fair to say that [antisemitism] has virtually ceased to exist." Yet the fear of being labeled antisemitic had stymied real discussion of Israel between Jews and Christians.[27] Oxtoby's assessment of widespread American Protestant support for the Israelis and the conflation of anti-Zionism and antisemitism reflected the justification that members of the ACPC offered for their disbandment. American Protestants fully supported Israel, even if pockets of criticism remained among some liberal Protestant leaders.

Evangelicals Celebrate Israel's Triumph

However frustrated some Jews may have been by the response of mainline Protestants to the Six-Day War, the enthusiastic evangelical reaction was impossible to miss. Indeed the reality of Israeli victory, overwhelmingly celebrated by evangelicals and fundamentalists, heralded a new era for Protestant interest in the Holy Land and Judaism. As soon as the fighting ended, evangelicals and fundamentalists addressed the prophetic significance of Israel's territorial acquisitions. Excited by images of Jews praying again at the Western Wall, American fundamentalists and evangelicals dove headfirst into the waters of prophecy interpretation. Unlike the liberal Protestants, prophecy watchdogs viewed Israel's control of Jerusalem with cautious optimism.

In a radio broadcast in Chicago (home of the Moody Bible Institute) that aired four days after hostilities ended in the Middle East, three scholars from the Institute addressed questions about the significance of the war. While all three experts advised caution in interpreting events in Israel too specifically, all agreed that Americans should recognize that the outcome of the war could be a sign of the end of days.[28] When the panel moderator asked about the significance of the Israeli occupation of Jerusalem, all three panelists expressed their optimism, although each noted that it was too early to tell whether Israel would retain control. Clearly, for them, Israeli control over Jerusalem would be an ideal outcome of the war. The idea of international control over the Old City or return of the territory to Jordan did not enter the conversation. C. I. Scofield's "prophetic interpretation" that "Israel is God's prophetical clock and this clock moves only when God is dealing directly with Israel in their land," pointed to, as one panelist insisted, the importance of Israel to American Protestants concerned with the end of days.[29]

John F. Walvoord, president of the Dallas Theological Seminary, appeared less cautious than the three Moody Bible Institute panelists in his assessment of the Israeli victory. In the cover story for the October 1967 issue of *Moody Monthly*, Walvoord proclaimed that the "dramatic victory of Israel over the Arab states electrified the entire world."[30] Most significant of all, according to Walvoord, the Israeli control over Jerusalem surely heralded the "end of the time of the Gentiles" and the beginning of the end of days. Tracing the history of the ancient Israelites to the present situation in the Middle East, Walvoord noted that for Scripture to be fulfilled, and the end of times to begin, sacrifices must be resumed in the Temple in Jerusalem. Before the war such a fulfillment had seemed impossible. "Now," Walvoord pointed out, suddenly a dispossession which has endured for 1900 years has at least temporarily ended. Many therefore predict early erection of a temple by the victorious state of Israel."[31] The erection of the third temple marked the most significant precursor to the end of days, and evangelical and fundamentalist American Protestants waited with great anticipation for the first signs of construction.

Hal Lindsay, of the evangelical organization Campus Crusade for Christ, echoed Walvoord's optimism that the world was entering the end of days and the coming return of the Messiah. In reviewing recent world events, Lindsay argued, "we must see these [pieces of a puzzle] as part of a plan which is leading to the culmination of history thus far—the second coming of Christ. And," he added, "I believe a careful study of biblical prophecy reveals that this climactic event is drawing so close that we may be at its very threshold." The reestablishment of Israel constituted "the most important development, of course." The Israeli control of Jerusalem meant, according to Lindsay, that "we only await the rebuilding of the temple and this piece of the puzzle will be complete."[32] Many publications echoed these sentiments. The *Baptist Bible Tribune* hailed the Israeli victory because it would allow the rebuilding of the temple: "The Israeli state must have a temple. She will have one."[33] The fundamentalist journal *Eternity* recorded a minister's take on the threat posed by Egypt and Syria: "This is more a prophetic question than a military one," to which the Bible apparently guaranteed Israeli victory.[34] The readers of *Eternity*, then, found nothing very surprising in Israel's six-day military victory.

Eternity's excitement in viewing the events in Israel through prophetic lenses marks a significant shift in the Protestant assessment of Israel's significance. Prior to 1967 many fundamentalists remained cautious about Israel as a nation founded in "unbelief." More and more Protestant prophecy watchdogs appeared to have abandoned such caution in the months following the war, however, and plunged forward in assessing its significance.[35] An *Eternity* editorial, published in January 1968, proclaimed that the Arab-Israeli War made 1967 a significant year because of the war's prophetic importance: "Prophetic overtones echoed over the brief battle, as Jerusalem was controlled by the Jews for the first time since Nebuchadnezzar."[36]

Christianity Today, the evangelical journal founded in 1956, also viewed the war through a religious lens. Nasser, a "Muslim," had been assisted in his "revenge" campaign—"an adventurous anti-Israeli program"—by the "Buddhist" U Thant. "Israel," the editorial board noted, "hedged on three sides by Arab foes and outnumbered twenty to one, began fighting to ensure its survival as a nation." Commenting on the Israeli occupation of Jerusalem after nineteen hundred years, the editors explained that "the popular Israeli toast, 'next year in Jerusalem!' was crowned last week by anticipatory fulfillment when a rabbi in soldier's garb blew a ram's horn at the Wailing Wall." The editorial noted Americans' overwhelming support for Israel and pointed out that "history must acknowledge the grim irony of the battle between hawks and doves in the United States, for doves quickly became hawks when Israel was in danger."[37]

American Christians had the ability to understand the recent "imbroglio in the Middle East" through an understanding of prophetic scriptures, the editors insisted. Jewish control of Jerusalem served as a harbinger of the end of days and "even if they do not keep the old city now," the editorial prophesied, "they will get it someday." Ultimately, the editorial concluded, "the prophetic clock of God is ticking while history moves inexorably toward the final climax. And as that clock ticks, the Christian believer lifts his head high; for he knows that a glorious redemption draws near."[38]

For fundamentalists and evangelicals, the Israeli victory only increased the urgency with which they addressed missionizing efforts toward the Jews.[39] An advertisement by the American Association for Jewish Evangelism that appeared in *Moody Monthly* in the weeks after the 1967 War declared: "God Isn't Finished with His People Whom He Foreknew, Are You?" The ad continued: "Recent events confirm that Israel will continue as a nation, and must be recognized in world affairs. Scripture has warned that those who seek Israel's harm will not prosper—but God will reward those who seek Israel's health and happiness."[40] Such an advertisement had significant foreign policy implications for American Protestants: evangelism remained a responsibility of Christians, and those who oppose Israel or "seek Israel's harm" (including hostile Christians and the Arab nations) would "not prosper." Consequently American Protestants who sought "Israel's health and happiness" would surely be rewarded. The same issue of *Moody Monthly* highlighted evangelical efforts to reach out to Jewish congregations. In one article Louis Goldberg recounted the experience of the Highland Park Baptist Church in Chattanooga, Tennessee ("one of the leading evangelical churches in the nation") in implementing their first "Adventure in Understanding"—a dinner sponsored by the evangelical congregation to welcome several Jewish congregations and the local chapter of B'nai B'rith into an inter-religious celebration.

The Baptist congregation, in a dining hall draped with blue and white decorations reflecting the Israeli flag, presented a slide show from an Israeli trip to the 156 Jewish audience members who attended. Goldberg noted that "the Jewish guests seemed impressed by the Christians' acute interest in the land of Israel as well as in the Israelis themselves." While the sermon itself, led by Highland Park's minister and titled "The Debt We Owe Judaism," presented the evangelical message of Jesus as Messiah, other aspects of the service celebrated Jewish traditions including the singing of the Psalms with traditional Jewish music, two rabbis of the community making a blessing over the dinner, and the singing of the Hatikvah at the evening's conclusion.[41] The purpose of the dinner, for the evangelicals, appeared twofold: "to witness to the claims of Jesus the Messiah" while simultaneously offering the "hand of friendship and love to Jewish friends." Goldberg concluded his summation of the dinner by noting that Protestant ministers had, in the weeks following the event, received reciprocal invitations by rabbis to come to their congregations and that many more evangelical congregations had started their own "Adventure in Understanding" events.[42]

However much evangelical and fundamentalist Protestants celebrated the Israeli victory in the 1967 War and however much these celebrations sparked a renewal of missionizing efforts toward Jews, theological reevaluations of Christianity's relationship to Judaism did not occur. Holding fast to orthodox teachings of the necessity of a personal relationship with Jesus for salvation, fundamentalists and evangelicals did not, in any way, reassess their theology. If anything, the Israeli capture of Jerusalem *confirmed* their eschatology. John F. Walvoord's excitement about the Israeli victory in the Six-Day War and the capture of Jerusalem only fortified his theological assessment of the significance of current events for biblical prophecy.

In the conservative theological journal *Bibliotheca sacra*, Walvoord addressed the possibility of the return to animal sacrifice in a restored temple and added that premillennialists supported the idea as the fulfillment of biblical prophecy that predicted a return to the ancient rite in the last days before Christ's return.[43] Now, he insisted, "the facts of history" provided new encouragement to both orthodox Jews and Christians that a temple would be rebuilt and the sacrifices restored. Walvoord assessed the American Christian excitement about the possibility, including the rumors that a town in Indiana had shipped "500 railroad carloads of stone to Jerusalem" to help rebuild the temple, and other Christians in the United States had recast the bronze pillars necessary to restore the new temple to its original specifications. Although Walvoord noted that the Israeli government "flatly denied" such plans and noted that, should a temple be rebuilt, native stone would be used, the significance of such rumors lay in the hope that a restored temple would symbolize "the heart of Israel as both a nation and as a religious group."[44]

Walvoord offered a close reading of Daniel, chapter 12, which predicted that the return of Christ would be preceded by the cessation of the sacrifices in the temple. For the sacrifices to stop, they must first begin, Walvoord pointed out. Although problems existed to prevent the fulfillment of this prophecy, Walvoord argued, many issues that appeared impossible prior to the Six-Day War had been overcome: the restoration of Jews to Palestine, the reformation of the nation of Israel, and the Israeli recovery of Jerusalem. "History has recorded that Israel did return in spite of the difficulties. It is safe to conclude," Walvoord argued, "that future history will also record a rebuilding of the temple"—in fulfillment of the premillenial interpretation of scripture.[45]

While the events of June 1967 no doubt excited a prophetic assessment of world events, Israel's survival and victory in the Six-Day War prompted other evangelical Christians to remind themselves of the importance of the Jews to God. Although, as discussed previously, theological reevaluations did not result from this acknowledgment, still a new appreciation for what Judaism could teach Christians surfaced in the wake of the war. In an article that appeared in *Eternity* in August of 1967, author G. Douglas Young, director of the American Institute of Holy Land Studies in Jerusalem and professor of the Old Testament at Trinity Evangelical Divinity School in Illinois, urged "conservative Christians" to remember that "God still has something to teach us through the Jewish people"—a conclusion liberal Protestants had earlier embraced. Young concluded his article with a final reminder to his readers that "God is speaking to us today through them."[46] Young reaffirmed the significant shift evangelicals had undertaken in their approach to Jews and Judaism: both the individuals and the faith should be protected and celebrated as integral parts of the Christian story.

Ecumenical Implications of the War

As noted above, the reaction of liberal Protestants to the events of June 1967 resulted in a split in liberal Protestantism. Those liberal Protestants who had historically supported Israel, including former ACPC members, continued to voice their support for Israel and unequivocally condemned the Arab provocation. Other liberals who had appeared critical of Israel before the hostilities grew increasingly so in the war's aftermath. As a result, the previous decade's advances in improved Jewish-Christian dialogue halted, as American Jews voiced their consternation over the Protestant establishment's inability or unwillingness to support the Israeli cause. Some liberal Protestants, such as Martin Marty, denied the Jewish claim of Christian silence and pointed out that because of the fractured nature of Protestantism, no single body could speak for all American Protestants. Moreover, he explained, events happened so quickly that convening a committee on short notice to produce a unified statement condemning Arab hostility proved impossible.

Regardless, mainline Protestantism's self-assessment of the importance of the State of Israel and the continued problem of antisemitism in traditional Protestant theology took on new significance. Even if some liberal Protestants condemned Israeli action, they nonetheless recognized the need to address Israel theologically in a more systematic manner. Ironically, as relations cooled between American Jews and their liberal Protestant counterparts in the war's wake, liberal Protestant theologians prolifically engaged the theological and political significance of Israel's rebirth.

Unlike the evangelical and fundamentalist journals, liberal Protestants had, especially prior to the Six-Day War, eschewed theological engagement of the significance of Israel, often remaining entrenched in the traditional teachings of supercessionism that relegated Israel to theological insignificance. Israeli control over Jerusalem and larger areas of the Holy Land prompted a flood of theological reevaluations. Although theological reassessments of historic Christian antisemitism had occurred with increasing frequency in the preceding decades, the war opened a torrent of new concern. Moreover, constant Jewish comparisons of Christian silence on the eve of the 1967 War with Christian silence during the Holocaust led to one of the most significant outcomes of the 1967 War: the beginning of liberal Protestantism's assessment of the role of Christian theology in the perpetration of the Holocaust and a continued engagement with the reality of Christian antisemitism. While the political issues surrounding the war divided many liberal Protestants, attempts to engage the Christian responsibility in the Holocaust began.

In countless articles appearing in a wide variety of journals, including the *Christian Century*, the *Journal of Ecumenical Studies, Interpretation, International Review of Missions*, and *Theological Studies*, Protestant and Jewish theologians offered a wide-ranging interpretation of the importance of the Six-Day War in Christian theology, the need for improved Jewish-Christian relations, Christian guilt regarding the Holocaust, and issues of antisemitism versus anti-Zionism. Journals confronted theological tugs-of-war over the correct Christian interpretation of events and behavior in the war's aftermath. Books appeared by Abraham Joshua Heschel, Markus Barth, and others that presented new Jewish and Christian theologies concerning Jews, Judaism, and Israel. Theologians discussed the Christian's responsibility in preventing further conflict and issues of supercessionism and its political implications, and offered methods for improving dialogue without conceding principles.[47] American Jews, though frustrated by liberal Protestants' prewar lack of response, responded nonetheless to the new ecumenical spirit by encouraging the increased interest in Israel's theological significance to Christians while simultaneously affirming the reality of Israel's existence and the need for its security.

Often articles addressing theological issues also proposed political solutions. In an article for the *Journal of Ecumenical Studies*, Markus Barth suggested creating a federation of the Holy Land, in which the Israelis would relinquish their "Jewish character and name" in exchange for peace. He argued that politics, foreign policy, and religious dialogue, so intimately connected, could be separated only at great peril to each. "It might appear that the political and the theological issues just described were unrelated to one another," he noted, "but it is more probable that they are closely connected. The Israeli-Arab conflict . . . has a theological core which makes it as acid and acrid as it is. Theology and politics, matters of faith and questions of daily conduct can by no means be left in separate compartments. The threatened futures of the Israeli state, but equally the impossible future of the present curtailed to Jordan, require that Christians take a stance in these issues." Barth concluded: "Unless they seek a strengthening of faith, they will be incapable of finding a solid footing."[48]

In the summer of 1968 an article in the *Journal of Ecumenical Studies* by a Dutch Protestant theologian, H. Berkhof, encouraged Protestants to more actively engage the question of the theological significance of the modern nation of Israel. Disagreements about the place of Israel in Christian theology had resulted in two positions, Berkhof argued: the idea that the Church had replaced the Jews as God's chosen people, thereby effectively severing any theological relevance of the Jews or the nation of Israel to the Christian Church today; or the position that modern Israel represented the literal fulfillment of biblical prophecy and therefore existed as an integral part of God's plan for the world. Addressing both positions, Berkhof argued for a middle ground that denied literal interpretations of Scripture with regard to Israel but recognized, as the theologian Karl Barth insisted, that "the Jews are the other half of God's people" and that geography remained a relevant and vital part of understanding God's plan for the world, and Israel in particular.[49]

Israelis could teach the modern nations much about the fallacy of nationalism: both in their extreme Zionist position and in their easy acceptance of dual loyalty (to Israel and to their nations of origin). Berkhof concluded his article by urging Christians to engage the theological significance of Israel more deeply, to resist the extreme supercessionist theologies of Arab Christians, to prevent the Six-Day War from dominating religious discussions, and to engage the question among Christians first. Excluding Jews from these initial theological engagements would make some uncomfortable, Berkhof acknowledged, "but at the same time they will be convinced that such conversations will necessarily create a wholesome feeling of incompleteness in the ecumenical movement—a feeling which is yet absent."[50]

Professor of rabbinics and theology at Hebrew Union College, Jakob Petuchowski applauded Berkhof's prescription for intra-Christian conversations on the role of Israel and the Jews in modern theology. "From the wide range of options available on the Christian continuum, he chooses the one which is most favorable to the Jews and most in accord with the reality of Jewish existence," Petuchowski noted.[51] Yet, as Petuchowski pointed out, Berkhof himself admitted that such theological wrangling constituted intra-Christian problems rather than interfaith ones. Petuchowski listed the issues he would like Christians to recognize: that "Jews are not pagans," that Christianity did not supersede the special relationship between Jews and God, and that the joint biblical heritage possessed by both Jews and Christians is significant. He condemned the Christian criterion of assessing Israel's significance only from the perspective of the fulfillment of "the Christian playwright's script."[52] He pragmatically noted, however, that "to the extent to which the church still wields some political influence, it cannot be a matter of indifference to the Jew just how the church manages to come to terms with the reality of the State of Israel."

The readers of the *Journal of Ecumenical Studies* were further challenged to confront the meaning of Israel and its implications for Jewish-Christian dialogue in an article by Rabbi Jacob Agus of the Beth El Congregation in Baltimore, Maryland. Clearly, Agus argued, the Six-Day War had forced Christians to address the issue of Israel's theological importance: "was Israel a sign of the *eschaton*, just another nation-state, or a new ecumenical opportunity presenting itself?" Agus acknowledged that the Christian response in the United States to the Six-Day war presented a stumbling block to interfaith dialogue. Jews viewed the war as a threat of annihilation, whereas "Christian churchmen tended to disregard the Arab threats as idle rhetoric[53] Both Jews and Christians must "abandon their medieval conceptions" regarding each other and recognize the spiritual significance each faith offered the other. Israel remained partly a Christian creation, after all, argued Agus:

> Christian sympathy generated that atmosphere of international acceptance which made the homeland possible. Moshe Sharett, the one-time Foreign Secretary of Israel, noted after a journey through Asia and Africa that wherever the Bible was unknown, the Zionist movement was totally incomprehensible. Sympathy for the idea of a Jewish homeland in Palestine could only have emerged in cultures that were rooted in the Scriptures.[54]

Agus's analysis points to a bold implication—that without Christian sympathy for Zionism, Israel's existence might not have occurred. In the year following the 1967 War, then, some mainline Protestants like Agus offered a direct connection between Christianity and Zionism.

American Jewish reaction to the Christian response to the Six-Day War revealed deep divisions within the community over the proper Jewish and Christian response to the event.[55] Two pamphlets published in 1968 revealed the split among American Jews, each offering radically different assessments of the role Israel should play in Jewish-Christian dialogue.[56] The first, written for a primarily Christian audience, protested the silence of official Protestantism on the eve of the war and insisted that Israel's establishment and victory in the war "should be celebrated by Jews as an act of God comparable to the Exodus."[57] The other pamphlet, written by Michael Selzer of the American Council of Judaism, conversely ascribed no theological importance to either Israel's establishment or the war and lamented the assertion that American Jews held a vested interest in Israeli matters. Furthermore, Selzer decried the supposition of American Jews that religious dialogue "be predicated on the political endorsement of the State of Israel's actions."

For one Christian reviewer of the pamphlets, three factors complicated Christian participation in interreligious conversations about Israel: Christian guilt over the Holocaust, "our political ineptitude on the onset of the June 1967 war," and concern for the plight of Arab refugees.[58] The reviewer condemned the idea that the starting point for Jewish-Christian dialogue in the United States should come at the cost of "an uncritical acceptance of everything which the State of Israel does." Ultimately, the reviewer concluded, "perhaps we can atone for our guilt" by insisting to government officials that Israel's existence remained nonnegotiable. Yet Christians retained the moral imperative to care for the Arab refugees from Israeli wars and to "save the Arabs from the Jews, and vice versa."[59]

According to Abraham Heschel, Christian celebration of Israel's establishment and survival followed an important tradition of the early Church as revealed in the Book of Acts: "The Apostles were Jews and evidently shared the hope of their people of seeing the kingdom of God realized in the restoration of Israel's national independence."[60] Heschel pointed to Luke 17, verses 20–21: "Jerusalem will be trodden down by the Gentiles, until the time of the Gentiles are fulfilled"—a favorite of fundamentalists—as evidence that Christianity contained its own emphasis on the restoration of the nation of Israel. Heschel's point would have found a ready and sympathetic audience in the evangelical and fundamentalist persuasions. Clearly, however, his article—appearing in a liberal ecumenical journal—was intended to address traditional liberal Christian objections. For Heschel, Protestants must accept Israel's theological significance to Judaism for real dialogue to begin, and should also recognize the messianic importance of Israel and Jerusalem in their own eschatology. Throughout his analysis, Heschel clearly pointed to the reality of the Holocaust as proof of the necessity of Israel's establishment. As noted above, he rejected the idea that Israel served as "an atonement." The relationship between the Holocaust and Israel's establishment. however, could not be fully understood apart from each other.

In an editorial appearing in the *Journal of Ecumenical Studies*, Elwyn Smith pointed out that recent events in the Middle East had prompted new interest in evaluating the significance of the Holocaust: "What is notable at the present moment is that many who had never regarded the holocaust as a personal concern are changing."[61] More Christians now recognized that "the holocaust was precisely a Christian catastrophe." Smith surveyed the role of Christianity in Germany in perpetuating the Holocaust and, though challenging the argument that Christianity led directly to the murder of six million Jews in Europe, he noted that Christians' lack of effort to systematically protest or prevent it must be considered a failure. Christian theology could be partially blamed, however: "only too frequently Christian theology and attitude have been prone to see in disasters to Jews further proof that God is displeased with their failure to recognize Jesus as Messiah."[62] Such an attitude prevented Christians from acknowledging their inability to "love thy neighbor"—the most basic of Christian principles—and resulted in the failure to pass "the terrible test" of the Holocaust. Christians should recognize that standing with the Jews whenever they are in peril constituted a basic fulfillment of the biblical command. "Who would have thought that it could now be seen that insofar as Christians willingly share with Jews a common human fate amid the vagaries of politics, they stand more faithfully with their own biblical Word and Gospel?" Smith asked. "Perhaps," he concluded, "that is what the holocaust should mean to them."[63]

In the summer of 1970 the *Christian Science Monitor* published a five-part series titled "The Judeo-Christian Dialogue" that considered the importance of continuing attempts to recognize antisemitism within Christianity and eliminate it in order to foster improved relations between Christians and Jews. The first article, written by Louis Garinger, the religious affairs editor, noted that the Six-Day War presented "the most serious threat to improved Jewish-Christian relations."[64] Jews viewed the war as a war for Israel's survival and "expected Christians to do likewise." When American Christians did not respond as expected, "Jewish religious leaders found it disillusioning to the point that their ardor for the dialogue cooled considerably."[65] The lack of support from Christians motivated Jewish leaders to encourage Christians to "face the question of Israel and acknowledge what Jews believed to be the justice of their cause."

Although Garinger noted the recent *New York Times* advertisement sponsored by Karl Baehr's Interfaith and University Committee, signed by 250 leading American Protestants, that condemned continuing Arab terrorism on the Israeli-Lebanese border and revealed the concern that many influential Protestants expressed for Israeli security, he also noted the divide that separated many Protestants on the issue.[66] "Many Christians," he noted, "separate Zionism as a political philosophy from Judaism as a religion and condemn the former while sympathizing with the latter."[67] Garinger also noted that while evangelicals and fundamentalist eschewed interfaith dialogue because of their adherence of orthodox Protestant theology, they had nonetheless attacked antisemitism through a variety of methods. He noted the Reverend Billy Graham's vocal admiration for "his love of the Jewish people and the land of Israel and the city of Jerusalem," the fact that Graham's son and daughter had worked on an Israeli kibbutz, and that Franklin Graham "served with support forces during the June 1967 war."[68]

In his articles, Garinger recounted the long, troubled past of interfaith relations and placed the blame for its history on Christians, who, through traditional theologies, had relegated Jews to theological insignificance at best, or damned them to "divine punishment" (and thereby justified persecution) at worst. Even today, Garinger noted, Americans could witness "verbal antisemitism" in the rhetoric of extreme elements in both the American Right (the John Birch Society) and the Left (the Weathermen, the Revolutionary Youth Movement II, the Young Workers Liberation League, the Young Socialist Alliance, the Black Muslims, and the Black Panthers). Christians should also accept blame, he charged, because "Christian sins of omission" contributed to the existence of antisemitism. "Christians . . . who failed to speak out or act" in the prevention of the Holocaust facilitated the Jewish persecution.[69] More needed to be done to face the troubled past of Jewish-Christian relations and improve outreach efforts to the Jewish community.

Echoing some of Grainger's concerns about growing anti-Zionism, an article appeared in the *Christian Century* addressing the growing trend of anti-Zionism within the American Left as a result of the Six-Day War and charged that, although conceivably different from antisemitism, the two were often closely connected. While anti-Zionists "passionately repudiate" any suggestion that anti-Zionism and antisemitism are related, author Alan

Davies, a Protestant minister, noted, "Anti-Zionism sooner or later reveals a distressing tendency to shade into antisemitism." Even if Jews themselves are divided on the issue, "every expression of opposition to the Zionist movement everywhere" did not make those criticisms "legitimate."[70] Although Christians may not recognize a "connection between Auschwitz and Israel" or "Auschwitz and Christendom," Jews did. In order to achieve true dialogue, Protestants must come to terms with the emotional nature of Jewish support for Israel. "It is exceedingly difficult on the emotional level for the victims of the Holocaust to distinguish anti-Zionism from antisemitism, however clear the distinction may seem to gentiles."[71] Moreover, Davies argued, "Christians are confused about Auschwitz. The frequent journalistic comparisons between Zionist militarism and Nazi militarism are instructive. To find Israel in a morally ambiguous situation releases the Christian from thinking too much about Auschwitz and his own vicarious participation in one of the darkest moments in Western history."[72]

Davies concluded his article with an admonition to the Christian community: "First, take the plank out of your own eye, and then you will see clearly to take the speck out of your brother's." Davies's article highlighted a common theme among pro-Israel mainline Protestants: hypercritical assessments of the state ignored problems faced by American society itself and revealed a tendency to ignore the problems of anti-Judaism inherent in Protestant theology. Protestants could be too quick to offer sweeping indictments of Israel without a deep introspection of their own problems. In short, linking the Holocaust with Protestant attitudes toward Israel and Jews was not just being pushed by the American Jewish community. Loud voices within certain Protestant groups were doing it as well.

Conclusion

By the outbreak of the Yom Kippur War in 1973, those liberal Protestants who lobbied for increasing American Protestant support for Israel found their concerns shared by a growing number of liberal Protestants—despite bureaucratic and "official" Protestant reluctance to endorse the U.S.–Israeli alliance. "The general responses have been amazingly good," former ACPC member Franklin Littell wrote to Niebuhr regarding the establishment of the pro-Israel activist group Christians Concerned for Israel. "They strengthen my conviction that once you get behind the bureaucrats in the church boards, there is a vast reservoir of goodwill toward the Holy Land that can be channeled into intelligent and critical support of Israel."[73]

In the following years, tapping the reservoir of American Protestant support for Israel remained a goal of those liberal Protestants who believed that American Christian support of Israel was a moral imperative. On the theological front, even Protestants who appeared ambivalent or even critical of Israel nonetheless embarked upon urgent reevaluations of traditional Protestant attitudes toward Jews and Judaism—a process that had begun in the 1950s but continued with renewed vigor in the 1960s and 1970s. The frustration that American Jews voiced in response to a lack of Protestant institutional condemnation of Arab provocation resulted in 1967 in a sense of urgency among American Protestant theologians to address the theological significance of Israel and repair the damage to Jewish-Christian relations.

Meanwhile, the excitement over the Israeli victory in the Six-Day War and the capture of Jerusalem pushed evangelical and fundamentalist Protestants toward unqualified support for the Israeli cause. The increasing resemblance of the current map of Israel to the biblical Holy Land catalyzed evangelical Protestants to support the land acquisitions of the Six-Day War as a sign of the fulfillment of biblical prophecy and the coming end of times. While evangelicals did not reevaluate their orthodox theology in response to current events, they nonetheless embraced a new tactic in their missions to the Jews, one that emphasized a common Judeo-Christian heritage and love for Israel. Evangelicals and fundamentalists would continue to employ this strategy, and it would have profound implications in the coming decades for U.S.–Israeli relations and U.S.–Middle East foreign policies. The decline of the influence of liberal Protestants in politics in the 1960s and 1970s would be matched by the political rise of evangelicals and fundamentalists. With new political prowess came a determination to influence foreign affairs on behalf of Israel and in accordance with their understanding of biblical prophecy. Those liberal Protestants who had worked to promote a strong U.S.–Israeli alliance for politically pragmatic and humanitarian reasons found themselves overpowered by an increasingly large and politically engaged group of Protestants who supported Israel for their own eschatological reasons.

The Individual and
the U.S.–Israeli Alliance

Ursula Niebuhr, the Jerusalem Committee,
and Christians Concerned for Israel

Although the American Christian Palestine Committee had disbanded by 1967, liberal Protestants who had actively pursued a strong U.S.–Israeli alliance continued to participate in new interfaith organizations and engaged in continuing efforts to strengthen the relationship. Israeli appreciation for these efforts resulted in governmental recognition of the role American Protestants played in creating a "special relationship" between the United States and Israel. Among those recognized for their efforts, Reinhold Niebuhr had long been considered one of Israel's most ardent and influential supporters in the United States. In appreciation for his efforts on behalf of Israel, Hebrew University in Jerusalem awarded him an honorary doctorate in 1969—two years before his death. Too sick to fly to Israel to accept the award, former Israeli ambassador to the United States and Hebrew University president Avraham Harman and Nathan Rotenstreich, the pro-rector, traveled to Niebuhr's residence, Yale Hill, in Stockbridge, Massachusetts, to present the award to Niebuhr on 15 December—the first time an honorary degree from an Israeli university was presented outside Israel. Upon the presentation of the degree, Niebuhr noted, "I am an old man, and I assume that this will be my final degree, and I will regard this as a degree that comes from the University of Jerusalem . . . I am a friend of the Jewish people . . . and I have never ceased to be favorable to the State of Israel."[1]

In February 1971 Reinhold Niebuhr died. The Jewish community, among many others, noted his death with sorrow.[2] Jerusalem mayor Teddy Kolleck, the first person to call the morning after Niebuhr's death, offered Niebuhr's widow both condolences and thanks from "the people of Jerusalem" for Niebuhr's unwavering support of Israel.[3] Articles in Jewish journals celebrated his life. In one article appearing in *Conservative Judaism*, author Seymour Siegel hailed Niebuhr as a trailblazer in Jewish-Christian relations. His belief that "Christian missionary activity among the Jews [was] wrong" and his support for "the thrilling emergence of the State of Israel" explained why, as one scholar noted, after Niebuhr delivered an address before the joint faculties of the Jewish Theological Seminary (JTS) and Union Theological Seminary, another listener declared: "After listening to this remarkable lecture, I know why the slogan at J.T.S. is "Love thy Niebuhr as thy self."[4] The noted Jewish theologian Abraham Joshua Heschel delivered the only eulogy at Niebuhr's funeral. He praised Niebuhr's efforts to "strengthen the Hebraic prophetic content of the Christian tradition." Niebuhr was, Heschel noted, "a lover of Zion and Jerusalem, was imbued with the spirit of the Hebrew Bible, [and] was a staunch friend of the Jewish people and the state of Israel, of the poor and downtrodden here and everywhere."[5]

After Niebuhr's death, his wife Ursula, a retired professor of religion at Barnard College, took up the cause of Protestant political support of Israel and the improvement of Jewish-Christian relations. Although less public than her husband, the efforts of Ursula Niebuhr to develop closer relationships between the United States and Israel, and between Christians and Jews, grew increasingly significant in the years preceding Reinhold's death and in the decades following, and is an example of the intimate connections that were established between important individual Israelis and American Protestants in an attempt to effect policy. In 1969 Teddy Kolleck invited Ursula to join his Jerusalem Committee, an organization established to advise the mayor on the development of the city following the 1967 War. Made up of "architects, planners, conservationists, and scholars" from across the globe, the Committee regularly met in Jerusalem to discuss the city's development and consolidation under the Israeli government.

One of the most remarkable developments stemming from Niebuhr's inclusion in the Jerusalem Committee was the evolution of a lifelong correspondence with Kolleck. They wrote to each other over the course of several decades, visited each other in New York and Jerusalem, and discussed challenges that the U.S.–Israeli alliance encountered. For example, after visiting Washington, D.C., for a memorial service for Reinhold, Ursula reported to Kolleck the "political gossip" overheard during her visit in a letter marked "confidential." "Several of my very pro-Israel friends are concerned that the Israeli Embassy is being too active in the American political scene with regard to possible presidential candidates," she wrote. "Mrs. Meir [Israel's prime minister] was in Washington when I was there," she added, "and there were several remarks to the effect that if she went to see Senators Humphrey and Jackson, she should have also paid a call on the other candidates." Niebuhr conceded that, "I know you have enough problems to deal with, but my conscience is clearer if I pass this on."[6] Niebuhr's efforts to aid the Israeli cause in Washington drew an immediate reaction from Kolleck. He presented Niebuhr's letter to the director of the Israeli prime minister's office who then passed it on to Golda Meir herself. "Mrs. Meir asked that we convey to you her thanks for your interest and your friendship," Kolleck wrote to Niebuhr. Kolleck explained that the Israeli Embassy maintained political contacts with both the government and the "opposition party," and that Meir had met with Democratic hopefuls, including Muskie, Humphrey, Kennedy, Jackson, and Lindsay, but that a scheduled meeting with George McGovern had been canceled because of scheduling conflicts.[7]

At the conclusion of the Yom Kippur War in 1973, Kolleck asked Niebuhr to work to counter the increasing demands from the international community to once again divide Jerusalem between Jordan and Israel. "I hope you will be able in your respective circles to clear up the misrepresentation and distortion which have been increasingly prevalent," Kolleck wrote, and added, "Please help us impress upon others the importance of a unified Jerusalem as the capital of Israel."[8]

Ursula Niebuhr's advocacy on behalf of Israel extended to working with American organizations as well. Even before Reinhold's death and her first visit to Israel, Ursula had grown increasingly active in American organizations that promoted improved Jewish-Christian relations and a strong alliance. Such activism connected Ursula to former members of the American Christian Palestine Committee who had now focused their efforts on other organizations. One such organization, the Youth Committee for Peace and Democracy in the Middle East, founded by former ACPC members Bayard Rustin and Franklin Littell, worked to encourage support for Israel in colleges and universities across the nation. Approving of their activities on behalf of the Israeli cause, Niebuhr agreed to sponsor the organization.[9] She also supported Littell's Christians Concerned for Israel. In an effort "to build bridges to the Jewish community," the religion professor at Temple University argued that "the murder of the Jews was possible because of the wholesale apostasy of the baptized" and that "a rebirth of Christian life must begin with an agonizing reappraisal of the whole matter of Christian-Jewish relations." He lamented the "thunderous silence" of the Christian Church on the eve of the Six-Day War which, he insisted, left the Jews convinced that "the Christian churches—your particular concern, and mine—had not changed their

attitudes and actions since Auschwitz and Theresiendstadt and Dachau."[10]
The organization would publish a newsletter dedicated to celebrating Christian efforts to both improve Jewish-Christian relations and inform American readers of the "positive" Christian presence in Israel at such places as the Tantur Ecumenical Institute, the Christian Kibbutz (Nes Ammim), and the Institute of Holy Land Studies.[11]

Significantly, unlike previous pro-Israel Christian organizations, CCI would represent *both* evangelicals and mainline Protestants. Evangelicals who supported the organization included some of the most powerful leading evangelicals in the United States, such as G. Douglas Young, founder and president of the American Institute of Holy Land Studies, and Arnold T. Olson, president of the Evangelical Free Church of America and former president of the National Association of Evangelicals. In a letter to Littell, Niebuhr noted, "I have wished for many months that something like the 'Christian News from Israel' would be put out by a non-Israeli or non-Jewish group. There is such a need . . . both to express and extend the interest of Christian individuals, as well as the Christian churches, in what has happened and is happening in Israel." Moreover, she added, "this interest and concern should be the overdue expression of our historic guilt and our present responsibility for Israel."[12]

A. Roy Eckardt, professor of religion at Lehigh University and coauthor, with Alice Eckardt, of a theological reassessment of Christian antisemitism and the theological significance of the founding of Israel,[13] served as the cofounder of CCI—a move that delighted Niebuhr, as the Eckardts had dedicated their book to Reinhold. In the book the authors argued that Israel enjoyed the right to exist based on its historical claims to the land and that an overly critical assessment of the state's shortcomings produced a "double standard" that demanded a perfection from Israel that no other nation faced. Furthermore, the authors argued that failure to support Israel's right to exist amounted to politicide, which in Israel's case necessarily constituted genocide. The Eckardts' theological interests translated into activism with the establishment of CCI and the publication of its newsletter, *Christians Concerned for Israel Notebook*.

Between 1970 and 1977 the organization produced approximately thirty issues of its newsletter. It considered itself the watchdog of antisemitism and anti-Israel sentiment in American Christianity. The issues the newsletter addressed included information about study tours and other opportunities for American Christians to travel to Israel, commentary on U.N. events, books, and articles dealing with theological reassessments of the relationship between Christianity and Judaism, academic conferences on the Holocaust and Jewish-Christian relations, and general foreign policy concerns.

The organization's sensitivity to criticism of Israel by some liberal American Protestants resulted in a public dispute with the editors of *Christianity and Crisis* in March 1972. The Reverend Francis B. Sayre of the Washington Cathedral (and the grandson of Woodrow Wilson) delivered a sermon highly critical of Israel on Palm Sunday, 26 March 1972. In the sermon Sayre quoted an article by Israel Shahak, an anti-Zionist Israeli scholar at Hebrew University, which had been published in the 20 March issue of *Christianity and Crisis*. In the article Shahak wrote: "I consider the annexation of East Jerusalem by my Government to be an immoral and unjust act. My first demand," he added, "is to give non-Jews of Jerusalem freedom," or "the present situation of one community oppressing the other will poison us all and us Jews first of all." Reverend Sayre, using Shahak's comments as a symbol of the crucifixion of Christ by mankind's sinfulness, declared: "We could look at contemporary Jerusalem if we wished and see the moral tragedy of mankind enacted there all over again in the politics of latter-day Israel. Now the Jews have it all. But even as they praise their God for the smile of fortune, they begin almost simultaneously to put Him to death." Sayre, quoting Shahak, insisted that the unification of Jerusalem under the Israeli government and the neglect of the Arab refugees constituted a moral outrage comparable to the crucifixion of Jesus.[14]

Both Protestants and Catholics responded with anger to the sermon. Franklin Littell immediately wrote to Wayne Cowan, the editor of *Christianity and Crisis,* to express his displeasure over the publication of Shahak's article. "It is a bitter shame and a scandal that *Christianity and Crisis* should have descended to the level that it has, and that both Jews and Christians concerned for mastering the lessons of the Church Struggle and the Holocaust should have to take it for granted that a once great magazine is now the predictable exponent of a position which on this issue—both politically and theologically—is indistinguishable from *Deutsches Christentum*," Littell wrote. Moreover, Littell added, "when you feature a renegade Jew as part of your continuing attack on the Jewish people, their faith and hope, you in fact simply document why Christianity has lost credibility in this generation."[15]

Ursula Niebuhr wrote to Teddy Kolleck to inform him of the sermon and express her displeasure at both Reverend Sayre and *Christianity and Crisis*. "There is someone called Israel Shahak, who has been rather a nuisance," she told Kolleck. She also informed him that "there has been quite a reaction [against Sayre's sermon], locally."[16] Kolleck wrote a letter to inform Sayre of the inaccuracy of his assessment of the state of affairs in Jerusalem, and Niebuhr forwarded a copy of the letter to Sayre. The *Notebook* published a condemnatory assessment of the affair and included excerpts from Kolleck's letter. Meanwhile, Niebuhr contacted the editors of *Christianity and Crisis* and asked them to remove Reinhold's name from the masthead of the magazine.[17]

Niebuhr's response to the editorial board illustrates the common perspective of Protestants working to eliminate antisemitic tendencies in both Christian theology and in foreign policy. Christians faced a heavy burden when considering their long history of antisemitism, a burden that should prompt self-evaluation and theological reassessments, and also serve to guard against hypocritical attacks upon Israel. The reaction of liberal Protestants to the perceived biases of the major Protestant journals and the public condemnation that followed Sayre's sermon reveal the increasingly passionate conviction that Protestants must reevaluate traditional attitudes toward and teachings about Jews and must, as a Christian responsibility, confront the reality of Israel and offer the nation moral and political support.

6

A New U.S.–Israeli Alliance, 1973–1979

Speaking before the New York Board of Rabbis while on the campaign trail, presidential candidate Jimmy Carter assured his audience of his concrete commitment to Israel. For Carter, American support for Israel could not be extricated from biblical faith. He explained: "I have a feeling of being at home when I go to Israel. I have a feeling, coincidentally, that the foundation of the nation of Israel in 1948 is a fulfillment of biblical prophecies." Confidently Carter concluded his remarks by noting that the majority of Americans agreed with his position on Israel. "It's not just that I'm a candidate that causes me to feel the way I do," he explained. "I think my position accurately represents the overwhelming majority of the opinions of the American people."[1] Carter was right.

The 1967 War had ushered in a new approach to Israel among American Protestants. Opinion polls revealed that the majority of Americans supported a strong U.S.–Israeli alliance. Challenges to the alliance stemming from the 1973 Yom Kippur War and the United Nation's condemnation of Zionism as a form of racism would prove too weak to upset the alliance and instead reaffirmed the United States' commitment to Israel. Theological assessments of traditional Protestant teachings toward Jews and Judaism reflected a new sensitivity toward Jewish-Christian relations, as mainline Protestants continued to grapple with the reality of Israel and the meaning of Judaism. The societal upheaval of the 1960s and 1970s, however, created a crisis for mainline Protestants.

These mainline denominations lost members to evangelical Protestant churches that emphasized adherence to orthodox theology. The decline of liberal Protestantism would have profound implications for American Protestant support for Israel. The decline of mainstream Protestantism signaled the abandonment of the pragmatic and humanitarian advocacy for a strong U.S.–Israeli alliance. The alliance indeed grew stronger but for prophetic and eschatological reasons that were anathemas to the liberal Protestants preceding it. A new alliance would arise, more politically powerful than the one it preceded, and would alter the relationship between American Protestants, Jews, and Israel.

The Yom Kippur War of 1973

Six years after the 1967 War Israel was embroiled in yet another war with its neighbors. Continuing terrorist attacks into Israeli territory from Syria and Egypt, the murder of eleven Israeli athletes at the Munich Olympics the previous year by members of Yasser Arafat's Fatah organization, and Egyptian rearmament on the Sinai border created a siege mentality for Israelis. Israel responded to Syrian border raids and the murder of the Israeli athletes with massive reprisals. For Egypt and Syria, in particular, the humiliation of the Six-Day War could only be rectified through military victory over Israel. To that end, on 6 October 1973, Egypt and Syria launched a surprise attack on Israel. Israelis, caught off guard celebrating the High Holy Day of Yom Kippur, endured battlefield setbacks for several days. Hoping to press their advantage against the Israelis, Egyptian troops overextended themselves, and, after a few days of fighting, Israel reoccupied lost ground, gained more territory, and inflicted severe damage on Syrian and Egyptian forces.

Meanwhile, just as they had during the Six-Day War, both the Soviets and the Americans moved to support their respective sides in the conflict. President Richard Nixon, ignoring King Faisal of Saudi Arabia's threat to impose an oil embargo should the United States assist Israel, sent over $2 billion to the Israelis during the conflict. Nixon, fearful that Israel would resort to the use of nuclear weapons, believed it was imperative to persuade the Israelis to fight conventionally. The Soviet Union assisted the Egyptian cause by providing improved technology and war material, and offered to send its own troops to the region as U.N. peacekeepers—a proposition the United States flatly refused. Nineteen days after the conflict began, Israel, Egypt, and Syria agreed to a U.N.-sponsored cease-fire. Both sides suffered heavy losses, including seven thousand deaths and the destruction of almost five hundred aircraft and sixteen hundred tanks.[2] Both sides claimed victory. The Arabs viewed their ability to launch a surprise attack and not be destroyed by the Israelis as evidence that Israel could be defeated by Arab forces. The Israelis pointed to the significant gains they had made at the time of the cease-fire—several hundred square miles of newly acquired territory—as evidence that, should the fighting have continued, the Arabs would likely again have faced a crushing defeat.[3]

Two significant outcomes followed the 1973 Yom Kippur War. Saudi Arabia imposed an oil embargo on the United States and other Israel allies, creating a worldwide oil shortage and plunging the economies of Europe and the United States into an economic recession that contributed to the era's stagflation. Second, in the years that followed, Egyptian leader Anwar Sadat turned to diplomacy to achieve an economically desirable peace with Israel. Egypt desperately needed to open the Suez Canal and reduce military spending. Therefore, the importance of stabilizing relations with Israel in order to achieve economic growth grew paramount. Henry Kissinger, Nixon's secretary of state, embarked upon an intense effort to work for a diplomatic solution to the Israeli-Egyptian standoff. In what became known as "shuttle diplomacy," Kissinger flew back and forth to the Middle East, visiting Egypt and Israel in an effort to achieve concrete diplomatic resolutions. The results of Kissinger's shuttle diplomacy—Sinai I (1974) and II (1975)—reduced armaments and troop buildups along the Egyptian-Israeli border, brought in peacekeeping forces, and reopened the Suez Canal. Yet peace and official Egyptian recognition remained elusive goals. President Jimmy Carter finally brought both sides to the negotiating table in 1978.

Protestants React

Mainline Protestants, while spending a great deal of effort on their theological reevaluations of traditional Christian teachings about Judaism, nonetheless found themselves unable to address, in any unified way, the realities of continued warfare in the Middle East. The annual meeting of the National Council of Churches, held during the Yom Kippur War, approved a motion to establish a new program of Jewish-Christian relations but, after much debate, found itself unable to pass a resolution on the war itself. It issued a statement deploring "the current fighting" and "called for the U.S. and the U.S.S.R. to stop sending arms to the area and urged that peace be sought through the United Nations." Members of the American Jewish Committee, in attendance as observers for the conference, issued a statement criticizing the "inability of the NCC governing board to morally condemn Egypt and Syria." The AJC promised that in the future it would work only "with those responsible Christian bodies and leaders who understand that Israel is now engaged in a struggle for her survival."[4]

The *Christian Century* addressed the war with the publication of a point-counterpoint series of articles by a theologian critical of Israel and a response by one of its supporters. Robert E. Cushman, of the Duke Divinity School, offered a strong critique of Israel, asking his readers: "With what wisdom and what right in the order of international justice have we persistently supported the Jewish State of Israel" in defiance of U.N. resolutions, and added "are we to pay the price [of supporting Israel] alone and in contravention of 'decent respect to the opinion of mankind?'" America's pro-Israel policy had been a mistake from its inception; nonetheless Americans should avoid "inertia" in addressing the problems of Israel and the Middle East. Zionism should be rejected as "messianic Judaism gone secular at the expense of Arabic Islam." Democratic action to end American support of Israel would languish so long as political leaders remained overshadowed by the "American Zionism's powerful lobby in Washington."[5]

Franklin Littell offered his own assessment of the Yom Kippur War in response to Cushman. Littell pointed to the disconnection between the response of liberal Protestant leadership and laity to the war. He contrasted the comment by "another Protestant board secretary that 'Israel might have to die for the peace of the world'" with "the response of pastors and laymen in congregations across the country—[which] judging from long-distance calls and letters—has been a good deal more spontaneous and less calculated."[6] Unlike the response of Christians to the outbreak of the Six-Day War, Littell argued that "many Christians have this time risen up to express their identification with Israel's right to live." Liberal Protestant leaders, in their response to Israel and the war, hardly represented the convictions of the laity, he insisted.

Christian Century editor James Wall traveled to Jerusalem in the wake of the Yom Kippur War in an effort to get a sense of Arab and Israeli attitudes and future expectations. Neither the intense need for security, expressed by war-ravaged Israelis, nor the adamant calls for independence conveyed to Wall by Arabs in Christian Bethlehem surprised the editor, although both made an impression. Yet, as Wall explained in his article, he was surprised by the reaction of retired former American rabbi (now Israeli citizen) Israel Goldstein to the perceived antisemitism of American Protestants. "I was not prepared for Dr. Goldstein's strong insistence that antisemitism is behind much of the reluctance of Christians to rally to Israel's support," he noted. "Showing me a well-marked *Christian Century* editorial, he said: 'In all frankness, when I look at a document like this, I say to myself, 'They try to be fair and yet they are unfair.' How come? Is it because they haven't reconciled themselves to the theological hang-up of the destiny of the Jews as a result of the alleged part the Jews had in the death of Jesus?'"[7]

Wall noted that, in considering Israel's history, "had it not been for the Holocaust, the spirit of Zionism might have died with the rising tide of anti-colonialism, and the new State of Israel might never have come into existence."[8] Reflecting upon this history, Wall concluded by noting that while Palestinian Arabs—Christian and Muslim—deserved American Protestant support, so did Israel. "The Jewish State of Israel, with its ambiguous identity as a nation and a religious entity, looks to American Christians for support. Somehow," Wall argued, "we must find a way to provide that support."[9]

Christians Concerned for Israel unreservedly offered Israel its support in its assessment of the Yom Kippur War. An editorial in the organization's *Notebook* declared: "One thing is sure, for believing Christians the survival of Israel is a religious as well as a political issue." The editorial concluded, "Today with the image of the Holocaust and the lessons of the Church Struggle before us, we are completely without excuse if we remain silent and inactive."[10] Ursula Niebuhr confided to Littell that she had "such an uneasy conscience about the whole matter" and was particularly disturbed by Teddy Kolleck's frustration with the international community's continued demand, stronger in the wake of the 1973 Yom Kippur War, for the Israelis to relinquish control of Jerusalem to an international committee. "Do you think there is anything that some of us should do, as Christian Scholars?" Niebuhr wrote to the Littells. "I think those of us who are obviously Christian and obviously well-acquainted with Jerusalem, should perhaps speak of what we know."[11]

In late 1975 the United States was presented with another challenge to its alliance with Israel, this time in the United Nations. After a conference in Mexico and following an October speech by Ugandan dictator General Idi Amin calling for Israel's "extinction," the U.N., on 10 November, passed U.N. Resolution 3379 declaring that "Zionism is a form of racism and racial discrimination." The United States and Western Europe debated the appropriate response after having lost a furious battle to defeat the resolution against the Arab and Soviet bloc nations. Prior to the vote and in response to Amin's speech, U.N. Ambassador Daniel Patrick Moynihan, instead of, as the *New York Times* had suggested, "looking the other way, implicitly acknowledging that Amin was a fat African lunatic," confronted him in the media and described Amin as a "racist murderer."[12]

In a draft of his official U.N. speech, Moynihan angrily pointed out that to allow this resolution to pass "meant that lunatics were taking over the asylum." In a later, slightly toned-down official version of the speech Moynihan proclaimed: "The United States rises to declare before the General Assembly of the United Nations and before the world, that it does not acknowledge, and it will not abide by, it will never acquiesce in this infamous act." Furthermore, he added, "whatever else Zionism may be, it is not and cannot be, 'a form of racism.' In logic," he continued, "the State of Israel could be, or could become, many things, theoretically including many things undesirable, but it could not be and could not become racist unless it ceased to be Zionist."[13]

The American public response, overwhelmingly negative to Resolution 3379, elevated Moynihan to hero status. "It was a great day for the Irish!" declared the *New York Times*. Although many in the State Department worried that Moynihan's firm rejection and condemnation had made the issue greater than it might have been, American "civil society" backed both Moynihan and Israel. More than fifty major U.S. newspapers and a large number of civil rights leaders endorsed Moynihan's response and affirmed their support for Israel.[14] American Protestants rejected the equation of Zionism to racism and criticized the U.N. for allowing such a resolution to pass. Many worried that the relevance of the U.N. to the modern world and its ability to resolve international disputes had been thrown into question. Liberal Protestants urged Americans not to entirely abandon the U.N., even as they acknowledged the mistake of Resolution 3379. One example of such a response came from the Presbytery of Genesee Valley Synod which issued a statement on 13 November 1975 describing the resolution as "A Violent and Harmful Action." The moderator of the Presbytery of Genesee, in a statement sent to members of the New York Synod explained to congregates that the resolution "puts Zionism in the same category as apartheid and other forms of racism." The Council expressed concern over three issues: the effect of such a resolution on "our Jewish neighbors"; the need for awareness "of the antisemitism this resolution sanctions"; and the need for continued unwavering support for the United Nations, despite its "violent and harmful action." Moderator C. Fredrick Yoos concluded the statement by urging congregants to "share these concerns with your people; and that they consider writing our congressional leaders of this concern."[15] Yoos also sent copies of the statement to the House of Representatives and the Senate, and to the Jewish Community Federation.

The Election of Carter

The election of Georgia's governor Jimmy Carter as president of the United States surprised politicos who had hardly heard of Carter before his announcement in 1975. Raised in rural southern Georgia as a Southern Baptist, his explosion onto the political scene resulted in a reevaluation of religion and politics, and a renewed interest in evangelicalism—a movement in Protestantism that had grown in numbers during the past few decades. The year Carter assumed the presidency, *Newsweek* magazine dubbed 1976 "The

Year of the Evangelical." Carter's wholesome goodness contrasted with the corruption following Nixon's Watergate scandal and Gerald Ford's unpopular pardon of the former president. Carter's frankness about his faith fascinated Americans who were desperate to restore decency to the office of the White House. Carter's most successful achievement, brokering the Egyptian-Israeli Camp David Accords, found its origins in his religious evangelical faith.

Carter had grown up attending Sunday School classes that studied the Old Testament and the geography of the Holy Land. As one historian noted, "as a child he had studied maps of the Holy Land and identified the sites of Bible stories. By the time he was three years old, he had a greater knowledge about Palestine than he did about the rest of America." In his autobiography, *The Blood of Abraham*, Carter stated that he "considered this homeland for the Jews to be compatible with the teachings of the Bible, hence ordained by God."[16] Carter's religious frankness and sympathy for Israel appealed to both evangelicals and American Jews, both of whom enthusiastically endorsed his first presidential bid. In a meeting with the New York Board of Rabbis on 31 August 1976 Carter reiterated his commitment to Israel's security. Israel's security, he insisted, "is a matter of great importance to our country and I think is a major reason that wherever I go in our nation during the campaign months, I find an almost unanimous commitment to . . . the nation of Israel." He emphasized the near universality of the commitment among Americans: "This is a feeling among all our people, regardless of religious or other backgrounds that's almost unanimous and . . . I've never had a dissenting voice raised and I feel I ought to be a cause for assurance."[17] He added that in visits with Israeli officials they emphasized the special relationship between Israel and the United States. Carter reiterated the importance of that alliance and noted, "That friendship must be firm and must never be in doubt." Yet he also pointed to the importance of the U.N. Resolution 242, which called for the withdrawal of Israel from some of the territories acquired during the Six-Day War. While noting the importance of secure borders and Arab recognition of Israel's right to exist, Carter added that true peace in the region would come only through working with Resolution 242 as a framework for negotiations.[18]

In addition to evangelical support for his presidency, Carter also received the endorsement of the Jewish community in the United States. American Jews, historically Democrats, applauded Carter's commitment to social activism as well as his avowed support for the strengthening of the U.S.–Israeli alliance. Members of the Atlanta Jewish community, from Carter's home state of Georgia, issued a press release on 25 May 1976 endorsing him. The sole reason for the endorsement stemmed from his support of Israel. "We have personally known him to be a long-time friend and unwavering supporter of the State of Israel," the signers noted. They added that Carter's support for Israeli control of the Golan Heights and East Jerusalem, his refusal to recognize the Palestinian Liberation Organization, and his insistence on face-to-face negotiations between Israel and her neighbors proved his commitment to Israel and therefore warranted the endorsement.[19]

Later in Carter's campaign his platform for U.S.–Middle East foreign policy received the endorsement of members of Congress and the Jewish community. In a press release dated 20 September 1976 Congressman William Lehman from the Florida's 13th District outlined the platform and offered his endorsement. The "six steps for a Middle East peace" included Arab recognition of Israel, the establishment of diplomatic relations based on peace treaties, open frontiers, cessation of embargo and "hostile propaganda," and public declarations by Arab leaders of their recognition of Israel.[20]

The press noted Carter's biblical support for Israel's existence in a variety of articles. In one *New York Times* article journalist Eli Evans interviewed southern Jews about Carter. One "Atlanta doctor" noted: "We Jews are paranoid and for good reason. Given petro-dollars, we can't trust anyone." But, he added, "Carter's support for Israel is biblical. It's deep. He doesn't have to be convinced there ought to be a Jewish state. He knows that in his heart."[21] Evans pointed out Carter's public declaration in March 1976—"I think God wants the Jews to have a place to live"—as evidence of "that tradition." Evans also pointed out that southerners' support for Israel had remained consistent for the past twenty-eight years, with "virtually every Southern Senator and Congressman" voting for favorable policies toward Israel. This stemmed, Evans explained, not just from "fundamentalist prophecy" but also from southern admiration of Israeli military prowess. "Time and events have translated it into Southern myth," Evans wrote, "the appeal of the underdog, the respect for toughness and scrappiness, the admiration for military daring and bravery in the face of overwhelming odds." Such ideas had, Evans insisted, changed southern stereotypes of Jews. He offered, as evidence, a comment made to him by "a filling station attendant in south Georgia" who told him, "I always thought the Jews were yellow, but them Israelites, they're tough."[22]

The Egyptian-Israeli Peace Accords

Carter's honeymoon with American Jews and evangelicals did not last long. Polls taken in late 1977 revealed increasing displeasure among American Jews over Carter's Middle East policy.[23] Carter's public criticism of Israeli settlements on disputed land acquired during the 1967 War—"an obstacle to peace"—angered Israelis, American Jews, and American evangelicals. Carter insisted that adherence to U.N. Resolution 242 necessitated an Israeli willingness to barter land for peace with its Arab neighbors. Moreover, in an effort to avoid alienating the Arab nations, Carter offered to sell military jet planes to Saudi Arabia—a move that angered constituents in both Jewish and evangelical communities.

In particular, Carter's National Security Advisor, Zbigniew Brzezinski, received a significant amount of hostility from American Jews for his advice to Carter to remain a neutral broker in Middle East disputes. Brzezinski countered the criticism by insisting that Israeli willingness to return land, avoid building settlements in the West Bank and Gaza, and American willingness to sell arms to Arab countries remained in the best interest of both the United States and Israel. In an interview with the *New York Times*, Brzezinski pointed out that "the key question is whether the Arab countries will be moderate and friendly to the United States and accommodating to Israel or whether they will be radical, unfriendly to the United States, allied with the Soviet Union, and hostile to Israel." Arab alliance with the Soviet Union and hostility to Israel meant that "the Western system will suffer and ultimately Israel will perish."[24]

Early in his presidency Carter turned his attention to working for Egyptian and Israeli peace. In attempting to create such a peace, Carter focused on the relations between Israel and her largest enemy, Egypt. In Israel the 1977 Knesset elections brought the right-wing Likud Party into power with Menachem Begin as its leader. The Likud Party, deeply resistant to bartering any land in exchange for peace with its Arab neighbors, resented Carter's belief in the importance of the establishment of a Palestinian state and trod carefully in its negotiations with the United States on this point. During a White House reception for newly elected Begin, Carter reiterated his support for Israel and tied his own support of Israel to the horrors of the Holocaust and a biblical mandate to return to Palestine: "Out of the ashes of the Holocaust was born the State of Israel, a promise of refuge and security, and of return at last to the Biblical land from which the Jews were driven so many hundreds of years ago." While Carter emphasized America's "unshakable commitment to Israeli security," he nonetheless added that "we remain deeply committed to a just and lasting peace with its neighbors."[25]

Despite Begin's hard-line approach to territories acquired in the 1967 War, Begin and Egypt's President Anwar Sadat began the tentative steps in establishing diplomatic relations. Sadat embarked upon such tender negotiations with the goal of reducing Egypt's enormous military budget by opening the

Suez Canal for trade and thereby increasing revenue for his country while ridding it of the Palestine Liberation Organization ("a cancer in our midst"). In a surprising move, Sadat traveled to Israel to speak before the Knesset. He offered peace and recognition in exchange for the return of land acquired in the 1967 War and the recognition of a separate Palestinian state. Begin remained unmoved, however, and a deadlock descended on the negotiations. Carter offered to break the deadlock by inviting both leaders to Camp David, the presidential retreat in Maryland, to work on the terms of peace.

The meeting lasted fourteen days, during which the explosive personalities of each side, as well as the explosive nature of the issues, pushed Carter, Secretary of State Cyrus Vance, and National Security Advisor Zbigniew Brzezinski to the limits of their diplomatic skills. Although the fate of the Palestinians remained unresolved, despite the affirmation of U.N. Resolution 242 by both parties, Egypt and Israel agreed on terms of peace on 17 September 1978. Seven months later, the official peace treaty outlining the return of the Sinai to Egypt, access to Sinai oil for Israelis, the establishment of a U.N. observer to oversee the three-year pullout plan, and, most important, Egypt's recognition of Israel received the endorsement of both Sadat and Begin—both of whom won the Nobel Peace Prize for their actions. The move astonished and angered much of the Arab world (Sadat was assassinated on 6 October 1981) but was cheered by the West and Israel as a move to eventually establish normalized relations throughout the Middle East.

In an editorial appearing after the first negotiations in September the *Christian Century* praised the important steps taken by Egypt and Israel to establish peace. The Accords offered the first real opportunity to "break this vicious cycle" of war with Israel and her neighbors. Although the Palestinians' fate remained an important unresolved part of the negotiations, the article explained, important steps had been taken to work toward a Palestinian state. "Over the next five years, the Palestinians will have an opportunity not only to govern themselves in a limited fashion, but also to display their willingness to live in peace with Israel." The article praised Israeli moves toward Palestinian self-rule and concluded that "responsibility for peace has now shifted to the Palestinians."[26] Another issue praised Carter's use of "heart religion" to negotiate peace in a hard-politic realm—foreign policy. Editor James Wall noted that "Carter brought something to Camp David which worked. And since there are no political textbooks that explain it, the answer must lie in another realm. 'Heart-oriented' religion may itself have experienced something of a rebirth in public perception."[27]

Christianity and Crisis also praised Carter's achievements in the Camp David Accords. In an open letter to Carter, John Linder and Robert Hoyt noted that "almost from the beginning you have been subjected to the harsh criticism that your policy entailed a weakening of the U.S.'s commitment to Israel's survival and security." Now, however, the authors pointed out, "this criticism is slackening." Carter's perseverance "kept the process alive," with the result that "Israel today has reason to feel more secure than at any time since October 1973, if not since 1948." Yet the authors cautioned Carter to clarify his intentions for U.S.–Middle East foreign policy, particularly regarding "the kind of future open to the Palestinians and the unique character of human rights problems peculiar to the Middle East." Despite the domestic problems Carter might face in his reelection campaign, Linder and Hoyt insisted that enforcing clear and humane policies in these areas would be the only way to create true peace in the region. "After Camp David," the authors concluded, "it was possible to accept at face value what you had been quoted as saying at the outset: 'Peace is more important than my reelection.'"[28] These journals' response to Carter's concern for the Palestinian problem reflected their long-standing objection to Israel's lack of initiative in dealing with the refugee crisis and the question of Palestinian statehood, and their endorsement of Carter's priorities.

Theological Adjustments

Increasing interactions between liberal American Protestants and Israelis changed the nature of the Jewish-Christian dialogue and U.S.–Israeli relations in the late 1970s. Prominent American Protestants visited Israel, and many spent time at the Tantur Ecumenical Institute in Jerusalem for intensive theological study courses. Franklin Littell, Ursula Niebuhr, Roy and Alice Eckardt, and Martin Marty, among many others, visited Tantur and wrote about the impact of traveling to Israel on their own perceptions of both Israel and Protestant theology. In an article for the *Christian Century*, Marty detailed a recent trip to Tantur and noted his participation in a seminar led by Franklin Sherman on "Jewish-Christian Relations." After his stay at Tantur, Marty declared that "while a dove; I am fanatically pro-Israel, which means that I am 50.01 per cent pro and 49.99 percent critical."[29] Albert R. Ahlstrom, a Lutheran Pastor at Columbia University in New York, also visited Israel while staying as a Scholar-in-Residence at Tantur in the summer of 1978. He detailed his impressions and experiences in an eighteen-page report submitted to the Lutheran World Federation, Department of Studies of the American Lutheran Church.

In his report Ahlstrom dealt with two primary issues: the political scene and its theological implications. In his discussion of the politics of the region, Ahlstrom commented on the serious presence of the United States in the Middle East. In Israel and the occupied territories, Arabs and Israelis view "the U.S.A. as the most powerful presence in the areas: and that presence is often seen as consumptive and decadent."[30] For the United States to help broker peace, a "piece-by-piece approach" must be taken, he urged. "We are seeing this now as we await the renewal of the Camp David Agreements. In this sense," he added, "I return to the Niebuhrean sources:

> Real peace can only be a system of interdependent political interests poised upon [a] delicate arrangement of flexible alliances which will assure security for Israel and a nation state for the Palestinian Arabs. This is hardly based upon "historical rights" or "biblical claims." These will be political and always temporary solutions.[31]

Along with political action, American Protestants must take the theological implications of the State of Israel and Zionism seriously within their own theology, Ahlstrom insisted. "Christian theologians find it very difficult to deal with the Return as portrayed in Zionist hope," he noted. Yet Christians must find a way to confront it since "the Return" remained "integral to Jewish self-identity."[32] Christians tended to distinguish between Zionism and Judaism, and, as a result, Christians "spiritualized the latter so that it is in our day barely recognizable." In confronting the implications of Israel and Judaism to Christian theology, Christians must address two issues—"Who is Israel?" and "The Church's Task" in Israel. In considering the first, Ahlstrom described the three main views of Christians in defining "Israel": supercessionism that "shunted Judaism into irrelevance if not damnation," the belief that Israel and Christianity hold "parallel covenants" with God, and the third, held by evangelicals, that "Israel is in storage awaiting the Second Coming and eventual conversion."[33] For Christians, defining "Israel" remained a necessary step not only for greater Christian theology but also as imperative to undertaking religious dialogue with Jews in Israel who consider the question of Israeli identity "very much alive within Judaism."

For Ahlstrom, theology and geopolitics seemed inseparable. In order to undertake the task of theological reevaluation and to promote greater Jewish-Christian dialogue, American Christians must do three things, Ahlstrom insisted. They must serve as greater advocates for Arab Christians in the area; they must find ways to "increase [our] presence as *inquirers* among

Israeli Jewish citizens and scholars"; and, perhaps most important, Ahlstrom concluded, "we need to be able to counter any antisemitism that is couched in terms of anti-Zionism."[34]

The effort to define and understand Israel, Ahlstrom argued, is important not only for liberal Protestant self-understanding but is also imperative for countering the "strong appeal of Christian fundamentalism" which offered "a very narrow and ultimately destructive view of the Palestinian issues." Mainstream American Protestants "need to hear voices that offer clear alternatives" to the evangelical worldview that sees "in a restored Israel a signal for the messianic time and the requisite conversion of Jews before the Second Coming." Ahlstrom noted with alarm that "some Israeli forces find these Christian voices momentarily and politically helpful."[35] With such an observation, Ahlstrom clearly rejected evangelicals' attempts to convert Jews for their own eschatological reasons and considered the idea that the establishment of Israel marked an important fulfillment of biblical prophecy prohibitive to establishing a just peace that considered both Palestinian and Israeli issues.

The *Christian Century*, too, recognized the importance of Israel's survival for Jewish identity and Jewish-Christian relations. Yet editor James M. Wall pointed to the difficulties of this identity for U.S. foreign policy and American ecumenism. Wall noted that American Christendom had recently embraced significant theological changes: Niebuhr's call to cease evangelizing the Jews and the Vatican II decision, under the inspiration of an American priest John Courtney Murray, to abandon the Catholic claim to be the "one true church." Jews, too, had embraced theological changes; in embracing the "process of acculturation" they had abandoned their "chosenness" for a special relationship with Israel.[36]

The final years of the 1970s witnessed a dramatic surge of conferences, articles, and organizations established to promote improved Jewish-Christian relations and reformation of liberal Protestant theologies in response to historical Christian antisemitism and the Holocaust. In 1974 Ursula Niebuhr noted this development in a letter to Jerusalem Mayor Teddy Kolleck. Commenting on a recent symposium, "After Auschwitz," held at the Cathedral of St. John the Divine in New York City (and covered by the *New York Times*), Niebuhr noted, "I think it shows that a few people in the Christian churches are becoming more sensitive not only to contemporary events but the past history."[37] Other organizations, dedicated to encouraging improved relations between Christians and Israelis, sponsored their own meetings and conferences. One such organization, the Jerusalem Conference of Christians and

Israelis, held its second annual meeting in Jerusalem in 1977. Its sponsors represented a wide variety of American Christian denominations, American Jews, as well as notable Israelis.

In addition, a fourteen-member delegation from the American religious communities participated in the annual conference of the International Council of Christians and Jews in Jerusalem in August 1976. American Christian Palestine Committee veteran Carl Hermann Voss headed the delegation and, upon his arrival, enjoyed a personal greeting from Israeli President Ephraim Katzir.[38] Likewise, the first meeting of the International Congress for the Peace of Jerusalem, held in Jerusalem from 31 January through 2 February 1978, boasted significant American religious figures as well, including those from the evangelical and fundamentalist persuasions, and featured Prime Minister Menachem Begin as the keynote speaker.[39]

Domestically the theological shift was apparent in the amount of attention Jewish-Christian relations and Israel received in the pages of theological journals and texts. Indeed, between 1973 and 1979, more than seventy articles appeared in the major theological journals and more than a dozen books were published that addressed the Holocaust, Jewish-Christian relations, the theological significance of Israel, and the need for the reevaluation of Protestant relations toward Jews and Judaism. What had begun as a trickle in the 1950s had now become a theological flood. Receiving intense scrutiny were issues such as the Jewishness of Jesus, the religious and political importance of land to Jews, the role of Christians in coming to terms with the Jewish understanding of land, the continuing debate over the biblical claim to Palestine, the question of missions to Jews, and the role of Christian antisemitism in the perpetuation of the Holocaust.[40]

Evangelical scholarly journals also addressed these topics. Unlike their liberal brethren, however, evangelicals had never abandoned the idea of the continuing significance of the Jewish people in Christian eschatology, and the land of Israel remained central to their understanding of God's covenant with the Jews. Charles M. Horne, professor of theology at Wheaton College Graduate School, in an article in the *Journal of the Evangelical Theological Society,* insisted that God had not rejected his people, that living Jews remained essentially bound to a continuing covenant with God. While Horne rejected the idea that the Jews would be saved in their entirety (such a view would be at odds with evangelical orthodox theology that emphasizes the centrality of Christ to salvation), he noted that "eschatological implications" of the salvation of "a remnant [of Jews] according to the election of grace" deserved careful consideration among evangelicals.[41]

Marvin Wilson, professor of biblical studies at Gordon College also denounced liberal Christians who preached that the Church superseded the old covenant between God and the Jews. The people of Israel and their land remained central in evangelical theology. Wilson did not insist that missions should be abandoned but emphasized instead that the land of Israel and Zionism should be appreciated as evidence of both God's existence and his continuing bond with the Jews. Despite the U.N.'s condemnation of Zionism as equivalent to racism, Jews should not relinquish their notion of "chosenness." "From this writer's perspective," Wilson noted, "it is a serious error for today's Jew to alter or renounce the Biblical concept of chosenness in order to avoid the charge of triumphalism. . . . If the Jew has a Biblical destiny to fulfill—and it is my conviction that he does," Wilson added, "then that destiny is inescapably tied to the concept of election."[42] Central to the concept of chosenness, Wilson argued, the land of Israel remains integral to the relationship between the Jews and God. Paul's argument in Romans 9:11, Wilson argued, makes clear that "the destiny of the Jew and Gentile is so interlaced that the latter does not find God except through the former." While Wilson noted that he remained unsure if "Israel's return to the land is clearly a fulfillment of biblical prophecy" (a reference to Israel's return in "unbelief"—a stumbling block for premillennialists)—he insisted that "the modern Zionist state of Israel could be a fulfillment of prophecy and is most surely a remarkable sign of God's continuing love, preservation and purpose for his people."[43] Christians must come to terms with the theological importance of the modern Israeli state and for its continuing relationship with the Jews.

The preservation of the Jews as the chosen people who returned to the modern State of Israel remained central to evangelical theology, even as its emphasis reflected a shift in evangelical-Jewish relations. Although some evangelicals, such as Wilson, remained unsure that Scripture had literally been fulfilled in Israel's establishment, they were clearly unwilling to dismiss its significance and encouraged Christians to recognize the importance of Jews and Judaism to Christianity.

The Rise of Evangelical Political Power

Beginning in the late 1950s the mainline Protestant churches began steadily losing congregants to evangelical and fundamentalist denominations.[44] This statistical shift resulted in an erosion of the cultural dominance of mainline Protestantism in American society and left evangelicals poised to organize into a formidable political force by the 1980s. Historians and social scientists disagree over the causes of the mainline defections. Some argue that the cultural permissiveness of the 1960s alienated many American Protestants who grew increasingly unhappy with their churches' perceived willingness to accommodate modernity by abandoning biblical literalism, embracing evolution and German higher criticism while simultaneously working to remain culturally relevant. For many Americans, the orthodox theology that required sacrifice and strictness of its members appealed to Protestants put off by the shrinking doctrinal differences between the mainstream denominations and American culture at large. Other scholars, though not disputing the decline in mainline memberships, nonetheless argue that such trends reflected not so much a reaction to contemporary events of the 1960s and 1970s but rather longer populist impulses visible in American culture since the Revolutionary War.[45]

Whatever the reason for mainline decline, the rise in membership numbers for evangelical and fundamentalist Protestants augured important implications for U.S.–Israeli relations. The tendency among these Protestants to regard the establishment of Israel as the fulfillment of biblical prophecy and to support Israeli land acquisition in wars with its neighbors since 1948 meant that a majority of American Protestants now viewed Israel as an important ally, not simply for strategic purposes but for religious purposes as well. Americans must support Israel not simply because Israel held important prophetic implications but also because, according to these Protestants, nations would be judged according to their behavior toward the Jewish state.

From a foreign policy perspective, this meant that evangelicals must work to develop close U.S.–Israeli ties and ensure that politicians honored this alliance. It also meant that nations that opposed or criticized Israel worked counter to God's purposes and should be opposed. Arab nations particularly encountered evangelical opprobrium in this regard. Unlike liberal Protestants who considered the plight of Arab refugees and the importance of Middle East peace paramount in considering U.S.–Israeli relations, evangelicals dismissed Arabs, and Palestinians in particular, as working counter to God's purposes and as historical enemies of Israel who would never be reconciled. These Protestants ridiculed attempts by politicians and the U.N. to barter land for peace as useless at best and dangerous at worst. This stance held important implications for Protestant-Jewish relations in the United States as well.

Although evangelicals and fundamentalists had eschewed theological reevaluations that liberal Protestants had begun in the previous decade, they nonetheless altered their approach to Jews at home and abroad. Conversion, while still remaining of utmost importance, took a public relations back seat to general expressions of goodwill toward the Jews and Israel. Evangelicals and fundamentalists had historically rejected the liberal Protestant ideas of supercessionism and the tendency to consider the theological significance of Israel's establishment as unimportant or nonexistent. Evangelicals pointed to the continuing significance of both Jews and Israel in understanding eschatology and highlighted this significance in their relations with both the State of Israel and the Jews.

By the beginning of the 1970s the evangelicals studying world events through their eschatological lens found much to be excited about. As Timothy Weber noted, in *On the Road to Armageddon*, by 1970 "dispensationalists were full of confidence. Despite great difficulties, the nation of Israel has been established and had expanded its borders in the Middle East. Antipathy and hatred for Israel was unquenchable among Muslim nations and the Communist Bloc. The threat of nuclear war was increasing." World events appeared to be falling into perfect place for the beginning of the end of days. Social upheavals during the 1960s added to international instability and created a perfect storm for dispensationalists to sweep through American society and culture. Indeed, as Weber explained, "Bible teachers were about to enter the glory days of their movement, in which they reached more people and developed more markets than ever before."[46]

One example of the increasing influence of premillennialism in American culture was Hal Lindsey and Carole C. Carlson's best-selling book, *The Late Great Planet Earth* (1970). It offered a more accessible apocalyptic tale than did William Hull's earlier work by describing the end of days in terrifyingly modern terms. In the book the authors outlined the biblical prophecies detailed in the Book of Daniel and the Book of Revelation and offered a contemporary assessment of world events in relation to these ancient prophecies. In posing the question, "Where is mankind headed?" Lindsey and Carlson suggested the grave fate that awaited nonbelievers and those nations hostile to Israel. As a traveling lecturer for the evangelical group, Campus Crusade for Christ, Lindsey used his skills as a public speaker, his comfort with contemporary jargon, and accessible language to explain biblical eschatology in a way that appealed to a wide variety of Americans troubled by world events. As noted in the introduction to the book, "this is not a complex theological treatise, but a direct account of the most thrilling, optimistic view of what the future could hold for any individual."[47] The nation of Israel figured prominently in Lindsey and Carlson's explanation of world events and prophecy. How the nations of the world treated Israel would serve as a litmus test for righteousness and judgment by God. The seven years of tribulation that preceded the return of Christ to earth would occur "sometime in the near future," the authors explained, but could not begin "until the Jewish people reestablished their nation in their ancient homeland of Palestine."[48]

The *Late Great Planet Earth* attacked Christian "scoffers" who "denied the possibility of accepting the prophecies concerning the restoration of Israel as a nation in Palestine." Theologians of the "liberal school" still insisted that prophecy had no literal meaning for today and that it could not be taken seriously. It is difficult to understand this view," the authors argued, "if one carefully weighs the case of Israel's rebirth as a nation."[49] The Jewish people's survival as a nation who still remained faithful to God testified to the accuracy of prophetic scripture and should serve to bolster prophetic teachings of Daniel and Revelation, Lindsey and Carlson insisted. Specifically, two of the three most important prophetic events had been fulfilled in the last few decades, they pointed out. "First the Jewish nation would be reborn in the land of Palestine. Secondly, the Jews would repossess old Jerusalem and the sacred sites." Until the third day of fighting during the 1967 War, the authors had remained puzzled as to its prophetic significance. But after the third day of fighting "when Moshe Dayan, the ingenious Israeli general marched to the wailing wall, the last remnant of the Old Temple, and said, 'We have returned to our holiest of places, never to leave her again,'" the prophetic puzzle pieces fell into place. The third most prophetic event, the authors concluded, would be the rebuilding of the third temple on Mount Moriah—the only place it could be rebuilt in fulfillment of prophecy.[50]

The *Late Great Planet Earth* became a national best-seller in 1970 and eventually sold thirty-five million copies. Weber argues that the success of the book reflected the authors' ability to point to specific events in 1948 and 1967 that allowed them to "make connections between the Bible's prophecies and current events." For the book's audience, reading the book "was like getting an advance copy of tomorrow's newspaper."[51] American society appeared primed to consider the premillennial dispensationalist explanation of world events.

Not all contemporary events dealing with the State of Israel captured the attention of American evangelicals. Jimmy Carter's Camp David Accords did not fit with fundamentalist eschatology—trading land for peace—and, consequently, was virtually ignored in the pages of the conservative Christian press. The conservative journals appeared less enthusiastic about the peace accords than their liberal counterparts.[52] In the same *Moody Monthly* issue that carried only the briefest mention of the Peace Accords (with an unfavorable assessment of them as "a long step backward" by Bethlehem's mayor Elias Freij) the periodical published an advertisement that filled the first two pages from the Friends of Israel Gospel Ministry, an organization dedicated to evangelizing the Jews.

The first full page was a graphic depicting an orthodox Jew standing in a graveyard surrounded by tombstones of the nations of the world that had persecuted the Jews, including Greece, Babylon, Assyria, Rome, Persia, Egypt, and "Nazi Fascist" Germany. The Jew stands over a freshly dug grave with a question mark on the tombstone above it. The next page asks, "Who's Next?" The obvious implication, in the second page of the advertisement, was that, unless the United States did all it could to assist Israel, its name would soon appear on the gravestone. Beneath the question, "Who's Next?" appeared the verse from Zechariah 2:8 "For he that toucheth you [Israel], toucheth the apple of his eye." The concern expressed in the advertisement was that, since the Yom Kippur War and the growing recognition of the importance of "Middle East oil," support for Israel "has rapidly and universally deteriorated" and given rise instead to growing antisemitism. Though the United States remained loyal to Israel, would such support continue? wondered author Marvin Rosenthal, international director of the Friends of Israel Gospel Ministries. Antisemitism constituted a direct effort by Satan to eliminate the necessary precursor for Christ's return, the advertisement explained. The return of Christ and defeat of Satan in the battle of Armageddon required Israel's existence. "Therefore," Rosenthal pointed out, "those in opposition to Israel stand, in the larger sense, in opposition to God himself."[53]

As long as America's foreign policy and Israel's welfare coincided, support for Israel appeared stable. Now, however, new opposition from Arab states threatened this connection and, by extension, America's ultimate welfare. America, Rosenthal warned, "will feel the angry wrath of God in judgment" should she abandon her ally. Christians had a particular responsibility to support Israel as an act of atonement for the crimes committed in the name of Christianity.[54]

The Friends of Israel's advertisement in *Moody Monthly* signaled the changing emphasis among evangelicals toward their relations with Jews and Israel. Although these Protestants continued their missionizing efforts toward Jews, their emphasis, particularly regarding their contact with Jews, was evangelical support for Israel above all else. With missionary attempts subsumed under the banner of Israeli support, American Jews, and certainly the Israeli state, cautiously began to welcome their new allies into the pro-Israel fold. Another article in the same issue of *Moody Monthly* provides another example of this shift in emphasis and Israeli reciprocity. In that article, author William F. Willoughby noted a new development between the Israeli government and American evangelicals. "For the first time in Israel's thirty year history," the leaders of Israel's kibbutz movement endorsed a proposed project, "Project Kibbutz," that would allow evangelical Americans to work for a year on one of Israel's kibbutzim.

In August 1978 forty American evangelicals flew to Israel for year-long kibbutz assignments. The director of the program, Charles Farah, professor of theological and historical studies at Oral Roberts University, noted that "for many years Christians who love Israel have faced the problem of finding a concrete means of demonstrating their concern." Project Kibbutz allowed Christians to "make a direct contribution to Israel's prosperity while gaining the benefits of the cultural and religious exchange with modern Israelis."[55] While noting that evangelicals "are among the most enthusiastic supporters of the well-being of Israel," the article did not mention missionizing opportunities or goals in the program.

Not all conservative evangelicals offered their support of Israel and the increasingly close connection between American evangelicals and the Israeli government, however. Most notable of these included the Reverend Bob Jones II, president of Bob Jones University in Greenville, South Carolina. In an article that appeared in his university's newsletter, *Faith for the Family*, Jones lamented the U.S.–Israeli alliance as antithetical to true U.S. interests in the Middle East and insisted that "Israel as it now exists is not the Messianic state from which blessing shall flow out to the whole world during the reign of the Lord Jesus Christ."[56] He claimed that Israel had been reborn in disbelief and remained hostile to evangelical attempts at missions. The willingness of evangelical leaders such as Liberty University founder and president Jerry Falwell to minimize the call to evangelize the Jews in order to develop closer ties to the Israeli government appeared to Jones as the abandonment of orthodox Protestant principles.[57]

Despite the public rejection of Israel by the ultra-conservative Bob Jones, American Jewish organizations in the United States appeared cautiously optimistic about evangelical support for Israel. In 1975 Stanley F. Chyet, director of the American Jewish Archives, approached Elmer A. Josephson, president of Bible Light Ministries, to inquire about the organization and its relationship with the American Jewish community and whether its publications might be useful in the archival collection. Josephson replied to Chyet by informing him that the sole purpose of the organization lay in "bringing about a better understanding between Jews and Christians, informing the latter of the debt we owe the Jews for all the light and knowledge of God there is in the world, counteracting antisemitism and assisting the State of Israel by every available means, believing they are destined to be instrumental in bringing about world redemption."[58] Josephson noted that the "greatest thrust" of the Bible Light Ministries lay in their support of Israel—"selling Israeli bonds, helping to provide blankets, linens, and clothing"—and added that during a recent five-year trip to Israel he had written *Israel, God's Key to World Redemption*, a copy of which he had donated to the head of the Department of Religion at Hebrew University. Josephson concluded his letter by offering to send Chyet a copy of his book and back issues of *Bible Light* for the archive's collection. Josephson's letter refrained from discussing missionary efforts in Israel or in the United States toward Jews and instead focused on efforts to improve Jewish-Christian relations through greater appreciation for Jewish contributions to Christianity and humanity in general and through financial support for Israel.

Jewish organizations recognized the potentially powerful support the evangelical community offered Israel. Meir Kahane of the Jewish Defense League noted that "the most potent weapon that Israel has within the United States are evangelicals who convince others that the United States' true interest is total and unconditional backing for the Jewish State."[59] Evangelical leaders who offered such a viewpoint were celebrated by the American Jewish community. The evangelical leader Billy Graham's receipt of the American Jewish Council's Interreligious Award, conferred by Rabbi Marc Tanenbaum in October 1977, marked another example of the improving relations between evangelicals and American Jews and the willingness to deemphasize evangelical missions. Having been presented the award in recognition of "his contributions to human rights, the support for Israel, combating antisemitism and strengthening mutual respect and understanding between the Evangelical and Jewish communities," Graham emphasized common religious heritage between Jews and Christians and affirmed evangelical support of Israel. In Graham's acceptance speech, he noted that "a vast majority of evangelical Christians in this country and abroad support the State of Israel's right to exist."[60]

On the occasion of Israel's thirtieth birthday, eighty-four notable Christian leaders, including Arnold T. Olsen, president-emeritus of the Evangelical Free Church in America, Pat Robertson, and David Hyatt, president of the National Conference of Christians and Jews, issued a joint statement that crossed theological lines in support of Israel. The statement, issued during the one-day National Christian Leadership Conference for Israel, praised the efforts of Sadat and Begin to achieve peace and reaffirmed Christian support of Israel. The statement recognized Christianity's roots in "the history and life of the people of Israel" and noted the "new ecumenical spirit of the world, the remembrance of the Holocaust, and the present situation in the Middle East" as necessary reasons to support Israel.[61] The statement furthermore condemned terrorist activities and border skirmishes by surrounding Arab nations and supported "Israel's legitimate need for secure and defensible borders." It concluded with a biblical verse that instructed believers to "pray for the peace of Jerusalem, they shall prosper that love thee."[62]

Recognition among Israeli and Egyptian leaders of the growing power and influence of evangelical Protestants in the United States prompted an invitation for several prominent evangelical leaders to visit both countries. In May 1978 evangelical minister Jerry Falwell accompanied four other leading evangelicals to visit Egypt and Israel at the invitation, and expense of, Anwar Sadat and Menachem Begin. Michael Praggai, the Israeli adviser on church matters, told the press that the invitation reflected Israel's interest in "viewing the situation from an evangelical point of view."[63] Egyptian press minister Mohammed Hakki explained that "I'd like them—the American religious leaders—to hear firsthand from President Sadat and other Egyptian officials their point of view." Falwell reported to the media that his purpose in going was to convince Israel and Egypt to "be as open to the preaching of the Gospel as we have opened the United States to religious freedom of all groups." The four men chosen as "conservative leaders" of American evangelicalism, Falwell, John Warwick Montgomery, Billy Zioli (President Ford's former spiritual advisor), and James Tozer, met with the Egyptian president and the Israeli prime minister. Falwell communicated his hope to both leaders that peace could be achieved and carried messages from Sadat to Begin. Yet Falwell hesitated to endorse Carter's efforts: "I personally think the U.S. government should not impose undue pressure on either government," he explained. "Peace must be negotiated by both Israel and Egypt."[64] Yet Falwell's initial appearance of neutrality would be altered with the founding of the Moral Majority that same year. One of the four founding principles of the organization included support of Israel, and in the following years Falwell would go on to develop close relationships with the Likud Party and Prime Minister Menachem Begin in particular.

Even for that small number of conservative evangelicals who remained critical of Israel and Judaism, such as Bob Jones, the political power of the vast and ardent pro-Israel support of evangelicals in the United States remained undeniable. In 1979 a Canadian right-wing religious journal, *The Researcher,* published an article commending Jones for his attack on Falwell. The author noted that attacks on "Scofield Zionism" left critics branded as "the Anti-christ" and that Israeli propaganda had "misled" Christians. Now, the article complained, "every so-called Christian country has two lines of sabotaging fifth columnists, who are constantly working to prevent their countries from refraining from involvement in Israel's guilt and suicidal ventures"—Christians and Jews. In fact, the article claimed that evangelical support of Israel was so great that "should the impossible happen that the United States, Britain or France should decide to help the Arabs to defend their natural rights and boundaries, nearly every evangelical church and assembly would become a seething hotbed of protest and active or passive resistance against their country's war effort."[65] Although Falwell would have certainly rejected Jones's criticism of his abandonment of orthodox evangelical theology, he would most likely have agreed with *The Researcher*'s assessment of the intensity of evangelical support for Israel in the United States. In the decades to come, building that support and organizing it into a powerful political voting bloc would occupy much of Falwell's and the evangelical communities' efforts.

A Solid Alliance

To those liberal Protestants who had worked to increase American Protestant support for Israel since its inception and establishment, the end of the 1970s revealed success in the grass-roots response. By January 1975 Franklin Littell noted that "CCI now has some 7,200 individuals, pastors and leading laymen who receive mailings of the *Notebook* and work for the survival of Israel."[66] In March 1975 the editors of *Christians Concerned for Israel Notebook* reported that the Wisconsin Council of Churches had organized an "Interfaith Coalition and the State of Israel" committee dedicated to organizing grass-roots support for Israel among American Protestants. The organization's platform declared that "as concerned Christians and Jews, it is important that we reaffirm our common heritage and affirm our moral and spiritual support for the people of the state of Israel in modern times." Their founding principles included the recognition of the right of Israel to exist, requiring that we "support the need for secure borders, recognize the problem of the displaced Arab population and urge the resolution of it as soon as possible."[67] Such grass-roots activism had become the norm, according to the editors of the *Notebook*. "In recent months we have heard from a number of cities and states where local committees have been formed to express Christian identity with Israel," they noted. The Wisconsin Council of Churches was one of the most recent examples among many. In an editorial published a few months later, the *Notebook* explained that "once we get beyond the church bureaucracies to the congregations, there is obviously a groundswell of sympathy and understanding for Israel. We receive at CCI dozens of letters weekly from rank and file pastors who want to know what they can do to help Israel, to oppose those who want to destroy her, to wipe out Christian antisemitism and get our teaching about the Jews on the right track."[68]

By November of 1975 Littell reported to subscribers to the *Notebook* that the CCI office now received approximately seventy-five letters a week, mainly from three groups. The majority of letters came from "enthusiastic pastors, laypeople, and some graduate students" who recognized the necessity of "a fundamental repentance and reorientation." Other letters came from "conservative Christians" who, while supporting a close U.S.–Israeli alliance, nonetheless "cannot understand why we are critical of missions to the Jews." The third and the smallest group of letter writers included "chiefly liberal Protestants that cannot discuss questions like 'holy history,' 'covenant,' 'divine election' and other mysteries of the faith." Such liberal Protestants "would prefer to talk about anything but the significance of a continuing, vital Jewish people for Christian theology."[69] Yet grass-roots efforts by American Protestants to effect changes within the hierarchy of American Protestantism showed signs of success when, for example, the U.N.'s resolution equating Zionism with racism resulted in cries of protest in the United States.

The Christian churches' response to Israel received the attention of the secular press as well. For example, in an article appearing in the *National Review*, author Malachi B. Martin argued that "among the changes in the teaching of Christian doctrine that have taken place during the last decade, the most revolutionary concerns the attitude of Christians toward Jews." Recent teachings by both Catholics and Protestants that emphasized the obligation of Christians to "study the Jewish people" and "listen to what the Jews have to say" contained profound implications for the State of Israel, Martin wrote. "According to the new view, Christians, because of their special obligations toward the Jewish people, have a special duty to see that nothing interferes with the continued well-being of Israel," he explained. While many within Christendom remained unsure of how traditional Christian orthodoxy should react to Jews and Israel, Martin concluded that "they will soon have to recognize that this new view is another aspect of the profound changes we see in every sector of our lives today."[70]

As American Protestants cautiously embraced theological changes, they also began to come to terms with the legacy of the Holocaust. The broadcast of the television mini-series "Holocaust" in 1978 marked a significant moment in American religious history. The show reported approximately 120 million viewers and, as Richard M. Harley of the *Christian Science Monitor* noted, offered profound implications for U.S. foreign policy: "Whether it was intended or not, the past plight of the Jews as depicted in the film would inevitably be used to attract support for present Israeli positions." Harley noted the recent trend in American education to incorporate Holocaust studies into mainstream curriculum and pointed out that "700 campuses and high schools are offering Holocaust courses this year." Harley highlighted CCI director Franklin Littell's establishment at Temple University of a Ph.D. program in Holocaust Studies. In the article, Harley pointed out Littell's insistence that "the idea is an admirable one—to make the Holocaust theme an educational tool to heighten concern for the value of human life." Harley noted that the Holocaust had recently become "a rallying point" for Christian and Jewish leaders to express "mutual concern about global violations of human rights" and to fight antisemitism in America. Krister Stendahl, dean of the Harvard Divinity School, noted that such educational opportunities should not devolve into a "mere buildup of guilt" but should remind Americans that "these things did happen in a highly sophisticated and cultured world" and should motivate Christians to "unmask similar things today."[71]

The significant changes in American Protestant attitudes toward Jews, Judaism, and Israel since 1933 captured the attention of the notable mainline Protestant religious historian Martin Marty in a 1978 article written for the *Christian Century*. In the article Marty addressed the theological reevaluations of Christendom in light of the Holocaust and the Camp David Accords. Motivated in part by the "new friendliness between Jews and those conservative Protestants who see Israel as part of a premillennial vision," Marty attempted to evaluate Protestant attitudes in response to two hypothetical questions posed by Jews: "Are you sympathetic with our situation?" and "Can we count on you for support of Israel—no matter what?"[72] Like Yoos, Marty insisted that "Israel plays an unimaginably large part" in the question of Jewish survival and "has therefore become *the* focus of conflict and concords between Jews and Christians." Marty identified eleven "rungs" on the "ladder" of Christian sympathy for Israel—from pacifists who could not be counted on to support Israel for principled reasons to premillennialists whose "reliance level is so high that it now tends to cancel out Jewish interest in other Christians." In between the two extremes, Marty noted those who supported Israel out of "practical concern," Niebuhrian "mutual self-interest" and "moral commitment." Other Christians supported Israel out of a sense, with varying levels of literal interpretation, that Israel's existence revealed "divine action."[73]

In this "concept of Israel as biblical promise," Marty pointed out that the view of President Jimmy Carter insisted that "the formation of the modern State of Israel is a fulfillment of biblical prophecy, God acts in history, and God's acts when enscriptured are most discernible." Such Christians therefore believe that both America and Israel are "nations under God." If, Marty argued, "people who hold this view can use the word of God to criticize American policy, they can do so in respect to Israel as well, but they have a deep sympathy in any case, and can be counted on."[74] Furthermore, those within the most conservative "divine action" spectrum—particularly premillennialists—resent any attempts to "carve up [Israel's] boundaries in ways that deviate from the maps of ancient Israel in the Sunday [S]chool books." Marty noted the irony in premillennial support of Israel—those most "counted on" to support Israel were, nonetheless, those most likely to reject Judaism as a legitimate religion. "Many of them care about Jews as Jews," he noted, "but much of their literature shows that their support for Israel and of evangelization to be marked chiefly by interest in the part Jews play in their reading of divine plans."[75]

Mainline Protestants had previously enjoyed the closest relationship to American Jews, chiefly because of their lack of missions and de-emphasis of "theological differences." Marty noted that "a few influential people in the mainline camp . . . are pro-Arab," but "the polls suggest their numbers are tiny." Jews therefore, historically, "always brought the strongest appeals for theological support of Israel" to liberal Protestants. Yet the growing "numerical strength" and financial support of Israel by premillennialists in the 1960s and 1970s threatened this relationship: "To have their support of Israel, even when it means denying the integrity of the faith of Israel, has been valuable to American Jews seeking support of Israel." Marty pointed to the AJC's recent praise of Billy Graham for his support of Israel. While noting that such praise was "richly deserved," Marty insisted nonetheless that it revealed confusion among Jews and Protestants about both premillennial motivations and Christian ideas about Israel. Mainline Protestants needed to continue evaluating their own ideas about Jews and Judaism and Israel but so, too, did conservative evangelicals, Marty insisted. "Whoever reads the signs of the times," he observed, "will soon conclude that almost all of us will be busy revisionists in the years ahead."[76]

Conclusion

In fact, revisions—theological and political— had already begun. The reality of the Jewish genocide in Europe prompted mainline Protestants to reevaluate their traditional theological teachings about Jews and Judaism and led to increased ecumenical dialogue among themselves and Jews. The Jewish refugee and humanitarian crisis had bolstered the initial support for Zionism and was propelled by a powerful group of politically influential mainline Protestants who successfully lobbied for sympathetic policies on Israel's behalf. As Israel grew more secure, general Protestant support for the state did as well. Israeli land acquisitions and apparent reluctance to accommodate the Palestinian refugees into Israeli society garnered criticism from mainline Protestants as the years progressed. By the time Carter brokered the first Middle East peace treaty between Israel and her neighbor Egypt, however, Israel could count on widespread American support and enjoyed a strong alliance with the United States. The initial, crucial, mainline Protestant support for the new state proved to be a significant part of understanding how the alliance developed and grew still stronger.

Evangelicals further tightened the embrace. Their rise to political power by the end of the 1970s inaugurated a new chapter in the story of the U.S.–Israeli alliance. Their support for Israel for biblical and prophetic reasons followed after the initial mainline Protestant pragmatic and humanitarian support and continued to strengthen the American Protestant–Israeli alliance. While evangelicals ignored theological reevaluations (even as they underwent changes in theological *emphasis*), their increasing insistence on support for Israel for religious reasons nonetheless altered their interactions with Jews and their understanding of Judaism. Most important, it signaled a new approach in the Protestant–Israeli alliance that emphasized religion over humanitarian and pragmatic concerns.

7

The Political and Religious
Landscape Shifts, 1980–2008

"To stand against Israel is to stand against God," declared Jerry Falwell in his 1980 missive, *Listen America.*[1] Falwell's explosion on the political
scene with the formation of the religious political activist group, the Moral
Majority, signaled a dramatic shift in the relationship between religion and
politics in America. The cultural and political relevance of liberal mainline Protestants dissipated in the 1980s, the result of a trend begun in the
previous decade. It was replaced by the growing numbers and power of a
new political player—American evangelicalism. Falwell's declaration about
God and Israel represented a new strain of religious foreign policy interests,
which, in the midst of the Cold War, emphasized the coming Armageddon
and the role Israel would play in the end of days. Although the tendency
to emphasize end times eschatology among certain fundamentalist and
dispensationalist evangelicals had existed since the turn of the century, its
adherents had remained small in number and politically unimportant. Reaction to the political and cultural upheavals of the 1960s and 1970s catalyzed
a sophisticated counterattack to liberalism among many American Protestants. Mainline Protestants reeled from the shock of their seemingly sudden
displacement.

Contemporary assessments of religious definitions echo earlier scholarly
frustration. In the scholarly literature of the 1980s, one can easily detect a
collective hand wringing among religious scholars and other academics
over the question of evangelicalism. Reaction to the waning of liberal, mainstream Protestants in numbers and influence produced a range of responses
from shock to self-examination to surprise. Who were the evangelicals and
how had they risen to power in numbers and political influence? The rise
of Ronald Reagan and the birth of the New Religious Right (and its many
forms, including the Moral Majority and later the Christian Coalition) had
rapidly shifted the political and religious landscape in the United States and

had profound implications for U.S.–Israeli policies in the following decades. Moreover, a particularly potent tendency within conservative Protestantism—dispensational premillennialism—appeared to be growing increasingly influential politically. With it came distinct views of the role of Israel in end-times eschatology and the responsibility of American Christians to remain faithful to pro-Israeli policies. Liberal Protestants and intellectuals worried that their evangelical brethren of this particular strain appeared to be trigger-happy endorsers of "Armageddon theology."[2] Figuring out who these Protestants were and what they believed became a near obsession among researchers and liberal Protestant leaders alike.

Far from appearing to be the "consensus religious landscape" described by historians in the 1950s, the American religious landscape of the 1980s appeared more fractured than ever.[3] Americans abandoned their historical mainline denominations in the heart of the city and struck out to form new suburban evangelical churches with increasing emphasis on orthodox Protestant theology. "The fundamentalist, Pentecostal, and evangelical churches have clearly gained in visibility, morale, and strength: their code-words have become part of American culture," religious scholar Martin E. Marty explained.[4] Once considered "marginal," these churches could no longer be viewed as such, he argued, especially when one evaluated the Gallup Poll statistics that revealed an increasing number of Americans self-identifying as "born-again," the evangelical claims made by Presidents Carter, Ford, and Reagan (and third-party candidate John Anderson), and the decline of mainline church memberships.[5] One scholar, in 1991, referred to the newly powerful set of Protestants as "the evangelical mainstream."[6] What seemed to startle Marty and others, however, was the nature of the rise of evangelical power. Marty characterized it as "organized, belligerent and aggressive, lumpish, unwilling to be filtered."[7] All defined it as a reaction against modernity. Most important, all recognized it as a force to be reckoned with.

Theological Considerations

While many liberal mainline Protestants embraced the spirit of ecumenism that pervaded the mainline churches and world church organizations in the 1960s and 1970s, evangelicals defined themselves as defenders of orthodox theology. Such a protective stance of traditional Protestant theology resulted in ever larger evangelical congregations as the laity increasingly distanced themselves from their leaders. James R. Kelly, in an article assessing the nature of ecumenism in the United States in 1979, concluded that "a spirit of ecumenism was found to be widely affirmed and generally non-relativistic, but it still is not appreciably linked to actual clergy behavior."[8] Moreover, the study concluded that although religious leaders in Judaism and Christianity (both Protestant and Catholic) affirmed the importance of ecumenism, most noted the lack of interest or practice among the laity themselves. The finding revealed a clear distinction between the leadership and laity in their approaches to denominational and doctrinal differences. Conservative Christians defended traditional theology and reasserted orthodoxy in the face of the perceived excesses of the 1960s and 1970s—and grew more popular as a result of their eschewing the embrace of "tolerance" in the 1960s and 1970s. Kelly noted that research by other scholars suggested that the difficulties of embracing tolerance lay in the challenge of relativism: "it is in accord not only with human nature, but also with the logic of having convictions to wish in some fashion to silence those who disagree."[9] Conservative Protestants who led the vanguard of the Religious Right could convincingly argue that sincerity of their beliefs necessitated intolerance of others. For those Americans whose religious convictions necessitated strong support for right-wing Israeli policies and the development of a sympathetic and supportive pro-Israel foreign policy, religious relativism negated the importance of Israel on a religio-political level. Ecumenism, though important to liberals, alienated conservatives who were intent on preserving and defending biblical orthodoxy and a black/white worldview.

The surge of evangelical pro-Israel platforms piqued the curiosity of American Jews. Jewish intellectuals grew curious to understand the motives of their new "ally" in the 1980s, and a variety of articles were devoted to reexamining older relationships between fundamentalist premillennialists and Jews. In a 1985 article, for example, William Glass revisited fundamentalism's legacy of Zionism and antisemitism in the 1930s. He highlighted the dual nature of fundamentalists' attitude toward Jews and Israel: Jews retain a unique and significant role in Christian eschatology and, as such, are to be honored, and yet the tendency of premillennialists to see world events as an unstoppable part of God's plan prevented them from taking a more active role in fighting antisemitism in the 1930s. For many fundamentalists, Glass argued, the antisemitism of the 1930s fulfilled a "sign of the times," however horrible, and discouraged a more activist stance in preventing persecution because God would never allow his chosen people to be destroyed.[10] Fundamentalism thus left an ambiguous legacy: its condemnation of antisemitism coupled with its interpretation of prophecy led to a strange pro-Israel, pro-Jew inheritance, but its unwillingness to join in the crusade against Hitler's genocidal policies left it impotent. Glass's contemporary assessment of the "ambiguous legacy" of fundamentalism reflected a cautious interest in evangelicals' rising power in America. Glass and others struggled to understand where their theology and history fit into the American religious landscape.

Political Shifts: "The Collapse of the Liberal Vision"

The resurgence of evangelicals, particularly of fundamentalists, could be explained, according to some scholars, through their appeal to order, laity longing for authority, the effective use of technology, the appeal to nostalgia, fulfillment of spiritual experiences, and the appeal of premillennialism (the latter of which offered "its adherents a sense that they alone know exactly where history is going").[11] Other liberals began to call attention to the evangelicals' effective mobilization efforts, particularly during the 1984 presidential election. Running for his second term, Reagan employed the evangelicals to great advantage, capitalizing on momentum that had started in his first presidential campaign. Their influence appeared so significant that, in an article for *The Review of Religious Research*, Richard V. Pierard wondered if perhaps the "religious backers of President Reagan in their enthusiasm exceeded the bounds of propriety," and questioned whether their efforts on Reagan's behalf had, in fact, secured his reelection.[12] Although Pierard ultimately concluded that Reagan won reelection based on his political record, the active involvement of the Religious Right pushed the political agenda into a decidedly more conservative realm. Employing effective campaign strategies, including the distribution of literature supporting Reagan's Christian values, voter registration drives, direct mailings—a general "media blitz"—the Religious Right rallied voters to Reagan's side.[13] Significantly Reagan spent little effort in courting the leadership of the mainline churches, preferring to focus on evangelicals, speaking at their conventions instead, including the National Association of Evangelicals and Baptist Fundamentalism Conventions. Evangelicals mobilized by creating their own lobbying groups, including the American Coalition for Traditional Values, headed by evangelical writer and speaker Tim LaHaye (whose dispensational premillennialist book series, *Left Behind*, highlighting the significance of Israel in the end of days, would become a *New York Times* best-seller in the 1990s).[14]

Although American Jewish voters had abandoned Carter in the 1980 election, many remained cautious about Reagan's alignment with the New Religious Right. In an October 1984 issue of *Commentary*, neoconservative Irving Kristol tried to allay Jewish fears by pointing out that the Moral Majority was "unequivocally pro-Israel" and its support important to the security of Israel.[15] Others—Protestants, Catholics, Jews, and the nonreligious alike—worried about the influence of premillennial dispensationalism, "Armageddon theory," on Reagan's attitude toward the Soviet Union and the possibility of arms reduction. In the second presidential debate, held on 21 October 1984, Reagan noted his conversations with premillennialist dispensationalist preachers who prophesied that Armageddon would occur soon (although he did not discuss their activities on behalf of his reelection campaign) but dismissed the possibility that "a nuclear war could be fought and won."[16]

In 1985 sociologist Jeffery K. Hadden, in a scholarly address to peers, also contemplated the powerful political rise of evangelical Americans. He identified several reasons for the success of the evangelical political platform including the use of religious broadcasting by charismatic leaders, the appeal of the idea of American exceptionalism and providential grace, the adaptation of urban revival techniques to the late twentieth century, and the misunderstanding of fundamentalism by "scholars and the mass media alike." Finally, Hadden identified the "collapse of the liberal vision" as the fifth explanation for the profound social and political shift under way.[17] Evangelical and fundamentalist Christians blamed the failings of the liberal vision of the 1960s for the malady then affecting the United States. They emphasized repentance and self-correction to rectify the tilting ship—an old message, Hadden argued, that found new life with new techniques to spread it.[18]

The liberal examination of evangelical and fundamentalist beliefs continued and moved beyond an attempt to understand the movement's origins and rise to power, and encompassed its increasingly popular emphasis on U.S.–Israeli policies and attitudes in the light of prophecy. A shift in the meaning and direction of Christian Zionism—from its early years as a humanitarian and politically pragmatic policy supported by mainline Protestants to one that emphasized Israel's role in end times eschatology—alarmed and alienated liberal Protestants. Ronald Stockton, a political scientist writing for the *Middle East Journal* in 1987, argued that one of the most important factors in explaining the persistent and strong popular support for Israel, despite "periodic fluctuations" in the U.S.–Israeli crisis, lay in the doctrine of "Christian Zionism" and its adherents' belief that U.S. support for Israel was essential in making the U.S. a "godly" nation in line with biblical commands and prophecies.[19] Stockton argued that "Christian Zionism is a mainstream phenomenon firmly rooted in those religious and cultural groups from which it historically sprang, but also transcending them."[20] He pointed to the Falwell Model—the idea that American "Christians are obligated to support Jews and Israel" in order to be blessed as a nation by God.[21] Christian support for Israel closely aligned with the biblical understanding of ancient Israel, specifically its ancient boundaries (parts of Jordan, Syria, Iraq, and Egypt), and therefore tended to reject land for peace treaties and supported Israeli expansionist tendencies. The Falwell Model, according to Stockton, viewed Israel as the absolute fulfillment of biblical prophecies and tied the fate of the United States to Israel. Televangelist Jimmy Swaggart mirrored such ideology when he noted, "I feel that America is tied with the spiritual umbilical cord to Israel. The ties go back to long before the founding of the United States of America. The Judeo-Christian concept goes all the way back to Abraham and God's promise to Abraham which I also believe included America."[22] This idea clearly influenced Reagan. In a meeting with Thomas Dine of the American Israel Public Affairs Committee (AIPAC), Reagan noted: "You know, I turn back to your ancient prophets in the Old Testament and the signs foretelling Armageddon, and I find myself wondering if—if we're the generation that's going to see that come about. I don't know if you've noted any of those prophecies lately, but believe me, they certainly describe the times we're going through."[23] Reagan's interest in Israel as a fulfillment of prophecy, and his concern for the end-of-days timeline certainly worried non-dispensationalist premillennialists. In 1988, however, sociologist Andrew J. Weigert suggested that the growing popularity of fundamentalist premillennialism theology made sense because its description of the end of days seemed suddenly plausible in the context of a nuclear war— the previously abstract appeared literal.[24]

Not all evangelicals endorsed the premillennial dispensationalist worldview. Wes Michaelson of *Sojourners*, for example, rejected the wide endorsement of all Israeli policies by other evangelicals. Firmly rejecting modern Zionism, he explained that "many evangelicals have unabashedly provided a theological justification for Zionism, granting divine sanction to and even glorifying the violence of modern Israel." Zionism, he charged, "is foreign to the heart of Judaism and the biblical message."[25] *Sojourners* rejected Christian Zionism as a perversion of Palestinian rights. Jim Wallis, leader of the group of evangelicals who publish *Sojourners*, also rejected much of the political agenda of his fellow evangelicals. Wallis and other sojourners tended to eschew hyper-patriotism, distrusted military buildup, and disagreed with much U.S. foreign policy. Their journal focused on social justice issues, humanitarian causes, and advocacy for the economically disadvantaged.[26] Such a focus aligned with the mainline Protestant view, particularly its criticism of Israeli policies—a perspective that, as we have seen, became a source of great conflict within the mainline journals and leadership. Liberal mainline Protestants' focus on human rights issues, particularly concerning Palestinians, coupled with their historic tendency to sever the formation of the modern nation of Israel from biblical prophecy, led to protests against Israeli policies in the West Bank and Gaza, support for Palestinian statehood, and protest over continued U.S. financial and military support for Israel.

By the 1980s many within the leadership of mainline denominations had embraced a generally critical view of Israeli policies, even as the laity had not. For mainline Protestant leaders, questions of Israel's right to exist faded as Israel continued to survive, and the sense of Christian guilt that had led to much mainline support for Israel in the previous decades was replaced by criticism of illegal settlements on the West Bank and Gaza, the continuing plight of refugees, and the cause of Palestinian statehood. Moreover, the increasing popularity of the dispensationalist premillennialist worldview alarmed the mainline leadership. More and more they pointed to the apparent contradiction inherent in such theology: Israel is important to God's plans yet all Jews must be converted to Christianity in the end of days. Mainline denominations had gradually embraced, particularly in the 1960s and 1970s, a lessening, if not total cessation, of missions to the Jews. The moral and theological relativism of those two decades negated the need for active, cross-religious evangelism. Mainline leadership seized upon what they viewed as the inherent antisemitism of some evangelical and fundamentalist Protestants. Tom Driver, a Union Theological Seminary professor writing in *Christianity and Crisis,* noted that "the most pro-Israeli group in American Christianity is also the most anti-Semitic," since they believe it is Israel's "providential role to protect American interests." He added:

> Israel is viewed by them as an instrument of America's manifest destiny. By this sort of Christian *realpolitik* the Jews are to be kept in their place and used for an end not of their own but that of a zealous, fanatical and self-righteous Christian mission which cannot tell the difference between Jesus Christ and the American nation. This bigotry proposes a marriage of convenience with a certain kind of Zionism—a kind which cannot tell the difference between Yahweh and the state of Israel.[27]

The mainline Protestant churches during the 1980s and 1990s articulated a vastly different U.S.–Israeli agenda than did their fellow evangelicals. The 1991 vote in the National Council of Churches to support the U.N.'s resolution that Israel should withdraw from the Palestinian territories it occupied signaled an important shift in Protestant–Jewish–U.S.–Israeli relations. While mainline Protestants appeared to be increasingly absorbed in human rights issues in Third World countries, including Palestinian territories, American Jews viewed this emphasis as a betrayal. As we have seen, original political support for Zionism emerged from the mainline churches, even though the post-1967 years revealed increasingly sharp criticism of Israeli policies. Even in the 1980s Marc Tanenbaum of the American Jewish Committee had noted the shift in the Protestant alliance:

> The evangelical community is the largest and fastest growing block of pro-Israeli, pro-Jewish sentiment in this country. Since the 1967 War, the Jewish community has felt abandoned by Protestants, by groups clustered around the National Council of Churches, which because of sympathy to third world causes, gave an impression of support for the PLO. There was a vacuum of public support to Israel that began to be filled by the fundamentalist and evangelical Christians.[28]

In fact, there had never been a "vacuum of public support to Israel"; the support simply arose from a camp that mainline Protestant and Jewish Americans had virtually ignored. By the 1990s, however, American Jews and Israelis began to recognize that evangelicals presented a powerful new ally in protecting the U.S.–Israeli alliance.

Attitudes and Activism

Evangelical Protestants' support for Israel over the Palestinians reflected basic attitudes in American society at large. In mainstream American television, film, and news coverage, Arabs "remain one of the few ethnic groups who can still be slandered with impunity in America."[29] Analysis of polling data revealed that most Americans not only viewed Arabs negatively ("barbaric, cruel, treacherous, cunning, mistreat women, warlike, bloodthirsty"), but, as a result, most overwhelmingly sided with Israel in the Arab-Israeli conflict.[30] Most Americans polled expressed concern over the perceived antisemitic attitude of most Arabs and viewed antisemitism as "un-Christian" and "anti-American." Those polled overwhelmingly identified the United States as a Christian nation and antisemitism as a threat to its values.[31] Unsurprisingly, then, polls revealed that, of all Arab organizations or nations, Americans viewed least favorably the Palestinian Liberation Organization specifically and Palestinians generally.

While most liberal Protestant leaders had grown increasingly critical of Israeli policies toward the Palestinians, this criticism reflected a break with mainstream Americans. Though only 32 percent of Americans viewed Palestinians favorably, the numbers dropped even lower within the context of the Palestinian-Israeli conflict. Research in the 1980s revealed that 57 percent of Americans sided with Israel, whereas only 16 percent sided with the Palestinians. Conservative Protestants could confidently claim, then, that liberal Protestant organizations and leadership critical of Israel had lost touch with the American people. For many conservative Protestants, the "abandoning" of Israel by liberal Protestants only revealed another way that liberals had generally abandoned their faith. A poll conducted by political scientists in 1987 revealed the growing divide between conservative and liberal Protestants over the issue of Christian Zionism.

The study highlighted significant differences among Christians. Whereas 57 percent of Protestants considered themselves Christian Zionists, only 35 percent of Catholics did. In the liberal/conservative Protestant divide, 77 percent of Protestants considered themselves "Born Again," whereas only 33 three percent did not, and 69 percent of American Protestants considered themselves evangelical as opposed to 35 percent who did not.[32] The political scientists concluded that the impact of such statistics on U.S.–Israeli policies proved significant when the issues were framed in the context of "Israel" versus the "Arabs." After analyzing the social agenda of the Religious Right, they concluded that Christian Zionism, unlike the Religious Right, "is more a mainstream cultural theme linked to American self-identity and to the perception of America as a moral community. Christian Zionism is disproportionately associated with the evangelical Christian base from which it historically sprang." They noted that "the survey data indicate that it transcends these origins and has support in all religious, ideological and political strata."[33] Clearly, then, by the end of the 1980s, the Christian Zionist ideology represented mainstream American Protestantism.

Meanwhile, evangelical Protestants' growing numbers and influence challenged and eventually defeated the hegemony of liberal mainstream Protestantism in U.S. politics. Many scholars attribute the rise of evangelical Protestant political activism to the establishment of the Moral Majority in 1979 by the evangelist Jerry Falwell, Minister Ed McAteer, and New Rightest Howard Phillips. One of the largest conservative lobby groups in the United States, the Moral Majority represented a concerted effort by evangelical Christians to enact domestic and foreign policies on behalf of the values of conservative Protestants. Its membership roster numbered in the millions and reflected a veritable who's who of significant American evangelicals including, among others, Tim and Beverly LaHaye, Jim and Tammy Baker, and well-known Atlanta minister Charles Stanley. Echoing Nixon's call to the "Silent Majority" during the 1960s, the Moral Majority claimed that its platform reflected the concerns of the majority of Americans. Its four founding principles included opposition to abortion, the upholding of traditional marriage, strong U.S. defense, and support for Israel.

Clearly Israel was not the only factor influencing the increasing political activism of evangelical Protestantism. Certainly other issues, such as abortion, prayer in school, the teaching of evolution, and gay rights, created platforms to rally around for these Protestants. Although issues of foreign policy were not this group's only concern, the way the modern nation of Israel became engrained into their religious eschatology became a matter of paramount importance. In addressing its support for Israel and a strong national defense, the Moral Majority focused on foreign policy issues and stringently lobbied Congress and the president to enact policies favorable to Israel's security. Israel and its role in the fulfillment of biblical prophecy factored heavily into the Moral Majority's theological interests, making it sympathetic to Israeli claims to the Holy Land.

Political mobilization on behalf of Israel began with a general rejection of Carter's recognition of Palestine's right to statehood and the exchange of land for peace. Many American evangelicals declared that such a position directly contradicted the biblical mandate for Israeli claims to all the Holy Land (although, as we shall see later, they were not inflexible in their objection to land-for-peace deals). Although other factors played a role in Reagan's defeat of Carter, exit polls revealed that he lost both the Jewish and evangelical vote—a significant part of his previous base. Willing to ignore Carter's outspoken faith in favor of hard-right Israeli interests, Falwell urged his followers to support Ronald Reagan's campaign.

Under Reagan, Israel received $3 billion annually in the form of grants as well as Reagan's vocal support in the United Nations.[34] For example, after coming under increasing fire in the U.N. for its activities in Lebanon, Israel found a strong ally in Reagan.[35] While Jerry Falwell enjoyed friendly relations with Reagan during his presidency, Falwell's connection to significant figures in the Israeli hard-right Likud government created what one scholar termed a "theopolitical alliance."[36] After meeting Israeli prime minister Menachem Begin during Falwell's first trip to Israel, Falwell and several other prominent ministers wrote a letter to the prime minister that pledged their unwavering support for Israel and emphasized America's common interests with its Middle East ally:

As Americans who are dedicated to the cause of freedom, we share love of liberty, commitment to democratic institutions, and respect for the dignity of the individual fashioned in the image of God with the people of Israel. We also know that the State of Israel plays a crucial and strategic role in protecting the security of our own country and of all freedom-loving peoples. Israel stands as a bulwark of strength and determination against those, who by terror and blackmail, threaten our democratic way of life. At a time when the reliability of America's traditional allies is increasingly called into question, we salute the State of Israel for your steadfast friendship and for your loyalty and devotion to the ties which bind our nations together. Israel has always upheld America, and as Christian leaders, we pledge to uphold Israel.[37]

The statement went further than simply an expression of pragmatic support for a democratic ally in the Middle East, however. Reiterating their objection to land-for-peace negotiations, the statement continued: "On theological, as well as historical grounds, we proclaim that the Land, Israel, encompasses Judea and Samaria, as integral parts of the Jewish patrimony, with Jerusalem as its indivisible capital." Furthermore, they noted, "we acknowledge the rights of Jewish settlements in these areas."[38] Evangelical and fundamentalists' opposition to land negotiations had broad implications for U.S. policy in the Middle East. Palestinian claims to statehood constituted a "grave threat" to Israeli security, and these Protestants believed that pressure by the United Nations and Europeans to force Israel to return to its 1967 borders should be resisted at all costs. Such concessions not only jeopardized Israeli rights to a biblical mandate to possess all the Holy Land but also "the strategic interests of the U.S. and the Western world."[39] In stark contrast to the liberal Protestant agenda, many evangelicals argued that land negotiations with Palestinians, Jordanians, Syrians, and Lebanese endangered Israeli and American security.

When Menachem Begin bombed the Iraqi nuclear reactor in 1981, his first call to the United States was not to President Reagan but to Falwell, asking him to explain Israel's rationale in the preemptive strike to evangelicals in the United States. Falwell responded: "Mr. Prime Minister, I want to congratulate you for a mission that made us very proud that we manufacture those F-16s. In my opinion," he added, "you must've put it right down the smokestack."[40] Falwell, like Begin, believed that Israel and the United States had common enemies. In this respect, theirs was "a common stand" and tied America's fate unambiguously to Israel's. Falwell argued that biblical mandate necessitated American support of Israel, and he condemned the National Council of Churches for its public criticism of Israel's action in Iraq. "These ecclesiastical leaders do not speak for a majority of Christians in America," Falwell told reporters.[41] Falwell insisted that "God promises to bless those who blessed the children of Abraham and curse those who cursed Israel. I think history supports the fact that he has been true to his word. When you go back to the pharaohs, the Caesars, Adolf Hitler and the Soviet Union, all those who dared to touch the apple of God's eye—Israel—have been punished by God. America has been blessed because she has blessed Israel."[42] Such a position—a reiteration of Israel as "the apple of God's eye"—would remain one of the most important justifications for continued evangelical support for Israel. Eventually such emphasis would supersede the stress on the coming of Armageddon (and, more important, the destruction of the Jews who refused to convert during the end of days) that evangelicals in the late 1960s had expressed. This shift in emphasis—away from prophecy toward the promises of blessings to those who supported Israel— served to help allay Jewish concerns about the possible antisemitic nature of evangelical support of Israel.[43]

Evangelicals across the United States echoed Falwell's conviction of the necessity of support for Israel in order for America to prosper. Missionary and Bible Light International founder Elmer Josephson highlighted the promise of Genesis 12:3—"I will bless them that bless thee"—when considering the attitude Christians should take toward Jews in the United States and Israelis.[44] Such evangelical insistence that American support for Israel was vital to American prosperity resonated with Pastor John Hagee of the nondenominational Cornerstone mega-church in San Antonio, Texas.

Shocked by the U.S. public condemnation of the Osirak nuclear reactor bombing in Iraq, on 10 September 1981, Hagee orchestrated a "Night to Honor Israel" in which his church raised $10,000 for a local chapter of Hadassah. Hagee would continue to hold more "Nights to Honor Israel" in his own church and in churches across the nation, raising millions of dollars over the following decades. Motivated by issues of foreign policy, Hagee ensured through his fund-raising efforts that the position of evangelicals in the United States toward Israel would have sure financial backing in the years to come.

Hagee's political activism on behalf of Israel reflected an increasingly powerful religio-political movement of evangelicals in the United States. The organized lobbying efforts of evangelical Protestants to effect changes in American politics that reflected their Christian values alarmed many political observers. While the first election of Reagan had signaled a political shift among Christian voters (the abandonment of Sunday School teacher Jimmy Carter for the dubious evangelical credentials of his challenger, Ronald Reagan), the 1984 election received even more attention from political watchdogs. Here, many observed, the Religious Right appeared to be coming into its political own.

Part of the Religious Right's growing influence increased with the establishment of the Christian Coalition by Pat Robertson following his unsuccessful bid for the presidency in 1988. The Christian Coalition, following on the heels of the Moral Majority (which effectively disbanded in 1989), created a highly influential political advocacy group and voter mobilization program that galvanized evangelicals to continue political agitation. With membership reaching well over one million, the Christian Coalition significantly contributed to successful political lobbying for the Christian Right and conducted substantial funds for pro-Israeli causes in the last few decades of the twentieth century.[45]

Not all have agreed, however, that evangelical and Jewish agendas are so closely intertwined. Criticism from Robert Zimmerman, president of the American Jewish Congress, for example, highlighted the uneasy alliance many American Jews feel toward pro-Israel American evangelicals. Zimmerman pointed to the conflict of interest between the Religious Right and liberal Jews in American politics. He noted that Jews, who traditionally support issues that are an anathema to the Religious Right, including abortion, separation of church and state, and the opposition of prayer in public schools, had allied themselves with a political agenda that "threatens the freedoms that make Jews safe in America."[46] Others within the American Jewish community remained less concerned about fundamentalists' conservative domestic agenda and focused instead on the most basic shared values—monotheism and strong Israeli defense. "Praise God and pass the ammunition," responded Nathan Perlmutter, director of the Anti-Defamation League of B'nai B'rith, to Jewish concerns about fundamentalist agendas. Lenny Ben David, formerly associated with AIPAC and the Israel Embassy in Washington, stated that "until I see Jesus coming over the hill, I am in favor of all the friends Israel can get."[47] Attitudes within Israel echoed David's pragmatism. The Israelis who discounted fundamentalist theology were nonetheless happy to take evangelical tourist dollars, benefit from political lobbying efforts of Christian Zionists, and nurture close relationships with important fundamentalist figures in America. In the 1980s, while courting Falwell's support, former prime minister Begin stated: "I tell you, if the Christian fundamentalists support us in Congress today, I will support them when the Messiah comes tomorrow."[48] Whatever differences existed between Jewish groups about the nature of evangelical and fundamentalist support of Israel, one thing had grown increasingly clear: a growing number of Americans were identifying as evangelicals, and these evangelicals were working to strengthen the U.S.–Israeli alliance even further.

The increasingly tight embrace between Israeli policy makers and American Christian Zionists alarmed many within the mainline Protestant leadership. In an effort to counterbalance the enormous influence of the Christian Zionists, more than twenty-four mainline denominations joined forces with several Catholic organizations and non-Protestant leaders to form the Churches for Middle East Peace (CMEP) in 1984. Its stated purpose, to effect a "sound and balanced U.S. policy" that promoted "lasting peace and justice" involved encouraging members and supporters to "engage directly with policymakers at every level." According to CMEP's mission, the development of a viable Palestinian state, as well as secure borders for Israel, necessitated a more coordinated and vocal presence on Capitol Hill. Its advisory board included "prominent diplomats (retired), politicians, church leaders, academicians, businesspeople and media persons with a particular interest and connection to the Middle East."[49] In December 1987 the first Palestinian intifada began in response to Israeli crackdowns on security in the Palestinian territories, resulting in the deaths of more than one thousand Palestinians and more than one hundred Israelis. That year, through workshops, political dinners, and lobbying efforts, CMEP advocated balanced media coverage of the Palestinian-Israeli conflict and encouraged a sympathetic U.S. policy response to the Palestinians.

While condemning the violence and bloodshed on both sides of the conflict, liberal Protestants sympathized with the Palestinian perspective and considered it "understandable" in light of the continued Israeli occupation of Palestinian lands. Many decried the perceived bias in the media reporting of the intifada, and embarked on their own letter-writing campaign to influence U.S. policy makers to pressure the Israeli government to end its military campaign in the Palestinian territories.

The End of the Cold War and a Shift in Focus

Even after Reagan's two-term presidency ended in the election of his vice president, George H. W. Bush, evangelicals continued to push their foreign policy agenda—support for Israel. Cautiousness about the Israeli-Palestinian conflict characterized Bush's approach to Middle East affairs. Although

Bush's circumspect realistic approach to foreign policy negated romantic notions of Armageddon theology, the declaration of war against Iraq occupied most of the first Bush administration's foreign policy and simultaneously further fueled the end-times speculation among dispensational premillennialists.[50] One researcher in 1991 noted that after the Gulf War, book sales with an Armageddon theme rose sharply, and speculation increased that the final battle of the end times would take place in the near future.[51] Liberal Protestants, in contrast, vigorously objected to the buildup of military preparedness in the Gulf prior to the war.

The National Council of Churches called for the removal of all U.S. military personnel from the region—a request unacknowledged by President George H. W. Bush in a telling revelation about the lack of liberal Protestant political power. In fact, as the *New York Times* pointed out, the "heyday" of administration concern for mainline Protestant agendas had passed. Prior to the Reagan era, *New York Times* journalist Ari Goldman noted, "Presidents and Cabinet officials would call in the leaders of [the National Council of Churches] for consultation." However, he pointed out, "Evangelical Christians, especially the Moral Majority, stole the political limelight."[52] But with the end of the Cold War, and a necessary shift in interpretation of the end of days, evangelicals found themselves in a foreign policy dilemma. The Evil Empire no longer existed, but Israel remained vital to their eschatology. In the meantime, the Republican Party encouraged the Christian Right to continue to attract evangelicals to the Republican Party. The polling information gathered from the election of Democrat Bill Clinton in 1992 revealed that the shift of white evangelicals to the Republican Party remained intact, despite Clinton's Southern Baptist affiliation.[53]

The direction of U.S. foreign policy during eight years of the Clinton administration appeared adrift. No longer were American resources concentrated on defeating a monolithic enemy. Other issues occupied the attention of foreign policy makers, including the Balkans, terrorism in Somalia, targeting Bin Laden's training camps in Afghanistan, and peace efforts in Northern Ireland and the Palestinian territories. The role of Israel as America's strategic ally in the Cold War evaporated, leaving policy makers to question the pragmatism of continuing to promote a strong U.S.–Israeli alliance.[54] Even as policy makers struggled to define U.S. foreign policy objectives, Clinton embarked upon an ambitious attempt to end the Israeli-Palestinian violence of the first intifada. Palestinian President Yasser Arafat and Israeli Prime Minister Yitzak Rabin met with Clinton in Oslo, Norway, to hammer out negotiations. Although the Oslo Accords resulted in an "official" end to the intifada, and resulted in Israel-PLO letters of recognition, issues over Israeli settlement expansion, among other disagreements, failed to deliver the promised peace.

Some evangelical Americans, already wary of a Democrat in office, responded to Clinton's efforts to broker peace between Arafat and the Israeli Labor Party's Rabin, and eventually with Shimon Peres, but with suspicion. Under the Clinton administration, Israel agreed to phase out financial assistance from the United States, prompting many evangelicals to question the solidity of the U.S.–Israeli alliance. The Oslo Accords presented further challenges to the hope of fundamentalist dispensationalist evangelicals to expand the borders of modern Israel to match those of the Bible. Yet even as many Zionist evangelicals disapproved of land-for-peace deals, support for Israel in general, including liberal Labor Party prime ministers, remained firm— even showing a remarkable degree of flexibility and respect for Israel's democratic process.[55] Remaining loyal to Israel, and concerned with its security, whatever the political climate, remained central to fulfilling God's command to bless those that bless Israel.

Immediately upon his election in 1996, Binyamin Netanyahu of the conservative and hawkish Likud Party reached out to Jerry Falwell in an effort to garner American public support to help him stave off the concessions Bill Clinton requested of Israel in the stalled peace talks. After a meeting with Netanyahu, Falwell declared: "There are about 200,000 evangelical pastors in America, and we are asking them all, through e-mail, faxes, letters and the telephone, to go into their pulpits and use their influence in support of the State of Israel and the prime minister."[56] The meeting symbolized the odd symbiotic relationship between Israel and American evangelical Zionists at the turn of the century: the Israeli Right needed evangelical public support for its Palestinian policies, and the fundamentalists needed to support right-wing Israeli polices for what they perceived as the spiritual and physical well-being of the United States.

Meanwhile, the liberal Protestant call for a "shared Jerusalem" ignited a propaganda war between Zionist evangelicals and mainline denominations.[57] While organizations like the Churches for Middle East Peace actively lobbied for a shared status in Jerusalem, evangelical Zionists considered the city sacrosanct to their vision of Israel and saw Israel's maintenance of sole control nonnegotiable. Although land-for-peace deals remained unpopular but tolerable, Jerusalem's status inspired fierce reactions from evangelicals. After touring Israel at the invitation of Prime Minister Netanyahu, seventeen prominent evangelical Zionist leaders, including Pat Robertson, Ralph Reed,

Jerry Falwell, and Ed McAteer, publicly pledged to support a "united Jerusalem" under Israeli sovereignty.

Before leaving office, Clinton once again attempted to fulfill the promise of the Oslo Accords by pushing for another Israeli-Palestinian summit. Placing a great deal of U.S. prestige on the negotiations, the July 2000 Camp David Summit brought together Clinton, Ehud Barak and Yasser Arafat in an attempt to negotiate a final settlement. Frustrating evangelical Zionists, Barak extended an offer to return Gaza and over 90 percent of the West Bank territory to Arafat, who refused, demanding the Palestinian right of return to Israel as a nonnegotiable factor. Once again, negotiations ended without achieving peace.

In September 2000 a second intifada, the Al-Aqsa Intifada, erupted in response to a provocative visit to the Temple Mount by Ariel Sharon. Mainline Protestants again voiced their frustration at the media coverage. While Fred Strickert, professor of religion at Wartburg College, writing for the *Christian Century,* acknowledged the ability of the Internet to convey a more balanced interpretation of the intifada and the Israeli response, he noted that "the Web also gives voice to those Christians who see the conflict as evidence of a Palestinian refusal to recognize Israel's right to exist, or who see the establishment of the state of Israel as a major step on the way to the Rapture."[58] Though hopeful that the Internet would allow better mobilization of mainline Protestant support of the Palestinian cause, Strickert noted, with regret, that that mobilization still appeared ineffective in influencing Congress. While groups such as the Churches for a Middle East Peace had initiated "Action Alerts" in an attempt to influence Congress, Strickert conceded that such efforts on behalf of the Palestinian cause were unsuccessful in defeating House Bill 426, which condemned Arafat for the violence and blamed Palestinians for the perpetuation of the intifada.[59]

The election of George W. Bush in 2000, for which evangelicals came out in significant numbers, brought about speculation regarding the role that religion would play in the self-professed "born-again" Christian president's U.S. Middle East policy. At first, determined not to repeat the mistakes of his predecessor by staking too much prestige on an unsuccessful peace negotiation as Clinton had done in the 2000 Camp David meetings, Bush did not make the region a priority. Coming into office with little foreign policy experience and a sweeping domestic agenda, Bush, despite the hopes of evangelical supporters and fears of mainline Protestant critics, did not appear heavily influenced by end times eschatology.[60] In fact, in response to the continued violence of the Al-Aqsa Intifada, Bush appeared critical of the harsh Israeli reaction, supportive of an independent Palestinian state, and worried about alienating valuable alliances with other Middle Eastern nations—hardly a dispensational premillennialist approach. According to Richard Land of the Southern Baptist Convention, Bush's support of Israel appeared to stem from other considerations besides religion. In justifications strangely echoing the pragmatism of Reinhold Niebuhr's Zionism, Land suggested that Bush's support "is founded on humanitarian and geopolitical grounds"—the necessity of a safe haven after the Holocaust and Israel's usefulness as a valuable democratic ally in the Middle East.[61] Keeping the U.S. policy on the same course as had former presidents, Bush publicly supported general attempts at negotiations and consistently called for moderation.

The terrorist attacks on 11 September 2001 and the Israeli response to the high-profile assassination of a public figure a month later changed the importance of the region to the Bush administration. Conflicted between viewing Israel as an ally in the new war on terrorism and a liability in creating support for the U.S. invasion of Afghanistan and Iraq among Middle Eastern nations, Bush appeared to vacillate between supporting and condemning Israel's militant response to terrorism in the West Bank. When Bush called for Prime Minister Ariel Sharon to withdraw from the West Bank "without delay," evangelicals rallied in support of Israel and, in April 2002, orchestrated, along with other pro-Israel advocates, a Rally for Israel in Washington, D.C.[62] Whether or not evangelical criticism of Bush's policies toward Sharon altered the president's perspective, in April 2002 Bush gave a speech in the White House Rose Garden that signaled a shift back to a policy that appeared to favor Israel.

The Rose Garden Speech changed U.S. foreign policy in the Middle East by emphasizing the development of democracy in the Palestinian territories rather than defining the boundaries of a future Palestinian state. Such an emphasis was consistent with Bush's policy of democracy building in the Middle East in general, but critics of the policy charged that it took necessary pressure off Sharon to make concessions to the Palestinians. This did not, however, soften evangelical Zionists' disapproval of the 2003 Road Map to Peace initiative proposed by the United States, Russia, the European Union, and the United Nations, which called for the gradual withdrawal of Israel from the West Bank, nor of Sharon's preemptive withdrawal from Gaza in 2005. Nor did it mute the criticism of mainline Protestant leaders who continued to condemn Israeli policies in the Palestinian territories.

Concerned about the growing criticism of Israeli policies toward the Palestinians among the mainline churches, Glen Tobias, Abraham Foxman, and

Eugene Korn of the Anti-Defamation League wrote a guide for addressing the criticism. In it the authors noted that although American Christians did not hold a uniform position, they could, nonetheless, be organized into three main groups. The first group, "the Christian 'right' or Evangelical positions" were "strongly pro-Israel and activist," and the second, mainline Protestants, tended to sympathize more with the Palestinian perspective and were hostile to Israel in varying degrees. The third group, the Roman Catholic Church, appeared to offer a fairly balanced approach to the Israeli-Palestinian conflict, with some exceptions.[63]

The second group constituted the primary focus of the study. The authors systematically chartered the consistently pro-Palestinian activism of the mainline liberal Protestant denominations and organizations such as Churches for Middle East Peace, the National Council of the Churches of Christ in the U.S.A., and the supranational World Council of Churches. They repeatedly charged that groups such as the United Methodists, Lutherans, Episcopalians, and Presbyterians failed to condemn Palestinian violence, and even in some cases sympathized with it. They noted the letters, meetings held with U.S. officials, public statements, and lobbying efforts of these denominations to pressure the United States into taking a harder stance against Israel. According to the authors, members of these dominations openly supported the Palestinian cause as one of justice, and noted the Episcopal Church's website that designated Israel as an "apartheid" state. They also highlighted a statement by Mark Brown, a Lutheran leader and World Council of Churches member, in which he declared "the church is partisan. We are on the side of the poor and oppressed." The authors concluded that the main cause of mainline criticism of Israel lay in the "occupation" of Palestinian territory, the status of Jerusalem, and the Palestinian right of return, and lamented that the "churches devote much more time to denouncing the 'occupation' and violence against Palestinian civilians than they do denouncing terrorism against Israeli civilians." The authors suggested that such criticism by liberal Protestants stemmed from their theological unwillingness to acknowledge the "biblical promise of the land to the Jews" and "do not deal with biblical passages that promise the land to the Jewish people," even as they acknowledged that "Israel was a necessary creation after the Holocaust."[64]

Such a platform stood in stark contrast to the "Christian Zionists, i.e., Evangelicals," the authors noted, who privilege the biblical mandate for Israel over the guilt of the Holocaust in their support. "They are," the authors remarked, "staunch advocates for Israel's security." The authors urged their readers to engage in dialogue with mainline Protestants to correct their "misstatements" by emphasizing Israel's legitimacy, need for security, and multiple attempts to broker peace with the Palestinians. The emphasis on dialogue with mainline Protestants would take on added urgency in 2004 when the mainline Presbyterian Church of the United States of America (PCUSA) initiated a divesture campaign aimed at punishing selective businesses that had profited from "the occupation" of Palestinian territory and construction of the security wall isolating sections of the West Bank and the Gaza Strip from Israel.[65]

The Presbyterian divesture campaign alarmed American Jews and Israelis. Writing from the Jerusalem Center for Public Affairs, Eugene Korn again offered an analysis of the "liberal churches" attitudes toward Israel, this time in the context of the divesture campaign. He concluded that the campaign constituted "part of a larger anti-Zionist campaign to weaken and delegitimize Israel."[66] Significantly, however, Korn noted that such attitudes remained the domain of a "focused minority, while the majority of liberal American Christians remain sympathetic to Israel." Echoing earlier assessments by sociologists, religious scholars, and political scientists, Korn highlighted the differences in attitudes toward Israel between the elite ("a small group of ideologues") and the "pew level." Korn added that "all polls taken in America over the past twenty years on attitudes toward the Israeli-Palestinian conflict yield consistent results," with most Americans polling "between 3:1 and 4:1 sympathy for Israel over the Palestinians"—with increasing levels of sympathy following 9/11 and Hamas's electoral victory in 2005.[67] Still, the move from anti-Israel rhetoric to action alarmed American Jews and Israelis, taking many, Korn noted, "by surprise." Korn's explanation for the PCUSA's campaign reflected a common charge by both evangelical Zionists and Jews: mainline Protestants refused to acknowledge the "national characteristics" of the Jewish faith. Instead, they divorced any claim to nationhood from Judaism.

In an effort reminiscent of the ACPC's strategy, the National Christian Leadership Conference for Israel invited well-placed leaders in the PCUSA to conduct a "fact finding mission" in Israel a month before the General Assembly was to reconvene to vote on whether to continue the divesture campaign. Since its passage by the General Assembly in 2004, the divesture campaign had provoked controversy among the congregants, including former CIA director James Woolsey, who spoke against it before the General Assembly in 2006. The fact finding mission ended in success, according to Korn, who accompanied the visitors. The church leaders, after spending eight days in Israel, "were transformed from propagandists to eye witnesses, and . . . they became the most effective voices against divestment." In a vote of 483 to 28, the PCUSA General Assembly ended its divesture campaign.[68]

The divesture campaign not only alarmed American Jews and Israelis but it also further solidified the differences between the liberal elite and evangelical Zionists. For example, religious studies scholar Stephen Spector recalled attending one evangelical prayer service held on behalf of Israel in October 2005 in which a congregant fervently prayed for "a fresh wind of revelation to the parts of the Church that are rising up against Israel"—a direct reference to the liberal Protestant divesture campaign.[69] For Zionist evangelicals, such action by mainline Protestants reaffirmed two factors: that mainline churches remained out of touch with the pulse of most Protestant Americans and that evangelicals' continued fervent support for Israel remained a dominant priority.

Conclusion

It is hard to know what would have more greatly astonished the editors of the *Christian Century* in the 1930s who directed Jews to celebrate Christmas and negated Jewish claims to nationhood: the fact of Israel's establishment and survival or that American Protestants, by the turn of the twenty-first century, could be safely considered Israel's staunchest allies. Even Karl Baehr, the ACPC's tireless advocate of pro-Israel U.S. foreign policy, might have been surprised at the power and influence of pro-Israel evangelicals. He had worried that the Israeli land acquisitions of the 1967 War had damaged Protestant support for Israel and had undone decades of pro-Israel activism among the churches. Ironically the 1967 War did, in fact, change the nature of American Protestant support for Israel.

Though Israel's establishment had excited evangelicals and fundamentalists, it was the capture of Jerusalem in 1967 that solidified their support for the Jewish state. For American Protestants who interpreted Scripture literally—and their numbers were steadily growing in the latter half of the twentieth century—Israel's victory appeared prophetic. Many liberal Protestants *did* condemn the land acquisitions, but within ten years it did not matter. A new kind of Protestant Zionism had surfaced which relied less on the humanitarian and pragmatic impulses of earlier Protestants and more on prophecy and philosemitism. These evangelicals were now the mainstream, and they solidified American Protestant support for Israel.

The beginning of the twenty-first century revealed the importance of religion's influence on U.S. foreign policy in the Middle East. Small grass-roots efforts to atone for the sins of Christian Europe grew into a mainstream movement. Individual activists such as Reinhold Niebuhr, lobby groups like the American Christian Palestine Committee, and effective Protestant-Jewish political coordination changed the religious and political landscape in the United States and helped build a strong U.S.–Israeli alliance. Although mainline liberal Protestants were hardly united in uncritical support of Israel, the pro-Israel Protestants outmaneuvered their opponents to build a solid foundation. Later, inspired by prophecy that assigned Israel a primary role in the end of days and convinced that antisemitism hurt America's national interest, evangelicals capitalized on the earlier liberal Protestant-Israel alliance. Using an already friendly relationship to their advantage, evangelicals tightened the connection by raising enormous amounts of money and exerting significant political influence on Israel's behalf. Israeli prime ministers now looked directly to American evangelicals for their unwavering support.

The mainline Protestants, who had supported the early years of Israeli statehood out of concern first for the refugee and humanitarian crisis of the Holocaust and then as a stalwart ally during the Cold War, faded in numbers and influence and disappeared into near political irrelevance by the twenty-first century. The transformation that began with Jewish genocide in Europe and that had prompted mainline Protestants to support the idea of Zionism found its completion in the rise of evangelical power in the United States.

Liberal Protestants embarked on profound theological transformations in mainline Protestant theology, even as their remaining numbers grew increasingly critical of post-1967 Israeli-Palestinian policies. Forced to confront their assumptions about supercessionism and Jewish nationalism, liberal Protestants openly wrestled with appropriate responses to the Holocaust and Israel's survival, and inaugurated profound improvements in Jewish-Christian relations. The Protestant response to Jewish physician and Holocaust survivor Samuel Newman's letter-writing campaign aimed at the Southern Baptist convention's assertion that unconverted Jews "were lost without hope" revealed the intensity of Protestant self-examination regarding traditional Protestant attitudes and theology toward Jews and Judaism. Ultimately, by the turn of the twenty-first century, the once uniform idea that Jews had lost their chosen status and claim to statehood after the crucifixion of Christ would be swept into the dustbin of liberal Protestant theological thought.

The now politically powerful evangelical Protestants undertook their own theological innovations through a de-emphasis on end-of-times eschatology to focus more on the command to bless Israel in order to garner blessings for the United States. The earlier evangelical excitement over Israel's establishment that centered on bloody end-times scenarios, exemplified in the 1967 letter from an American Protestant to the Israeli Ministry of Religious Affairs inquiring about whether animal sacrifices in Jerusalem had resumed, shifted focus. Now an emphasis on attacking antisemitism as un-Christian, and supporting Israel and its land acquisitions as part of a biblical mandate, dominates the evangelical–Jewish–Israeli relationship. To these powerful Protestants, support of Israel protects America with the shield of biblical righteousness. The politically pragmatic and humanitarian Zionism of Niebuhr's era had been utterly replaced by a different Christian Zionism. Understanding how the Holocaust, Israel's establishment, and the 1967 War deepened American Protestants' relationship with Jews, Judaism, and Israel offers a more complete appreciation of the role religion plays in American politics and in U.S.–Israeli relations.

Notes

1. George Marsden, *Understanding Fundamentalism and Evangelicalism* (Grand Rapids, MI: Eerdmans, 1991), 1. See also Alan Mittleman, Byron Johnson, and Nancy Isserman, eds., *Uneasy Allies? Evangelical and Jewish Relations* (Lanham, MD: Rowman and Littlefield, 2007).

2. For a more thorough and cogent analysis of evangelicalism, see Gary Dorrien, "Evangelical Ironies: Theology, Politics, and Israel," in Mittleman, Johnson, and Isserman, *Uneasy Allies*, 103–126.

3. James Davison Hunter, "Operationalizing Evangelicalism: A Review, Critique & Proposal," *Sociological Analysis* 42, no. 4 (winter 1981): 363–372.

4. Ibid., 369–370. Hunter notes that the following denominational list serves as a fairly (although not entirely exhaustive) assessment of the major evangelical denominations in the United States: the Baptist tradition includes the Southern Baptist Convention of the United States, the Disciples of Christ, many of the Churches of Christ, Plymouth Brethren, the Independent Fundamentalist Churches of America, the Independent Fundamentalist Bible Churches, the Seventh-Day Adventists, the Worldwide Church of God, and the Church of God International; the Holiness-Pentecostal traditions include the Churches of God in North America, Church of God (Anderson, Indiana), the Wesleyan Church, the Church of the Nazarene, and the Church of Christ (Holiness) U.S.A., and (Pentecostal) the Church of God (Cleveland, Tennessee), the Church of God of Prophecy, the Full-Gospel Church Association, and the Assemblies of God; the Reformed-Confessional tradition includes the Christian Reformed Church, the Orthodox Presbyterian Church, the Reformed Presbyterian Church, the Evangelical Synod, the Lutheran Church—Missouri Synod, the Evangelical Lutheran Synod, and the Association of Evangelical Lutheran Churches; and denominations representative of the Anabaptist tradition include the Mennonite Church, the General Conference Mennonite Church, the Brethren in Christ Church, the Evangelical Mennonite Church, and the churches of the Evangelical Friends Alliance.

5. David Harrington Watt, "The Private Hopes of American Fundamentalists and Evangelicals, 1925–1975," *Religion and American Culture: A Journal of Interpretation* 1, no. 2 (summer 1991): 155–175.

6. Scholarship on the issue has been hitherto limited. In *American Protestantism and a Jewish State* (1973), historian Hertzel Fishman traced the reaction of liberal Protestantism to the idea of a homeland for the Jews in Palestine through the establishment of the State of Israel and the Six-Day War. Fishman concluded that "standard Protestant theology"

rejected the idea of a modern Jewish nation for theological reasons. Characterizing any theology as "standard Protestant theology" is, of course, problematic, as reviewers of Fishman's book have pointed out, including Melvin I. Urofsky in *Reviews in American History* 3, no. 3 (September 1975): 383–388. See Hertzel Fishman, *American Protestantism and a Jewish State* (Detroit: Wayne State University Press, 1973). Yaakov Ariel addresses the rise of pro-Zionist sympathies among premillennial dispensationalists in *On Behalf of Israel: American Fundamentalist Attitudes Toward Jews, Judaism, and Zionism, 1865–1945* (Brooklyn: Carlson, 1991). Ariel examines the birth of dispensational premillennialism in England and the United States in the late nineteenth and early twentieth centuries, and emphasizes the negative aspects of Protestant sympathy for the Zionist cause. Ariel concentrates his study on three major figures in the premillennialists' dispensationalist movement: John Nelson Darby, William Blackstone, and Arno Gaebelein. He argues that increased interest on the part of these Protestant leaders reflected ambivalence about Jews as individuals and concern for Israel only in the context of eschatological hopes. He adds that Israel's welcoming embrace of contemporary pro-Israel dispensational premillennialists represents a grave error of judgment—a misunderstanding of "the connection between the aggressive missionary work premillennialists carry out among Jews and the political support they give the State of Israel." Most recently, like Yaakov Ariel, historian Timothy Weber, in *On the Road to Armageddon: How Evangelicals Became Israel's Best Friend* (Grand Rapids, MI: Baker Academic, 2005), has addressed evangelicals' changing attitude toward Jews in light of end-times eschatology and the birth of Israel. His study provides a broad analysis of American evangelicalism's interest in Jews and Israel from the late nineteenth century to the present. He argues that, until 1967, fundamentalists were content to observe world events but did not act to affect political or foreign policies to their particular eschatological viewpoint. Yet the victory of Israel in the war of 1967 changed fundamentalists who now actively entered the game of global politics in order to speed up the end of days. Weber is concerned, however, only with fundamentalists and does not consider the role of liberal Protestants in laying the foundation for a close U.S.–Israeli alliance in the twentieth century that evangelicals would later commandeer for their own theological purposes.

CHAPTER 1. AMERICAN PROTESTANTS AND JEWISH PERSECUTION, 1933–1937

1. Editorial, "Jews and Christmas," *Christian Century* (20 December 1939): 1566–1567.

2. Jerome Karabel, *The Chosen: The Hidden History of Admission and Exclusion at Harvard, Yale, and Princeton* (Boston: Houghton Mifflin, 2005).

3. Fredrick M. Schweitzer, "Introduction," in Robert Michael, *A Concise History of American Antisemitism* (Lanham, MD: Rowman and Littlefield, 2005), viii.

4. Ibid., xx.

5. Michael, A Concise History, 127–128.

6. Other historians of American antisemitism dispute Michael's assertion that religion formed the basis for discrimination and prejudice against Jews. Eric Goldstein, for example, argues that the problems of modernity, questions of acculturation and assimilation of recent Jewish immigrants from Eastern Europe, and the economic depression served as the primary causes for the rise of antisemitism in the 1930s. Eric Goldstein, *The Price of Whiteness: Jews, Race, and American Identity* (Princeton, NJ: Princeton University Press, 2006).

7. See Deborah Dash Moore, *At Home in America: Second Generation New York Jews* (New York: Columbia University Press, 1981).

8. Douglas Strong, *Organized Antisemitism in America* (Westport, CT: Greenwood, 1941), 18.

9. As quoted in Michael, *A Concise History*, 127.

10. Originally published in 1891 in Russia, *The Protocols of the Elders of Zion* was a fabrication that its proponents claimed outlined a worldwide Jewish conspiracy to dominate and subjugate Christians. Its contents contained common libels against the Jews such as, among others, the use of Christian children's blood in Jewish rituals, attempts to poison Christian wells, and the desire to promote world warfare. *Protocols* appeared in the United States in 1920 as a series in Henry Ford's *Dearborn Independent* titled "The International Jew." The series ran until 1922.

11. Letter from G. George Fox to Roger Straus (3 December 1936), Antisemitism File III, Jacob Rader Marcus Center of the American Jewish Archives, Cincinnati Campus, Hebrew Union College, Jewish Institute of Religion.

12. Letter from Roger Straus to George Fox (7 December 1937), Small Collections 389, Jacob Rader Marcus Center of the American Jewish Archives, Cincinnati Campus, Hebrew Union College, Jewish Institute of Religion.

13. Other founding members included noted sociologist George E. Vincent, political scientist and noted philanthropist Charles Merriam, Baptist minister and University of Chicago Trustee Charles Gilkey, Washington University Chancellor and Nobel-prize winning physicist Arthur H. Compton, and Congressman W. A. Milliken.

14. Founding Statement of the National Foundation for the Preservation of Democracy (1936), Antisemitism File, Jacob Rader Marcus Center of the American Jewish Archives, Cincinnati Campus, Hebrew Union College, Jewish Institute of Religion.

15. Strong, *Organized Antisemitism,* 75.

16. Arno Clemens Gaebelein, *The Conflict of the Ages: The Mystery of Lawlessness: Its Origin, Historic Development and Coming Defeat* (New York: Publication Office *Our Hope,* 1936).

17. Yaakov S. Ariel, *On Behalf of Israel : American Fundamentalist Attitudes toward Jews, Judaism, and Zionism, 1865–1945* (Brooklyn, NY: Carlson, 1991).

18. Balfour Declaration, Library of Congress Archives.

19. Donald Wagner, "From Blackstone to Bush: Christian Zionism in the United States, 1890–2004," in *Challenging Christian Zionism: Theology, Politics and the Israel-Palestine Conflict,* ed. Naim Ateek, Cedar Duaybis, and Maurine Tobin, Proceedings of the Fifth International Sabeel Conference (Jerusalem: Sabeel Ecumenical Liberation Theology Center, 2004), 54.

20. Weber, *On the Road to Armageddon,* 85.

21. Fishman, *American Protestantism and a Jewish State,* 24.

22. Mark Twain, *The Innocents Abroad* (New York: New American Library, 1980 [1869]).

23. Fishman, *American Protestantism and a Jewish State,* 24.

24. Ibid., 27.

25. Letter from Judah Magnes to John Haynes Holmes (24 October 1937), Correspondence File, Jacob Rader Marcus Center of the American Jewish Archives, Hebrew Union College, Jewish Institute of Religion, Cincinnati Campus.

26. Editorial, "What Is Palestine's Future?" *Christian Century* (11 December 1929): 1535.

27. Ibid.

28. Editorial, "Jews and Jesus," *Christian Century* (3 May 1933): 582–584.

29. Ibid.

30. Editorial, "The Jewish Problem in Germany and Palestine," *Christian Century* (29 November 1933): 1491.

31. *Great Britain Parliamentary Papers*, vol. 14 (1936/1937); as quoted in Fishman, *American Protestantism and a Jewish State*, 44.

32. "The Palestine Commission's Report: From the Point of View of the Church," *International Review of Missions* 36 (1937): 468.

33. Fishman, *American Protestantism and a Jewish State*, 71–72.

34. Ibid., 66.

35. Papers of the Pro-Palestine Federation, Central Zionist Archives; also quoted in Fishman, *American Protestantism and a Jewish State*, 67.

36. W. A. Visser't Hooft, "Christ or Caesar in Germany?" *Christian Century* (3 May 1933): 589.

37. Ernst Modershohn, "The Jews in Germany," *Moody Bible Institute Monthly* (July 1934): 506.

38. Henry Smith Leiper, "The German Church Problem," *Reformed Church Messenger* (16 November 1933): 10.

39. The German Christians, like the Confessing Church, were a splinter organization of the Evangelical Church in Germany. They supported the Nazi Party ideology and sought to implement its ideas of racial purity into liturgy, theology, and membership.

40. Reinhold Niebuhr, "Religion and the New Germany," *Christian Century* (28 June 1933): 843–844.

41. Ibid., 844.

42. "Topics of the Times: Germany's Non-Aryan Millions," *New York Times* (4 November 1933): 18.

43. "Mixed Race Group Unites in Germany," *New York Times* (6 November 1933): 9.

44. "The Nazification of German Protestantism Continues," *Christian Century* (20 September 1933): 1164.

45. Editorial, *Watchman Examiner* (4 January 1934): 4; "German Missions to the Jews," *Alliance Weekly* (28 April 1934): 267.

46. Rev. Dr. Samuel M. Zwemer, "Far Horizons," *Presbyterian* (28 June 1934): 14.

47. "Christian Jews in Germany," *Moody Bible Institute Monthly* (August 1934): 539.

48. Ibid., 540.

49. Ibid.

50. Editorial, "Demonic Germany and the Predicament of Humanity," *Christian Century* (30 November 1938): 1456–1459.

51. Editorial," Jewry and Democracy," *Christian Century* (9 June 1937): 735.

52. Editorial, "The Jewish Problem," *Christian Century* (29 April 1936): 25.

CHAPTER 2. AMERICAN PROTESTANTS RESPOND TO
ZIONISM AND THE JEWISH GENOCIDE IN EUROPE, 1938–1948

Certain discussions in chapter 2 emerge from an earlier work titled "The American Christian Palestine Committee, the Holocaust, and Mainstream Protestant Zionism," which appeared in *Genocide and Holocaust Studies* 24, no. 2 (fall 2010): 273–296, and appear here by the kind permission of Oxford University Press.

1. Loy W. Henderson, State Department, Division of Near East Affairs, Office Memorandum, 23 May 1945, Anglo-American Committee of Inquiry File, Manuscript Collection 163, Jacob Rader Marcus Center of the American Jewish Archives, Hebrew Union College, Jewish Institute of Religion, Cincinnati Campus, Cincinnati.

2. Robert Ross, *So It Was True: The American Protestant Press and the Nazi Persecution of the Jews* (Minneapolis: University of Minnesota Press, 1980), 83–84.

3. Editorial, "Terror in Germany," *Christian Century* (23 November 1938): 1422–1423.

4. J. Frank Norris, "Protocols of the Wise Men of Zion," *Fundamentalist* (22 October 1937): 5–7; quoted in Weber, *On the Road to Armageddon*, 140–141.

5. Weber, *On the Road to Armageddon*, 148–149.

6. Charles Clayton Morrison, "Palestine—Pawn of Empire," *Christian Century* (31 May 1939): 695–696.

7. Fishman, *American Protestantism and a Jewish State*, 50.

8. "Jewish Women from Many Lands Are Neighbors in Palestine," *Christian Science Monitor* (26 May 1939): 14.

9. Editorial, "The Forbidden Theme," *Christian Century* (24 September 1941): 1167–1169.

10. Press Release, Office of Senator Robert F. Wagner, 28 March 1941, American Christian Palestine Committee (ACPC) File, Central Zionist Archives (CZA) F40/16, Jerusalem.

11. Its first membership list included seventy-three senators and seventy-six congressmen. Among the most notable members were Senator Harry S. Truman; Attorney General Robert H. Jackson; Secretary of the Interior Harold L. Ickes; Secretary of Agriculture Claude A. Wickard; Wendell L. Willkie; Alfred E. Smith; Clarence A. Dykstra, director of Selective Service and head of the Defense Mediation Board; Paul V. McNutt, federal security administrator; John M. Carmody, Federal Works administrator; William Allen White; Senator Alben W. Barkley, then Senate Majority Leader; Senator Walter F. George, chairman of the Senate Foreign Relations Committee; Senator Arthur H. Vandenberg of Michigan; Senator Robert A. Taft of Ohio; Senator Henry Cabot Lodge Jr., of Massachusetts; Sam Rayburn, Speaker of the House; John W. McCormack, House Majority Leader; and Joseph W. Martin Jr., House Minority Leader and Chairman of the Republican National Committee. ACPC File, CZA F40/16, Jerusalem.

12. Press Release, American Palestine Committee, 28 March 1941, ACPC File, CZA F40/16, Jerusalem.

13. Ibid.

14. Ibid.

15. American Palestine Committee, "America and Zion," 30 April 1941, ACPC File, CZA F40/16, Jerusalem.

16. Ibid.

17. Ibid.

18. Charles Clayton Morrison, "How Their Minds Have Changed,"*Christian Century* (25 October 1939): 1302.

19. Reinhold Niebuhr, "If America is drawn into the war, can you, as a Christian, participate in it, or support it?" *Christian Century* (8 December 1940): 1578–1580.

20. Reinhold Niebuhr, *Christianity and Crisis* (10 February 1941): 6.

21. For a thorough analysis of the American Press and its reporting of the destruction of the European Jews during the Nazi Regime, see Deborah Lipstadt, *Beyond Belief: The American Press and the Coming of the Holocaust 1933–1945* (New York: Free Press, 1986).

Lipstadt argues that the American press and government remained largely indifferent in its coverage of the Holocaust during the war, despite considerable knowledge of the Nazi genocide. See also Robert W. Ross, *So It Was True: The American Protestant Press and the Nazi Persecution of the Jews* (Minneapolis: University of Minnesota Press, 1980). Ross examined the religious press during the war and came to conclusions similar to those of Lipstadt: knowledge of the Holocaust was widely available, even in the religious press, but readers found it difficult to believe.

22. Editorial, "Horror Stories from Poland," *Christian Century* (9 December 1942): 1518–1519.

23. Rabbi Theodore Lewis to Charles C. Morrison, 10 December 1942, Manuscript Collection 49, Stephen Wise Papers, Jacob Rader Marcus Center of the American Jewish Archives, Hebrew Union College, Jewish Institute of Religion, Cincinnati Campus.

24. Theodore Lewis, Letter to the Editor, *Christian Century* (23 December 1942): 1597.

25. Felix Frankfurter to Reinhold Niebuhr, 24 December 1941, Reinhold Niebuhr Papers, Box 63, Library of Congress Archives, Washington, D.C.

26. Niebuhr, "Jews after the War," *The Nation* (28 February 1942): 254.

27. Ibid.

28. Felix Frankfurter to Reinhold Niebuhr, 1941, Reinhold Niebuhr Papers Box 63, Library of Congress Archives, Washington, D.C.

29. Henry Atkinson, "The 'Jewish Problem' is a Christian Problem," *Christianity and Crisis* (28 June 1943): 3–4.

30. Editorial, "European Jews Are in a Desperate Plight," *Christian Century* (8 September 1943): 1004–1005.

31. "American Palestine Committee Calls on Christian America to Back Up Jewish Homeland," 23 December 1943, ACPC File, CZA F40/17, Jerusalem.

32. Ibid.

33. "Resolutions by the Executive Committee of the Christian Council on Palestine," 1943, ACPC File, CZA F40/20, Jerusalem.

34. Henry Atkinson and Carl Hermann Voss, "More Light on the Jewish Question," *World Alliance Newsletter* (September 1943), ACPC File, CZA F40/26, Jerusalem.

35. Ibid., 4–9.

36. Ibid.

37. Press Release, American Palestine Committee, 9 March 1944, ACPC File, CZA F40/17, Jerusalem.

38. Resolutions of the International Pro-Palestine Committee, October 1945, ACPC File, CZA F40/17, Jerusalem.38. Ibid.

39. Press Release, American Palestine Committee, 9 March 1944, ACPC File, CZA F40/17, Jerusalem.

40. Ibid.

41. Carl Hermann Voss, "Christian Ministers Speak Out," *New Palestine* (31 March 1944): 339.

42. Ibid.

43. Ibid. The CCP program was very specific about ways to increase Jewish immigration. It advocated that "America take the lead in helping save millions of Jews from the horror created by the Nazi terror in Europe. We suggest that our government consider the possibility of utilizing the immigration quotas from all nations for 1944, by which a total of 155,000 visas may be issued, and that 100,000 of these be issued to an equal number of

Jews now homeless and stateless in Europe. In taking this action we are not unmindful of the grave political difficulties involved, but our faith in our British Allies in this world-wide war against tyranny and on behalf of the Four Freedoms is sincere."

44. "Palestine in War in Peace," Radio Address for *University of the Air* series, 28 June 1944, ACPC File, CZA F40/26, Jerusalem.

45. "Methodist Conference Demands Fulfillment of Jewish National Home Pledge," American Palestine Committee Press Release, 13 June 1944, ACPC File, CZA F40/17, Jerusalem.

46. Ibid.

47. Harry Rimmer, "Palestine: The Coming Storm Center," *Moody Monthly* 41 (October 1941): 113.

48. Arno Gaebelein, "The Increasing Antisemitism," *Our Hope* 44 (1939): 687.

49. Weber, *On the Road to Armageddon*, 148.

50. Editorial, *Moody Monthly* 43 (April 1943): 472.

51. Arno Gaebelein, "The Poor Jews," *Our Hope* 46 (1940): 625.

52. Will Houghton, *Moody Monthly* 40 (July 1940): 592.

53. Arno Gaebelein, "Anti-Semitic Tentacles Spread," *Our Hope* 47 (1940): 263.

54. Arno Gaebelein, "Jewish Problems," *Our Hope* 48 (1942): 839–840.

55. Arno Gaebelein, "The New Great World Crisis," *Our Hope* 50 (1943): 22.

56. Gaebelein, "Jewish Problems," 813–814.

57. Ibid.

58. Arno Gaebelein, "The Jewish Problem," *Our Hope* 50 (1943): 250–251.

59. "Report on American Jewish Organizations and Attitudes of American Jews Toward Palestine," in Manuscript Collection 163, Anglo-American Committee of Inquiry File, Box 1, Jacob Rader Marcus Center of the American Jewish Archives, Hebrew Union College, Institute for Jewish Religion, Cincinnati Campus.

60. "Christian Opinion on Jewish Nationalism and a Jewish State, with a Foreword by Morris S. Lazaron," Jewish-Christian Relations Nearprint File (1940s), Jacob Rader Marcus Center of the American Jewish Archives, Hebrew Union College, Institute for Jewish Religion, Cincinnati Campus.

61. Ibid.

62. Ibid.

63. Ibid.

64. Fishman, *American Protestantism and a Jewish State*, 84.

65. John Haynes Holmes to Judah Magnes, Correspondence File, Jacob Rader Marcus Center of the American Jewish Archives, Hebrew Union College, Institute for Jewish Religion, Cincinnati Campus.

66. Ibid.

67. Letter from William A. Eddy of the Legation of the United States of America, writing from Saudi Arabia on 11 April 1945 to the Secretary of State regarding "Statements of Najib Salha regarding the conversations between the President and the King Abdul Aziz," Anglo-American Committee of Inquiry File, Manuscript Collection 163, Jacob Rader Marcus Center of the American Jewish Archives, Cincinnati.

68. In one letter to Wallace Murray, dated 15 June 1945, the U.S. ambassador in Iran, Gordon P. Merriam, addressed Roosevelt's complicated legacy on Palestine: "The President . . . authorized Wise to say that the President would continue President Roosevelt's

policy with respect to Palestine. We did not feel particularly alarmed at the result of this opening round since, as we know, Mr. Roosevelt had two Palestinian policies. . . . We have taken . . . occasions to brief the President on the subject. he is a very sensible and reasonable man, and we now feel that he is well grounded in the essentials of the Palestine question and will go pretty slow in the future."

69. Secret Memo for the President prepared by Paul H. Alling, Department of State, Division of Near Eastern Affairs and approved by the Assistant Secretary of the Department of State, Anglo-American Committee of Inquiry, Manuscript Collection 163, Jacob Rader Marcus Center of the American Jewish Archives, Hebrew Union College, Jewish Institute of Religion, Cincinnati Campus, Cincinnati.

70. Gordon P. Merriam to Wallace Murray, American Ambassador, Tehran, 15 June 1945, Anglo-American Committee of Inquiry File, Manuscript Collection 163, Jacob Rader Marcus Center of the American Jewish Archives, Hebrew Union College, Jewish Institute of Religion, Cincinnati Campus.

71. Loy W. Henderson, State Department, Division of Near East Affairs, Office Memorandum, 23 May 1945, Anglo-American Committee of Inquiry File, Manuscript Collection 163, Jacob Rader Marcus Center of the American Jewish Archives, Hebrew Union College, Jewish Institute of Religion, Cincinnati Campus.

72. Memorandum for the President, Subject: Palestine, 28 May 1945, Anglo-American Committee of Inquiry Correspondence File, Manuscript Collection 163, Box 1, Jacob Rader Marcus Center of the American Jewish Archives, Hebrew Union College, Jewish Institute of Religion, Cincinnati Campus.

73. Helen Gahagan Douglas, "To Christian Youth," speech delivered at Christ Church in New York City, 14 October 1944, ACPC File, CZA F40/44, Jerusalem.

74. Ibid.

75. Wendell Phillips, Press and Radio Address, 16 October 1945, ACPC File, CZA F40/17, Jerusalem.

76. Katherine Hayden Salter, "The Gentile Problem," *Christian Century* (28 August 1940); found in the Jewish–Christian Relations Nearprint Collection, Jacob Rader Marcus Center of the American Jewish Archives, Hebrew Union College, Jewish Institute of Religion, Cincinnati Campus.

77. John Haynes Holmes, "Christianity's Debt to Judaism: Why Not Acknowledge It?" Sermon delivered to Community Church in New York City, 17 January 1943, Jewish Christian Relations Nearprint File, Jacob Rader Marcus Center for American Jewish Archives, Cincinnati.

78. "Conference Urges Fight on Bigotry," *New York Times* (9 February 1945): 12.

79. The National Conference of Christians and Jews was founded by a Catholic priest from Denver, Colorado, in 1933.

80. "Conference Urges Fight on Bigotry," *New York Times* (9 February 1945): 12.

81. "Interfaith Group Notes Rise in Bias," *New York Times* (11 April 1945): 21.

82. "Plans Bias Fight Fund," *New York Times* (2 November 1945): 21.

83. The NCCJ was founded in response to Jewish desires to eliminate proselytizing efforts by Protestants and reflected an early attempt to eliminate Christian antisemitism and foster greater interfaith interaction in the United States. See William R. Hutchinson, ed., *Between the Times: The Travail of the Protestant Establishment in America, 1900–1960*

(New York: Cambridge University Press, 1989); and Lance Sussman, "Toward a Better Understanding": The Rise of the Interfaith Movement in America and the Role of Rabbi Isaac Landerman," *American Jewish Archives Journal* 43, no. 1 (April 1982): 35–51.

84. "Dr. Latz Is Honored," *New York Times* (10 April 1946): 21.

85. "Church Leaders to Meet," *New York Times* (1 July 1946): 22.

86. "Jews and Christians Hold Rally in London," *New York Times* (30 July 1945): 5.

87. "Interfaith Group for World Urged," *New York Times* (23 October 1946): 24.

88. Ibid.

89. "Resolutions by the World Council of Churches," *Federal Council Bulletin* 29, no. 5 (May 1946): 8–9.

90. Ibid.

91. "Winant Calls for Unity," *New York Times* (8 January 1947): 26.

92. "Two Million Dollars Sought for Anti-Bias Task," *New York Times* (16 February 1947): 46.

93. "Pastor Sees Bias in Bible," *New York Times* (7 April 1947): 16.

94. "World Fight Is Set on Antisemitism," *New York Times* (6 August 1947): 5.

95. Ibid.

96. "Did Hitler Win?" *Christianity and Crisis* (12 November 1945): 3.

97. Press Release from the Christian Council on Palestine, "Christian Ministers Urge President Truman to Insist that Jewish Refugees Detained at La Spezia Be Granted Immediate Passage to Palestine," 12 April 1946, ACPC File, CZA F40/24, Jerusalem.

98. Arno Gaebelein, "Zionist Demands to Atlee," *Our Hope* 52 (1945): 188–190.

99. E. Schuyler English, "The Judgment of the Nations," *Our Hope* 51 (1945): 563.

100. Telegram from Gallman to Byrnes, 6 October 1945, Anglo-American Committee of Inquiry File, Manuscript Collection 163, Box 1, Jacob Rader Marcus Center of the American Jewish Archives, Hebrew Union College, Jewish Institute of Religion, Cincinnati Campus.

101. Ibid.

102. Secret Memo from the State Department, 19 October 1945, Transcription of a conversation between Lord Halifax and James Byrnes, Anglo-American Committee of Inquiry, Manuscript Collection 163, Box 1, Jacob Rader Marcus Center of the American Jewish Archives, Hebrew Union College, Jewish Institute of Religion, Cincinnati Campus.

103. Daniel Poling testimony before the Anglo-American Committee of Inquiry, transcript in the Reinhold Niebuhr Papers, Box 63, Library of Congress Archives, Washington, D.C.

104. Reinhold Niebuhr's testimony before the Anglo-American Committee of Inquiry, Reinhold Niebuhr Papers, Box 63, Library of Congress Archives, Washington, D.C.

105. Ibid.

106. Ibid.

107. Letter from Rabbi Stephen Wise, Reinhold Niebuhr Papers, Box 63, Library of Congress Archives, Washington, D.C.

108. Fishman, *American Protestantism and a Jewish State*, 81–82.

109. Record Group 59, General Records of the Department of State. Office of Public Opinion Studies, 1943–1965. Public Opinion on Foreign Countries and Regions; Near East and Middle East, 1945–1965, Box 41.

110. The report quoted Roosevelt's letter to Wagner in which Roosevelt stated: "I am convinced that the American people give their support to this aim [of the establishment of a Jewish homeland in Palestine] and if re-elected I shall help to bring about its realization." Memorandum–Plan II (Arab state only), Anglo-American Committee of Inquiry File, Manuscript Collection 163, Box 1, Jacob Rader Marcus Center of the American Jewish Archives, Hebrew Union College, Jewish Institute of Religion, Cincinnati Campus.

111. Record Group 59, General Records of the Department of State, Office of Public Opinion Studies, 1943–1975. Monthly Surveys of Public Opinion on International Affairs, 1944–1948, Box 11 (November 1947), Survey 79.

112. Ibid.

113. Ibid. (February 1948), Survey 82.

CASE STUDY 1

1. Extensive scholarship exists regarding the question of Christian accommodation and resistance to national socialism and the genocide of the Jews, with most scholars concluding that little resistance and a great deal of accommodation occurred in Germany and Europe between 1933 and 1945. See, for example, Doris Bergen, *Twisted Cross: The German Christian Movement in the Third Reich* (Chapel Hill: University of North Carolina Press, 1991); Ernst Christian Helmreich, *The German Churches under Hitler* (Detroit: Wayne State University Press, 1979); and Klaus Scholder, *The Churches and the Third Reich*, vols. 1 and 2 (Philadelphia: Fortress, 1988).

2. Virginia Lee Warren, "Jews Future Seen Better in Europe," *New York Times* (18 June 1945): 8.

3. The German Confessing Church broke away from the mainline German church in 1933 in response to increasing influences of Nazi ideology and control.

4. Reinhold Niebuhr, "Reveal German Chaplains Carried on Anti-Nazi Activity," *Christianity and Crisis* (2 April 1945): 7. The editors explained that the pamphlet was presented to American soldiers occupying the German army barracks at the conclusion of the war. This is the only account I am aware of in which anti-Nazi literature was circulated by German chaplains inside the army barracks.

5. Editorial, "Dutch Churches Praised for Uncompromising Stand against Persecution of Jews," *Christianity and Crisis* (30 April 1945): 7; Editorial, "France Praises Interfaith Cooperation," *Christian Century* (20 June 1945): 740.

6. Editorial, "France Praises Interfaith Cooperation," 740.

7. Editorial, "Jewish Congregation in Holland to Help Rebuild Catholic Churches," *Christianity and Crisis* (29 October 1945): 7.

8. Ben L. Rose, "As Niemöller Sees Germany's Future," *Christian Century* (10 October 1945): 1155.

9. Editorial, "Message of the German Evangelical Church to the German People," *Christianity and Crisis* (29 October 1945): 7.

10. "Editorial Notes," *Christianity and Crisis* - (23 July 1945): 2.

11. According to Niemöller, 45 Protestant clergy and 450 Roman Catholic priests were imprisoned in Dachau.

12. Martin Niemöller, "Niemöller about the Question of Guilt," *Christianity and Crisis*-(8 July 8 1946): 6.

13. Letter to Stephen Wise from Samuel Cavert, 20 February 1947, Record Group 18, Box 16, Folder 1, Federal Council of Churches Collection, Presbyterian Historical Society, Philadelphia.

14. "End of Hate Urged by Dr. Niemöller," *New York Times* (20 January 1947): 35.

15. Ibid.

16. Ibid.

17. Eleanor Roosevelt, "Germans' Guilt," *New York Times* (4 January 1947). Found in Record Group 18, NCC, Box 15, Series II—General Secretary 1898–1951, Presbyterian Historical Society Archives, Philadelphia.

18. Letter from Samuel Cavert to Eleanor Roosevelt, 6 January 1947, and Letter from Eleanor Roosevelt to Samuel Cavert, 13 January 1947, both in Record Group 18, Box 16, Folder 1, Federal Council of Churches Collection, Presbyterian Historical Society, Philadelphia.

19. Letter to the Editor, W. Maylan Jones of the First Methodist Church, 24 January 1947, Record Group 18, Box 16, Folder 1, Federal Council of Churches Collection, Presbyterian Historical Society, Philadelphia.

20. Letter from Mrs. George Friedman to Samuel Cavert, 9 January 1947, Record Group 18, Box 16, Folder 1, FCC Collection, Presbyterian Historical Society, Philadelphia.

21. Joseph Alliger to Harper Sibley, 7 January 1947, Record Group 18, Box 16, Folder 1, FCC Collection, Presbyterian Historical Society, Philadelphia.

22. "German Pastor Replies to His Critics—Says Era of Antisemitism Is Over," *New York Times* (21 January 1947): 8.

23. Ibid.

24. Delbert Clark, "Antisemitism End in Germany Denied," *New York Times* (25 January 1947): 4.

25. Letter from J. G. Weiser to Federal Council of Churches, 22 January 1947, Record Group 18, Box 16, Folder 1, FCC Collection, Presbyterian Historical Society, Philadelphia.

26. Letter from Paul Hirsch to FCC, 20 January 1947, Record Group 18, Box 16, Folder 1, FCC Collection, Presbyterian Historical Society, Philadelphia.

27. "The Truth about Niemöller," Record Group 18, NCC, Box 15, Series II—General Secretary 1898–1951, Presbyterian Historical Society, Philadelphia.

28. Victor Bernstein, "Answering Niemöller," *PM* (21 January 1947): 2.

29. Letter from Frank Matthias to Federal Council of Churches, 26 January 1947, Record Group 18, Box 16, Folder 1, FCC Collection, Presbyterian Historical Society, Philadelphia.

30. "Masaryk Assails Niemöller Visit," printed in the *New York Sun* (11 February 1947), Record Group 18, Box 16, Folder 1, FCC Collection, Presbyterian Historical Society, Philadelphia.

31. Letter from Stephen Wise to Samuel Cavert, 24 January 1947, Record Group 18, Box 16, Folder 1, FCC Collection, Presbyterian Historical Society, Philadelphia.

32. "Niemöller Says God, Not Man, Beat Hitler," *New York Times* (25 January 1947): 2.

33. Reinhold Niebuhr, "Our Chances for Peace," *Christianity and Crisis* (17 February 1947): 1–2.

34. Letter from Daniel Poling to Samuel Cavert, 27 January 1947, Record Group 18, Box 16, Folder 1, FCC Collection, Presbyterian Historical Society, Philadelphia.

35. "Play Fair with Niemöller!" *Christian Century* (15 January 1947): 1.

36. Letter from Samuel Cavert to Stephen Wise, 27 January 1947, Record Group 18, Box 16, Folder 1, FCC Collection, Presbyterian Historical Society, Philadelphia.

37. Letter from H. C. Furstenwalde to Stephen Wise, 25 January 1947, Record Group 18, Box 16, Folder 1, FCC Collection, Presbyterian Historical Society, Philadelphia.

38. "Pastor Niemöller," Editorial, *B'nai B'rith Messenger*, 14 February 1947, Record Group 18, Box 16, Folder 1, FCC Collection, Presbyterian Historical Society, Philadelphia.

39. "Gazing into the Pit," *Christian Century* (9 May 1945): 575.

40. Ibid.

CHAPTER 3. THE CHALLENGES OF STATEHOOD, 1948–1953

1. Public Opinion Survey August 1947–July 1948 and Public Opinion Surveys 1945–1965, General Records, Department of State, Record Group 59, Box 41. The survey assessment noted that between January and June of 1948, the State Department received 461,199 pieces of mail on Palestine. It added that, "for the purposes of comparison it may be noted that the Department mail in November, 1946, included approximately 10,300 comments on Yugoslavia, largely in connection with the arrest of Archbishop Stepanic. And in one week at the first of April, 1947, approximately 5,000 comments on Greece were received. These are examples of peaks reached on other questions that drew a large volume of comment mail, but in neither case was the volume as great, nor did it continue as long as in the case of comment on Palestine."

2. Public Opinion Survey March 1950 and Public Opinion Surveys 1945–1965, General Records, Record Group 59, Box 41.

3. Public Opinion Survey August 1947–July 1948 and Public Opinion Surveys 1945–1965, General Records, Department of State, Record Group 59, Box 41.

4. See Michael J. Cohen, *Truman and Israel* (Berkeley: University of California Press, 1990); Zvi Ganin, *Truman, American Jewry, and Israel, 1945–1948* (New York: Holmes and Meier, 1979); and John Snetsinger, *Truman, the Jewish Vote, and the Creation of Israel* (Stanford: Hoover Institution Press, 1974).

5. Michael T. Benson, *Harry S. Truman and the Founding of Israel* (Westport, CT: Praeger, 1997).

6. Harry S. Truman to Edward Jacobson, 27 February 1948, Truman Institute Archives, C292/ F3498, Hebrew University, Jerusalem.

7. Harry S. Truman to Honorable Dean Alfange, 13 May 1948, Truman Institute Archives, C292/ F3498, Hebrew University, Jerusalem.

8. Uri Bialer, "'Our Place in the World'—Mapai and Israel's Foreign Policy Orientation 1947–1952," *Jerusalem Papers on Peace Problems 33* (Jerusalem: Magnes, 1981).

9. Ibid., 20.

10. Ibid.

11. For a comprehensive examination of Israeli-Vatican relations in the first two decades of Israeli independence, see Uri Bialer, *Cross on the Star of David: The Christian World in Israel's Foreign Policy, 1948–1967* (Bloomington: Indiana University Press, 2005).

12. "Largest Protestant Affiliations Groups in the United States" memo, Israeli Ministry for Religious Affairs File, Israeli State Archive (ISA) 5807/7, Jerusalem.

13. "Truman's Palestine Trouble Grows," *Christian Century* (11 February 1948): 165.

14. Virginia Gildersleeve, *Many a Good Crusade: Memoirs of Virginia Gildersleeve* (New York: Macmillan, 1959), 184–185; quoted in Fishman, *American Protestantism and a Jewish State*, 84.

15. "Palestine—Whose Holy Land?" *Christian Century*, (16 June 1948): 587.

16. "Do the World's Jews Want to Be Feared?" *Christian Century* (16 June 1948): 589.

17. Editorial, "Israel Knows No God," *Christian Century* (9 June 1948): 565.

18. Benjamin Kreitman, "'God' and Israel's Declaration," *Christian Century* (14 July 1948): 711.

19. Daniel Bliss, "Justice and Peace in the Holy Land," *Christian Century* (8 September 1948): 908–910.

20. Millar Burrows, "Jewish Nationalism," *Christian Century* (30 March 1949): 401.

21. Copy of Statement by Garland Evans Hopkins titled "Garland Hopkins Finds Palestinian Conditions Serious," Ministry of Religious Affairs File, ISA 85/22, Jerusalem.

22. Henry Sloan Coffin, "Perils to America in the New Jewish State," *Christianity and Crisis* (21 February 1949): 9–10.

23. H. A. Fischel, "Correspondence," *Christianity and Crisis* (21 March 1949): 30.

24. Ibid., 31.

25. Editorial Note, *Christianity and Crisis* (3 October 1949): 122.

26. Karl Baehr, "The Arabs and Israel," *Christianity and Crisis* (3 October 1949): 125.

27. Ibid., 126.

28. Editorial, "UN Takes Over Jerusalem Problem," *Lutheran* 23, no. 12 (21 December 1949): 5–6.

29. Elias Haddad, "Postmark: Bethlehem," *Lutheran* 23, no. 12 (21 December 1949): 12–14.

30. Elias Haddad, "Orphanage Opens in Bethlehem," *Lutheran* 32, no. 21 (22 February 1950): 16–17.

31. Karl Baehr, "For the Record," 4–7 December, 1951, ACPC File, CZA F40/36, Jerusalem.

32. Ibid., 29, 30, November 1951.

33. Ibid., 13 December 1951.

34. Ibid., 4–7 December 1951.

35. Fishman writes: "Though the American Christian Palestine Committee continued its public relations work during the hectic period when the United Nations was considering the Palestine question and long after the state of Israel was established, its *primary* task, helping to arouse the Christian conscience of America with respect to a Zionist solution to the Jewish problem, had been successfully achieved." Fishman, *American Protestantism and a Jewish State*, 82.

36. The Israeli government, particularly the Ministry of Religious Affairs, consistently worked with members of the ACPC to encourage American Protestant support for the state of Israel. Members of the government commented frequently on the importance of cooperation and the usefulness of the ACPC-Israeli alliance in promoting a close Israeli-American alliance. See CZA File 40 and Israeli State Archives File 366.

37. Eliahu Elath to Blanche J. Shepard, 17 March 1949, American Christian Palestine Committee, Ministry for Religious Affairs File, ISA 366/5, Jerusalem.

38. Abba Hillel Silver, Zionist Emergency Council, 11 February, 1949, Ministry for Religious Affairs File, ISA 85/22. See also Mark A. Raider, *Abba Hillel Silver and Ameri-*

can Zionism (London: Cass, 1997); and Marc Lee Raphael, *Abba Hillel Silver: A Profile in American Judaism* (New York: Holmes & Meier, 1989).

39. The Vatican supported the idea of the internationalization of Jerusalem to protect the holy sites from Israeli or Jordanian hegemony. "Jerusalem and the Christian World: A Letter to the President of the United States," published in 1949 by the American Christian Palestine Committee, argued that "as Christian ministers and laymen, the status of Jerusalem and its future are a source of anxiety" and noted that "as Christians we have been particularly concerned with the relationship between the State of Israel and the Christian Institutions and population of that part of the Holy Land under Israeli jurisdiction. We have closely followed the development of this relationship, and are convinced that the state and the people of Israel would, in administering Jerusalem, abide by the principle of freedom of religion as formulated in the Israeli draft constitution, as repeatedly pledged by official spokesmen of the government, and as now practiced in the State of Israel." ACPC File, CZA F40/79, Jerusalem.

40. ACPC Press Release, "Report by Christian Fact-Finding Mission on Jerusalem Rejects Internationalization Plan after Investigation There," 19 January 1950, ACPC File, CZA F40/69, Jerusalem.

41. Carl Herman Voss to Moshe Sharett, 24 September 1949, Ministry for Religious Affairs File, ISA 85/22, Jerusalem.

42. Jerome Unger to Hon. Aubrey S. Iban, 29 September 1949, Ministry for Religious Affairs File, ISA 85/22, Jerusalem.

43. Press Release, American Christian Palestine Committee, November 1949, Ministry for Religious Affairs File, ISA 85/22, Jerusalem.

44. "TVA on the Jordan," Dinner, ACPC File, CZA F40/87, Jerusalem.

45. Ministry of Religious Affairs to Ambassador Eliahu Elath in Washington, D.C., 30 January 1950, Ministry of Religious Affairs File, ISA 375/13, Jerusalem.

46. Lillie Schultz to Ambassador Eliahu Elath, 11 March 1950, Ministry of Religious Affairs File, ISA 375/13, Jerusalem.

47. Ibid.

48. Letter from Samuel Cavert, 28 February 1950, Federal Council of Churches Records, Record Group 18, Box 17, Folder 7, Presbyterian Historical Society, Philadelphia.

49. Lillie Schultz to Ambassador Eliahu Elath, 27 March 1950, Ministry of Religious Affairs File, ISA 374/12, Jerusalem.

50. Ambassador Eliahu Elath to Lillie Schultz, 5 April 1950, Ministry of Religious Affairs File, ISA 374/12, Jerusalem.

51. Lillie Schultz to Moshe Karen, Counselor to the Israeli Embassy, 1 June 1950, Ministry for Religious Affairs File, ISA 374/2, Jerusalem.

52. Ibid.

53. Carl Hermann Voss to the Israeli Consulate, 6 January 1950, Ministry for Religious Affairs File, ISA 85/22, Jerusalem.

54. Daniel Poling to Louis Lipsky, 24 January 1951, Ministry of Religious Affairs File, ISA 338/24, Jerusalem.

55. Ibid.

56. See ISA files 113/21 and 338/24.

57. James M. Watkins to Eliahu Elath, 5 March 1952, Ministry for Religious Affairs File, ISA 338/28, Jerusalem.

58. Uri Bialer, *Cross on the Star of David: The Christian World in Israel's Foreign Policy, 1948–1967* (Bloomington: Indiana University Press, 2005).

59. "Jews Demand Jerusalem," *Pentecostal Evangel* (30 April 1949): 9.

60. U. S. Grant, "Things to Come," *Pentecostal Evangel* (21 May 1949): 2.

61. James Kensley Reeves to Chaim Weizmann (4 November 1949), Office of the Prime Minister File, ISA 5807/7, Jerusalem.

62. Letter from E. Etayen, Information Office of the Ministry for Religious Affairs to. James Reeves, 22 December 1949, Ministry for Religious Affairs File, ISA 5807/7, Jerusalem.

63. Louis A. Bauman, "Israel Lives Again!" *King's Business* 41 (September 1950): 7.

64. Ibid., 8.

65. Ibid., 9.

66. Editorial, "Israel Lives Again!" *King's Business* 43 (March 1952): 5.

67. Louis A. Bauman, "The Nations Marshalling for Armageddon," *King's Business* 41 (December 1950): 13.

68. Ibid., 14.

69. W. O. H. Garman, radio address on ABC, "The Jew" (29 May 1948), Garman Files, Fundamentalist Archives, Bob Jones University.

70. Ibid.

71. Letter from Samuel Newman to J. Frank Norris, 20 October 1950, Small Collections SC-9074, Jacob Rader Marcus Center of the American Jewish Archives, Cincinnati, Ohio.

72. Ibid. No record is given of whether Norris responded to Newman's invitation to join the ACPC, but his name never appeared on membership records. This is not surprising as many fundamentalists approached the liberal theology of ACPC members with caution, despite common goals to support Israel.

73. Robert A. Ashworth, "The Story of the National Conference of Christians and Jews" (March 1950), 16, Small Collections 13557, Jacob Rader Marcus Center of the American Jewish Archives, Hebrew Union College, Jewish Institute for Religion, Cincinnati Campus.

74. See Stuart Svonkin, *Jews Against Prejudice: American Jews and the Fight for Civil Liberties* (New York: Columbia University Press, 1997).

75. Ibid., 44.

76. Ibid.

77. Svonkin, *Jews Against Prejudice*, 33.

78. Jacob Chinitz, "Is a Christian-Jewish Dialogue Possible?" *Jewish Spectator* (March, 1952): 20. Small Collections, SC—9074, Jacob Rader Marcus Center of the American Jewish Archives, Hebrew Union College, Jewish Institute for Religion, Cincinnati Campus.

79. Ibid., 21.

80. Ibid., 22.

81. Ibid., 27.

82. "Proselytizing and the Jews," *The Facts* 4, no. 1 (January 1949): introduction, Ministry for Religious Affairs File, ISA 374/12, Jerusalem.

83. Ibid., 6.

84. A. Roy Eckardt, *Christianity and the Children of Israel* (New York: King's Crown, 1948).

85. W. E. Garrison, "The Christian and the Jew," *Christian Century* (26 May 1948): 512–513.

86. "Some Thoughts on Modern Israel," *Ecumenical Review* 4 (October 1951): 19–20.

87. Ibid., 17.

88. Fishman, *American Protestantism and a Jewish State,* 102.

89. Ibid.

90. As quoted in ibid., 104.

91. Ibid., 106–107.

92. Abe Harman to Rabbi Jerry Unger, Zionist Emergency Council, 6 July 1951, Ministry for Religious Affairs File, ISA 111/50, Jerusalem.

93. Carl Hermann Voss to Abe Harman, 2 July 1952, Ministry for Religious Affairs File, ISA 111/50, Jerusalem.

94. "Report on 45-Minute Interview with Mr. Eric W. Bethman, Director of Publications, American Friends of the Middle East," ACPC Memo, 28 March 1952, ACPC File, CZA F40/57, Jerusalem.

95. Karl Baehr, "Memorandum: Garland Evans Hopkins Reception," 2 June 1952, ACPC File, CZA F40/57, Jerusalem.

96. Karl Baehr, "For the Record: Garland Evans Hopkins," ACPC Memo, 18 June 1952, ACPC File, CZA F40/57, Jerusalem.

97. S. Margoshes to the American Christian Palestine Committee, 11 February 1953, ACPC File, CZA F40/57, Jerusalem.

98. Ibid.

99. Ibid.

100. S. Margoshes to the American Christian Palestine Committee, 11 February 1953, ACPC File, CZA F40/57, Jerusalem.

101. Ibid.

102. Ibid.

103. At a lunch meeting in February 1953 Garland Evans Hopkins praised Eisenhower and "his Administration of 'big men who are going to do big things,'" according to Margoshes in her letter to the members of the ACPC executive council, 11 February 1953, ACPC File, CZA F40/57, Jerusalem.

CHAPTER 4. POLITICAL AND THEOLOGICAL DISSENT, 1953–1967

1. Letter from Karl Baehr to Alisa Klausner Ber, Israeli Foreign Office, 25 June 1957, CZA F40/55.

2. On the evening of 14 October 1953 Israel Defense Forces (IDF), led by Ariel Sharon, conducted a covert raid on a West Bank village, Qibya, in which the U.N. estimated that fifty-five Palestinians, mainly civilians, were killed. Israelis claimed that the raid was conducted in order to eliminate border infiltrations from Palestinian militants. The U.N. Security Council and the U.S. State Department condemned the raid on 18 October 1953, and the United States temporarily suspended aid to Israel in response.

3. Statement by the Reverend Karl Baehr, Executive Director of the American Christian Palestine Committee before the Senate Foreign Relations Subcommittee on the Near East, 25 May 1953.

4. Ibid.

5. Ibid.

6. Ibid.

7. Press release regarding three-day ACPC annual conference in Washington, D.C., 17 February 1954, ACPC File, CZA F40/31.

8. Ibid.

9. Ibid.

10. Resolutions of the National Conference of the ACPC, Washington, D.C., 16 February 1954, CZA F40/31.

11. Karl Baehr, ACPC Memo, Garland Evans Hopkins Luncheon, 31 January 1952, ACPC File, CZA F40/53.

12. Ibid.

13. Ibid.

14. Observer A, ACPC Memo, Coffee Hour Meeting of the American Friends of the Middle East, 15 October 1953, ACPC File, CZA F40/54.

15. Observer B, ACPC Memo, American Friends of the Middle East, 16 October 1953, ACPC File, CZA F40/54.

16. Garland Evans Hopkins, "Memo to Americans," 28 May 1954, AFME File, CZA F40/55.

17. Letter of Membership from Marion Oexle to S. Ralph Harlow, 27 April 1956, AFME File, CZA F40/55.

18. Press Release, "Elson Leaves for Seven-Week Mideast Tour," 20 June 1956, AFME File, CZA F40/55.

19. Resolution of the Palestine Conciliation Commission, 19 November 1951, United Nations.

20. "Zionism vs. Arab League," *Christian Science Monitor* (22 June 1956): 20.

21. Mary Hornaday, "'Friends' Ask Political Lid on Palestine," *Christian Science Monitor* (30 January 1956): 5.

22. Ibid.

23. ACPC advertisement ". . . before it is too late!" *New York Times* (27 January 1956): 12.

24. Letter from Garland Evans Hopkins to Karl Baehr, 6 March 1956, AFME File, CZA F40/109.

25. Ibid.

26. *The Department of State Bulletin* 36, no. 917 (21 January 1957): 83–87.

27. Ibid.

28. Ibid.

29. R. Park Johnson, "The Arab-Israeli Impasse: Can American Christians Help Remove Roadblocks to Reconciliation?" *Presbyterian Life* 9 (14 April 1956): 15–18.

30. Editorial, "What Lies behind the Israeli Attacks?" *Christian Century*(10 October 1956): 1155.

31. Editorial, "Insulation," *Christian Herald* 79 (October 1956): 11.

32. Editorial, "Principle," *Christian Herald* 79 (November 1956): 11.

33. Editorial, "International Crisis on the Sandy Wastes of Sinai," *Christianity Today* (12 November 1956): 4.

34. Oswald T. Allis, "Israel's Transgression in Palestine," *Christianity Today* (24 December 1956): 8.

35. Ibid., 9.

36. Wilbur M. Smith, "Israel in Her Promised Land," *Christianity Today* (24 December 1956): 7.

37. Ibid.

38. Robert Van Deusen, "Mideast Policy," *Lutheran* (23 January 1956): 11.

39. Letter to the Honorable Dwight D. Eisenhower, 28 December 1956, ACPC File, CZA F40/55.

40. Ibid., 17 January 1956, CZA F40/55.

41. Garland Evans Hopkins, "Some Reflections" speech, by, 17 January 1956, CZA F40/55.

42. Ibid.

43. Ibid.

44. Ibid.

45. Ibid.

46. "Freda Utley at AFME," 19 December 1957, ACPC File, CZA F40/53.

47. Letter to ACPC members from Karl Baehr and Samuel Guy Inman, 30 September 1958, CZA F40/53.

48. Ibid.

49. Dorothy Thompson, "There Is Only One Way for Israel to Proceed," Bell Syndicate, 22 September 1958, CZA F40/53.

50. Ibid.

51. Internal ACPC Memo, "Erich Bethmann Lifts Curtain on AFME," 10 October 1958, CZA F40/54.

52. Ibid.

53. ACPC Memo to Rabbi Unger, 17 December 1958, CZA F40/54.

54. The ACPC continued to organize roughly one study tour a year with the assistance of the Israeli Ministry of Religious Affairs, making sure that participants met with high-level Israeli officials (ISA 494/19 and ISA 85/22). Karl Baehr even asked for Israeli assistance in organizing a study tour for the fundamentalist organization American Association for Jewish Evangelism—a sensitive request in the context of Israeli resistance to Christian missions to the Jews (ISA 494/19). Likewise, the Israeli government often asked the ACPC for assistance in countering negative publicity in the Protestant press (ISA 58221/21).

55. Karl Baehr, "A Proposal: The Association of the AIS with the AICF," 2 November 1966, CZA F40/83.

56. Ibid.

57. Mark Silk, "Notes on the Judeo-Christian Tradition," *American Quarterly* 36 (spring 1984): 65–80; quoted in Patrick Allitt, ed., *Major Problems in American Religious History* (Boston: Houghton Mifflin, 2000): 352.

58. Ibid.

59. *The New Delhi Report: The Third Assembly of the World Council of Churches 1961* (New York: Association Press, 1962), 148.

60. "Logumkloster Speaks to the Church," *National Lutheran* (November 1964): 18–19.

61. Ibid.

62. "The Church Speaks," *Christian Social Relations at General Convention, 1964* (New York: Protestant Episcopal Church), 9–10.

63. "Of Antisemitism," *Christian Friends Bulletin* (New York, 1965): 1, Bob Jones University Archives.

64. Jeffery Hadden and Bruce Vawter, "Churchly Particularism and the Jews," *Christian Century* (10 August 1966): 987.

65. Ibid.

66. Ibid., 988.

67. Markus Barth, "The Christ in Israel's History," *Theology Today* (11 October 1954): 348.

68. For example, see also Richard Batey, "'So All Israel Will Be Saved,'" *Interpretation* (20 April 1966): 218–228; E. A. Speiser, "'People' and 'Nation' of Israel," *Journal of Biblical Literature* (June 1960): 157–163; Ben Meyer, "Jesus and the Remnant of Israel," *Journal of Biblical Literature* (June 1965): 123–130; Andre Chouraqui, "The Messiah of Israel," *Cross Currents* (fall 1961): 331–342; and Andre Neher, "The State of Israel: A Reflection on Its Inner Meaning," *Cross Currents* (spring 1959): 150–159.

69. T. F. Torrance, "The Israel of God: Israel and the Incarnation," *Interpretation* (10 July 1956): 310.

70. Ibid., 312.

71. Ibid., 315.

72. Ibid., 319.

73. See, for example, John F. Walvoord, "The New Covenant with Israel," *Bibliotheca sacra* (July 1953): 193–205; Charles L. Feinberg, "The State of Israel," *Bibliotheca sacra* (October 955): 311–319; Howard Ferrin, "All Israel Shall Be Saved," *Bibliotheca sacra* (July 1955): 235–247; Bernard Ramm, "A Review of 'Antisemitismus and Eschatologie,' by Rudolph Pfisterer," *Bibliotheca sacra* (January–March 1961): 22–26; and Carl Armerding, "Asleep in the Dust," *Bibliotheca sacra* (April–June, 1964): 153–158.

74. William Hull, *Israel—Key to Prophecy: The Story of Israel from the Regathering to the Millennium as Told by the Prophets* (Grand Rapids, MI: Zondervan, 1957), 11.

75. Ibid., 36.

76. Although this literary technique will appear in Hal Lindsay and Carole C. Carlson's *Late Great Planet Earth* more than a decade later, it is interesting to note that the apocalyptic genre, starring Israel and the Jews, had already begun. For reference to the Catholic takeover of America, see Lindsay and Carlson, *The Late Great Planet Earth* (Grand Rapids, MI: Zondervan, 1970), 49–50.

77. Ibid., 83.

78. Ibid., 98.

79. George T. B. Davis, "A Divine Promise That Changed History," *Sunday School Times* (16 March 1957): 205–206, 222.

80. Ibid., 222.

81. Ibid.

82. Weber, *On the Road to Armageddon*, 17.

83. Noel Smith, "Basic Principles of Zionism," *Baptist Bible Tribune* (7 April 1960): 4, Bob Jones University Archives.

84. Noel Smith, "Who Owns Palestine?" *Baptist Bible Tribune* (20 December 1957):1, Bob Jones University Archives.

85. Ibid.

86. Noel Smith, "The Revolution and the Jews," *Baptist Bible Tribune* (3 March 1961): 3–4, Bob Jones University Archives.

87. Noel Smith, "The Significance of Israel," *Baptist Bible Tribune* (5 May 1961): 4, Bob Jones University Archives.

88. Ibid., 5.

89. F. Kenton Beshore, "The Christian and Antisemitism," *Bible Research Monthly* (October 1964): 183, Bob Jones University Archives.

90. Ibid.

91. "God gave Isaac great potentialities, thus enduing the Jewish nation with greater potentials than any other nation the world has ever known. We read that God wanted this unusual nation to spread His truth over the face of the earth. He gave them distinctive opportunities and keener mental capacities in every realm, fitting them to take the truth of God to the world. Some will say they have failed God, and therefore He has turned his back on them, and today God is looking to the Church to evangelize the world. I can find nowhere in Scripture where God commands the Church to win the world to Jesus Christ. He told us to preach the Gospel to the whole world, but never does the Lord Jesus declare that the Church will convert the world." F. Kenton Beshore, "Israel, My Glory," *Bible Research Monthly* (October 1964): 185, Bob Jones University Archives.

92. Roy Grace, "The Christian's Debt to the Jew," (Philadelphia: Spearhead, 1966): 3, Weniger File, Bob Jones University Archives.

93. Ibid., 9.

94. Isaac Alteras, *Eisenhower and Israel: U.S.–Israeli Relations, 1953–1960* (Gainesville: University Press of Florida, 1993); and Douglas Little, "The Making of a Special Relationship: The United States and Israel, 1957–68," *International Journal of Middle East Studies* 25 (1993): 563.

95. Little, "The Making of a Special Relationship," 567.

96. Ibid., 563.

97. Ibid., 573.

98. H. W. Brands, *Into the Labyrinth: The United States and the Middle East, 1945–1993* (New York: McGraw-Hill, 1994): 89.

99. Lecture by Carl Hermann Voss, of the American Christian Palestine Committee, at Hebrew University, Jerusalem, Israel, 21 June 1966, Small Collections 12633, Jacob Rader Marcus Center of the American Jewish Archives.

100. Ibid.

101. Ibid.

102. Ibid.

103. Ibid.

CASE STUDY 2

1. Letter from Samuel Newman to the Reverend Herschel H. Hobbs, 26 May 1961, SC-9074, Jacob Rader Marcus Center of the American Jewish Archives.

2. Ibid.

3. Letter from Harry Emerson Fosdick to Samuel Newman, 3 October 1966, SC-9074, Jacob Rader Marcus Center of the American Jewish Archives.

4. Letter from William Hamilton to Samuel Newman, 13 December 1965, SC-9074, Jacob Rader Marcus Center of the American Jewish Archives.

5. Letter from Samuel H. Miller to Samuel Newman, 10 January 1962, SC-9074, Jacob Rader Marcus Center of the American Jewish Archives.

6. Letter from Paul Ramsey to Samuel Newman, 29 July 1963, SC-9074, Jacob Rader Marcus Center of the American Jewish Archives.

7. Letter from H. H. Hobbs to Samuel Newman, 7 June 1961, SC-9074, Jacob Rader Marcus Center of the American Jewish Archives.

8. Letter from Samuel Newman to H. H. Hobbs, 17 June 1961, SC-9074, Jacob Rader Marcus Center of the American Jewish Archives.

9. Letter from H. H. Hobbs to Samuel Newman, 31 July 1961, SC-9074, Jacob Rader Marcus Center of the American Jewish Archives.

10. Letter from David M. Stowe to Samuel Newman, 8 February 1961, SC-9074, Jacob Rader Marcus Center of the American Jewish Archives.

11. Letter from Harold Lindsell to Samuel Newman, 7 August 1961, SC-9074, Jacob Rader Marcus Center of the American Jewish Archives.

12. Letter from John H. Gerstner to Samuel Newman, 3 January 1967, SC-9074, Jacob Rader Marcus Center of the American Jewish Archives.

13. Letter from Leon H. Sullivan to Samuel Newman, 2 October 1962, SC-9074, Jacob Rader Marcus Center of the American Jewish Archives.

14. Letter from Jack P. Lewis to Samuel Newman, 7 June 1962, SC-9074, Jacob Rader Marcus Center of the American Jewish Archives.

15. Letter from Marc Tanenbaum to Samuel Newman, 2 March 1967, SC-9074, Jacob Rader Marcus Center of the American Jewish Archives.

CHAPTER 5. THE TIDE TURNS, 1967–1973

1. John F. Walvoord, "The Amazing Rise of Israel!" *Moody Monthly*, (October 1967): 22.

2. Robert J. Donovan and the Staff of the Los Angeles Times, *Six Days in June: Israel's Fight for Survival* (New York: Signet Books, 1967): 157–160.

3. Ibid.

4. Ibid., 10.

5. Ibid., 98.

6. Official U.S. and Israeli investigations of the USS *Liberty* event concluded that the attack was accidental and reflected problems of communication and misidentification in the midst of battle. Some members of the U.S. intelligence community disputed the official conclusion.

7. George T. Hilliard, Letter to the Editor, *Boston Herald* (June 12, 1967), Small collections 11590, Box No. 2286, Jacob Rader Marcus Center for the American Jewish Archives, Cincinnati, Ohio.

8. The noted religious historian Martin E. Marty published the transcript of an interview he conducted with an Israeli in 1969 that addressed the perceived silence of the American churches on the eve of the Six-Day War. When the Israeli mentioned the silence of the churches, Marty replied: "I've never been able to accept all the criticism of Christians that followed upon that war. American Jews do not understand how hard it is for Protestants to speak out officially on anything! We Protestants are still not urban, not concentrated, not authorized to 'speak out'—and certainly cannot mobilize much within six days! Martin E. Marty, "Christians and Jews: An Inconclusive Quest for Accord," *Christian Century* (12 February 1969): 206–207.

9. "Staff Safe, Hospital Damaged in Middle East War," *Lutheran* (5 July 1967): 24.

10. Ibid., 25.

11. "Churches Seek Lasting Peace in Settlement of Mid-East War," *Lutheran* (19 July 1967): 24.

12. The *Lutheran* reported the remarks of Abraham Soetendorp, chairman of one of England's Israel emergency committees, who added, "In a day when we speak about the dialog between Jews and Christians, it is disappointing to find that in a time of mortal danger for the Jewish community, the church does not stand behind the Jews." Los Angeles rabbi Balfour Brickner, the journal noted, also argued that "organized American Christianity failed to give Israel visible support" (ibid.).

13. "World Concern Focused on Fate of Jerusalem," *Lutheran* (2 August 1967): 25.

14. J. A. Sanders, "Urbis and Orbis: Jerusalem Today," *Christian Century* (26 July 1967).

15. "Jews in Old Jerusalem! A Historic Re-Entry," *Christianity Today* (23 June 1967): 38.

16. Advertisement in *New York Times* (12 July 1967).

17. Reinhold Niebuhr, "David and Goliath," *Christianity and Crisis* (26 June 1967): 141.

18. Ibid., 142.

19. John Bennett, the acting editor of *Crisis*, appeared more circumspect in his reaction. Bennett addressed the apparent contradiction in the American response to intervention in Israel but growing calls for withdrawal from Vietnam. The two cases were different, Bennett argued, since "Israel was threatened with extermination [and] no one threatens the extermination of South Vietnam. To aid Israel would be to help an existing nation to defend itself, to be itself." Yet the victory had placed a burden on Israel, Bennett charged, to address the problem of the Arab refugees as magnanimously as possible, and thereby earn improved relations with her Arab neighbors. The United States should assist Israel in alleviating its plight and, therefore, by extension, improve its international reputation. Bennett insisted, however, that the Arab/Soviet attempt to label Israel as the aggressor "would seem to most of us in the West to be so one-sided that it would discredit the General Assembly at a time when the UN is desperately needed as a means of overcoming American unilateralism." John Bennett, "Further Thoughts on the Middle East," *Christianity and Crisis* (26 June 1967): 142.

20. Alan Geyer, "Christians and 'The Peace of Jerusalem,'" *Christianity and Crisis.* (10 July 1967): 161.

21. Balfour Brickner, "No Ease in Zion for Us," *Christianity and Crisis* (18 September 1967): 200.

22. The remainder of Brickner's lengthy article addressed the hurt the Jewish community felt at Protestant silence on the eve of the 1967 War and explanations for Jewish responses to both the war and its criticism of the American Christian community. Ibid., 202–203.

23. John Bennett answered Brickner's plea for greater Protestant understanding about the war by insisting that *Christianity and Crisis* had, in fact, "emphasized the right of Israel to live" on the eve of the war. Bennett noted that the editorial board was "at first controlled by the fear that she might be annihilated and that the Jews as a people might suffer another holocaust." Bennett pointed out that major Protestant organizations had remained neutral in their response but that major Protestant leaders had expressed their solidarity with Israel. Nonetheless, of most concern to "Protestantism" now, after the Israeli victory, remained the fate of the territories acquired by conquest. Bennett insisted that "we cannot proceed as though Israel as a modern nation has a biblical deed to Jerusalem." Israel, Bennett explained, should hold onto the newly acquired territories only long enough to use them to negotiate for peace with her Arab neighbors. John C. Bennett, "Theological Premises Must Not Override Issues of Justice: A Response to Rabbi Brickner," *Christianity and Crisis* (18 September 1967): 204–205.

24. Willard G. Oxtoby, "What Is the Christian Stake in a Jewish Dream?" *Presbyterian Life* (1 July 1967): 26.

25. Ibid.

26. Ibid., 27.

27. Ibid., 28.

28. "Bible Prophecy and the Mid-East Crisis" (transcript of radio broadcast), *Moody Monthly* (July/August 1967): 22.

29. Ibid., 24.

30. John F. Walvoord, "The Amazing Rise of Israel!" *Moody Monthly* (October 1967): 22.

31. Ibid., 25.

32. Hal Lindsay, "The Pieces Fall Together," *Moody Monthly* (October 1967): 28.

33. Noel Smith, "The Israel State Today: They Are There in Unbelief; What Lies Ahead for Them?" *Bible Baptist Tribune* (June 30, 1967): 1.

34. Raymond Cox, "Eyewitness: Israel," *Eternity* (July 1967): 6–8.

35. Yet not every article concerning the prophetic importance of the war found an unequivocally positive response. One author, William Sanford LaSor, appeared more cautious in ascribing biblical significance to the events of June. He insisted that the question of whether the current Israeli state should consider the former boundaries of the ancient nation of Israel demanded a careful assessment: "At present, I am not willing to concede that the State of Israel is to be identified as the Israel described in Holy Scripture. But at the same time, I am willing to admit that it seems quite likely that the regathering of the Jews, the establishment of the State of Israel, and the almost incredible military successes of Israeli armies against what appeared to be overwhelming odds, are somehow to be related to God's promises." Christians should remember, even "in the excitement of studying signs of the times," that their purpose remained in doing "the will of God. And the will of God is to bring men to know Him. We are debtors, not only to the Jew but also to the Arab." LaSor conceded that "most evangelical Christians are more sympathetic to the Israeli than to the Arabic side of the conflict." The common biblical heritage, the promise given to Abraham to inhabit the Holy Land, and the American proclivity to "cheer for the under-dog" had eclipsed American Christian duties to the Arab. Both the Jew and Arab deserved Christian consideration, and Christians should remain "positively impartial" encouraging "our own governments to act with the same principles" of concern for both parties. William Sanford LaSor, "Have the 'Times of the Gentiles' Been Fulfilled?" *Eternity* (August 1967): 32.

36. "What Made 1967 a Significant Year?" *Eternity* (January 1968): 6.

37. "War Sweeps the Bible Lands," *Christianity Today* (23 June 1967): 20.

38. Ibid., 21.

39. An editorial in *Christianity Today* argued that the most important consequence that could arise from Jerusalem's uncertain future would be the creation of greater religious freedom that would allow evangelicals to witness to Israelis more openly. The editors noted that "NCC advisers and consultants are in dire confusion about the Gospel and the Jew. Some contend that to evangelize the Jew is antisemitic; others share [Reinhold] Niebuhr's notion that Israel is already a segment of Western Christianity. Evangelical Christians consider non-evangelization of the Jew a supreme act of lovelessness. It is important to remember, continued the editorial, "in casting lots for Jerusalem, those who profess to be the friends of freedom ought not to overlook freedom to proclaim the good news." Editorial, "Casting Lots for Jerusalem," *Christianity Today* (18 August 1967): 30.

40. "God Isn't Finished," *Moody Monthly* (September 1967): 46.

41. Louis Goldberg, "The Church That Said 'Shalom,'" *Moody Monthly* (September 1967): 54.

42. Ibid.

43. John F. Walvoord, "Will Israel Build a Temple in Jerusalem?" *Bibliotheca Sacra* (April–June, 1968): 99–106.

44. Ibid., 100.

45. Ibid.

46. G. Douglas Young, "Lessons We Can Learn from Judaism," *Eternity* (August 1967): 22.

47. See, for example, Murray Saltzman, "Will Judaism Survive the Seventies?" *Christian Century* (4 March 1970): 263–266; Monika Hellwig, "Christian Theology and the Covenant of Israel," *Journal of Ecumenical Studies* (winter 1970): 37–55; "Convocation Presses toward a New Theology of Israel," *Christian Century* (16 December 1970): 1521–1522; Peter Richardson, *Israel in the Apostolic Church* (Cambridge: Cambridge University Press, 1969); Pinchas E. Lapide, "Jesus in Israeli Literature," *Christian Century* (21 October 1970): 1248–1253; Johan M. Snoek, *The Grey Book: A Collection of Protests against Antisemitism and the Persecution of Jews, Issued by Non-Roman Catholic Churches and Church Leaders during Hitler's Rule,* with an introduction by Uriel Tal (New York: Humanities, 1970); Abraham Joshua Heschel, *Israel: An Echo of Eternity* (New York: Farrar, Straus and Giroux, 1969); Jacob Agus, "A Jewish Response to Anti-Zionism and Antisemitism," *Journal of Ecumenical Studies* (summer 1970): 556–558; Markus Barth, *Israel and the Church: Contribution to a Dialogue Vital for Peace* (Richmond, VA: John Knox, 1969); Herbert B. Huffmon, "The Israel of God," *Interpretation* (23 January 1969): 66–77.

48. Markus Barth, "Shall Israel Go It Alone?" *Journal of Ecumenical Studies* (spring 1968): 346–352.

49. H. Berkhof, "Israel as a Theological Problem in the Christian Church," *Journal of Ecumenical Studies* (summer 1969): 329–347.

50. Ibid., 347.

51. Jakob J. Petuchowski, "A Jewish Response to 'Israel as a Theological Problem in the Christian Church,'" *Journal of Ecumenical Studies* (summer 1969): 348–353.

52. Ibid., 351.

53. Jacob Agus, "Israel and the Jewish-Christian Dialogue," *Journal of Ecumenical Studies* (winter 1969): 18–36.

54. Ibid., 34.

55. See, for example, Emil L. Fackenheim, "The People Israel Lives," *Christian Century* (6 May 1970): 563–568; Jacob P. Rudin, "On World Reaction to Developments in the Middle East," *Christian Century* (22 June 1969): 110; and Stuart Gottlieb, "Judaism, Israel and Conscientious Objection," *Christian Century* (3 September 1969): 1136–1137.

56. Henry Siegman, ed., *The Religious Dimensions of Israel: The Challenge of the Six-Day War* (New York: Synagogue Council of America, 1968); and Michael Selzer, *Israel as a Factor in Jewish-Gentile Relations in America* (New York: American Council of Judaism, 1968).

57. Siegman, *The Religious Dimensions of Israel*, 68.

58. Thomas M. Raitt, *Journal of Ecumenical Studies* (summer 1969): 452.

59. Ibid.

60. Abraham Heschel, "Christian-Jewish Dialogue and the Meaning of the State of Israel," *Cross Currents* (fall 1969): 425.

61. Elwyn A. Smith, "The Christian Meaning of the Holocaust," *Journal of Ecumenical Studies* (summer 1969): 419.

62. Ibid., 421.

63. Ibid., 422.

64. Louis Garinger, "A Path away from Bitterness," *Christian Science Monitor* (14 August 1970): 2.

65. Louis Garinger, "Mideast Clash Muffles Dialogue," *Christian Science Monitor* (17 August 1970): 12.

66. "A Christian Response to Arab Terrorism," advertisement sponsored by the Interfaith and University Committee, *New York Times* (8 May 1970): 14.

67. Garinger, "Mideast Clash Muffles Dialogue," 12.

68. Louis Garinger, "How Various Groups Approach Interfaith Relations," *Christian Science Monitor* (25 August 1970): 4.

69. Garinger, "A Path away from Bitterness," 2.

70. Alan T. Davies, "Anti-Zionism, Antisemitism, and the Christian Mind," *Christian Century* (19 August 1970): 987–989.

71. Ibid., 988.

72. Ibid., 989.

73. Letter from Franklin Littell to Wayne Cowan, 10 April 1972, Reinhold Niebuhr Papers, Box 49, Library of Congress Archives.

CASE STUDY 3

1. Speech on the occasion of receiving an honorary doctorate degree from Hebrew University in Jerusalem, 15 December 1969, Reinhold Niebuhr Papers, Box 62, Library of Congress Archives.

2. Sir Isaiah Berlin, a friend of both Reinhold and his wife Ursula, wrote to Ursula after Niebuhr's death. Niebuhr, he wrote "really was, quite apart from his intellectual and spiritual attainments, a touchstone in whom one believed, or wanted to believe in: I would be ready to march behind him in any revolution, in any moral or social crisis, in the full knowledge that whatever else, one could not, if one followed him, ever find oneself in a morally dubious or even uncertain position." Letter from Isaiah Berlin to Ursula Niebuhr, June 1971, Reinhold Niebuhr Papers, Box 49, Library of Congress Archives.

3. Letter from Ursula Niebuhr to Teddy Kolleck, 3 July 1978, Reinhold Niebuhr Papers, Box 63, Library of Congress Archives.

4. Seymour Siegel, "Reinhold Niebuhr: An Appreciation," *Conservative Judaism* (summer 1971): 57.

5. Abraham Joshua Heschel, "A Last Farewell," eulogy delivered at Reinhold Niebuhr's funeral, February 1971, Reinhold Niebuhr Papers, Box 62, Library of Congress Archives.

6. Letter from Ursula Niebuhr to Teddy Kolleck, 14 December 1941, Reinhold Niebuhr Papers, Box 63, Library of Congress Archives.

7. Letter from Teddy Kolleck to Ursula Niebuhr, 21 February 1972, Reinhold Niebuhr Papers, Box 63, Library of Congress Archives.

8. Letter from Teddy Kolleck to Ursula Niebuhr, 18 December 1973, Reinhold Niebuhr Papers, Box 63, Library of Congress Archives.

9. Letter from Ursula Niebuhr to Bayard Rustin and Franklin Littell, 18 May 1970, Reinhold Niebuhr Papers, Box 49, Library of Congress Archives.

10. Letter from Franklin Littell to Reinhold Niebuhr, 21 October 1970, Reinhold Niebuhr Papers, Box 49, Library of Congress Archives.

11. Ibid.

12. Letter from Ursula Niebuhr to Franklin Littell, 28 October 1970, Reinhold Niebuhr Papers, Box 49, Library of Congress Archives.

13. Alice Eckardt and A. Roy Eckardt, *Encounter with Israel: A Challenge to Conscience* (New York: Association Press, 1970).

14. Francis B. Sayre, Jr. Sermon on Easter Sunday at the Washington Cathedral (26 March 1972), Antisemitism 1970, Miscellaneous File, Jacob Rader Marcus Center for the American Jewish Archives.

15. Letter from Franklin Littell to Wayne Cowan, 10 April 1972, Reinhold Niebuhr Papers, Box 49, Library of Congress Archives. Littell also wrote to Sayre, who had been his college roommate, to express his disappointment in the Palm Sunday sermon. "I think your use of the Palm Sunday occasion to attack Israel was not only wrong, but wicked, and since I am convinced that it reflected not personal malice but rather the sickness of Christendom, I must not keep still," he declared. "If we want to repent, as we should, we Christians have a great deal to repent of in Jerusalem!" he added, "Most important, when did the notion arise that it is our business to repent of sins attributed to others? Letter from Franklin Littell to Francis B. Sayre, 11 April 1972, Reinhold Niebuhr Papers, Box 49, Library of Congress Archives.

16. Letter from Ursula Niebuhr to Teddy Kolleck, 19 April 1972, Reinhold Niebuhr Papers, Box 63, Library of Congress Archives.

17. She explained to the editors that, "some of us, and this includes my husband, as well as me, have felt very deeply the weight of responsibility that we, as Christians, bear for past history. The Christian Church in the early and middle ages, as well as the Christian Churches since the Reformation, by their antisemitism, have denied the very principles of their faith. I would say Christians have denied Christ, who was the Jewish teacher, Jesus, who taught love. So, as Christians, therefore, we stand convicted. The fate of millions of Jews lies heavily on our conscience." Letter to the Editors of *Christianity and Crisis* from Ursula Niebuhr, 26 May 1972, Reinhold Niebuhr Papers, Box 49, Library of Congress Archives.

CHAPTER 6. A NEW U.S.–ISRAELI ALLIANCE, 1973–1979

1. Text of meeting of the New York Board of Rabbis with Governor Jimmy Carter, 31 August 1976, Fifth Avenue Synagogue, New York City. Nearprint File "Jimmy Carter," Jacob Rader Marcus Center of the American Jewish Archives, Hebrew Union College, Jewish Institute for Religion, Cincinnati Campus.

2. Frank Aker, *October 1973: The Arab-Israeli War* (Hamden, CT: Archon Books, 1985), 2.

3. Ibid., 126–128.

4. Tracy Early, "Churchmen Steer Liberal Course," *Christian Science Monitor* (19 October 1973): 7.

5. Robert Cushman, "What Price Israel?" *Christian Century* (7 November 1973): 1093.

6. Franklin Little, "A Plea for Israel," *Christian Century* (7 November 1973): 1095.

7. James Wall, "A Report from Israel: What Price Security?" *Christian Century* (26 December 1973): 1269.

8. Historian and member of the Israeli Ministry of Education Hertzel Fishman rejected Wall's assessment of Israeli history in a response to the *Christian Century* ("Security and Israel's Future: Reader's Response (6 February 1974): 155: "I am aware, of course, that for many reasons—theological, missionary and others—some Christians are still not prepared to acknowledge the facts of Jewish history and the validity of its religio-nationalist culture [as separate from the Holocaust]. But surely they should try to rid themselves of these hang-ups if they wish to understand Judaism authentically and to contribute to a meaningful ecumenical dialogue." Another reader considered Wall's editorial as an example of "soft-core antisemitism"—"the pious 'It grieves me to say this, but I must protest against the aggression of those Jews' tone of voice."

9. Ibid.

10. Editorial, *Christians Concerned for Israel Notebook* (October 1973), Small Collections 1867, Jacob Radar Marcus Center of the American Jewish Archives, Hebrew Union College, Jewish Institute of Religion, Cincinnati Campus.

11. Letter from Ursula Niebuhr to Frank and Harriet Littell, 31 December 1973, Reinhold Niebuhr Papers, Box 63, Library of Congress Archives, Washington, D.C.

12. Tom Buckley, "Brawler at the U.N.," *New York Times* (7 December 1975): 307.

13. Ibid. 14. Jonas Hagen, "Promoting Tolerance: Historical Perspectives on Zionism and Racism," *UN Chronicle Online Edition,* http://www.un.org/Pubs/chronicle/2007/webArticles/022307_zionism.htm.

15. C. Fredrick Yoos, "Statement of Presbytery of Genesee Valley Synod of New York Conveying Concern over United Nations Resolution Equating Zionism with Racism, Describing It as a 'Violent and Harmful Action,'" 13 November 1975, Jewish-Christian Relations File, Miscellaneous Collection, Jacob Rader Marcus Center for the American Jewish Archives, Hebrew Union College, Jewish Institute for Religion, Cincinnati Campus.

16. Allitt, *Major Problems in American Religious History,* 150.

17. Text of Meeting of the New York Board of Rabbis with Governor Jimmy Carter, 31 August, 1976, Fifth Avenue Synagogue, New York City. Nearprint File "Jimmy Carter," Jacob Rader Marcus Center of the American Jewish Archives, Hebrew Union College, Jewish Institute for Religion, Cincinnati Campus.

18. Ibid.

19. "Jimmy Carter Presidential Campaign: For America's Third Century, Why Not Our Best?" Press Release distributed by "Members of the Atlanta Jewish Community," 25 May 1976, Jimmy Carter Nearprint Box, Jacob Rader Marcus Center for the American Jewish Archives, Cincinnati, Ohio.

20. Press Release from Congressman William Lehman, 13th District of Florida, "Lehman Lauds Carter Peace Plan for Middle East," 20 September 1976, Jimmy Carter Nearprint Box, Jacob Rader Marcus Center for the American Jewish Archives, Hebrew Union College, Jewish Institute for Religion, Cincinnati Campus.

21. Eli Evans, "Southern Jews, Baptists, and Jimmy Carter," *New York Times* (20 October 1976).

22. Ibid., 12.

23. See, for example, "Carter Terms Israel's Decision on Settlers an Obstacle to Peace," *New York Times* (29 July 1977); "U.S. Jews Have Growing Doubts about Carter," *Christian Science Monitor* (7 October 1977); Daniel Southerland, "Carter Repairs Ties to Jewish Community," *Christian Science Monitor* (7 October 1977); and Seymour Martin Lipset and

William Schneider, "Carter vs. Israel: What the Polls Reveal," *Commentary* (November 1977).

24. Bernard Gwertzman, "Jewish Leader Says Mideast Policy Makes a 'Question Mark' of Carter" *New York Times* (10 March 1978): A1.

25. Comments by President Jimmy Carter at the White House Reception Honoring Prime Minister Menachem Begin and Jewish Leaders, 1 May 1978, Jimmy Carter Near-print File, Jacob Rader Marcus Center for the American Jewish Archives, Hebrew Union College, Jewish Institute for Religion, Cincinnati Campus.

26. "After Camp David," *Christian Century* (4 October 1978): 908.

27. James Wall, "Heart Religion after Camp David," *Christian Century* (25 October 1978): 1003.

28. John Linder, with Robert Hoyt, "Mid-East Agenda for the President: Up from the Summit," *Christianity and Crisis* (13 November 1978): 266–272.

29. Martin Marty, "Sojourn at Tantur," *Christian Century* (12 May 1976), Reinhold Niebuhr Papers, Box 56, Library of Congress Archives, Washington, D.C.

30. Albert R. Ahlstrom, Report to the Lutheran World Federation, Department of Studies of the American Lutheran Church, Reinhold Niebuhr Papers, Box 56, Library of Congress Archives, Washington, D.C..

31. Ibid., 11.

32. Ibid., 13.

33. Ibid., 14.

34. Ibid., 17.

35. Ibid.

36. James M. Wall, "Going beyond the 'Special Relationship,'" *Christian Century* (31 May 1978): 579–580.

37. Ursula Niebuhr to Teddy Kolleck, 6 June 1974, Reinhold Niebuhr Papers, Box 63, Library of Congress Archives, Washington, D.C.

38. Carl Hermann Voss to Solomon Liptzin, 11 August 1976, Small Collections SC-12634, Jacob Rader Marcus Center of the American Jewish Archives, Hebrew Union College, Jewish Institute for Religion, Cincinnati Campus.

39. Franklin H. Littell, "Readers of the CCI Notebook Memo," 1 October 1977, Reinhold Niebuhr Papers, Box 49, Library of Congress Archives, Washington, D.C.

40. See, for example, "On Palestinians in Israel: A Report on a Journey to Israel From May 23–June 9, 1972," *Journal of Ecumenical Studies* (winter 1973): 121–127; George H. Tavard, "On Israel: Reflections with Sadness," *Journal of Ecumenical Studies* (spring 1973): 367–369; Franklin H. Littell, "Christendom, Holocaust, and Israel: The Importance for Christians of Recent Major Events in Jewish History," *Journal of Ecumenical Studies* (summer 1973): 483–497; Thomas E. Ambrogi, "Dialogue in Jerusalem: Christian Support for Israel?" *Journal of Ecumenical Studies* (winter 1974): 114–120; Pinchas Lapide, "Christians and Jews—A New Protestant Beginning," *Journal of Ecumenical Studies* (fall 1975): 485–492; Robert E. Willis, "Christian Theology after Auschwitz," *Journal of Ecumenical Studies* (fall 1975): 493–519; Elmer A. Martens, "The Promise of the Land to Israel," *Directions* (April 1976): 8–13; Devon H. Wiens, "The Promises to National Israel in the Preaching of the New Testament Apostles," *Directions* (April 1976): 14–18; William E. Phipps, "Jesus, the Prophetic Pharisee," *Journal of Ecumenical Studies*. (winter 1977): 17–31; George W. E. Nickelsburg, "Good News/Bad News: The

Messiah and God's Fractured Community," *Currents in Theology and Missions*(December 1977): 324–332; Edward H. Flannery, "Zionism, the State of Israel, and Jewish-Christian Dialogue," *Judaism* (summer 1978): 313–317; Marcus Barth, "Jesus the Jew: Israel and the Palestinians" (Atlanta, GA: John Knox, 1978); Marvin R. Wilson, "Zionism as Theology: An Evangelical Approach," *Journal of the Evangelical Theological Society* (March 1979): 27–44.

41. Charles M. Horne, "The Meaning of the Phrase 'And Thus All Israel Will Be Saved' (Romans 11:26)," *Journal of the Evangelical Theological Society* (21 December 1978): 329.

42. Marvin R. Wilson, "Zionism as Theology: An Evangelical Approach," *Journal of the Evangelical Theological Society* (March 1979): 29.

43. Ibid., 41.

44. See *The Yearbook of American and Canadian Churches* (1960–1980) for a full examination of the numeric trends in American Protestant church memberships.

45. Roger Finke and Rodney Stark, *The Churching of America 1776–1990: Winners and Losers in Our Religious Economy* (New Brunswick, NJ: Rutgers University Press, 1992).

46. Weber, *On the Road to Armageddon*, 186.

47. Lindsay and Carlson, *The Late Great Planet Earth,* introduction.

48. Ibid., 42–43.

49. Ibid., 48–49.

50. Ibid., 57.

51. Weber, *On the Road to Armageddon,* 189.

52. John Kenyon, "Dateline Tomorrow," *Christian Herald* (November 1978): 3.

53. Marvin Rosenthal, "Who's Next?" *Moody Monthly* (October 1978): 1–2.

54. This was an argument similar to those of liberal Protestants such as Franklin Littell.

55. William F. Willoughby, "Special Report: A Chance for Christians to Help Israel," *Moody Monthly* (October 1978): 26–27.

56. Bob Jones, "Palestine in Perspective," *Faith for the Family* (January 1979): 1–7.

57. Ibid., 7.

58. Letter from Elmer A. Josephson to Stanley F. Chyet, 15 September 1975, Small Collections 5522, Jacob Rader Marcus Center for the American Jewish Archives, Hebrew Union College, Jewish Institute for Religion, Cincinnati Campus.

59. Meir Kahane, "Christians for Zion," *Jewish Press* (24 January 1975): 34.

60. "Graham Cites Support for Israel's Existence," *Statesville Record & Landmark* (29 October 1977): section 2.

61. "Christian Leaders Reaffirm Their Support of Israel," *Religious News Service* (26 April 1978), Weniger File, Bob Jones University Archives.

62. Ibid.

63. "Falwell Visits Mid-East," *Bible Baptist Tribune* (19 May 1978): 13. The same story appeared in two other journals: "Trusted Christian Leaders Counsel with Arab and Jewish Leaders," *Sword of the Lord* (26 May 1978): 12–13; and "Fall, Religious Leaders Confer with Sadat, Begin," *Journal—Champion* (12 May 1978): 1, 10.

64. "Falwell Visits Mid-East," 14.

65. "Problems in Palestine," *Researcher* (spring 1979): 1–3.

66. Editorial, *Christians Concerned for Israel Newsletter* (January 1975), Small Collections 1867, Jacob Radar Marcus Center for the American Jewish Archives, Hebrew Union College, Jewish Institution for Religion, Cincinnati Campus.

67. "Wisconsin Coalition Formed," *Christians Concerned for Israel Notebook* (March 1975), Small Collections 1867, Jacob Radar Marcus Center for the American Jewish Archives, Hebrew Union College, Jewish Institution for Religion, Cincinnati Campus.

68. Editorial, *Christians Concerned for Israel Notebook*, (June 1975), Small Collections 1867, Jacob Radar Marcus Center for the American Jewish Archives Hebrew Union College, Jewish Institution for Religion, Cincinnati Campus.

69. Franklin Littell, Letter to Readers of the *Christians Concerned for Israel Notebook* (November 1975), Reinhold Niebuhr Papers, Box 63, Library of Congress Archives, Washington, D.C.

70. Malachi B. Martin, "The Church and Israel," *National Review* (9 December 1971): 1435.

71. Richard M. Harley, "Holocaust Lessons—Not Just from TV," *Christian Science Monitor* (8 May 1978): 31.

72. Martin Marty, "Which Christians Can Israel Count On? A Ladder of Sympathies," *Christian Century* (8 March 1978): 233–236.

73. Ibid., 234.

74. Ibid.

75. Ibid., 236.

76. Ibid.

CHAPTER 7. THE POLITICAL AND RELIGIOUS LANDSCAPE SHIFTS, 1980–2008

1. Jerry Falwell, *Listen America* (New York: Bantam Books, 1981).

2. See, for example, Andrew J. Weigert, "Christian Eschatological Identities and the Nuclear Context," *Journal for the Scientific Study of Religion* 27, no. 2 (June 1988): 175–191. Weigert argues that the "plausibility attached to Liberal versus Fundamentalist types of Christian eschatologies has undergone an historical shift from the former to the latter. Fundamentalist eschatology offers a social psychological context for the formation of meaningful identity and motivation with explicit reference to the nuclear context." See also Martin E. Marty, "Fundamentalism as a Social Phenomenon," *Bulletin of the American Academy of Arts and Sciences* (November 1988): 15–29; Stephen Kierfulff, "Belief in 'Armageddon Theology,' and Willingness to Risk Nuclear War," *Journal for the Scientific Study of Religion* (March 1991): 81–93.

3. Martin E. Marty, "Religion in America since Mid-Century," *Daedalus* 11, no. 1 (winter 1982): 149–163.

4. Ibid., 151.

5. Ibid., 154.

6. Watt, 155.

7. Ibid., 157.

8. James R. Kelly, "The Spirit of Ecumenism: How Wide, How Deep, How Mindful of Truth?" *Review of Religious Research* (spring 19791): 180–194.

9. Ibid., 182.

10. William R. Glass, "Fundamentalism's Prophetic Vision of the Jews: The 1930s," *Jewish Social Studies* (winter 1985): 63–76.

11. Marty, "Religion in America since Mid-Century," 159.

12. Richard V. Pierard, "Religion and the 1984 Election Campaign," *Review of Religious Research* (December 1985): 98–114.

13. Ibid., 100.

14. Ibid., 102.

15. As quoted in Pierard, "Religion and the 1984 Election Campaign," 107.

16. Ibid., 110.

17. Jeffery K. Hadden, "Religious Broadcasting and the Mobilization of the New Christian Right," *Journal for the Scientific Study of Religion* (March 1987): 1–24.

18. Ibid., 22.

19. Ronald R. Stockton, "Christian Zionism: Prophecy and Public Opinion," *Middle East Journal* (spring 1987): 234–253.

20. Ibid., 235.

21. Ibid., 240.

22. Quoted in Jan Nederveen Pieterse, "The History of a Metaphor: Christian Zionism and the Politics of Apocalypse," *Archives de sciences sociales des religions* (July–September 1991): 75.

23. As quoted in Stockton, "Christian Zionism," 241.

24. Weigert, "Christian Eschatological Identities and the Nuclear Context," 176. He notes, "In a stunning reversal, the nuclear context, in the historical instate of a few decades, has rendered mythic, cosmic Fundamentalist eschatology *closer to empirical projections and more plausible* in imagery and calculability than demythologized Liberal versions. Literal reading of the Bible gains prima facie legitimacy in a world with sufficient targeted nuclear throw weight to justify scientists constructing empirical scenarios similar to the ideological enemies' literal applications of ancient apocalyptic writings."

25. As quoted in Stockton, "Christian Zionism," 241.

26. Martha Abele MacIver, "Mirror Images? Conceptions of God and Political Duty on the Left and Right of the Evangelical Spectrum," *Sociological Analysis* (fall 1990): 287–295.

27. Tom F. Driver, "Hating Jews for Jesus' Sake," *Christianity and Crisis* (November 24, 1980): 325ff.; as quoted in Stockton, "Christian Zionism," 241.28. Ibid., 91.

29. Shelley Slade, "The Image of the Arab in America: Analysis of a Poll on American Attitudes," *Middle East Journal* (spring 1981): 143–162.

30. The negative view of Arabs, Slade points out, was not "monolithic." Most Americans had a high view of Egypt and Sadat, a "balanced" view of Saudi Arabia and Jordan, while most had a "very low opinion of the PLO, Libya, Syria and Iraq." Ibid., 144.

31. Ibid., 148. Notably Slade found that "when asked which words or phrases come to mind with the mention of the words 'Christian' or 'Christianity,' 'USA' or 'America' is cited the second most often, surpassed only by the mention of 'Jesus Christ.'"

32. Stockton, "Christian Zionism," 246.

33. Ibid.

34. Mitchell G. Bard, "Reagan's Legacy on Israel" (25 June 2004), http://www.israelinsider.com/views1/3779.htm.

35. On 4 December 1983 Reagan declared, "If Israel is ever forced to leave the U.N., the United States and Israel will leave together." "Reagan Pledges Aid for Israel in the United Nations," *New York Times* (5 December 1983): IA.

36. Donald Wagner, "Reagan and Begin, Bibi and Jerry: The Theopolitical Alliance of the Likud Party with the American Christian 'Right,'" *Arab Studies Quarterly* (November 2006), http://www.findarticles.com/p/articles/mi_m2501/is_4_20/ai_54895469/.

37. "Fellowship Pastors Meet with Begin: Falwell-Dixon-Zimmerman Welcome Him to U.S.," *Bible Baptist Tribune* (2 May 1980): 1–2.

38. Ibid.

39. "Israel's Begin Explains Attack on Reactor," *Moral Majority Report* (20 July 1981): 4.

40. Walter H. Capps, *The New Religious Right: Piety, Patriotism, and Politics* (Columbia: University of South Carolina Press, 1990), 38.

41. "Israel's Begin Explains Attack on Reactor," *Moral Majority Report* (20 July 1981): 4.

42. Weber, *On the Road to Armageddon*, 220.

43. David Brog, *Standing with Israel: Why Christians Support the Jewish State* (Lake Mary, FL: Frontline, 2006).

44. Esther L. Vogt, "Star over Israel," *Sunday School Times and Gospel Herald* (1 July 1981): 6.

45. Brog, *Standing with Israel*, 3.

46. Phyllis Bennis and Khaled Mansour, "Praise God and Pass the Ammunition!": The Changing Nature of Israel's U.S. Backers," Middle East Report no. 208, *U.S. Foreign Policy in the Middle East: Critical Assessments* (fall 1998), 18.

47. Ibid.

48. Thomas Friedman, *From Beirut to Jerusalem* (New York: Farrar Straus & Giroux, 1989); cited in Bennis and Mansour, "Praise God and Pass the Ammunition!"

49. See the website of the Churches for Middle East Peace, http://www.cmep.org.

50. As Susan Harding noted, in "Imagining the Last Days: The Politics of Apocalyptic Language," *Bulletin of the American Academy of Arts and Sciences* (December 1994): 14–44, "in December 1990, as the nation was poised on the brink of war, Zondervan Publishing House reportedly printed a million copies of an updated version of *Armageddon, Oil, and the Middle East Crisis* by John Walvoord. Over 600,000 copies had reportedly sold by early February, and Billy Graham was distributing another 300,000 copies free." She added that "weekly stories and editorials in Christian magazines located events in the Gulf in biblically based schemes. All over the country, born-again Christians pondered the Persian Gulf War in terms of Bible prophecy."

51. Pieterse, "The History of a Metaphor," 76.

52. Ari Godman, "Mideast Tensions; Council of Churches Condemns U.S. Policy in the Gulf," *New York Times* (16 November 1990): 13.

53. Clyde Wilcox, "Premillennialists at the Millennium: Some Reflections on the Christian Right in the Twenty-First Century," *Sociology of Religion* (fall 1994): 243–261.

54. Bennis and Mansour, "Praise God and Pass the Ammunition!" 16.

55. Stephen Spector, *Evangelicals and Israel: The Story of American Christian Zionism* (Oxford: Oxford University Press, 2009), 148.

56. Bennis and Mansour, "Praise God and Pass the Ammunition!" 17.

57. Donald Wagner, "The Evangelical-Jewish Alliance," *Christian Century* (28 June 2003): 20–24.

58. Fred Strickert, "War on the Web," *Christian Century* (16 May 2001): 20–22. Reprinted on http://www.religion-online.org.

59. Ibid., 4.

60. Spector, *Evangelicals and Israel*, 207.

61. Ibid., 209.

62. Ibid., 223.

63. Glen Tobias, Abraham Foxman, and Eugene Korn, "Meeting the Challenge: Church Attitudes Toward the Israeli-Palestinian Conflict," *Anti-Defamation League* (2002): 23.

64. Ibid., 27.

65. See the website of the Presbyterian Church of the United States of America, http://www.enddivestment.com/analysis3.html.

66. Eugene Korn, "Divestment from Israel, the Liberal Churches, and Jewish Responses," no. 52 (1 January 2007), http://www.jcpa.org.

67. Ibid.

68. Ibid.

69. Spector, *Evangelicals and Israel*, 12.

Selected Bibliography

UNPUBLISHED SOURCES

Manuscripts Division, Reinhold Niebuhr Personal Papers, Library of Congress, Washington, D.C.
Central Zionist Archives, Jerusalem, Israel
Israeli State Archives, Jerusalem, Israel
American Jewish Archives, Jacob Rader Marcus Center of the American Jewish Archives, Cincinnati Campus, Hebrew Union College, Jewish Institute of Religion
Truman Archives, Hebrew University, Jerusalem, Israel
Fundamentalism Files, Bob Jones University Archives, Greenville, South Carolina
Presbyterian Historical Society Archives, Philadelphia, Pennsylvania
U.S. Department of State Archives, National Archives, College Park, Maryland

NEWSPAPER

New York Times, 1933–1979

PERIODICALS

Christian Century, 1933–1979
Christianity and Crisis, 1941–1976
Federal Council Bulletin, 1933–1979
Christian Life, 1950–1980
Christian News From Israel, 1950–1980
Moody Monthly, 1933–1980

PRIMARY SOURCES

American Christian Palestine Committee (ACPC). *The Arab War Effort: A Documented Account*. New York: ACPC, 1946.
———. *A Christian Report on Israel: A Composite Account by the Members of the American Christian Palestine Committee Study Tour of Israel*. New York: ACPC, 1949.
———. *Problems of the Middle East: Proceedings of a Conference Held at the School of Education, New York University*. New York: ACPC, 1947.

———. *Questions and Answers on Palestine.* New York: ACPC, 1945.

———. *The Voice of Christian America: Proceedings of the National Conference on Palestine.*" Washington, D.C., 9 March. New York: American Palestine Committee and Christian Council on Palestine, 1944.

"Amsterdam: World Council Asks Church to Act against Anti-Semitism." *Christianity and Crisis* (20 September 1948): 120.

Baehr, Karl. *Arab and Jewish Refugees—Problems and Prospects.* New York: American Christian Palestine Committee, 1953.

Berlin, Sir Isaiah. *Personal Impressions.* New York: Penguin Books, 1982.

Bernstein, Phillip S. "Palestine and the Jew—A Reply." *Christian Century* (4 February 1948): 138–140.

Brandeis, Louis Dembitz. *Brandeis on Zionism: A Collection of Addresses and Statements, 1856–1941.* Westport, CT: Hyperion, 1976.

Buber, Martin. *Israel and Palestine.* New York: Farrar, Straus & Young, 1952.

Burrows, Millar. "Jewish Nationalism," *Christian Century* (30 March 1949): 401.

Carter, Jimmy. *The Blood of Abraham.* New York: Houghton Mifflin, 1986.

———. *Keeping Faith: Memoirs of a President.* New York: Bantam Books, 1982.

"Clergymen Appeal for a Jewish Commonwealth." *Christian Century* (11 April 1945): 477.

Dawidowicz, Lucy. "American Public Opinion." In *American Jewish Yearbook*, 1968.

"Did Hitler Win?" *Christianity and Crisis* (12 November 1945): 3.

"Do the World's Jews Want to be Feared?" *Christian Century* (16 June 1948): 589.

"Dutch Churches Praised for Uncompromising Stand against Persecuted Jews," *Christianity and Crisis* (30 April 1945): 7.

Eckardt, Alice, and A. Roy Eckardt. *Long Night's Journey into Day: A Revised Retrospective on the Holocaust.* Detroit: Wayne State University Press, 1988.

"Editorial Notes." *Christianity and Crisis* (23 July 1945): 2.

Einstein, Albert. *The Arabs and Palestine.* New York: Christian Council on Palestine and American Palestine Committee, 1944.

Fosdick, Harry Emerson. *A Pilgrimage to Palestine.* New York: Macmillan, 1927.

Frank, Waldo. *The Jew in Our Day.* With an introduction by Reinhold Niebuhr. New York: Duell, Sloan and Pearce, 1944.

Frankfurter, Felix. *From the Diaries of Felix Frankfurter.* With biographical essay and notes. New York: Norton, 1975.

"Gazing into the Pit." *Christian Century* (9 May 1945): 575.

"Germany: Message Concerning the Jewish Question." *Christianity and Crisis* (24 May 1948): 71.

Heschel, Abraham J. *Israel.* New York: Farrar, Straus & Giroux, 1969.

"Interfaith Conference Called Important Step in Fighting Increased Hatreds." *Christianity and Crisis* (22 July 1946): 8.

"Interfaith Goodwill Movement Launched in Frankfurt." *Christianity and Crisis* (4 March 1946): 8.

"Israel and Judaism." *Christian Century* (16 March 1949): 327–329.

"Israel Knows No God." *Christian Century* (9 June 1948): 565.

"Jewish Attitudes to Evangelism." *Christianity and Crisis* (31 March 1947): 8.

"Jewish Congregation in Holland to Help Rebuild Catholic Churches." *Christianity and Crisis* (29 October 1945): 7.

Kollek, Teddy, and Amos Kollek. *For Jerusalem: A Life by Teddy Kollek*. New York: Random House, 1978.

Little, Franklin H. "Essay: Reinhold Niebuhr and the Jewish People." *Holocaust and Genocide Studies* 6 (January 1991): 45–61.

Little, Franklin H. *The Crucifixion of the Jews*. New York: Harper & Row, 1975.

"Message of the German Evangelical Church to the German People." *Christianity and Crisis* (29 October 1945).

Niebuhr, Reinhold. "Editorial Notes." *Christianity and Crisis* (17 February 1947): 2.

Niebuhr, Ursula. "Christian and Jew—Need for New Attitudes." *British Weekly* (March 1970): 6–7.

———. "Guidelines for Christian-Jewish Relations." *British Weekly* (September 1973): 9.

———. "Jerusalem and Israel." *British Weekly* (November 1968): 3–4.

Niemöller, Martin. "Niemöller about the Question of Guilt." *Christianity and Crisis* (8 July 1946): 6.

"Pastor Niemöller's Visit." *Federal Council Bulletin* (April 1947): 3.

"Praises Interfaith Cooperation." *Christian Century* (20 June 1945): 740.

"Resolutions by the World Council of Churches." *Federal Council Bulletin* (May 1946): 8–9.

"Reveal German Chaplains Carried on Anti-Nazi Activity." *Christianity and Crisis* (2 April 1945): 7.

Rose, Ben L. "As Niemöeller Sees Germany's Future." *Christian Century* (10 October 1945): 1155.

Silcox, Claris Edwin. *Catholics, Jews, and Protestants: A Study of Relationships in the United States and Canada*. New York: Harper & Brothers, 1934.

Strauss, Lehman. *Is It Possible to Know God's Plan for the Future*. Grand Rapids, MI: Zondervan, 1965.

"Telegram to Mrs. Roosevelt." *Federal Council Bulletin* (January 1947): 11.

"Testifies Niemöeller Not an Anti-Semite." *Christian Century* (3 December 1947): 1477.

Thompson, Dorothy. *I Speak Again as a Christian*. New York: Christian Council on Palestine and American Palestine Committee, 1945.

———. *Let the Promise Be Fulfilled: A Christian View of Palestine*. New York: American Christian Palestine Committee, 1946.

Tobias, Glen, Abraham Foxman, and Eugene Korn. *Meeting the Challenge: Church Attitudes Toward the Israeli-Palestinian Conflict*. New York: Anti-Defamation League, 2003.

United States Department of State. *Anglo-American Committee of Inquiry: Report to the United States Government and His Majesty's Government in the United Kingdom*. Washington, D.C.: U.S. Government Printing Office, 1946.

Voss, Carl Hermann. *Answers on the Palestine Question*. New York: American Christian Palestine Committee, 1948.

Wall, James M. "Israelis Accept Fundamentalist Allies." *Christian Century* 103, no. 34 (12 November 1986): 995–996.

Walvoord, John F. *Israel in Prophecy*. Grand Rapids, MI: Zondervan, 1962.

Wendell, Phillips. *Before the Bar of History*. New York: American Christian Palestine Committee, 1945.

Wise, Stephen S., *Challenging Years*. New York: Putnam's, 1949.

Ariel, Yaakov. *Evangelizing the Chosen People: Missions to the Jews in America, 1880–2000.* Chapel Hill: University of North Carolina Press, 2000.

———. *On Behalf of Israel: American Fundamentalist Attitudes toward Jews, Judaism, and Zionism, 1865–1945.* Brooklyn: Carlson, 1991.

Armstrong, Karen. *The Battle for God.* New York: Knopf, 2000.

Bennis, Phyllis, and Khaled Mansour, "Praise God and Pass the Ammunition!": The Changing Nature of Israel's U.S. Backers." Middle East Report No. 208. *U.S. Foreign Policy in the Middle East: Critical Assessments* (fall 1998), 16–18, 43.

Bourne, Peter G. *Jimmy Carter: A Comprehensive Biography from Plains to Post-Presidency.* New York: Lisa Drew/Scribner, 1997.

Brog, David. *Standing with Israel: Why Christian Support the Jewish State.* Lake Mary, FL: Frontline, 2006.

Cargas, Harry James. *A Christian Response to the Holocaust.* Denver, CO: Stonehenge Books, 1981.

Chafets, Zev. *A Match Made in Heaven: American Jews, Christian Zionists, and One Man's Exploration of the Weird and Wonderful Judeo-Evangelical Alliance.* New York: Harper Perennial, 2008.

Clark, Victoria. *Allies for Armageddon: The Rise of Christian Zionism.* New Haven, CT: Yale University Press, 2007.

Cohen, Naomi W., ed. *Essential Papers on Jewish-Christian Relations in the United States.* New York: New York University Press, 2003.

———. *Jews in Christian America: The Pursuit of Religious Equality.* New York: Oxford University Press, 1992.

Cohn-Sherbok, Dan. *Holocaust Theology: A Reader.* New York: New York University Press, 2002.

Conway, John S., "The Founding of the State of Israel and the Responses of the Christian Churches." *Kirchliche Zeitgeschichte* 12, no. 2, (1999): 459–472.

Dehmer, Alan, "Unholy Alliance: Christian Fundamentalism and the Israeli State." *ADC Issues*, no. 16 (April 1984).

Dollinger, Mark. *Quest for Inclusion: Jews and Liberalism in Modern America.* Princeton, NJ: Princeton University Press, 2000.

Fackenheim, Emil L. *The Jewish Bible after the Holocaust: A Re-reading.* Bloomington: Indiana University Press, 1990.

Fisher, Eugene J. *Visions of the Other: Jewish and Christian Theologians Assess the Dialogue.* New York: Paulist, 1994.

Fishman, Hertzel. *American Protestantism and a Jewish State.* Detroit: Wayne State University Press, 1973.

Ganin, Zvi. *Truman, American Jewry, and Israel, 1945–1948.* New York: Holmes & Meier, 1979.

Gerber, David. *Antisemitism in American History.* Urbana: University of Illinois Press, 1986.

Glass, William R., "Fundamentalism's Prophetic Vision of the Jews: The 1930s." *Jewish Social Studies* 47, no. 1 (winter 1985).

Goldman, Shalom. *God's Sacred Tongue: Hebrew and the American Imagination.* Chapel Hill: University of North Carolina Press, 2004.

Goldsmith, Robin Squier. *Niebuhr and Martin Buber*. Ann Arbor: University of Michigan Press, 1986.

Gorenberg, Gershom. *The End of Days: Fundamentalism and the Struggle for the Temple Mount*. New York: Oxford University Press, 2000.

Gurock, Jeffery. *American Zionism: Missions and Politics*. New York: Routledge, 1998.

Gushee, David P. "Learning from the Christian Rescuers: Lessons for the Churches." *Annals of the American Academy of Political and Social Science* 548 (November 1996): 138–155.

Hadden, Jeffery K., "Religious Broadcasting and the Mobilization of the New Christian Right." *Journal for the Scientific Study of Religion* 26, no. 1 (March 1987).

Halperin, Samuel. *The Political World of American Zionism*. Detroit: Wayne State University Press, 1961.

Halsell, Grace. *Prophecy and Politics: Militant Evangelists on the Road to Nuclear War*. Westport, CT: Lawrence Hill, 1986.

Handy, Robert T. *The Holy Land in American Protestant Life, 1800–1948: A Documentary History*. New York: Arno, 1981.

Harding, Susan, "Imagining the Last Days: The Politics of Apocalyptic Language." *Bulletin of the American Academy of Arts and Sciences* 43, no. 3 (December 1994).

Harley, Richard, "Holocaust Lessons—Not Just from TV." *Christian Science Monitor* (8 May 1978).

Haynes, Stephen R. *Prospects for Post-Holocaust Theology*. Atlanta: Scholar's Press, 1991.

Haynes, Stephen R., and John K. Roth, eds. *The Death of God Movement and the Holocaust: Radical Theology Encounters the Shoah*. Westport, CT: Greenwood, 1999.

Hollinger, David A. *Science, Jews and Secular Culture: Studies in Mid-Twentieth Century American Intellectual History*. Princeton, NJ: Princeton University Press, 1996.

Hunter, James Davison, "Operationalizing Evangelicalism: A Review, Critique & Proposal." *Sociological Analysis* 42, no. 4 (winter 1981): 363–372.

Jacobs, Steven L., ed. *Contemporary Christian Responses to the Shoah*. New York: University Press of America, 1993.

Kelly, James R., "The Spirit of Ecumenism: How Wide, How Deep, How Mindful of Truth?" *Review of Religious Research* 20, no. 2 (spring 1979).

Kierfulff, Stephen. "Belief in 'Armageddon Theology,' and Willingness to Risk Nuclear War." *Journal for the Scientific Study of Religion* 30, no. 1 (March 1991).

Kraut, Benny. "Toward the Establishment of the NCCJ." *American Jewish History* (March 1988).

———. "A Wary Collaboration." In *Between the Times,* ed. William Hutchinson. Cambridge: Cambridge University Press, 1989.

Lederhendler, Eli, and Jonathan D. Sarna, eds. *America and Zionism: Essays and Papers in Memory of Moshe Davis*. Detroit: Wayne State University Press, 2002.

Lipstadt, Deborah. *Beyond Belief: The American Press and the Coming of the Holocaust, 1933–1945*. New York: Free Press, 1986.

Locke, Hubert G., and Marcia Sachs Littell, eds. *Remembrance and Recollection: Essays on the Centennial Year of Martin Niemöller and Reinhold Niebuhr, and the Fiftieth Year of the Wannsee Conference*. Lanham, MD: University Press of America, 1995.

MacIver, Martha Abele, "Mirror Images? Conceptions of God and Political Duty on the Left and Right of the Evangelical Spectrum." *Sociological Analysis* 51, no. 3 (fall 1990).

Malachy, Yona. *American Fundamentalism and Israel: The Relation of Fundamentalist Churches to Zionism and the State of Israel.* Jerusalem: Hebrew University of Jerusalem, 1978.

Marsden, George. *Fundamentalism and American Culture: The Shaping of Twentieth Century Evangelicalism, 1870–1925.* New York: Oxford University Press, 1980.

Mart, Michelle. "The 'Christianization' of Israel and Jews in 1950s America." *Religion and American Culture: A Journal of Interpretation* 14, no. 1: 109–146.

Martin, Malachi B. "The Church and Israel." *National Review* 29, no. 50 (December 1971).

Marty, Martin. "Fundamentalism as a Social Phenomenon." *Bulletin of the American Academy of Arts and Sciences* 42, no. 2 (November 1988).

——. "Religion in America since Mid-century." *Daedalus* 11, no. 1 (winter 1982).

——. "Which Christians Can Israel Count On? A Ladder of Sympathies." *Christian Century* 95, no. 8 (8 March 1978).

Mayer, Jeremy D., "Christian Fundamentalism and Public Opinion toward the Middle East: Israel's New Best Friends?" *Social Science Quarterly* 85, no. 3 (September 2004).

McGarry, Michael B. *Christology after Auschwitz.* New York: Paulist, 1977.

Medoff, Rafael. "Communication: A Further Note on the 'Unconventional Zionism' of Reinhold Niebuhr." *Studies in Zionism* 12, no. 1 (1991).

Melman, Yossi, and Dan Raviv. *Friends in Deed: Inside the U.S.–Israel Alliance.* New York: Hyperion, 1994.

Merkley, Paul Charles. *Christian Attitudes Towards the State of Israel.* Montreal: McGill-Queen's University Press, 2001.

Naveh, Eyal, "The Hebraic Foundation of Christian Faith according to Reinhold Niebuhr." *Studies in Zionism* 10, no. 1 (1990).

——. "Unconventional 'Christian Zionist': The Theologian Reinhold Niebuhr and His Attitude toward the Jewish National Movement." *Studies in Zionism* 11, no. 2 (1990).

Neusner, Jacob. *Israel and Zion in American Judaism: The Zionist Fulfillment.* New York: Garland, 1993.

——. *Stranger at Home: "The Holocaust," Zionism, and American Judaism.* Chicago: University of Chicago Press, 1981.

——. *Who, Where and What Is "Israel"? Zionist Perspectives on Israeli and American Judaism.* New York: University Press of America, 1989.

Oldmixon, Elizabeth, Beth Rosenson, and Kenneth D. Wald. "Why Members of Congress Support Israel: Explanations of Legislator Behavior." Paper prepared for the Annual Meeting of the Midwest Political Science Association, April 30, 2003.

Perkin, Harold. "American Fundamentalism and the Selling of God." *Political Quarterly* (2000).

Pieterse, Jan Nederveen. "The History of a Metaphor: Christian Zionism and the Politics of the Apocalypse." *Archives des sciences socials des religions* 36, no. 75 (July–September 1991).

Poliakov, Leon. *Harvest of Hate: The Nazi Program for the Destruction of the Jews in Europe.* Westport, CT: Greenwood, 1971.

Prior, Michael. *Speaking the Truth about Zionism and Israel.* London: Melisende, 2004.

——. *Zionism and the State of Israel: A Moral Inquiry.* London: Routledge, 1999.

Rashkover, Randi. "Jewish Responses to Jewish-Christian Dialogue: A Look Ahead to the Twenty-First Century." *Cross Currents* (spring/summer 2000).

Reichley, A. James. "Religion and the Future of American Politics." *Political Science Quarterly* 101, no. 1 (1986).

Reuther, Rosemary Radford. *Faith and Fratricide: The Theological Roots of Antisemitism.* New York: Seabury, 1974.

Robertson, D. B. *Reinhold Niebuhr's Works: A Bibliography.* Berea, KY: Berea College Press, 1954.

Ross, Robert W. *So It Was True: The American Protestant Press and the Nazi Persecution of the Jews.* Minneapolis: University of Minnesota Press, 1980.

Roth, John K., and Michael Berenbaum, eds. *Holocaust: Religious and Philosophical Implications.* New York: Paragon House, 1989.

Rubenstein, Richard L. *After Auschwitz: History, Theology and Contemporary Judaism.* Baltimore: Johns Hopkins University Press, 1992.

Sarna, Jonathan. *Religion and State in the American Jewish Experience.* Notre Dame, IN: University of Notre Dame Press, 1997.

Sharif, Regina S. *Non-Jewish Zionism: Its Roots in Western History.* London: Zed, 1983.

Singer, Michael, ed. *Humanity at the Limit: The Impact of the Holocaust Experience on Jews and Christians.* Bloomington: Indiana University Press, 2000.

Slade, Shelley. "The Image of the Arabs in America: Analysis of a Poll on American Attitudes." *Middle East Journal* 35, no. 2 (spring 1981).

Smidt, Corwin. "Evangelicals within Contemporary American Politics: Differentiating between Fundamentalist and Non-Fundamentalist Evangelicals." *Western Political Quarterly* 41, no. 3 (September 1988).

Smith, Robert O. "Reclaiming Bonhoeffer after Auschwitz." *Dialog: A Journal of Theology* (2004).

Sofer, Sasson. *Zionism and the Foundations of Israeli Diplomacy.* Cambridge: Cambridge University Press, 1998.

Spector, Stephen. *Evangelicals and Israel: The Story of American Christian Zionism.* New York: Oxford University Press, 2009.

Stevens, Richard. *American Zionism and U.S. Foreign Policy, 1942–1947.* Beirut: Institute for Palestine Studies, 1970.

Stockton, Ronald. "Christian Zionism: Prophecy and Public Opinion." *Middle East Journal* 41, no. 2 (spring 1987).

Stone, Jon R. *On the Boundaries of American Evangelicalism: The Postwar Evangelical Coalition.* New York: St. Martin's, 1997.

Tivnan, Edward. *The Lobby: Jewish Political Power and American Foreign Policy.* New York: Simon and Schuster, 1987.

Watt, David Harrington. "The Private Hopes of American Fundamentalists and Evangelicals, 1925–1975." *Religion and American Culture* 1, no. 2 (summer, 1991).

Weigert, Andrew J. "Christian Eschatological Identities and the Nuclear Context." *Journal for the Scientific Study of Religion* 27, no. 2 (June 1988).

Whalen, Robert. "'Christians Love the Jews!': The Development of American Philo-Semitism, 1790–1860." *Religion and American Culture* 6, no. 2 (summer, 1996).

Wieseltier, Leon. "Epistle to the Hebrews." *New Republic* (9 February 1998).

Wilcox, Clyde. "Premillennialists at the Millennium: Some Reflections on the Christian Right in the Twenty-First Century." *Sociology of Religion* 55, no. 3 (fall 1994).

Williamson, Clark M. *A Guest in the House of Israel: Post Holocaust Church Theology.* Louisville: John Knox, 1993.

Woodward, Joe. "The Church and the Holocaust." *Alberta Report* 25, no. 24 (1998).

Wyman, David S. *The Abandonment of the Jews: America and the Holocaust, 1941–1945.* New York: Pantheon Books, 1984.

———. *The World Reacts to the Holocaust.* Baltimore: Johns Hopkins University Press, 1996.

Index

David Accords, 168–171; election
of 166–168; political abandonment
by evangelicals, 201. *See also* Camp
David Accords; Egyptian-Israeli Peace
Accords
Catholics, 2–3, 7; Catholic Church in
Germany, 11; interest in status of
Jerusalem, 63, 72, 76; opposition to
antisemitism 49–50; Second Vatican
Council, 115
Cavert, Samuel, 52–57, 74–75
Chinitz, Jacob, 84–85
Christian Century, 1, 9, 12, 15, 18–20, 22,
24; anti-Jewish immigration, 28; anti-
Zionism, 33, 151–152; concern for
Palestinian refugees, 65, 68; criticism of
Israel, 63–64, 99; importance of Israel,
173; on the internationalization of
Jerusalem, 138; Niemöller controversy,
56–57; question of genocide, 29;
reaction to Camp David Accords,
170–171; response to Suez Crisis, 107;
response to Stephen Wise, 23; response
to 1973 War, 163; responsibility of
Christianity for antisemitism, 116;
theological reassessments of Judaism,
37, 39
Christian Coalition, 189, 191, 201
Christian Council on Palestine (CCP):
concern for Jewish refugees, 41;
establishment of, 25
Christian Herald, 55; response to Suez
Crisis, 107
Christian Science Monitor, 20, 150–151
Christianity and Crisis: concern
for Palestinian refugees, 65, 68;
establishment, 22; 39; Niemoeller
controversy, 51; reaction to Camp
David Accords, 171; removal of
Niebuhr's name from masthead, 159–
160; response to 1967 War, 138–139
Christianity Today, 108, 142
Christians Concerned for Israel (CCI), 60,
152, 157–160, 165, 183–184
Christians Concerned for Israel Notebook,
158–160, 165, 183–184

Churches for Middle East Peace (CMEP),
202, 204–205, 207, 244n49
Chyet, Stanley F., 180
Clark, Delbert, 54
Clinchy, Everett R., 38
Clinton, Bill, 203–204
Coffin, Henry Sloan, 32–33, 63; editorial in
Christianity and Crisis, 66–68
Cohan, Hoffman, 85
Cold War, 47, 62, 83, 87; end of, 203;
fundamentalist attitudes toward, 118;
Israel as a strategic ally in, 97–98;
Middle East foreign policy during,
94–97; 1967 War, 139; relationship to
eschatology, 189; rhetoric, 98
Commentary, 192
Committee for Justice and Peace in the
Holy Land: establishment, 33, 63–64,
71, 102
Communism, xv, 6, 28, 40–41, anti-
communist propaganda, 69; Arab, 87;
atheistic, 83, 97; military support for
Egypt, 104; spread of international, 106
Confessing Church (German), 12–13,
49–51, 222n3
Conflict of the Ages, 5
Congress of Industrial Organizations
(CIO), 26
Conservative Judaism, 156
Cowan, Wayne, 159
Cummings, Clark Walter, 66
Cushman, Robert E., 163
Curtis, Charles, 22

Darby, John Nelson, 7
David, Lenny Ben, 201
Davies, Alan, 151–152
Dayan, Moshe, 136, 178
Defender, 4–5
Defenders of the Christian Faith, 4
deicide, 115, 129
Dimona (Israeli nuclear reactor), 123
Dine, Thomas, 194
Dodge, Bayard S., 33, 63
Douglas, Helen, 26, 35
Driver, Tom, 195

Murray, Philip, 46
Murray, Wallace, 219n68

Nasser, Gamal Abdul, 94, 105, 108, 122–
    123; 1967 War, 134–136, 142
Nation, 23, 59; cooperation with Israeli
    Ministry of Religious Affairs, 73–78
National Association of Christians and
    Jews, 4
National Association of Evangelicals, 158,
    192
National Brotherhood Week, 38–39
National Conference of Christians and
    Jews (NCCJ), 3, 181; post-Second
    World War activities, 37–38, 83–84;
    response to 1967 War, 138, 220n83
National Council of Churches of Christ
    in America (NCC), 115, 138, 140, 163,
    195–196, 200, 203, 207
National Foundation for the Preservation
    of Democracy, 4
National Review, 184
National socialism, 11–13
Nazi: Party, 1; Christian accommodation
    with, 57; death camps, 23, 94; Europe,
    18, 22, 28; Germany, 25; influence on
    German churches, 50; number of Jews
    murdered by, 37; persecutions of Jews,
    2, 15–16, 29, 42; state, 11; terror, 13,
    17, 25
Nes Ammim, 158
Netanyahu, Binyamin, 204
Newman, Samuel, 82, 118; letter writing
    campaign, 127–131
Niebuhr, H. Richard, 32
Niebuhr, Reinhold, 13, 22, 206, 210, 211;
    conversion of Jews, 128; death of,
    155–156; Niemöller controversy, 50,
    55; response to 1967 War, 138; study
    tours to Israel, 73–78; testimony before
    Anglo-American Committee, 44
Niebuhr, Ursula, 156–160, 165, 171, 173
Niemöller, Martin, controversy over U.S.
    visits, 49–57
Nixon, Richard, 162–163
Non-Aryan Christians, 12, 14

Norris, J. Frank, 5, 19, 81–82
Nuremberg Racial Laws, 12

Olson, Arnold T., 158, 181
Oslo Accords, 203–205
Osservatore Romano, 63
Our Hope, 5; coverage of Holocaust, 28–30;
    opposition to British restrictions on
    immigration of Jews to Palestine, 42
Oxnam, G. Bromley, 73–78
Oxtoby, Willard G., 140–141

Palestine, 1; American attitudes toward,
    196; APC support for establishment of
    Jewish homeland in, 20–22, 24, 26–27,
    36; British immigration restrictions to,
    19, 42–47; Congressional support for
    unrestricted Jewish immigration to, 17;
    establishment of a Jewish homeland
    in, 6, 17; fundamentalist Protestant
    attitudes toward, 81; fundamentalist
    Protestant interest in, 15; Jewish interest
    in 8; Jews of Palestine's assistance of
    Allies in World War II, 27; liberal
    Protestant concern for Palestinian
    refugees, 195; Mandate, 119; Near
    East Division consideration of, 17,
    34; Palestinian statehood, 199; post-
    World War II Jewish refugees to, 41–47;
    pre-World War II Eastern European
    Jewish immigration to, 2, 5–6; right of
    return, 100–101. *See also* Arabs; British
    Mandate
Palestinian Arabs, 165
Palestinian Christians, 78
Palestinian Liberation Organization (PLO),
    168, 170, 196, 204, 243n30
Palestinian refugees, 65–68; fundamentalist
    attitude towards, 118
Pan-Arabism, 113
Pearson, Lester B., 106
Pentecostal Evangel, 79
Peres, Shimon, 122, 204
Perlmutter, Nathan, 201
Petuchowski, Jakob, 148
Phillips, Howard, 197

About the Author

CAITLIN CARENEN is Assistant Professor of History at Eastern Connecticut State University.